Practical Herbalism

Ordinary Plants with Extraordinary Powers

Including a Brief History of the Evolution of Herbal Medicine
and Specific Applications for Commonly Found or Easily Grown Herbs

by

Philip Fritchey, M.H., N.D., CNHP

Other titles by Philip Fritchey:
   The Practitioner's Guide to Holistic Skin Therapy (with Emily Fritchey, HST, CNHP – Licensed Clinical Esthetician)

Note to reader: This book is offered for informational purposes only and should not be construed as medical advice. For medical problems, always seek the help of a qualified health professional.

Copyright © 2004 by Whitman Publications

All rights reserved. No part of this publication may be reproduced, stored in a retrieval system, or transmitted in any form, by any means, electronic, mechanical, photocopying, recording, or otherwise, without the prior written permission of the copyright owner.

Printed in 2004, 2010, 2012, 2015, 2019 and 2022 by:
Whitman Publications
220 Parker Street
Warsaw, IN 46580

ISBN: 1-885653-22-0

Library of Congress Control Number: 2004112547

Printed in the United States of America.

Dedication

I dedicate this book to my Loving Father in Heaven, from Whom ALL healing flows. He gives us His forgiveness—for our spiritual transgressions, through Christ whose Love embraces us; and for our physical transgressions, through the herbs of the fields that surround us, placed here by Him in anticipation of our every need. To Him be the Glory.

And to my grandmother, Anna Bower Fritchey, and my loving wife, Emily—two angels placed in my life by His hand. Without their patience, knowledge, and inspiration, I would not have had the insight, nor probably even the life, to complete this work.

Foreword

Dr. Phil always said, "Patience and persistence can accomplish most anything" and this was demonstrated in his approach to everything he did—including loving me. Dr. Phil (as everyone called him) was a wonderful man, a gifted herbalist, a keen observer and a powerful and inspiring teacher of herbology and plant medicine.

He was an original—many believe he was born about 100 years too late. He was old school to the core, but his work was perfected in that. He had a very Will Rogers storytelling style about him, and his wit and wisdom inspired thousands of people to reconnect with nature and better understand how amazing plant medicine really is.

As this book goes into its 5th printing, I am touched by the messages I still receive from people all over the world whose lives have been powerfully influenced by this amazing man and his deep faith in a loving God. He always said these plants are a gift given to us by our loving Creator for the healing of all nations. He was highly intuitive and clearly understood the energetic vibration of plants in such a way. I called him "the plant whisperer" and he used that gift lovingly and willingly shared with others—almost to a fault.

He was my greatest inspiration and taught me so much. His life proved that a good teacher is like a candle—it consumes itself to light the way for others. I will spend the rest of my life keeping his mission alive and sharing the healing power of nature and the love of God with the world. Until we meet again, Poppa. Well done my good and faithful servant—well done.

Forever…

Emily Fritchey

Philip Leo Fritchey

July 7, 1947 – January 19, 2017

Acknowledgement

I would like to express my gratitude to the Lloyd Library and Museum in Cincinnati, Ohio for their dedication to the preservation of our herbal record and legacy, and for the hours of inspiration spent with the volumes in their care.

About the Author

Philip L. Fritchey
M.H., N.D., CNHP

Since rediscovering his family herbal heritage in the late 1980's, and recovering from a personal health crisis of his own, Dr. Fritchey has become a vocal advocate and nationally recognized lecturer on traditional herbalism. While working for nearly a decade alongside his wife in a busy natural health practice in central Georgia, he secured his Naturopathic degree and Master Herbalist letters from the Trinity College of Natural Health. He has written the Herbology curriculum for the National Association of Certified Natural Health Professionals, and now spends most of his time traveling and teaching the good news of the Biblical promise of herbs "for the healing of the nations." When not on the road, he formulates and compounds botanical remedies and skin care products that are distributed nationwide. He relies heavily on garden grown and wild-crafted native plants, and celebrates nature's abundant apothecary.

This book is a compilation of those years of study, experience, and observation. Focusing on ordinary plants that are commonly found or easily grown, Dr. Fritchey relays practical information on identifying, harvesting, and preparing good medicine from the "pharmacy underfoot." Whether you are an experienced herbalist, or a newly curious natural health seeker, you will find an enlightening historical perspective, and much reassuring information here—information made even more relevant in our troubled times.

Contents

CHAPTER 1: THE EVOLUTION OF HERBAL MEDICINE 9
    Ancient Roots to Modern Science...11
    Timeline..13
    Orchestrating the Demise of Botanical Medicine in America....................26
    The New Millennium – Reprieve or Reprisal?..31
    Also Recommended for Reading 33

CHAPTER 2: PRACTICAL HERBALISM 101 35
    Basic Herbal Preparations..40
    Traditional Methods for Preserving and Preparing Herbs.........................46
    Two More Traditional Herbal Remedies..56
    Tools of the Trade..58

CHAPTER 3: UNDERSTANDING HERBAL "ACTIONS"......................................63
    Alteratives..66
    Anodynes 66
    Antacids 67
    Anthelmintics..67
    Antiarthritics...68
    Antibiotics..68
    Anticatarrhals..69
    Antiemetics..70
    Anti-inflammatories...70
    Antiseptics...71
    Antispasmodics...71
    Aperients...72
    Aphrodisiacs 72
    Aromatics 73
    Astringents 73
    Bitters...74
    Blood Purifiers..74
    Cardiacs 75
    Carminatives...75
    Cholagogues 75
    Demulcents 75
    Diaphoretics 76
    Digestives 77
    Discutients...77
    Diuretics...77
    Emetics...78
    Emmenagogues..78
    Emollients 78
    Expectorants...78
    Febrifuges..79
    Galactagogues 79
    Hemostatics..80
    Hepatics...80
    Laxatives..80
    Lithotriptics..81
    Lymphatics..81
    Nervines...81
    Nutritives 83
    Parasiticides..83
    Parturients..83
    Refrigerants 84
    Rubefacients 84

- Sialagogues 84
- Stomachics 85
- Styptics 85
- Sudorifics 85
- Tonics 85
- Vulneraries 87

CHAPTER 4: NATURE'S APOTHECARY 89
- Birch Bark 90
- Black Cohosh 95
- Black Walnut 100
- Bugle 105
- Burdock 109
- Calendula Blossom 114
- Capsicum 118
- Catnip 123
- Cleavers 127
- Comfrey 130
- Cornsilk 135
- Dandelion 138
- Dill 142
- Echinacea 146
- Elderberry 153
- Fennel 159
- Garlic 164
- Gravel Root 168
- Hawthorn Berries 171
- Hops 175
- Horehound 180
- Horsetail 185
- Jewelweed 189
- Juniper Berries 194
- Lemon Balm 198
- Lobelia 202
- Marshmallow 207
- Mullein 214
- Nettles 220
- Oregon Grape 227
- Passion Flower 231
- Peppermint 236
- Plantain 240
- Pleurisy Root 245
- Poke 250
- Red Clover 254
- Red Raspberry 259
- Sage 266
- St. John's Wort 271
- Sassafras 275
- Thyme 278
- Vitex 283
- Wild Cherry 287
- Willow 291
- Yarrow 295
- Yellow Dock 300

APPENDIX A: GLOSSARY 305

APPENDIX B: CITATIONS 373

APPENDIX C: INDEX 433

CHAPTER 1

The Evolution of Herbal Medicine
with a History of Botanical Practice in the United States

"History repeats itself, a process which is virtually guaranteed by the fact that most people don't pay attention the first time." – Anon.

The World Health Organization has observed that even in this era of our technology-driven, chemically-oriented, medical industry, over three-quarters of the world's population still rely upon herbs and natural remedies as their primary form of health care. To some scientifically jaded practitioners of Western allopathic medicine, and to most of our cosmopolitan population, this may seem like a staggering proportion. It must be remembered, though, that as recently as two and a half centuries ago (a mere blip in the historical time frame), and for all time before, virtually all of the peoples of the earth sought solace and relief from their health issues in the plants of the field. The seemingly inexorable march of "progress" in medicine that has all but totally excluded our innate connection with the natural world has really only been apparent in the U.S./European sphere of influence. There, and only within the last hundred years, was the grip tightened to the threatened extinction of alternative views.

At the beginning of the twentieth century in the United States, the common citizenry and the medical professionals who served it were deeply divided over the philosophy and methods of medical care, and, perhaps more importantly, over the right of the people to choose the form of care they wanted. As it became empirically clear that the income potential of manufactured chemical medicines vastly outweighed the limited profits available from "home grown" remedies, the nation's monopolistic magnates of the Industrial Revolution began investing in the new industry. Flush with success in the battles to control rail lines, petroleum, electric power, and textile manufacturing, they once again used their enormous financial resources, social standing, and political influence in an all-out effort to discredit and destroy the "competitors" to the new industry of healing.

Disorganized, embattled, and embittered, the nation's once proud and outspoken sects of botanical practitioners soon found themselves outspent, outcast, and outlawed in every State of the Union. The term "quackery" came to mean any idea or approach to healing, no matter what its historical basis, that dared to question or contradict "the One True Belief" in allopathic medicine. With its poisonous drugs, invasive and often deadly surgical procedures, and utter dependence on the systematically indoctrinated graduates of industry-funded medical schools, the idea might have been a tough sell. On a stage of fear and despair set by the brutal disfigurements of war and the devastation of epidemics brought about by poor sanitation and overcrowded cities, the play found a receptive audience. Mesmerized by the dangling carrots of "the end of disease in our time" and "better living through chemistry," most of the population ultimately succumbed to the hype and promises, and gave up their traditional herbal practices. Looking for the light at the end of the tunnel, they blew out the candle that lit the way.

In a few short decades, thousands of years of our herbal legacy might have been lost forever, had it not been for a handful of daring and dedicated natural health advocates, some outspoken, some practicing "underground." Few, if any, people are living today who can actually remember the wrangling and political intrigue that brought about the near demise of botanical medicine under the monopolistic stranglehold of the allopathic medical industry in our country. The current resurgence of interest in herbal medicine and alternative therapies is the inevitable result of the people's frustration with the escalating costs, depersonalization of care, and the staggering increase in chronic and degenerative diseases under the present medical system. For preserving our most viable alternative to that system, we owe an enormous debt to the herbalists, nutritionists, and naturopaths that stood their ground against the derision and intimidation of an industry bent on controlling the business of pain, suffering, and disease. The most effective payment that we can offer for that debt is to carry on the battle. Like learning to walk again after a trauma, simple and natural healing practices that were once considered "common knowledge" need to be re-learned, used, and passed on to the next generation.

History has shown that dependence is the life-blood of monopoly, but that there need be no dependence where there is knowledge of an alternative. Are we paying attention this time?

ANCIENT ROOTS TO MODERN SCIENCE

Nobody was available to quantify the dose, identify the active constituents, or document the results when early man first chewed some leaves or pounded some bark to apply to a painful wound, or ease a feverous malady. Why and how specific plants were first chosen or prepared will always be a mystery. What is known is that whether by instinct, trial-and-error, or Divine Providence, peoples living in every corner of the globe gradually developed a working and healing relationship with their native flora. Disparate populations, with little or no possibility of contact, very often found similar uses for the same plants, and more often still, different plants to ease common ailments. Experience was passed on from generation to generation and tribe to tribe. Healers, medicine men, shamans, and wise-women became revered repositories of herbal traditions; preserving and protecting the means to ease pain and cure disease. As man became more mobile, these precious remedies were carried and shared through story, song, and ritual, and often became treasured items of commerce.

Gradually, the magic and medicine of plants moved from lore and tradition to the written word. Long before the first hard records of Western herbal medicine appeared in Europe and the Middle East, China and India began setting down the healing disciplines that have come to be known as Traditional Chinese Medicine and Ayurveda. Centered on the concept of restoring and maintaining balance in the vital life force known as Qi (Chi) or Prahna, and protected by the vast gulfs of distance and cultural isolation, these healing arts would remain an enigma to the West for nearly five thousand years.

In the West, it was left to the ancient Egyptians and the Persians to begin defining and recording herbal lore. Eventually the Greeks and then the Romans assimilated this knowledge. They combined it with discoveries and tales from conquered lands, and began setting it down as part of an approach to the healing of human ailments that would, with few changes, dominate the thinking of herbalists and physicians until the middle of the 18th Century. Hippocrates, Dioscorides, and Galen are still often quoted to this day. The Hippocratic Oath is a requisite for entry into the field of medicine, and traditional herbal remedies are still referred to as Galenic preparations.

With the advent of the "new Science" in Renaissance Europe, and the subsequent divisiveness between the scientists and the traditional Church in Rome, the face of medicine and healing began to undergo a tumultuous change. "Territorial disputes" over Body and Spirit turned the exploration of Natural Laws into life-threatening charges of heresy and witchcraft. The concept of healing the Body as a spiritless machine, and leaving the Soul, or Vital Force, to the Church was a compromise that protected everybody's "turf"—saving face for the Church, and allowing the new physicians to avoid a flaming stake. Four hundred years later, Western Medicine remains the only healing discipline on the planet that ignores any concept of a living connection to the vital energy of the Natural Creation.

A body without an accountability to the "living energy" of Nature also opened the doors to the use of lifeless mineral poisons and chemicals to manipulate and dominate its functions. The powerful effects of heavy metals and alchemists' brews on the human frame instantly became a source of fascination and deep controversy among healers and physicians. At the center of the storm, a physician/philosopher named Paracelsus rallied followers anxious to sweep away the ages-old traditions of nature-directed botanical medicine, and replace it with the new "science" of specific chemical drugs. Within the ranks of healing practitioners, the philosophical split opened into a bitter chasm, wider even than the rift with the Church. The divide would continue to course through the evolution of Western medicine until it reached the shores of the New World. There, throughout the 18th and 19th Centuries, it would become a great struggle for dominance that would culminate in the rise—and downfall—of the Golden Age of Botanical Medicine in America.

For all its bitter squabbles, ranker, and even occasional fisticuffs, the battle over which approach to healing (botanical or chemical) would dominate, did not ultimately turn on the philosophy, or even the efficacy, of either system. In the end, it was the simple reality that chemical drugs are more profitable which drove the great crusade to banish herbal medicine from the playing field. The spirits of the ancient physicians live on, though, in the common "weeds" that embrace us in Nature, and cushion our footsteps. Their voices are being heard once again, and the legacy of millennia of herbal healing has found a new generation in need.

TIMELINE

c.1500 B.C. – Ebers Papyrus

One of the best preserved records of the medical insights of the ancient Egyptians, this enormous scroll is filled with incantations, charms, magical formulas, symbols, prayers, and prescriptions for all sorts of ailments. The diversity of the pharmacopoeia and the high development of the art of pharmacy are very impressive. There were gargles, salves, inhalations, snuffs, suppositories, fumigants, enemas, poultices, and plasters along with specific instructions for the use of opium, hemlock, castor oil, and copper salts. Surgery was not highly developed, but surgical wound repair, excisions, and cauterization were frequently used.

c.460-c.370 B.C. – Hippocrates

Generally recognized as the "Father of Medicine" in the West, Hippocrates based his teaching of medicine on objective observation and deductive reasoning. Although he accepted the belief that disease results from an imbalance of the four bodily humors, he maintained that the humors were linked to glandular secretions and that outside forces influenced the disturbance. He believed strongly in the innate healing power of Nature—vis medicatrix naturae—and taught that medicine should build the patient's strength through diet and hygiene. More drastic treatments should only be resorted to as a last recourse. The Hippocratic Oath is an ethical code formulated in ancient Greece. It is still administered to medical graduates in many modern universities. It cannot be directly credited to Hippocrates, but it does accurately represent his ideals.

The Oath

> I swear by Apollo the physician, and Aesculapius, and Health (Hygieia), and All-Heal (Panacea), and all the gods and goddesses, that, according to my ability and judgment, I will keep this oath and this stipulation -- to reckon him who taught me this art equally dear to me as my parents, to share my substance with him, and relieve his necessities if required; to look upon his offspring in the same footing as my own brothers, and to teach them this art, if they shall wish to learn it, without fee or stipulation; and that by precept, lecture, and every other mode of instruction, I will impart a knowledge of my art to my own sons, and those of my teachers, and to disciples bound by a stipulation and oath according to the law of medicine, but to none others.

(Primum no nocere – "First do no harm.") I will give no deadly medicine to anyone if asked, nor suggest any such counsel; and in like manner I will not give to a woman a pessary to produce abortion.

I will follow that system of regimen which, according to my ability and judgement, I consider for the benefit of my patients, and abstain from whatever is deleterious and mischievous.

With purity and with holiness I will pass my life and practice my art.

I will not cut persons laboring under the stone, but will leave this to be done by men who are practitioners of this work. (This reference to surgery reinforced Hippocrates' belief that the physician should refrain from invasive procedures. It is usually left out of contemporary versions. – Ed.)

Into whatsoever houses I enter, I will go into them for the benefit of the sick, and will abstain from every voluntary act of mischief and corruption, and, further, from the abduction of females or males, of freemen and slaves.

Whatever, in connection with my professional practice, or not in connection with it, I see or hear in the life of men, which ought not to be spoken of abroad, I will not divulge, as reckoning that all such should be kept secret.

While I continue to keep this Oath inviolate, may it be granted to me to enjoy life and the practice of the art, respected by all men, in all times! But should I trespass and violate this Oath, may the reverse be my lot!

c.35-100 A.D. – Pedanius Dioscorides

As a Roman army surgeon under Nero's reign, Dioscorides compiled the first truly comprehensive reference of all known medicinal uses of plants throughout the empire. De Materia Medica, produced in the first century, was instantly acclaimed, and has been copied and quoted to the present day. It was, in effect and substance, the prototype for all herbals and pharmacopoeia that have followed.

c.130-c.200 A.D. – Galen

Born in Pergamum of Greek parents, the legendary physician and writer resided chiefly in Rome and was personal physician to several emperors. He is credited with some 500 treatises that correlated earlier medical knowledge with his own discoveries (based on experiments and animal dissections). He showed that arteries carry blood, not air, and added greatly to knowledge of the brain, nerves, spinal cord, and pulse. He developed elaborate theories about the humoral causes of disease, and equally complex prescriptions for their correction. Galen's was the strongest voice in the art of healing just before the fall of the civilizing force of the Roman Empire to the European barbarians. As a result, for fifteen centuries his ideas dominated medical thought in an intellectual vacuum much as did Aristotle's in the schools of philosophy. His virtually undisputed authority survived and took on dogmatic status through the Medieval era when there was very little original investigation, a blind allegiance that discouraged progress in both botanical and allopathic medicine until the sixteenth century.

It was not until the Renaissance that daring spirits began to question the infallibility of this medical icon. Unfortunately, when the constricting ties on exploration were loosened and many of Galen's teachings were discredited, there came a tendency to "throw the baby out with the bath water." Allopathic extremists rejected anything that had Galenic ties, and much of this great man's work was lost on their reactionary prejudice. By carefully peeling away the layers of myth and assumption that surrounded the world of Galen's time, contemporary herbalists still find a treasure trove of healing insights in his work. Viewed in the modern context, many of Galen's theories offer a unique order and effective methodology for the use of herbs even today.

Galen was the last and, in many ways, the greatest of the ancient Greek physicians. If he could visit our world today, he might teach us many lessons. He would sneer at the water supply of many of our cities, thinking of the magnificent aqueducts of Rome and of many of the colonial towns, some of which are still in use, and which stand as testimony to the astonishing skill of their engineers, and foresight of their physicians. There are still many communities in the world in which he would find imperfect drainage and poor sanitation, and could tell of the wonderful system by which Rome was kept sweet and clean. He could tour anywhere as a sanitary expert, preaching the gospel of good water supply and good drainage, two of the great elements in civilization. Most certainly, he would speak of the use of the herbs of the field to correct the maladies brought on by the ignorance of good sanitary practices, and the arrogance of our detachment from the natural world.

c.400-c.1400 A.D. – The Middle Ages

Following the glory that was Greece and the grandeur that was Rome, a desolation came upon the civilized world, in which the light of learning burned low, flickering almost to extinction. In our era of constant, nearly overwhelming technological change, it is hard to imagine a time when life and living conditions changed very little from generation to generation for nearly a thousand years. The tools, clothing, housing and lifestyle habits of a peasant farmer in the year 500 A.D. would have been readily recognized and comfortably assimilated by his successor on the land in 1500 A.D. So little did life change for such an extended period that the French coined the term "le longe duree" to describe it.

In medicine, too, the Middle Ages represent a simple perpetuation from century to century of the facts and theories of the Greeks and Romans, modified here and there by a trickle of insight from Arabian practice. Also evident was a growing shroud of superstition and magic creeping in from the gulf of folklore and ignorance of uneducated practitioners. There was, as Francis Bacon said, "much iteration, small addition." What schools there were bowed in humble, slavish submission to Galen and Hippocrates, taking everything from them but their spirits of exploration, observation, and discovery. There was no advance in our knowledge of the structure or function of the body. Only the Arabians carried on the torch lit from Greco-Roman lamps, and from the eighth to the eleventh centuries the healing profession reached among them a historically unparalleled position of dignity and importance.

640 A.D. – The Fall of Alexandria

After the fall of Rome in 410 A.D., the last bastion of Greek and Roman learning was in Egypt, in the city of Alexandria. Lacking the organization and resources of their predecessors, the barbarian hordes that swarmed over Europe saw Alexandria as remote and inaccessible. The Arabs did not, and in 640 A.D., they swept over the city. In the power vacuum left by the dissolving Roman Empire, the Arabs had turned from a disordered group of pastoral tribes into a well organized army fanatically bent on securing their place in the Middle East and North Africa. Suddenly they found themselves masters of half of the known world, and having once founded their empire, they immediately set themselves to acquire that knowledge of the sciences which alone was lacking to their greatness. Alexandria was the home of the world's greatest library and center of study for the natural sciences. Of all the invaders who competed for the last remains of the Roman Empire they alone pursued such studies. While the Germanic hordes, glorying in their brutality and complacent in their ignorance, took a thousand years to re-unite the broken chain of intellectual tradition, the Arabs accomplished this in less than a century. Before the ninth century had run its course, the Arabs were in possession of all the science of the Greeks, and they had produced from their own ranks students, philosophers, and healers of the highest order.

980-1037 A.D. – Avicenna

His Arabic name was Ibn Sina. A Persian philosopher and physician, he was to become the most renowned philosopher of medieval Islam. Avicenna's *Canon of Medicine*, a classic text, was particularly influential in the West from 1100 to 1500, and represented one of the period's few notable advancements in the field of botanical medicine in Europe.

1348-1350 A.D. – Black Plague

Sweeping inexorably across Europe, and killing nearly a third of its population, the Black Plague was a pivotal event in the history of science and medicine. Ironically, the fear it generated deepened the superstition and magic of healing rituals, and at the same time, the frustration and desperation of the era's physicians gave birth to a new sense of need for "a better way." Questions about the old assumptions of the cause and effect of disease quickly locked horns with the pragmatic declarations of the Church, though, and it would be another two centuries before genuine exploration and progress could once again be made.

1493-1541 A.D. – Paracelsus

Few fields of endeavor have been so consistently torn by dispute and ranker as the healing arts, and few figures within that field have been surrounded by the degree of division and controversy as the flamboyant and outspoken Swiss physician and alchemist, originally named Philippus Theophrastus Bombastus von Hohenheim. Studied in alchemy, chemistry, and metallurgy, his work was colored by the fantastic philosophies of the time, but he rejected Galen's humoral theory of disease, and advocated the use of specific remedies for specific diseases. He introduced many drugs and chemicals, including laudanum (tincture of opium), mercury, sulfur, iron, and arsenic. As a measure of the storm of divergent opinions surrounding him, he is still both heralded and derided to this day, as the father of allopathic medicine, and the first vocal proponent of chemical drugs.

1514-1564 A.D. – Andreas Vesalius

Flemish physician to Emperor Charles V and his son Philip II, he produced his chief work, the notably illustrated *De Humani Corporis Fabrica,* in 1543. This first great work in anatomy was based on studies made by dissecting human cadavers, a practice that had been suppressed for centuries. His discoveries in anatomy overthrew many hitherto uncontested doctrines of Galen, and generated a storm of criticism. It was the first non-theoretical, factually-based breach in Galen's thirteen century grip on medical philosophy.

1545-1607 A.D. – John Gerard

In 1562 Gerard went to London to become an apprentice to a barber-surgeon and, after seven years, was granted permission to establish his own practice. While studying in London, he became interested in plants and began a garden near his cottage in Holborn, London. Both the garden and its owner soon became popular, and Gerard was often presented not only with rare plants and seeds from different parts of the world, but also with offers to supervise the gardens of noblemen. In 1596 he compiled a list of the plants growing in his garden. Published in 1597, his celebrated *Herball, or Generall Historie of Plants,* containing more than 1,000 species, became, and still stands, as one of the great classic references of botanical medicine.

Contact with Native Americans and their strange, uniquely American plants prompted great curiosity among European herbalists. The Spanish were the first to introduce American plants to Europe, but other European explorers were soon to follow. Gerard was the first to incorporate New World plants in his *Herball.* Appearing at the genesis of the great divide in medical philosophies, Gerard's work was also the first comprehensive, common language compilation of western herbal practices in more than 13 centuries.

1578-1657 A.D. – William Harvey

This English physician is considered by many to have laid the foundation for modern medicine. At St. Bartholomew's Hospital in London, he was the first to demonstrate the function of the heart and the complete circulation of the blood. His renowned *On the Movement of the Heart and Blood in Animals* (1628) describes his theories, which were not fully substantiated until 1827. Harvey also made substantial contributions to the fields of comparative anatomy and embryology.

1616-1654 A.D. – Nicholas Culpeper

This famous physician, herbalist, and astrologer spent the greater part of his adult life ranging the hills and forests of England, where he catalogued literally hundreds of medicinal herbs. His driving purpose was to teach the common folk to minister to themselves by providing them with the tools and knowledge that would allow each family to better care for itself, independent of the reigning medical establishment. His mind and ambition was to reform the whole system of medicine that he felt was unnatural and unnecessarily mysterious. He set about translating the English Physician's Pharmacopoeia from the professional's Latin to the common man's English. As a result, he was maligned and assailed by his colleagues, and very popular in his community.

In 1652, he published his most noted work, *The Compleat Herbal & English Physitian*. Disgusted with some of the common practices of his peers, and frustrated with the continual assaults, Culpeper wrote: "This not being pleasing, and less profitable to me, I consulted with my two brothers, DR. REASON and DR. EXPERIENCE, and took a voyage to visit my mother NATURE, by whose advice, together with the help of DR. DILIGENCE, I at last obtained my desire; and being warned by MR. HONESTY, a stranger in our days, to publish it to the world, I have done it."

Always a man for the common people, Culpeper wrote with wit, intellect, and conviction. Though bound up in frequent arcane astrological references, the Complete Herbal remains one of the most quoted treatises on botanical medicine in history.

1670 A.D. – Invention of the Microscope

In Delft, Holland, a wealthy merchant named Anton van Leeuwenhoeck began grinding and stacking lenses. He named the sea of moving creatures he observed under his tool as "animacules." It would be nearly two more centuries, while Louis Pasteur was working on wine fermentation problems, before these tiny creatures would be associated with life processes that affected humans in any way.

1745?-1813 A.D. – Benjamin Rush

The only American physician to sign the Declaration of Independence, Dr. Rush was a vocal proponent of the "heroic" medicine of the time (blistering, purging, and bloodletting), and a great advocate of the use of calomel (mercury sub-chloride). He was the first professor of chemistry in the colonies, at the College of Philadelphia.

From 1769 to 1813, he served as Professor of Medicine at Pennsylvania University, by far the largest of the four medical schools in North America, and exerted an enormous influence over the medical practice of the time. Even in his own era, though, his callous bleeding and purging of patients aroused controversy, and his guidance was thought to be responsible for the tortuous death, among many others, of George Washington at the hands of three Rush-ite physicians.

While on the one hand, Dr. Rush was an outspoken critic of the practice of slavery, he was also the embodiment of ethnic arrogance. When presented with treatises on Native American health and botanical practices, he disdainfully stated to his students, "We have no discoveries in the materia medica to hope for from the Indians of North America. It would be a reproach to our schools of physic if modern physicians were not more successful than the Indians even in the treatment of their own diseases." Of course, tens of thousands of Native Americans died of the white man's diseases, while their own herbal insights might have saved countless colonists.

1749-1823 A.D. – Edward Jenner

This English physician's experiments, beginning in 1796 with the vaccination of James Phipps, proved that cowpox provided immunity against smallpox. He is often referred to as the Father of Immunology.

1755-1843 A.D. – Samuel Christian Hahnemann

Recognized as the Founder of Homeopathy, Hahnemann was born in Meissen, Germany. He studied allopathic medicine at Leipzig, and practiced there for 10 years. He observed that when some compounds are administered to a healthy person, they produced symptoms similar to those of other illnesses. In a moment of inspiration, he began experimenting with very small doses of these compounds with the hope that they would instill within the body an increased energy for healing. From this he developed his law of "similars" (like cures like), around which he built his system of homeopathy. His *Reine Arzneimittellehre (Precept of Pure Drugs)* published in 1811, became the first homeopathic drug catalog and repertory.

In stark contrast to the "heroic" bloodletting, purging, and blistering of conventional medicine at the time, the gentle and precise medicine of homeopathy quickly gained popular acceptance, and, of course, the scorn of the allopathic "regulars." Homeopathic medicines survive today as the only FDA approved form of "alternative" botanical medication.

1769-1843 A.D. – Samuel Thomson

The oldest son of an illiterate New Hampshire farmer, Thomson went on to found—and patent in 1813—a system of treating diseases with rigorous "courses" of indigenous plants and steam baths. His practice was spread by licensed agents over New England, the South, and the Midwest with a fervor that was only paralleled by the growth and popularity of religious sects in the early nineteenth century. Thomson's success would earn the unbridled scorn, rage, indignation, and persecution of the established medical community, and the total admiration, and even adulation, of nearly a third of the country's population who used his system to heal their families. Credited with being the Father of Modern Herbalism in America, Thomson and his system of botanical cures would set the stage for efforts towards grand reforms in medicine. Out of the Thomsonian ideal would rise Physio-Medicalism, Eclectic Medicine, and Naturopathy, which, along with Homeopathy, were the most popular alternatives to the "heroic" and often brutal therapies of the allopaths. Some would say that it was the threat of the popularity of Thomsonian medicine and its successors that brought about the A.M.A., to help fight for the very survival of the allopathic profession.

Crusader that he was, Thomson was also obstinate, cantankerous, and somewhat short sighted. He adamantly refused to license his system to regular physicians, and wanted no part of what he perceived as the intellectual elitism of medical schools. Even his most devoted followers saw the potential for improvements in his mostly intuitive system, and thought that the reform cause would be furthered more easily if a more traditional educational system and better qualified practitioners were available. Instead, the botanical reformers he inspired became embroiled in divisive ranker. The allopathic community seized on their disputes as evidence of contradiction and uncertainty, and the many factions that evolved from Thomsonian medicine ultimately succumbed one by one to the more unified front presented by the A.M.A.

1822-1895 A.D. – Louis Pasteur

This icon of the "Germ Theory" of disease was a chemist and microbiologist, born in Dôle, France. He studied at Besançon and Paris universities, and held academic posts at Strasbourg, Lille, and Paris, where in 1867 he became professor of chemistry at the Sorbonne. He established that putrefaction and fermentation were caused by micro-organisms, thus giving birth to the field of Microbiology. In a famous experiment in 1881, he showed that sheep and cows "vaccinated' with the attenuated bacilli of anthrax received protection against the disease. In 1888 the

Institute Pasteur was founded at Paris for the treatment of rabies, and he worked there until his death.

It has been said that at the end of his life, Pasteur acknowledged that his assumptions about the microbiological cause of disease had been erroneous, or at least incomplete. In a nod to a contemporary, Rudolf Virchow, Pasteur also concluded that "Le terraine est toute le monde," (the terrain is everything). In other words, the pathogens he had been studying were not, he felt, the sole cause of disease, but rather were dependent on the unhealthy state of the tissues they attack for their ability to flourish and produce the symptoms of disease.

1824-1897 A.D. – Father Sebastian Kneipp

Father Kneipp provided the link between European natural healing and American Naturopathy. As a priest, physical healing was as much a part of his ministry as was saving souls. His approach to healing was holistic, advocating the balance between work and leisure, stress and relaxation, and harmony between the spiritual, mental, emotional, physical, social, and ecological planes. In short, "he asked for a different life, not for better pills." He expected his patients to be active rather than passive in what came to be known as the Nature Cure.

1825-1939 A.D. – The Eclectic Medical Movement

Fathered by Wooster Beach, a conventionally trained though disillusioned medical doctor, the Eclectic Movement tried to incorporate both botanical and chemical therapies—an approach that by today's terminology might be known as integrative medicine. The movement spawned 24 Eclectic medical colleges and more than 65 journals over its 114 year history. Its most vibrant period was centered around the Eclectic Medical Institute of Cincinnati (Ohio) which opened in 1845, and graduated students until the decline of the movement forced it to close in 1939. The schools were a favorite of poor and disadvantaged students, and graduated the first female and black doctors in the country. The Eclectics accused the A.M.A. of engineering their decline by using aristocratic politics to legislate curriculum reforms that were prohibitively expensive for the students they served. In the end, the Eclectics' botanical bias, like that of the Naturopaths, brought little financial support to compete with the allopathic institutions that were lavished with funds from the pharmaceutical industry. Faced with overwhelming competition, and continuing financial troubles, the Eclectics were pushed aside in the rush to modern "scientific" medicine.

1836-1911 A.D. – The Physio-Medical Movement

Concerned with establishing a more permanent and respectable system of medicine built on a foundation of botanic medical colleges, Alva Curtis broke away from Samuel Thomson and organized the Independent Thomsonian Botanic Society. Though motivated by the lofty goals of general reform for the whole medical industry and avoidance of all chemical drugs, Curtis' followers had difficulty even settling on a name for their movement. They were known in various regions as botanico-medicals, physiopathics, medical reform, and physio-medical—the last appellation being the most persistent. Over the course of the movement, Curtis' faction of former Thomsonians opened and closed thirteen physio-medical colleges. Plagued by disorganization and contention, the last of these schools closed in 1911, and the remainder of the faithful allied themselves with the Eclectic Movement or the Naturopaths.

1847 A.D. – Formation of the American Medical Association

At the behest of New York physician, Dr. Nathan Smith Davis (1817-1904), some 250 doctors, representing 24 different states, 40 different medical societies, and 28 allopathic medical colleges gathered in Philadelphia on May 7, 1847. The purpose of the "urgent" meeting was to organize the "regular" profession in a stand against the growing army of "Irregulars"—Eclectics, Homeopaths, and neo-Thomsonians—that threatened to overwhelm the practices and livelihoods of the allopathic professionals. By the end of the day, the A.M.A. had been chartered, allopathic standards had been set for "acceptable" medical schools, and the members were forbidden to consult or even socialize with physicians whose views were contradictory to "the accumulated experience of the (allopathic) profession." A chasm of bitterness, mistrust, and monopolistic malice towards any alternative form of healthcare was written into official A.M.A. policy, where it existed, virtually unchanged, until August 27, 1987. On that day, the A.M.A. was found guilty of conspiracy in violation of the nation's antitrust laws (against chiropractors in particular), and was ordered to revamp their prejudicial "Principles of Medical Ethics."

The wording has been changed, so now we have only to wait for the attitude to follow.

1871 A.D. – Flush Toilet

It is doubtful that any invention has done more for the long-term health of the people than the invention made practical by English plumber, Thomas Crapper.

Sanitation, not medicine, has been responsible for the great advance in life expectancy in the last century.

1872-1945 A.D. – Benedict Lust

Benedict Lust, N.D., D.O., D.C., M.D., was born and educated in Germany. He introduced naturopathic healing to the United States in 1892, and established the Yungborn Health Institute in New Jersey, which later became the American School of Naturopathy. Suffering from tuberculosis in Germany, he had sought the aid of Father Kneipp. Feeling that he had been healed from certain death by the Nature Cure, he was commissioned by Fr. Kneipp, and sailed to America to spread the word about his healing miracle. By 1902, Lust had opened a Naturopathic sanatorium, established a Naturopathic college, begun a Naturopathic magazine, and opened a dispensary that featured Kneipp products. His ideas about natural healing were eclectic. While he was a proponent of the Kneipp Cure, he combined it with modalities he had learned from many of the other European nature doctors. He is credited with coining the term Naturopathy.

Like many of his contemporaries, Dr. Lust was a man of strongly held opinions. For example, he was opposed to the processing of foods "because such 'manufacture' tends to destroy their true nutritional values," and he opposed the administrations of all drugs and narcotics, "because they are unnatural elements which the human body is not capable of assimilating." He reviled against the regimentation of the American people under monopolistic medical laws, "because such legislation will wipe out other methods of treatment and bring inestimable damage to the health of every man, woman, and child affected." He fought any legislation that would prevent individuals from attending to their own ills, or choosing any type of treatment they might desire. "Such legislation," he held, "restricts personal liberty, and tends to take from the American people the right to use the beneficial, homespun, efficient remedies that have been handed down from generation to generation."

Throughout his career, Lust spent much time and energy fighting the American Medical Association and government persecution. Towards the end of his life, he was even embroiled in disputes within the organization of his own creation, the American Naturopathic Association. Shortly after he died in 1945, the organization split in two, forming the Eastern ANA and the Western ANA, each with its own constitution, officers, programs, and conventions. Personality conflicts as well as philosophical differences led to the split. The Eastern naturopaths were determined to follow the principles of Fr. Kneipp, and the example set by Dr. Lust, while those in the West seemed determined to "medicalize" naturopathy. The two camps developed their own schools and textbooks which reflected their different points of view. Today the factions are represented by the "traditional Naturopaths," who cling to the non-invasive and drugless ideals of Dr. Lust, and the "pseudo-medical naturopaths," who incorporate drugs and surgical procedures.

ORCHESTRATING THE DEMISE OF BOTANICAL MEDICINE IN AMERICA

1906 A.D. – Pure Food And Drug Act

By 1900 most American states had enacted food laws, but they were poorly enforced. The effort to enact a federal law was led by Dr. Harvey W. Wiley, head of the Bureau of Chemistry in the Department of Agriculture. Wiley enlisted the support of the largest food producers and pharmaceutical manufacturers, the American Medical Association, the General Federation of Women's Clubs, and other consumer groups. He faced the entrenched opposition of the politically powerful "Beef Trust," small producers of patent medicines, and southern congressmen concerned with the constitutional validity of the proposed law. The tide was turned in Wiley's favor by a series of sensational articles by muckraking journalists. Following the "embalmed beef" scandal of the Spanish-American War in 1898 (this concerned the quality of food supplied to U.S. troops), Charles Edward Russell produced a series of articles exposing the greed and corruption of the Beef Trust. Representing the pharmaceutical drug companies, Samuel Hopkins Adams also claimed that many commonly available patent medicines were often dangerous compounds of alcohol and other drugs. Then, in January 1906, Upton Sinclair published his best-selling novel, *The Jungle*, replete with hair-raising descriptions of the manner in which meat products were prepared in the Chicago stockyards.

Amid the storm of public indignation that followed, the Pure Food and Drug Act was passed on June 30, 1906. The act forbade foreign and interstate commerce in adulterated or fraudulently labeled foods, the source of the great controversy. Using the emotional outcry over tainted foods to stir up support, the major pharmaceutical manufacturers succeeded in including restrictive legislation aimed at curtailing the manufacture and distribution of drugs and "unproven" remedies by the scores of independent companies competing for their business. As a result of the Act, questionable products could be seized and condemned, and offending persons could be fined and jailed.

Some consider the Pure Food and Drug Act of 1906 as a triumph of progressive reform. Others think it was used as the first major step of the legislatively supported monopolization of health care in America.

1910 A.D. – "The Flexner Report"

On the heals of their success in regulating and reducing competition in the manufacture of botanical remedies, the allopathic community turned their sights on eliminating the major opposition to those measures—the educational institutions that turned out doctors who continued to support the use of plant medicines.

With a report entitled "Medical Education in the United States and Canada," Abraham Flexnor effectively sealed the fate of the botanical movements in North America. Commissioned by the Carnegie Foundation, and supported by funds from at least eleven other elite foundations, the Flexnor report severely criticized the state of facilities and curriculum at virtually every private medical school that did not subscribe to the wisdom of allopathic science. With the report as justification, and the financial power and prestige of the foundations and their corporate supporters as means, the A.M.A. set about an all-out crusade to close down and legislate out of existence their competition, once and for all. The next 25 years saw the near complete demise of every remaining botanical school, and the virtual outlawing of "non-standard" practice in every state of the Union.

Only a handful of outspoken practitioners had the fortitude to carry on the torch.

1928 A.D. – Food and Drug Administration

The FDA, an agency in the Public Health Service division of the U.S. Department of Health & Human Services, is charged with protecting public health by ensuring that foods are safe and pure, cosmetics and other chemical substances harmless, and products safe, effective, and honestly labeled. All new medicinal drugs must also be approved and licensed for use in the U.S. by the FDA. Presented to the public as the Federal enforcer of these lofty goals, the FDA immediately set about consolidating the power and political influence that would give it virtually uncontested control over the medical options available to the public.

Over its 72 year history, the FDA has maintained a close working relationship with the A.M.A., and has taken the large majority of its directors and regulators directly from the management ranks of the pharmaceutical industry. The attitude and regulatory posture of the agency towards botanical medicine, herbs and supplements, and alternative therapies in general has ranged from ambivalent to overtly hostile—dependent mostly upon the economic ebb and flow of the fortunes of the allopathic pharmaceutical corporations. By the middle of the twentieth century, interest in botanical remedies was assumed to be little more than a "folklore" residue in the light of the golden promises of the age of "Better Living Through Chemistry." Some herbs were still available as "teas"—as long as they were on the "GRAS" list (Generally Recognized As Safe), and some herbs and vitamins could be sold as "nutritional supplements" as long as neither made any medicinal claims. Any practice, use, or statement that suggested that herbs had health benefits was automatically labeled as "quackery," and subjected the practitioner to stiff legal penalties.

Enormously expensive campaigns—funded by public money—were initiated to "inform" the public about the "dangers" of "unproven" remedies, and to harass and remove from practice any individual—whether medically licensed or not—who dared to work with alternatives to the current medical "wisdom."

By the 1960's, the A.M.A./FDA campaign against non-allopathic approaches was on the verge of total eradication of thousands of years of botanical practice. Although shaken by the tragic ramifications of Thalidomide, the American public—most now two generations removed from any practical experience with botanical remedies—still maintained an uneasy confidence in the promise of allopathic medicine. The few remaining vocal proponents of herbs and natural alternatives were viewed as alarmists and eccentrics. More often than not, they were also characterized and persecuted by the FDA as "dangerous quacks" who were "preying on the pain and suffering of desperate people." Fortunately, it was only natural that any group that was so adamantly opposed by the "establishment" powers would be sympathetically embraced by the counter-cultural revolution of the 60's. With disdain for the oppressive power of government bureaucracy, and a deep mistrust of corporate propaganda, many young people began to rediscover, use, and advocate more natural alternatives.

To the chagrin of the FDA in the 60's, many of the "quacks" they were targeting were becoming cultural icons among the nation's youth. Concurrently, a surge of interest in Eastern philosophies and Native American spiritualism opened doors of awareness about ancient herbal heritages that had "new" and exciting implications to a restless generation. Environmental concerns began shedding light into the dark corners of the chemical industry's closet of horrors, and by implication, the pharmaceutical giants sheltered under the chemical corporate umbrellas were also exposed for their cruel and ineffective testing procedures, blatant influence peddling, and obscene profiteering. The winds of power had shifted, and the fortress of monopoly that had been crafted by the FDA and A.M.A. was being tested. Reinforced as it was, though, by the enormous wealth and influence of the industry it protected, it would not fall like a simple house of cards.

For the balance of the twentieth century, the FDA lashed out with even more stringent regulations, raids on practitioners, confiscation of products and educational materials, and the threat of criminal prosecution of individuals who would not toe the line. Using a tried and true formula, enormous amounts of public money were spent to "educate" a faltering public on the dangers of "unproven" remedies, attacking the public's interest in herbs like Comfrey, Sassafras, Chaparral and Ma Huang—herbs with long histories of safe and effective use. The FDA has even been known to confiscate a shipment of honey to a health-food store on the grounds that the presence of a book for sale nearby in which honey was described as particularly beneficial nutritionally constituted illegal "drug labeling."

1994 A.D. – Dietary Supplement Health Education Act

Despite the FDA/A.M.A. efforts to "educate" the public, interest in natural health and the use of nutritional supplements, including herbs, had reached an all-time high by the closing decade of the twentieth century. In the early 1990s, at the request of the FDA, Congress began considering two bills to greatly strengthen the ability of federal agencies to combat the growing trend. One would have increased the FDA's enforcement powers as well as the penalties for violating the Food, Drug, and Cosmetic Act. The other would have amended the Federal Trade Commission Act to make it illegal to advertise or publicize any nutritional or therapeutic claims for supplements that would not be permissible on supplement labels, while at the same time, the FDA was developing stricter regulations for those labels.

Alarmed by these developments and encouraged by growing public interest, the health-food industry rallied to urge Congress to "preserve the consumer's freedom to choose dietary supplements." It was apparent to supplement industry leaders that the FDA was making a last-ditch effort to put supplement retailers out of business. Consumers began to realize that unless they took action, the FDA would take away their right to buy the herbs, vitamins, and supplements that were having such a positive effect on their lives. The result was an unprecedented avalanche of communications to Congress, and the passage of the DSHEA.

Initially sponsored by Senator Orrin Hatch of Utah and Congressman Bill Richardson of New Mexico, the Dietary Supplement and Health Education Act of 1994 defined "dietary supplements" as a separate regulatory category and liberalized what information could be distributed by their sellers. (At the time of final passage, the legislation had been cosponsored by 65 Senators and 261 members of the House of Representatives—almost two-thirds of the Senate and more than half of the House.) Historically, the FDA has considered literature used directly in connection with the sale of a product to be "labeling" for the product. DSHEA exempts publications from "labeling" if they: (1) are not false or misleading, (2) do not promote a particular manufacturer or brand, (3) present a "balanced" view of pertinent scientific information, and (4) are physically separated from the items discussed.

DSHEA dramatically increased the amount of information about herbs and supplements that is available to a health hungry public. It also expanded the range of products that can be marketed as supplements by specifically including not only vitamins and minerals, but also many herbs and botanical preparations, enzymes, amino acids, natural hormones, as well as concentrates, extracts, natural metabolites, certain constituents, and combinations of these ingredients. DSHEA also created an NIH Office of Dietary Supplements and directed the President to appoint a Commission on Dietary Supplement Labels to recommend ways to implement the act.

In passing this landmark legislation, Congress set forth a number of "findings," including…

1. Consumers should be empowered to make choices about their own preventive health care programs based on data from scientific studies of health benefits related to particular dietary supplements;

2. National surveys have revealed that almost 50 percent of the 260,000,000 Americans regularly consume dietary supplements of vitamins, minerals, or herbs as a means of improving their nutrition;

3. Although the Federal Government should take swift action against products that are unsafe or adulterated, the Federal Government should not impose unreasonable regulatory barriers limiting or slowing the flow of safe products and accurate information to consumers.

THE NEW MILLENNIUM – REPRIEVE OR REPRISAL?

As we enter the twenty-first century, the DSHEA has given a little breathing space to the cause of botanical medicine in the United States. The battle for freedom of choice in health care is far from over, though. It is simply beginning again. Anyone who is interested in herbs and natural remedies, and the freedom to choose them as alternative methods of health care for themselves and their family must be aware that powerful interests are still hard at work trying to deny those simple God-given rights. It is both unrealistic and historically unjustified to think that the allopathic medical industry, with its enormous political and economic power, will simply "roll over," and allow the people to freely choose between their dependence on heavy handed and highly profitable drugs, and the gentle remedies made readily available by a benevolent Creator.

Unwilling to relax its iron grip on the grass-roots-driven supplement industry, DSHEA has provoked the FDA to become even more vigorous and creative with its persecution efforts. At the same time, the major pharmaceutical conglomerates have seen the economic writing on the wall, as more and more citizens return to herbs and natural remedies to either enhance or replace prescribed drugs. In an effort to recapture this blossoming market, the industry has given birth to the "new" world of "nutraceuticals" and standardized extracts. The "harmonizing" efforts centered around the German Kommission E monographs and the World Trade Commission are viewed by many as the pharmaceutical industry's effort to conquer the natural health movement by assimilation, while imposing unrealistic testing and regulatory standards on what are still, after all, the simple herbs of the field. Even the A.M.A., like the wolf volunteering to become a shepherd, has begun espousing the cause of "integrative" medicine, in an attempt to bring the errant cash flow back under its own umbrella.

Throughout the herbal "Dark Ages" of the twentieth century, after the engineered collapse of the botanical schools and systems, most of America, duped by these same forces, became complacent and ignorant about the health restoring power of common herbs. The total dependence on the allopathic system that followed yielded few miracles, enormous amounts of preventable pain and suffering, hundreds of thousands of deaths attributable directly to prescription drugs, and, of course, staggering costs. As a result, interest in herbs has been revived. New educational institutions have been formed. The biblical promise of "herbs for the service of man" is once again being realized.

To protect ourselves and our children, we must now invest ourselves in rediscovering—and passing on to the next generation—the nearly lost techniques for using the healing bounty of nature that lies beneath our very footsteps. That process has been made easier by the ready availability of the wisdom of our ancient herbalist predecessors, and by the contemporary writings and experiences of the handful of committed herbalists and natural healers who carried the torch through the last century.

The life stories and works of these individuals are well worth noting. It is they and the institutions they inspired, along with thousands of common "folk healers," who have preserved and defended the legacy of herbal healing that we are now witnessing as a near miraculous resurgence.

Edward Shook	Jack Ritchason	Rosemary Gladstar
John Harvey Kellogg	Gene & Christine Hughes	James Duke
John Christopher	Wendell W. Whitman	Norman Farnsworth
Bernard Jensen	Michael Tierra	Nathan Podhurst
John Uri Lloyd	Alfred Vogel	Jethro Kloss
Joseph E. Meyer	Jeanne Rose	Mark Blumenthal
David Hoffmann	Christopher Hobbs	Mark Pedersen
Paavo Airola	Amanda McQuade Crawford	

ALSO RECOMMENDED FOR READING

Golub, Edward S., Ph.D. The Limits of Medicine. Times Books—Random House, 1994. ISBN 0-8129-2141-0

Griggs, Barbara. Green Pharmacy—The History and Evolution of Western Herbal Medicine. Healing Arts Press, 1997. ISBN 0-89281-427-6

Haller, John S., Jr. Kindly Medicine—Physio-Medicalism in America. Kent State University Press, 1997. ISBN 0-8733-8577-2

Haller, John S., Jr. Medical Protestants—The Eclectics in American Medicine. Southern Illinois University Press, 1994. ISBN 0-8093-1894-6

Wilk, Dr. Chester A. Medicine, Monopolies, and Malice. Avery Publishing Group, 1996. ISBN 0-89529-647-0

CHAPTER 2

Practical Herbalism 101

Regaining the Independence of Our Herbal Heritage

The objective of this book is to help you learn how to identify, choose, and use some of the simple, God-given herbs of the field to make good medicine. It is NOT intended by that effort that you should eliminate the use of proprietary processed herbs and supplements, nor even to avoid conventional medical intervention when it is necessary. Rather, it is hoped that by this study, you will come to better appreciate and make more effective use of those options—as options—by adding additional practical choices in times of need.

There are, arguably, only six essential provisions necessary for the survival of the human animal: food, water, shelter, clothing, fuel, and medicine. (Two more elements—socialization and spiritual connection—must be added if man is not merely to survive, but to flourish.) The blessing of the great industrial and technological revolutions is that, at least here in the West, we no longer have to produce these things for ourselves. Grocery stores and restaurants, municipal water systems, building developers, clothing manufacturers, gas and electric companies, and our pharmaceutical and medical industry make these essentials of life available in great abundance.

Of course, the curse of this same industrial/technological cornucopia is that we have, both by design and complacency, become totally dependent on it. Few of us have retained the knowledge or the confidence to produce ANY of the core elements upon which our very survival depends. We are no longer consumers by choice, but of necessity, and out of necessity, we must now pay whatever price is demanded. As our dependence has grown, so has the price, and nowhere has that price escalated faster or has our dependence cost us more dearly than with medicine.

Of all the industries providing our basic needs, medicine is the only one that has been allowed to establish an unrestrained functional monopoly. For more than five generations, the A.M.A. and FDA have been joined in a focused and methodical program designed to disrupt, discredit, outlaw, and destroy every competing philosophy of healing. So successful and enduring has the campaign been that few, if any, people remain living today who remember when botanically trained M.D.s and Homeopaths stood in equal stature with "regular" physicians in the eyes of both the law and the citizenry. Gradually but unswervingly, and with but few notable exceptions, all modalities of medicine that didn't subscribe to the chemical drug and surgery model were slandered, coerced, or legislated out of existence, along with their supply lines and educational systems. Most previously accredited and established dissenting practitioners were simply allowed to die off—with no possibility of replacement.

As long as we can pay the price, our free market system makes available to us many kinds and sources of food, and multiple choices for fuel to warm our homes and drive our machines. We can have clothing made in a myriad of styles with fabrics and materials from around the world. We can have our homes built in a broad spectrum of forms from a staggering variety of materials. The suppliers of all these needs must compete with each other for our dollars. That, in spite of our dependence, has helped keep our costs in relative check and our options plentiful.

The "free market" in medicine, on the other hand, is a carefully cultivated illusion. We have been groomed by both the industry and our government, to believe that all "legitimate" medicine comes from only one philosophical source, and that all other forms must, at the very least, be viewed with suspicion. Our absolute psychological dependence on "conventional" medicine, reinforced by a constant and heavy-handed indoctrination of fear and guilt, has left most people feeling that they have but one direction to turn in times of health crisis. Not surprisingly, this has given the medical industry a virtual blank check to generate obscene profits from our pain and suffering.

There are, though, hopeful indications that this pendulum of dependence is swinging. You are reading this book after all, and exploring your options. All across our country, in fact, there is a fresh awakening of interest in herbs and other natural remedies. Millions of our citizens, with motives ranging from simple curiosity to absolute desperation, are also searching for alternatives for their health concerns. Many will likewise find the answers they seek in the natural gifts of a loving Creator—gifts that have been there all along.

It is not necessary to return to cave living to regain some of our lost sense of independence through the use of natural resources. We do not have to give up grocery stores and restaurants to experience the feeling of gratification that comes from gathering an armload of fresh vegetables from a well-tended garden plot. Nor do we have to go "off the grid" to know the spirit warming joy of sitting in front of a crackling fireplace on a cold winter night—a joy that is only deepened if we've actually had a hand in gathering and splitting the wood. It isn't just about extremes and necessity, it's about choices and self-determination. Gardeners don't just garden because they have no money for food, and these days, most fireplaces are lit in homes with fully functioning central heat. The primal fulfillment of those moments comes from realizing at some deep core level that we have directly produced something of essential importance for ourselves and our loved ones, and for those brief moments at least, we are dependent on no other earthly source for our sustenance.

Making simple but effective medicines from found or cultivated herbs offers an enhanced sense of self-sufficiency and a level of satisfaction that is directly proportionate to the degree of servility we have felt at the hands of conventional medicine. Few efforts are more liberating or empowering than those that help us recover some command of the most basic provisions of our life. The road back to complete independence and control over our health concerns is a long one, and certainly lies well beyond the scope of this book. As an old Chinese proverb observes, though, "The journey of a thousand miles begins with a single step."

Perhaps this could be that step for you.

Thinking Outside the Capsule

Since the dawn of time, man's reliance on the God-given remedies that were found in the natural world around him meant that he also had to learn to identify and collect the beneficial plants, and then prepare and take the often very disagreeable potions and elixirs. Only in the last quarter-century has it become commonplace to enclose herbal material in capsules for consumption.

That innovation is generally attributed to Kristine Hughes, co-founder of Nature's Sunshine Products in Provo, Utah. In 1972, she was seeking a means to make the Cayenne pepper powder that her husband, Gene Hughes, was taking to treat a gastric ulcer a little more palatable. The idea was so simple and successful that it fundamentally revolutionized the way people relate to herbal remedies. Like most innovations, though, the process of encapsulation has some very obvious advantages, and a few, perhaps less obvious, disadvantages.

Capsules provide convenience, the potential for greater consistency, and a barrier that protects our taste buds from the strong flavors associated with many herbal preparations. Commercially prepared remedies, now including pills, extracts, and unguents of various kinds, also relieve the consumer of the burdens of identification and preparation of crude plants. Newcomers to the world of natural healing may also find that the physical similarity of these preparations to familiar pharmaceuticals provides a psychologically more comfortable "bridge" to an otherwise unfamiliar world.

On the down-side, encapsulated herbs can be more difficult to digest and assimilate than simple teas and extracts. The input from the senses of taste and smell that may contribute to the effectiveness of the herbs in their natural form is also reduced. While commercially prepared herbal remedies may make us less dependent on pharmaceuticals, they are necessarily more costly than their "home-grown" counterparts, and they still keep us dependent on sources outside our own means to provide them. Since few of us have sophisticated, analytical equipment, the quality, efficacy, and even the proper identity of the plants in these products is largely a matter of faith in the company that produces them. Perhaps even more significantly, complete reliance on manufactured supplements and remedies does little to bridge the chasm between ourselves and the bounty of natural healing power that lies under our very footsteps.

Whether by perception of eons of mutually beneficial co-evolution, or through the benevolent hand of a loving Creator, our world has been filled with an abundance of medicinal plants and nutritional storehouses that wait in anticipation of each and every need of mankind. Every corner of the inhabited earth has been gifted with these botanical and natural resources, and the variety is as boundless as Creation itself. We will never have far to look, if we only take the time to learn what we are looking for. We can nurture and use this vast apothecary with gratitude and respect, destroy it through our ignorance, or ignore and abandon it through our arrogance. It is our choice.

For more than a century the powerful economic forces of the chemical drug and the allopathic medical industries have worked tirelessly to discredit and destroy our working relationship with nature's free and omnipresent healing tools. Within the confines of the Western industrialized world, this self-serving, profit-motivated effort very nearly succeeded. And yet, according to the World Health Organization, over three quarters of the world's population still rely on botanical medicine as their primary form of health care. That legacy persists, and frustration with the shortcomings of allopathic medicine in the West has created an environment that has allowed man's inescapable connections with his natural surroundings to once again bring the gentle power of herbal medicine back to its rightful prominence. Arguably—are we talking chicken or egg?—the surge in popularity and ready availability of encapsulated herbs and manufactured remedies has been an important factor in this rebirth.

The battle with the forces of pharmacy is not over, though. Dependence on outside resources implies the possibility that free access can be restricted or taken away again at any time; that our natural birthright will once again fall under the oppressive thumb of commercial interests. If we are to secure our right of access, we must fortify it with knowledge. Knowledge of the healing plants that grow in our own yards and environs; knowledge of medicinal wonders that can easily be cultivated in our gardens; and knowledge of simple and effective healing herbal preparations can forever break the bond of dependence on expensive, heavy-handed drugs and dangerously invasive, medical procedures. Knowledge of common herbs is an empowering comfort that keeps our health choices free from political threats and economic coercion.

An herbalist who gathers no herbs is like a bird that will not fly; a raindrop that will not fall; or a blossom that produces no seed. It is the consummate expression of faith to fulfill our God-given role in the natural processes; to soar to the heights of Creation's bounty, to aid and restore balance, and to pass on that faith. To do less is to deny the gifts of an eternally loving Father, who cares for all the needs of His children, in this world as well as the next.

The absence of Faith is fear, and it is fear that now keeps most people, many herbalists included, from confidently gathering and using medicinal herbs from the field. Contrary to popular "wisdom," though, it is not our knowledge of science that makes us wary of the plants around us, it is our ignorance of nature. We can forgive our uncertainty more readily, too, if we understand that our ignorance has been born of generations of apathy, and has been constantly reinforced by the commercial interests who profit by our dependence.

Learn how to identify, gather, and preserve common medicinal plants, and you have taken a significant step towards the restoration of faith and independence. Use your herbs to prepare simple, effective, time-tested botanical remedies; watch the results, and you have learned how to help restore health and vitality, gently and safely, for yourself and your loved ones. Build on those insights by reading, attending classes, and gathering in fellowship with other herbalists, and you have set yourself free from fear, dependence, and manipulation. Pass on that knowledge, and you have helped secure genuine freedom in health choices for future generations.

Nature's healing plants are there and waiting, all around us. They always have been. With interest, care, and respect, they always will be.

BASIC HERBAL PREPARATIONS

Identification, Gathering, Preservation, and Storage

Fresh herbs can be acquired from three basic sources: your own garden, another grower, or wildcrafting. Whatever the source, the first important factor to consider when selecting herbs for medicinal use is correct plant identification. Many different plants can look alike, especially at different stages of growth, and even herbs within the same species can be highly variable in appearance.

Fear of selecting or using the wrong plant is probably the biggest single concern of neophyte herbalists, and it is a concern that has a genuine basis in fact. Most common errors would simply have either disappointing or unexpected outcomes. Tragic results from mistaken identity, while uncommon, can and do occur, though. The leaves of the first year growth of common Foxglove (Digitalis purpurea), for instance, could be mistaken for the early growth of Comfrey, and Wild Carrot or Queen Anne's Lace bears a striking resemblance to the poisonous Hemlock. In either case, these mistakes could have disastrous consequences.

It isn't necessary to have a degree in botany to be a good herbalist, but if tree, flower, grass, or weed is your idea of plant identification, then there is some work left to do. Gaining confidence in herb identification will take time, study, and experience. An attention to distinguishing details is part of the herbalist's art. Not only appearance, but smell, feel, and taste, as well as environment and seasonal progress all combine to form each plant's unique fingerprint. As these factors are recognized, the herbs will become, one by one, first familiar, then unmistakable. Nature's great diversity is not an unfathomable puzzle. It is, for the patient observer, a clear and detailed blueprint with which we can restore, build, and maintain good health.

Whether you grow, buy, or forage for your fresh herbs, take some simple steps to help insure that you are getting the correct plant.

1. Invest in at least two good herb identification guide books.

2. Start with well-known, easy to identify plants.

3. Ask for advice from knowledgeable herbalists, gardeners, and friends.

4. Start your own notebook of identifying characteristics.

5. If there is ANY doubt, DON'T use it.

Growing Your Own

Growing herbs for medicinal (or even culinary) use is one of the best ways to insure the identity—and availability—of your materials. Follow these common-sense caveats.

1. Always get your plant stock and seeds from a reliable source, and make sure they are properly labeled, including botanical names.

2. Use markers in the growing beds to keep plants identified until they become familiar.

3. Separate plants with similar characteristics.

4. Never include toxic plants in medicinal herb beds.

5. Make a "map" of your herb beds, paying special attention to the perennial and biennial herbs that will die back in Winter and return in Spring. Include photos of the plants at various stages of growth.

6. Use only organic fertilizer and natural pest control for your medicinal plants.

Buying Fresh Herbs

Buying fresh herbs from another grower or wildcrafter is an act of faith. Growing and harvesting wild herbs has become a popular cottage industry, and suppliers are popping up all over the country. Most are ethical, and have the experience and expertise to provide good quality, correctly identified, herbal material to their customers. The ultimate responsibility for insuring the quality and identity of the herbs still lies with the user, though. These guidelines can help avoid problems.

1. **Know Your Source** – ask about experience and check references.

2. **Be Specific** – know the plant and plant part you require.

3. **Don't Ask for Trouble** – asking someone else to gather endangered plants does not relieve you of the responsibility.

4. **Double-Check Your Material** – be sure that what you requested is actually what you received.

5. **Be Prepared for What You Receive** – fresh cut herbs lose potency very quickly. Be ready to preserve your purchase as soon as it arrives.

Harvesting in the Wild

Wildcrafting, the process of gathering native herbs growing in their natural environment, ranks among the most gratifying experiences of an herbalist's life. Wildcrafting can be as simple as gathering some Dandelion greens from the boundaries of your own yard, or as intense as hiking through unspoiled forests in search of increasingly rare unmolested stands of wild Goldenseal or Ginseng. In between is the gathering of the great bounty of the plentiful, though often neglected, common herbs with extraordinary healing powers that nature has placed all around us. The healing energy concentrated in plants growing in their own natural habitat is unsurpassed by anything that can ever be cultivated. Perhaps the greatest treasure to be found by the wildcrafter is the reassurance that comes from realizing that the means to care for our most basic needs has been sprinkled over the landscape by a benevolent Creator—and it is NEVER far away.

Along with the obvious need for accurate plant identification, wildcrafting also involves other concerns over matters of ethical practices and environmental sensitivity. When gathering the healing gifts of nature from the wild, make sure you follow these principles and guidelines.

1. **Be Certain You Have the Right Plant** – use photographic guidebooks, or a knowledgeable guide.

2. **Be "Green" not Greedy** – take only what you can use.

3. **Never "Clear" an Area of Any Plant** – 30% of a stand of plants is the maximum that can be removed without jeopardizing the future of the colony.

4. **Never Harvest Endangered Plants** – there is ALWAYS an alternative.

5. **Be Conscious of Plant Life-Cycles** – let plants produce seed for the next generation.

6. **Leave the Area Better than You Found it** – restore natural leaf cover. "Pick-up and Pack-out" trash left by others.

7. **ALWAYS get Permission if You are Hunting Herbs on Someone Else's Land** – offer to share your find.

8. **Avoid Plants Growing Along Highways, Railways, or Heavily Traveled Roadsides.**

9. **IMMEDIATELY Label Your Material** – make a note of the plant name and the date and place gathered.

10. **Keep a Log of Your Finds** – make notes about the conditions surrounding the herbs you found. It can help you find your way back, and identify other areas that might yield equal results.

Harvesting – Timing Is Everything

Whether you are growing, buying, or wildcrafting, the quality and efficacy of your herbs depends on getting the right part of the herb at the right time in its life cycle.

The life cycle of a plant can be divided into five basic stages—dormancy, active growth, flowering, fruiting, and setting seed. Depending on the part of the plant you will be using, the time of harvest will vary. While there are occasional exceptions, the basic Rule of Thumb for determining when a part of an herb is at its peak of strength is simple.

Gather the part of the plant you wish to use just before the next phase of its life cycle begins. Using this principle, herbs should be gathered according to the following timetable.

1. **Roots, Bark** – may be harvested anytime after the plant has set and matured its seed (fruit), and before new growth begins in the Spring. In other words, roots and barks should ideally be harvested while the plant is dormant.

    Examples: Willow Bark, Gravel Root, Pike Root, Hydrangea

2. **Leaves, Tops and Shoots** – should be harvested just as flower buds have formed, and before they begin to open.

    Examples: Peppermint, Lemon Balm, Sage, Lobelia

3. **Flowers, Blossoms, Flowering Tops** – are at their peak of strength when the flowers are well-formed and fully open, and just before the petals begin to wither or fall, before setting fruit or forming seed.

    Examples: Calendula, Yarrow, Elder flowers

4. **Fruit** – should be gathered when they are plump, firm, and deeply colored, and before they show signs of decay.

    Examples: Hawthorn Berries, Juniper Berries, Vitex, Capsicum

5. **Seeds** – have their highest concentration of nutrients and medicinal properties when they are fully mature. Their carriers (pods, husks, calyxes) are usually dry and shriveled, and the plants themselves may be withered, dead, or dormant.

    Examples: Dill, Fennel, Milk Thistle

Notable exceptions:

Wild Cherry – The bark of this tree has its highest potency in the Fall, when it should be gathered to make cough and lung formulas.

Yellow Dock – The roots of this powerful cleansing herb can be gathered anytime the plant is not in bloom.

Comfrey root – Like Yellow Dock, it has great stores of healing power whenever it is not producing flowers. (Use the leaves and flowers then.)

Time of Day

The time of day that your herbs are harvested is not nearly so critical as the season. In general, the aerial parts of herbs should be collected after the morning dew has lifted, and before the heat of the day has sapped their vital energy. Timing on roots and barks is not a problem if harvested in the correct season.

Preserving Your Harvest

It would be a tidy world indeed if medicinal plants were always at the peak of their healing powers, or if the need for them only occurred when they were readily available. It is no small wonder that it does seem to work out that way so often. Wherever and whenever Poison Ivy is actively growing, there also will always be one of Nature's Poison Ivy "erasers" – Plantain, Jewelweed, or Hound's Tongue. At the same time that the summer sun threatens to burn our fragile skin, Comfrey and Aloe also flourish. When brutal winter winds bring coughs and respiratory distress, relief from the bark of the Wild Cherry tree is at its peak of strength. After a long winter of heavy foods and few naturally available fresh fruits and vegetables, the Spring fairly bursts forth with cleansing "tonics," ready to renew our bodies as nature renews herself.

Life is not always so orderly, though, and we are wise to plan for its twists and turns. Gathering and preserving herbs is a kind of insurance policy against those times when our health throws us an untimely curve, and presents us with a problem when our favored herbs are "out of season." Like our other insurance, we may hope that it will never be needed, but our preserved harvest also offers great comfort by its presence. In fact, the process of preserving and laying by our medicinal herbs can be very therapeutic in itself. There is little more satisfying than knowing that our own labors have contributed to the preservation of our own health, and that of our loved ones.

Traditional methods of preserving herbs—by drying, tincturing, oil extraction, and the making of salves and ointments—are tried and true. Our technological times offer us a few additional, if somewhat less "proven," options—juicing, freezing, and vacuum packaging, for instance. Whatever the method, the goal is the same; to capture the essence of the herb's natural healing powers and protect it from deterioration so that it can be used whenever it might be needed. To accomplish that goal, we must understand the forces that work against it.

The major factors that contribute to the breakdown or degradation of an herb's active principles are:

1. its own natural enzymes
2. bacteria, mold, and infestation
3. moisture
4. heat
5. light
6. air

Reducing or eliminating the influence of some or all of these factors stabilizes the herb—and its healing powers. How well these factors are controlled directly affects the herb's "shelf life," or how long the herb will remain efficacious.

TRADITIONAL METHODS FOR PRESERVING AND PREPARING HERBS

Drying

Enzymes, bacteria, and mold require moisture to survive and function. Reducing the level of moisture in an herbal material reduces the level of activity of these degrading factors. If herbs could be completely dried, and stored in a moisture-free environment, they might remain intact and effective virtually forever. Excavating the cool, dark, ancient tombs of the arid Egyptian desert, archeologists have unearthed seeds that remained viable and plant material that was readily identifiable and chemically indistinguishable from their modern progeny—over 6,000 years after they had been buried! Herbs that are gathered at the peak of their medicinal strength, carefully and effectively dried, and stored in a way that protects that state can be kept and used with confidence for quite a long time.

Traditional herb drying techniques call for hanging the herbs in loosely tied bundles, or arranging them in thin layers on baskets or screen frames and placing them in a sheltered location until they are brittle to the touch. This process can reduce the moisture level of the herbs down to a level at or near the ambient humidity. If the resulting material is then stored in a light proof, air tight container or dark glass sealed bottle, it may, depending on the herb and conditions, maintain its potency for two years or more. If the air-dried material is moved to a moderately heated cabinet or very low oven for a short time to drive off as much remaining moisture as possible, and then is stored in vacuum sealed light-proof containers, its effective life can be extended many fold. The shelf life of dried herbs is dependent on many factors, but mostly on the care with which they are processed and stored.

Drying herbs is simple, involves little cost, and yields a product that can be used and re-processed in a wide variety of ways. Virtually anything that can be done with fresh herbs, except expressing the juice, can be done with dried herbs. The limitations of dried herbs are that the process requires care and close attention, the resulting material is much bulkier than tinctures and prepared extracts, and the storage conditions are generally much more critical. Leaves and flowering tops can be air-dried. Small fruits and slices of larger fruits can also be air dried in arid climates, but are more safely done with low heat. Roots and barks almost always require low heat to drive the moisture out of the denser material, and to prevent the formation of mold and bacteria.

Herbs should be kept labeled and separated throughout the drying process. When they are dried, they can be easily confused or mixed up. Frequent inspections should be made while the herbs are drying to make sure that they are drying evenly and that no mold is developing. Herbs that show any signs of mold should be discarded. Dry herbs should also be kept as whole as possible. Crushing or grinding may reduce the volume, but it also exposes more surface area to degrading influences, and reduces their usable life. Containers of dried herbs should be immediately labeled with the name and date of collection, and, if they are to be shared, with the name of the collector.

Infusions and Decoctions

The simplest and most traditional method of taking herbs into the body is as an herbal beverage. Herbal "tea" may be made with either fresh or dried herbs, and may be either an infusion or a decoction. Either one can be made as a "simple"—using a single herb—or as a combination formulated to take advantage of the synergistic support of the selected herbs. In some cases, herbs may be added to a formula to help balance or offset some less desirable effects of the primary herb—unpleasant taste or excessive stimulation, for instance.

An infusion is made by pouring boiling water over the herbs in a cup or teapot, and allowing the mixture to stand for 15 minutes or so until the herbs have released their beneficial components to the water. The infusion may then be strained and sweetened to taste—preferably with a whole natural sweetener like raw honey or maple syrup. Occasionally, it may be recommended to let the infusion stand until it is cool to more thoroughly extract the constituents.

Infusions are usually made from the more delicate parts of the plants—flowers, leaves or flowering tops. When using aromatic herbs like Peppermint or Lemon Balm, it is especially important that the tea should be covered while it is infusing to prevent the loss of volatile elements to the atmosphere.

A decoction differs from an infusion in that the herb is combined with water in a small pot, and is brought to the boiling point over low heat. The mixture is then simmered slowly for 15-30 minutes, or sometimes until the amount of liquid is reduced by a specified amount—for instance, to one-half of the original volume. The resulting liquid extract is then strained, sweetened if desired, and taken according to directions.

Decoctions are usually made from the denser, more woody parts of the plants—roots, bark, and stems—or from herbal material whose primary actives are poorly soluble in water.

Infusions and decoctions should always be made with fresh, pure water. Spring water is ideal. They are best when prepared as needed, but they may be prepared ahead if they are kept refrigerated and used within 48 hours.

In addition to their obvious internal applications, infusions and decoctions can be used to great advantage externally as well. Detoxification baths, fomentations, washes for wounds, scalp and skin rinses, eye washes and drops, and vaginal douches may all be prepared from an infusion or decoction. External teas like these are usually made stronger than those intended for internal consumption. A "strong" infusion or decoction typically requires 2-4 times the amount of herb in proportion to the water, and a "strong" decoction may be simmered for a longer time or reduced to a greater extent, as well. Glycerin may be added to these mixtures to preserve them for a longer period. One part of vegetable glycerin to three parts of extract works well.

Tincturing

Tinctures are concentrated liquid extracts made with fresh or dried herbs. Herbal material is macerated (soaked) in a natural solvent called a menstruum. The menstruum—usually a mixture of distilled spirits and water—dissolves and carries the active constituents out of the fibrous plant material. When the mass is pressed and filtered, the resulting extract more or less contains the same proportion of naturally balanced "actives" as the original plant. Tinctures are, therefore, called whole herb extracts, and can be used with the same safety considerations and expectation for outcome as the herb itself.

The key advantages to tinctures are that they are concentrated and convenient to use, easy to mix into combinations, dosages are easier to control, and they have an excellent shelf life. They may be taken internally, applied directly to the skin, or used in external applications like fomentations. On the downside, tinctures are more costly and tedious to make when compared to drying herbs. Some people also find the alcohol that is usually used to make them to be objectionable.

The menstruum can be varied, and many tinctures are made with either cider vinegar or glycerin and water. Wine is also occasionally used. Aqueous alcohol solutions are generally preferred for two reasons. Many of the most active constituents of plants are alkaloids or resins, and these chemicals are most soluble in alcohol. Non-alcohol extracts may not retain the original balance of these important phyto-chemicals. Secondly, the alcohol itself acts as a disinfectant and preservative, helping to destroy contaminating bacteria and molds. When properly stored, alcohol tinctures will retain their potency for five years or more. Non-alcohol extracts have a shorter shelf-life, and should be used within one or two years.

Commercial tinctures are usually made according to strict proportional standards set in the U.S. Pharmacopoeia (U.S.P.), the National Formulary (N.F.), or in traditional homeopathic formularies. These standards require measuring the moisture content of fresh herbs, and varying the proportion of water and alcohol accordingly to precise tolerances. The percentage of alcohol (proof) in the menstruum also varies for each herb, based on the known solubility of its constituents. Commercial tincturing is an interesting process that attempts to get the most potency from every herb, but it is unnecessarily complex for tinctures that are for home and personal use.

If we consider tincturing as a method of preservation rather than a standardization process, then we can reduce the steps to a very manageable level. Our product will be as safe and effective as the original herb, and it will more closely resemble the tinctures and extracts that have been used since before the time of Galen. The sense of accomplishment and satisfaction at having prepared these traditional extracts is very gratifying.

Making a Basic Tincture

Materials Required

> 4 oz. of FRESH herb*
> OR
> 2 oz. of DRIED herb*
>
> 16 oz. 100 Proof Vodka (50 % aqueous-alcohol solution)
>
> 1 Quart Mason jar with lid
>
> * You may use any herb, but Comfrey Root is a good start.

Method:

1. Weigh out the amount of herb required.

2. If fresh herb material is used, it should be very finely chopped or crushed. A food processor makes short work of this task. Dried herbs also need to be reduced as much as possible. A food processor or blender works well for most dry herbs, but very hard material like some roots and barks may require a grain mill or coffee grinder (reserve it for this purpose).

3. Put the finely cut or ground herb into the jar.

4. Measure out the Vodka (Brandy, Rum or other good quality distilled spirits may also be used), and pour it over the herb.

5. Seal the jar and shake to mix thoroughly.

6. Set the jar in a warm place where you will pass it regularly. A sunny window sill or porch railing is ideal. Shake the jar at least twice daily to mix its contents.

7. After two weeks, strain off the liquid through a clean piece of muslin or linen fabric. Squeeze as much of the menstruum as possible out of the herb pulp. If desired, the liquid extract that is recovered can be filtered once more through an unbleached coffee filter paper, but any remaining particles will eventually settle out of the tincture once it is bottled.

8. Pour the tincture into dark amber glass bottles. Fill as completely as possible to eliminate air, and cap tightly. Label the bottles with the herb name, date made, and menstruum used. Store in a cool, dark cabinet until needed.

Many old time herbalists prepare their tinctures according to the phases of the moon; starting the tincture on the New Moon, and finishing it when the moon is full. Muscle response testing indicates that this lunar support may make a difference, and, like chicken soup, it can't hurt.

Tincture Notes and Recipes:
— If using glycerin as the menstruum, always use vegetable glycerin, and dilute it with two parts of distilled water. Simmering the mixture at the beginning of the process (as for a decoction) for 15 minutes or so may help extract the plant actives.

— Cider vinegar (raw) should be at least 5% acidity. Use it undiluted.

Oil Extracts

Oil extracts are used mainly for topical applications, and as the base for salves or ointments. Oil extracts can be taken internally, but they are readily absorbed through the skin, and can be as much as 70 times more effective at delivering oil-soluble phyto-chemicals into the bloodstream than when the same herbs are ingested. Most beneficial plant constituents, including alkaloids, are at least partially soluble in oil.

Oil extracts fall into two general categories, cold infusions and those prepared with heat. Generally speaking, dried herbs are more easily extracted in oil by cold infusion, while fresh herbs are more readily extracted with heat. Delicate herbs and flowers, and those with high concentrations of volatile oils, should always be prepared by cold infusion whether they are fresh or dried. Cold infusions may take two weeks or more to finish, while hot extracts can often be made in a matter of hours.

Most good quality, cold-pressed, vegetable oils—the only kind that should be used—are highly susceptible to oxidation. They will quickly turn rancid if storage conditions are less than ideal. Natural preservatives can be used to extend the shelf life of oil products, but they must also be protected from heat, light, and air if they are to maintain good quality. Refrigerating oil extracts, and gently warming them when needed, will dramatically increase their shelf life. Most cold-pressed, unrefined vegetable oils should NEVER be subjected to the high heat of cooking, even to make herbal extracts.

The two vegetable oils that are the most naturally resistant to oxidation are Extra Virgin Olive Oil and Grapeseed Oil. Extra Virgin Olive Oil holds up well under higher temperatures. It is the preferred oil for making hot extracts. Grapeseed Oil is very high in protective antioxidant compounds, and is an excellent choice for cold oil infusions.

Making Basic Oil Extracts

Cold Infusion

Materials required:

    1 cup of finely chopped fresh or ground dried herb (minced fresh Garlic is an excellent choice).

    10-12 oz. cold-pressed Grapeseed Oil

    1 Quart Mason jar with lid

Method:

1. Place the herb and oil in the jar and seal. The oil should cover the herb by at least an inch.

2. Set the jar in a warm place, preferably in direct sunlight.

3. Shake at least twice daily for two weeks.

4. Strain off the oil. Fill into dark glass bottles, and seal tightly.

5. Store in the refrigerator, or, if a natural preservative has been used, in a cool, dark cabinet.

Hot Oil Extract

Materials required:

A large heat resistant saucepan. Use un-chipped enamel ware, Pyrex, or stainless steel with a laminated bottom. NEVER use aluminum.

3-4 cups of chopped fresh herb (Try freshly gathered Plantain, Chickweed, or Comfrey leaves to start.)

Extra Virgin Olive Oil (Enough to just barely cover the herb in the pan.)

Method:

1. Leave the pan uncovered. On an electric range eye, or in the oven, very slowly raise the temperature of the oil until the mixture just starts to bubble. Back off the temperature slightly—no more than 200° F in the oven—until the bubbling is very slow but steady.

2. Simmer slowly this way and stir frequently until the herb material is completely crisp. This may take anywhere from 4-5 hours to a full day or more, depending upon the quantity and moisture content of the herb.

3. Strain, bottle, and store as for Cold Infusions.

Preserving Oil Extracts

There are several natural preservatives that can help extend the life of oil extracts. They may be used separately or in combination.

— Vitamin E oil – blends perfectly with other oils, and acts as an effective antioxidant. Use approximately ¼ teaspoon per ounce of oil extract.

— Tincture of Benzoin – extract of a tree resin with preservative properties. Use 1-2 drops per ounce of oil extract.

— Essential Oils – have varying levels of anti-microbial activity, and will help extend shelf life as well as add fragrance and therapeutic value.

— Myrrh – this Biblical resin may be tinctured, or simply crushed to a powder and added to oils as they are bottled. Use 4-5 drops of tincture or ¼ teaspoon of powdered resin per ounce of oil.

— Sage and Rosemary – adding some of either or both of these herbs (preferably fresh) to your mixture when preparing oil extracts will lend their antioxidant properties to the finished product. Wait until hot oil extracts are nearly finished before adding the Sage or Rosemary, and cover the pan to retain their volatile oils.

— Grapefruit Seed extract – a little difficult to find, but highly effective as a preservative. Varies in strength, so follow the manufacturer's recommendations.

Salves and Ointments

Sometimes, as with burns, cuts, or localized injuries, it is desirable to keep an oil extract in close, prolonged contact with a small area of the skin. An ointment or salve (the terms are interchangeable) is designed to do just that.

Essentially, an ointment is a mixture of fat soluble chemicals, extracted from herbs, that has been made so that it will hold together in a mass. It gradually melts at or near body temperature, and slowly releases its healing properties to the area of application.

Traditionally, ointments have been made by cooking herbs in mutton fat, beef tallow, lard, lanolin, or even petroleum jelly. The herbs are strained out, and the fatty material allowed to cool and re-harden, occasionally being thickened with a little paraffin. Not only are these fats (and the resulting products) pretty disagreeable, they can actually clog the skin's pores, and create as many problems as they might otherwise help resolve.

Keeping a healing oil in contact with the skin, and controlling its rate of absorption can be very useful. Fortunately, it isn't necessary to use noxious ingredients to accomplish this. Any oil extract, made according to the directions in the previous section, can be thickened with a little pure beeswax to make a wonderful healing ointment.

Making a Basic Ointment

Materials required:

- 4 oz. of herbal oil extract – See the previous section for directions on how to make this. A blend of Comfrey root, Calendula blossom, and Oregon Grape root makes a wonderfully healing salve for the skin.

- ½ oz. of pure beeswax – shaved or beads

- A natural preservative – See the previous section for suggestions. For a general healing salve, good choices would be Tincture of Benzoin (also healing for epithelial tissue), Myrrh (has antibiotic properties), and Vitamin E oil (protects new skin cells).

- Essential oils – For fragrance and therapeutic value, a skin salve might include several drops of Patchouli, Lavender, Frankincense, or Spruce.

- Several small wide-mouth jars or tins.

Method:

1. Slowly heat the oil in a small Pyrex or stainless steel saucepan. (DO NOT use aluminum.) If you have a gas range, this is best done in the oven.

2. Pay close attention to the process. Over-heated oils can be a serious fire hazard.

3. As the oil warms, stir in the beeswax slivers or beads. Stir frequently, and continue to heat just until the beeswax is melted and incorporated.

4. Remove the oil mixture from the heat, and stir in your preservative and essential oils.

5. Carefully pour the mixture into your containers, and allow to stand undisturbed until cool and firmly set. Cap securely, and store in a cool, dark cabinet until needed.

Notes and Recipes:
— Healing ointments are fun to make and make great gifts.

— Sore Muscle Rub: Combine equal parts of oil extracts of Capsicum (Cayenne peppers), Calendula flowers, and Bugle. Warm the oil and add beeswax in proper proportion for ointment (1 part beeswax to 8 parts oil). When beeswax is melted and incorporated, remove from heat and add 20 drops of Essential Oil of Peppermint and 2 drops of Tincture of Benzoin for each ounce of the oil/wax mixture. Pour into small containers, and allow to set. (NOTE: When applying this ointment, take care to avoid sensitive parts of the body.)

— Poison Ivy Balm: Combine oil extracts (any two, or all three) of Comfrey (leaf or root), Plantain (whole herb), and Jewelweed (flowering tops). Heat and combine with beeswax for ointment. When wax is melted, remove from heat, and add 5 drops of Essential Oil of Lavender and 2 drops of Tincture of Benzoin for each ounce of mixture. Pour into small containers and allow to set. (When all three herbs are used, this ointment is also excellent for insect bites and stings as well as all sorts of rashes.)

TWO MORE TRADITIONAL HERBAL REMEDIES

The outward application of botanical preparations to help heal wounds, relieve skin disorders, and ease inward ailments is a long-standing herbal tradition. The two most popular forms of this therapy are fomentations and poultices. The former is made with hot herbal extracts—an infusion or decoction, and the latter with prepared crude herbs.

Making a Fomentation

Generally used to relieve infections, swellings, acute inflammation, bruises, sprains, and fractures, a fomentation is nothing more than a hot compress made by dipping a flannel or woolen cloth into a strong hot tea or decoction of your chosen herbs. The cloth is applied to the body, and may be wrapped with plastic wrap or a towel to hold in the heat. Hot water bottles or and electric heating pad may also be applied. As the compress cools, it can be dipped back into the hot liquid, wrung out, and reapplied. Fomentations are usually applied in this way for several hours at a time, or until the desired result is achieved.

Fresh or dried herbs as well as tinctures added to hot water may be used to prepare fomentations.

Making a Poultice

Sometimes called a plaster, a poultice is a mass of chopped or mashed prepared herbs, usually layered between sheets of gauze or natural cloth, and bound to the body. They can be used much like fomentations, but also to aid more long-standing or severe injuries, and to draw out splinters and felons.

When available, fresh herbs with their natural juices intact are preferred for the preparation of poultices. Dried herbs can be moistened with hot water or aloe juice, and are sometimes mixed with ground flax seed, oatmeal, or whole wheat flour to form a thick paste. Tinctures can be added to the mixture to enhance its effects. The herbal material is spread over a cloth in a thick layer large enough to cover the desired area. The cloth is folded over to form a pouch, and the whole is bound to the body with an additional cloth or plastic wrap. A poultice is usually left in place for 1-3 days, at which time it can be removed and replaced with a freshly made application, if necessary.

Notes and Recipes:
— Dr. Christopher's favorite: Dr. John R. Christopher frequently used a combination of 3 parts of Mullein (leaf) and 1 part of Lobelia (flowering top) for poultices or fomentations to aid in the healing of boils, skin ulcerations, and swellings that he felt were the result of lymphatic congestion. He would also administer a tea made in the same proportions. I have had excellent success with this remedy as well, and I very often add 1 part of Peppermint herb to this formula as a "catalyst." (I'm probably not as patient as Dr. Christopher was, and the Peppermint helps to speed the process along.)

TOOLS OF THE TRADE

Apart from the identification guides and notebook that should accompany every herbalist to the field, a few well-selected tools and provisions will make the herb gathering and processing experience a lot more fun.

Gathering Tools
- Clothing appropriate to the quest
- Gloves
- Knife (sturdy enough for peeling bark)
- Snips
- Pruning saw (for limbs and roots)
- Shovel (the military style folding model is suitable for most forays)
- Hand axe
- Bags (large paper or zipper lock plastic)
- String or twine and an old newspaper (for bundling)
- Labeling pen and labels
- Magnifier
- A comfortable hiking pack (with outside straps)
- Insulated chest cooler (if you will be transporting your treasures for any distance)

Processing Aids

An herb dryer can be as simple as a length of cord strung across the attic, in a sheltered corner of the porch, or out in the garage (protected from chemicals and car exhaust). Loose bundles of herb tops will usually dry quite nicely in a few days when hung in warm shade. Smaller herbs and flowers may be dried on simple frames covered with plastic window screening. Heavier roots and barks are best done in a warm oven or with the aid of a food dehydrator.

A large wooden bowl (a recycled salad bowl, for instance) is perfect for garbling (hand cleaning and separating the usable parts of) your herbs. Meticulously inspecting and removing stems, discolored leaves, and foreign material from your precious medicinal herbs can be one of the most time-intensive aspects of herb collection. It can also be some of the most rewarding time spent. A bowl large enough to rest forearms on the rim while it sits comfortably in your lap is a worthwhile investment (though such an implement can often be found for a song at yard sales).

Herb storage containers can be made of any receptacle of appropriate size that can be made light and air tight. Mason jars, wrapped in paper, and stored in a cool dark cabinet serve the purpose very well, and economically to boot. When such jars are sealed using one of the commercially available, vacuum food-saver machines, the storage conditions approach ideal, and the usable life of the herbs will be improved dramatically.

The classic mortar and pestle that nostalgically adorns the covers of many herb books adds a wonderful bit of atmosphere to your kitchen apothecary. It is probably best maintained in that role. With few exceptions, the process of grinding and reducing herbal material for teas, tinctures, and extracts is far more easily accomplished with simple, inexpensive, and more user friendly power tools. A small electric coffee grinder (reserved exclusively for your herbs) will make short work of most seeds, root pieces, and bark chips. A basic blender can quickly mill most dried leaves and flowering tops to a fine powder. A food processor is probably the best choice for briskly reducing fresh plant material to fine shreds.

A good metric scale is a wise investment for all but the most casual herbal medicine maker. Don't waste money on the ultra-cheap and inaccurate kitchen/postage scales found at discount stores. Electronic digital models with a "tare" capability that allows you to use a variety of containers for weighing is ideal. Like most other electronic devices, good quality scales with a capacity of a kilo (2.2 lbs.) or more, and accuracy to a gram or better have come steadily down in price over the past few years. They can be found at office supply stores, restaurant equipment dealers, and some hardware stores.

Tinctures and cold oil extracts can be accomplished in clear glass mason jars of various sizes. A couple of gallon size jars (such as "sun tea" jars) are handy for making larger quantities. A stainless steel mesh strainer (make sure it's not aluminum wire) can be lined with muslin or cheesecloth to strain and filter tinctures. Small quantities of extracts can be pressed out with the aid of a potato ricer. Larger quantities may require a small cider or wine press for best results, and will pay for itself many times over in increased yield. A yard or two of unbleached muslin from a local fabric store will serve to press out a lot of herbal extract from the marc (the spent herb left after tincturing). Be sure to wash it before the first use to remove the sizing used in most new cloth, and cut it into substantial squares. Unbleached coffee filter papers can be used to finesse your extracts to nearly perfect clarity.

Dark amber or cobalt blue storage bottles of the pharmaceutical variety (called Boston Rounds) are ideal for finished extracts. Sizes up to 4 oz. are available with dropper tops for convenient dispensing. Collected bottles of various sizes and shapes are fine, as long as they are air tight. (Corked bottles are best left for decorative purposes.) Be sure they are scrupulously cleaned and sterilized in boiling water before re-use. When clear bottles are used for herbal preparations, they should always be stored in a dark, cool cupboard. Squat, wide-mouth, glass jars with leak-proof caps are the best choice for ointments and salves. Shallow metal containers with slip covers are readily available from many suppliers, but most of these "tins" are actually aluminum—not an ideal choice for medicinal herbs.

Labels are important at every step of the process. Keep plenty on hand, and be sure to label the container, not the lid. Lids can easily get switched.

A good collection of wooden spoons, rubber scrapers, funnels, and measuring cups with functional pouring lips makes an herbalist's life much easier. It is also something that seems to grow with each processing experience.

Stove Top Accessories

Most herbal "cooking" should be done on low even heat. An electric cook top with "European style" solid heating elements is ideal. Standard coil-type electric elements and gas ranges may require some means of moderating the contact between the pot and burner. Wire grids and metal "flame spreaders" are available for this purpose from most hardware stores. An "instant-read" probe thermometer (most can accurately register temperatures from below freezing to 300°F or so) will help keep your efforts from being cremated.

Pots used for herbal preparations should be made of flame-proof glass, porcelain enamel, or stainless steel. They should NEVER have aluminum interiors. It is also best to keep herbal cookware exclusively for that purpose, and not allow it to intermingle with food preparation pans. One pot should also be reserved solely for the making of ointments (residual melted beeswax is REALLY difficult to eliminate once it latches onto a pan or bottle).

Optional Joys

— *Dehydrator*

Herbal material CAN be effectively dried without one, and roots and barks CAN be dried in a (very) slow oven. A good quality Food Dehydrator will dramatically improve the dependability of the process, and the quality of the final product as well. Most of the countertop units available are adequate, but have too little capacity for serious production.

— *Vacuum Packaging Machine (with Mason jar sealing capability)*
Potentially the greatest single boon to herb storage and potency. Pulling a vacuum on jars of dried herbs minimizes air contact, seals the jars effectively, and virtually eliminates the chances that the herbal material can ever be contaminated or re-absorb moisture. If the jars are wrapped and stored in a cool, dark cabinet, the herbs might as well be residing in Tut's tomb. (Will you still need them in 6,000 years?) Make sure the sealer has an accessory port, and can, at least, be used to seal standard or wide-mouth Mason jars.

— *Yogurt Maker*
A very useful appliance for making low temperature extracts.

— *Commercial Blender*
Pulverize, chop, grind, puree, juice and compound the toughest herbs without ever breaking a sweat. But wait! Before you decide… A half-gallon size model of this Clydesdale workhorse can set you back $700 to $1,000 or more. Hang around used restaurant equipment dealers, and hope for a deal.

CHAPTER 3

Understanding Herbal Actions

Dis-ease is not something that happens to us. It happens through us. The body is designed to be healthy—and self-healing. If the natural state of health and vitality is disrupted, one or both of two basic events has occurred. We have either developed a deficiency of the essential resources necessary for the body to protect and maintain itself, or we have accumulated an excess of toxins and irritants—"bio-sludge" and invaders—that stand in the way of healing and balance, or that have overwhelmed what resources we have. The body expresses these conditions—and its efforts to restore balance—with symptoms. Far too often, these symptoms have come to be identified as the disease. Allopathic doctors, and many herbalists, focus on controlling the symptoms, and in the process allow the excesses and deficiencies at the root of the problem to become evermore deeply entrenched.

Of course, herbs can control symptoms, though they are seldom as effective at doing so as their heavy-handed chemical-drug counterparts. They are often chosen anyway, because they are "natural," and therefore assumed "safer" or, at least, less threatening. The often forgotten Natural Health axiom that "Suppressing symptoms does not heal," is just as true with herbs as it is with allopathic medicine, though. Just because most herbs are inherently less toxic than drugs does not mean that they are any more effective at restoring health if they are used like drugs are used. In order to employ herbs to their true advantage—the ability to support the body's effort to heal itself—we must learn to think of the body's actions—its symptoms—and the herb's actions, in synchronistic or synergistic terms. By working with the Natural processes instead of fighting them, we can empower and expedite the resolution of dis-ease, and the restoration of health.

Where there is dis-ease, it can only be eliminated if we correct the dichotomy of its cause—excess and deficiency. In short, we must take out the trash, and restock the pantry. Viewed in this context, herbs can be very powerful tools, indeed. Each general goal—detoxification and regeneration—has a subset of actions that can be taken to achieve the desired end. It is for these actions that we turn to the healing power of herbs.

Some herbs have the ability to detoxify the body through one or more of its several channels of elimination. Others have the capacity to nourish, strengthen, and tone various parts of the anatomy or physiological functions, utilizing their own unique and concentrated stores of nutrients. The most appropriate means for accomplishing each of the two primary objectives can be determined by the nature of the complex of symptoms that express how and where the dis-ease has manifested. If the body is blocked in the fulfillment of a natural function, we much remove the blockage where it occurs. If the body is struggling against an invading pathogen, we must bolster its resources and empower the means it has chosen for the struggle.

Certainly there are times when the symptoms themselves must be managed—whether as a palliative measure, as an emergency intervention, or to intercede with herbal substitutes and stimulants for natural functions until a cleansing and building program can restore balance and regain control. Herbs can justifiably and productively be applied to these ends. We must remain intimately aware, though, that many symptoms are part of the body's defense strategy. Each action we take that thwarts a natural defensive function of the body forces the body to revert to another, or suffer the consequences. It is for this most basic reason that allopathic medicine, whether chemical or herbal, consistently engenders side-effects. Balancing the desire for comfort and the need for some regulation of events with the body's choices and its own innate intelligence constitutes a great part of the herbalist's art.

The medicinal action of herbs, then, can be classified into three general groups; detoxifying, regenerating, and symptom regulating.

Detoxifying	Regenerating	Symptom Regulating
Alteratives	Aphrodisiacs	Anodynes
Anthelmintics	Aromatics	Antacids
Anticatarrhals	Astringents	Antibiotics
Aperients	Bitters	Antiemetics
Cathartics	Cardiacs	Anti-inflammatories
Cholagogues	Diaphoretics	Antipyretics
Deobstruents	Emmenagogues	Antiseptics
Diaphoretics	Galactagogues	Antispasmodics
Discutients	Hepatics	Carminatives
Diuretics	Nervines	Demulcents
Emetics	Nutritives	Emollients
Emmenagogues	Rubefacients	Febrifuges
Expectorants	Sialagogues	Hemostatics
Laxatives	Stomachics	Mucilages
Lithotriptics	Tonics	Parturients
Lymphatics	Vulneraries	Sedatives
Parasiticides		Stimulants
Purgatives		Styptics

Within these groups, the actions express themselves on one or more organs or systems of the body. When the action is focused on a particular organ or system, the herb is said to have an "affinity" for that area. Some actions that are primarily Symptom Regulating can also be viewed as Detoxifying or Regenerating, and vice versa, depending upon their application.

ELIMINATING BLOCKAGES AND EXCESSES

The first group of herb actions is Detoxifying. When toxins, irritants, and pathogens have accumulated in the body, they must be removed, or disease will manifest. To remove this "bio-sludge," herbs are used that have properties that tend to stimulate the self-cleansing processes of the system. Herbs that have an affinity for certain parts of the body are chosen based on the symptomology, and for best results are combined with those that have a more generalized effect. Herbs that have laxative properties cleanse the bowel, diuretics detoxify the kidneys, and herbs that have alterative properties aid in detoxifying the blood. Skin diseases, respiratory ailments, nervous system problems, heart disease and vascular insufficiencies, joint and connective tissue distress, and hormonal imbalances can all be relieved by these general detoxifiers, especially when enhanced by system-specific cleansing. In fact, the resolution of virtually every dis-ease of the human frame will be beneficially affected by clearing the metabolic and pathogenic debris that has accumulated in the body. Of course, the poor diet and lifestyle habits that brought about the problem in the first place must be corrected for detoxification to be possible.

RESTORING DEPLETED RESOURCES

The second set of herbal actions to consider is the Regenerating group. These are the herbs that build and tone depleted and overwhelmed tissues and functions. Regenerating herbs nourish and strengthen the body, improving the operating efficiency and recuperative powers of all its tissues and organs, and bolstering the body's resistance to disease. They are used to facilitate recovery from acute and chronic ailments, injury, surgery, and all the natural travails from fatigue to childbirth.

CRISIS MANAGEMENT, PAIN RELIEF, AND COMFORT AIDS

The third group of actions is Symptom Regulating. Once the detoxifying and regenerating processes are underway, this group of herbs can be used to mitigate the uncomfortable symptoms that called us into action in the first place. They will be the first actions we turn to in an emergency, and when used with good judgement, will make the journey back to health and balance a lot more pleasant.

Each of the actions listed below is followed by one or more letters that indicate their general application and effect: **D**etoxifying, **R**egenerating, **S**ymptom regulating.

ALTERATIVES (D)

Alteratives are herbs which cleanse (alter) the blood. Most herbs for blood cleansing support the functions of the liver, spleen, kidneys, and bowels. They take time to do their work, and should be used consistently over a long period of time, promoting the gradual detoxification of the entire blood stream. This will, in turn, help balance digestion, assimilation, and glandular secretions.

Alfalfa	Devil's Claw	Pipsissewa
Barberry	Echinacea	Plantain
Bayberry	Elder	Poke
Black Cohosh	Elecampane	Prickly Ash
Black Walnut	Garlic	Red Clover
Bladderwrack	Ginseng	Red Raspberry
Blessed Thistle	Goldenseal	Rhubarb
Blue Flag	Gotu Kola	St. John's Wort
Burdock	Heartsease	Sarsaparilla
Capsicum	Hyssop	Sassafras
Cascara Sagrada	Kelp	Squaw Vine
Chaparral	Licorice Root	Stillingia
Chickweed	Mandrake	Trillium
Cleavers	Marshmallow	Wood Betony
Comfrey	Nettles	Yarrow
Culver's Root	Oregon Grape	Yellow Dock
Dandelion		

Conditions aided by Alteratives: Blood toxicity can manifest as a wide variety of symptoms including skin eruptions and chronic diseases of the skin, allergies, headaches, chronic fatigue, chronic pain, cancer, nervous and mental disorders, dementia, and a host of other ailments. When the cause of disease is difficult to pinpoint, suspect blood toxicity.

ANODYNES (S)

Anodynes are herbs that relieve pain by lessening the excitability of the nerves and nerve centers. These are closely allied to the antispasmodics. Most of these herbs are used externally. When taken internally, they are referred to as Analgesics. Narcotics are a powerful class of pain relieving plants that are no longer accessible to the casual herbalist.

Bugle
Calendula
Chamomile
Cloves
Echinacea
Ginger
Hemlock Spruce
Hops
Horsenettle
Juniper Berries
Kava Kava

Lobelia
Meadowsweet
Mullein (flower)
Passion Flower
Poke Root
Pulsatilla
Red Poppy
Sassafras oil
Scullcap
Skunk Cabbage

Solomon's Seal
Tobacco
Valerian
Vervain
Virginia Snake Root
White Pond Lily
White Willow
Wild Lettuce
Wild Yam
Wood Betony

Conditions aided by Anodynes: Arthritis, sore muscles, joint pain, toothache, over-exertion, headache, sunburn, wounds, fractures, etc.

ANTACIDS (S)

Antacids is a term applied to herbs that correct over acid conditions in the stomach and bowels. Many can also be used to alkalize the blood.

Angelica
Apple
Barberry
Bladderwrack
Caraway Seeds
Catnip
Comfrey
Dill

Elder Flowers
Fennel
Flax Seeds
Hops
Irish Moss
Mullein
Parsley

Peppermint
Red Clover
Red Raspberry
Slippery Elm
Sweet Marjoram
White Poplar
Wood Betony

Conditions aided by Antacids: Dyspepsia, heartburn, reflux, bloating, belching, intestinal cramps, flatulence, irritable or inflamed bowel

ANTHELMINTICS (D)

Anthelmintics are herbs which have the capacity to expel or destroy intestinal worms and parasites. They should generally be followed by or combined with laxative or cathartic herbs to make sure that the parasites are eliminated from the intestinal tract.

American Wormseed	Garlic	Sage
Apricot Kernels	Gentian	Sorrel
Black Walnut	Hops	Tansy
Blue Flag	Horehound	Thyme
Buckbean	Hyssop	Turkey Rhubarb
Butternut	Male Fern	Turpentine (small dose)
Cajuput	Melon Seeds	White Birch
Cloves	Mulberry Bark	Wild Carrot
Culver's Root	Peach	Wood Sage
Dulse	Pumpkin Seeds	Wormwood
Elecampane	Rue	

Conditions aided by Anthelmintics: Intestinal worms and parasites create a variety of symptoms including chronic diarrhea, bloating, gas, indigestion, cramping, intestinal pains, rectal or anal itching, bloody stools, fluid retention, weight loss or gain, ulcers, colitis, and irritable bowel. They also contribute to toxic blood conditions, and that range of associated problems.

ANTIARTHRITICS (R, S)

These herbs are used to relieve and heal arthritic conditions.

Bitter Root	Dandelion	Saw Palmetto
Black Cohosh	Horsetail	Scullcap
Blackberry (fruit & root)	Hydrangea	Sheep's Sorrel
Buckthorn	Irish Moss	Wintergreen
Burdock	Licorice Root	Yellow Dock
Capsicum	Meadowsweet	Yucca Root
Chaparral	Sarsaparilla	

Conditions aided by Antiarthritics: Joint, connective tissue inflammation and pain

ANTIBIOTICS (D, R, S)

Antibiotics are agents that destroy or inhibit the growth of viruses and bacteria. Some of these herbs destroy germs by their direct action. Others promote and support the body's own immune reponses. They are sometimes called Antizymotics.

Black Walnut	Gentian	Mullein
Chaparral	Goldenseal	Myrrh
Cloves	Honey (raw)	Oregon Grape
Colloidal Silver	Hops	Rosemary
Echinacea	Juniper Berries	Sage
Garlic	Lobelia	Thyme

Conditions aided by Antibiotics: Any known, suspected, or threatened infection

ANTICATARRHALS (D)

Catarrh is an excessive accumulation of mucus and epithelial cells that forms on the mucus membranes anywhere in the repiratory and digestive systems. Anticatarrhals are herbs that help breakdown and eliminate excess mucus conditions. While ridding the body of catarrh, it is necessary to eliminate mucus forming foods, and very useful to aid the primary pathways of elimination by including aperient herbs for the bowel, or diuretic teas to eliminate excess fluid.

Angelica	Echinacea	Marshmallow
Anise (infants)	Elder Flowers & Berries	Milk Thistle
Barberry	Elecampane	Mullein
Bayberry	Eyebright	Pleurisy Root
Bistort	Fennel Seeds	Raisins
Bittersweet	Figs	Safflower
Black Walnut	Flax Seeds	Sage
Blood Root	Garlic	Sarsaparilla
Borage	Ginger	Sorrel
Burdock	Heartsease	Thyme
Capsicum	Horseradish	Vinegar & Honey
Cloves	Hyssop	Wild Cherry
Coltsfoot	Irish Moss	Wild Yam
Comfrey	Juniper Berries	Wintergreen
Coriander	Lemon	Wood Sorrel
Cranesbill	Lobelia	Yarrow
Cubebs	Lungwort	Yerba Santa
Dill Seed		

Conditions aided by Anticatarrhals: Chronic or excessive discharge from the nose, throat, lungs, stomach, intestines or urinary tract. Catarrh in the lungs is similar to colds, flu, and pneumonia; usually accompanied by chronic, hacking cough.

ANTIEMETICS (S)

These are herbs that relieve queasiness of the stomach, nausea, and vomiting.

Anise	Gentian	Pennyroyal (small doses)
Bilberry	Ginger	Peppermint
Bitter Orange	Goldenseal	Red Clover
Black Haw	Horseradish	Red Raspberry
Capsicum	Irish Moss	Sassafras
Catnip	Lavender	Spearmint
Cinnamon	Lemon Balm	Sweet Basil
Cloves	Lobelia (small doses)	White Oak
Fennel	Peach (leaves)	Wild Yam

Conditions aided by Antiemetics: Nausea, morning sickness, motion sickness, nausea from vertigo, chemotherapy, or radiation therapy. Acute or sudden onset nausea may be a defensive symptom. Do not interfere unless the condition lasts for more than a few hours.

ANTI-INFLAMMATORIES (S)

Anti-inflammatory herbs reduce inflammation, and relieve the associated swelling and pain. They can be applied topically, or taken internally (except as noted). They are sometimes called Antiphlogistics.

Abscess Root	Cornsilk (urinary)	Myrrh
Alder	Elder Flowers	Nettles (kidneys)
Arnica (external)	Fenugreek	Ox-eye Daisy
Balm of Gilead	Garlic	Peppermint
Balmony (external, breasts)	Heartsease	Pleurisy Root
Black Cohosh (nerves)	Hops	Sage
Borage	Hyssop	Self Heal
Bugle	Juniper Berries	Solomon's Seal
Calendula	Lady's Mantle	Sorrel
Capsicum	Licorice Root	Uva Ursi
Chamomile	Lily-of-the-Valley	Wintergreen
Chaparral	Marshmallow	Witch Hazel
Chickweed	Mugwort	Wormwood
Comfrey	Mullein	

Conditions aided by Anti-inflammatories: Inflammation is very often a defense or repair function, and as such it should be aided, not suppressed, until the cause is removed. Acute conditions may arise from abrasion, irritation, minor wounds or injuries, insect bites and stings, bumps, bruises, welts, shingles, chemical irritation or burns, etc. Once the cause has been addressed, the inflammatory response may be mitigated by the use of anti-inflammatories.

ANTISEPTICS (D,R,S)

Antiseptic herbs have the power to destroy or prevent the growth of bacteria, and to retard the decay of tissue and the formation of pus. Most essential oils have some antiseptic properties, and, of course, the alcohol base of many tinctures can provide some antiseptic protection, regardless of the herb that is tinctured. Glycerin, raw honey, and even refined white sugar can be used as antiseptics. Herbs that are known for their antiseptic properties include:

Balsam of Peru	Elder Bark	Rosemary
Barberry	Eucalyptus	Sage
Birch Bark	Garlic	Saw Palmetto
Bistort	Goldenseal	Smartweed
Black Walnut(hulls & leaves)	Horseradish	Southernwood
Blackberry	Ivy Berries	Thyme
Bladderwrack	Juniper Berries	Tobacco
Buchu	Lily-of-the-Valley	Trillium
Bugle	Mullein	Turpentine
Cajuput	Myrrh	White Oak Bark
Camphor	Nettles	White Pond Lily
Chaparral	Olive Leaf	White Willow
Comfrey	Oregon Grape	Wintergreen
Condurango	Plantain	Wood Sage
Culver's Root	Pleurisy Root	Wormwood
Echinacea	Prickly Ash	

Conditions aided by Antiseptics: Cuts, abrasions, wounds, indolent ulcers, abscesses, gangrene, frostbite, active infections

ANTISPASMODICS (S)

Antispasmodics are herbs that relieve nervous irritation, involuntary ticks, twitches and tremors, muscular spasms, hacking coughs, convulsions, and cramps.

Anise Seed (infants)	Hawthorn Berries	Red Clover
Black Cohosh	Kava Kava	Red Raspberry
Black Haw (Crampbark)	Lemon Balm	Red Root
Blue Cohosh	Linden Flowers	Rosemary
Boneset	Lobelia	Rue
Bugle	Mistletoe	Sage
Calendula	Motherwort	Scullcap
Capsicum	Mugwort	Self Heal
Cascara Sagrada	Mullein	Skunk Cabbage
Catnip	Oats	Spearmint
Chamomile	Ox-eye Daisy	Tansy
Chaparral	Passion Flower	Thyme
Clary Sage	Pennyroyal	Valerian
Coltsfoot	Peppermint	Vervain
Elecampane	Pleurisy Root	Virginia Snake Root
Fennel	Prickly Ash	Wild Yam
Garlic	Pulsatilla	

Conditions aided by Antispasmodics: Cramps, muscle spasms, nervous ticks and tremors, dry cough, asthma, hiccough, restless legs, involuntary muscle movements

APERIENTS (D,S)

Aperients are herbs that produce a mild laxative effect, without griping pains or purging.

Apple fiber	Figs	Prunes
Barberry	Flax Seeds	Psyllium Seeds & Hulls
Burdock	Fruit	Raisins
Butcher's Broom	Horehound	Rhubarb
Carob	Hyssop	Rose Hips
Chicory	Licorice Root	Safflower
Cleavers	Marshmallow	Watermelon
Dandelion	Olive Oil	Wood Betony
Elder Berries (cooked)	Oregon Grape	

Conditions aided by Aperients: Occasional mild irregularity, constipation

APHRODISIACS (See Sexual Tonics under Tonics)

These are herbs that correct conditions of impotence, and low sexual desire.

AROMATICS

Aromatics are herbs that have a fragrant, pungent, or spicy smell, and a spicy though usually agreeable taste. They have a stimulating effect on the gastrointestinal mucus membranes because of their essential oils, and are used to aid digestion and expel wind from the stomach and bowels. For this action, they are sometimes called Carminatives. They are also used to mask the taste or smell of other herbs. The stronger aromatics should generally be avoided if inflammation of the stomach or bowels is present.

Angelica	Horehound	Sage
Anise Seeds	Juniper Berries	St. John's Wort
Basil	Lemon Peel	Sassafras
Bayberry	Lovage	Southernwood
Benzoin	Meadowsweet	Spearmint
Buchu	Myrrh	Sweet Cicely
Cinnamon	Nutmeg	Sweet Flag
Cloves	Oregano	Vanilla
Coriander	Pennyroyal	Wintergreen
Dill	Peppermint	Wood Betony
Fennel	Rosemary	Wormwood
Ginger	Rue	Zedoary

Conditions aided by Aromatics: Gas, flatulence, bloating, dyspepsia, constipation, atonic conditions of the intestinal elimination

ASTRINGENTS (R,S)

These are herbs that increase the firmness and tone of the tissues. They are drying by nature, and lessen excessive discharges from the eyes, nose, intestines, urinary tract, vagina, draining abscesses, and indolent ulcers.

Agrimony	Calendula	Gravel Root
Alum Root	Capsicum	Hawthorn Berries
Barberry	Chaparral	Horsetail
Bayberry	Comfrey	Lady's Mantle
Black Walnut	Crampbark	Lungwort
Blackberry	Cranesbill	Mullein
Bugle	Elecampane	Olive Leaf
Bugleweed	Eyebright	Periwinkle

— continues on next page

— *continued from previous page*

Pipsissewa	Sandalwood	Trillium
Plantain	Self Heal	Uva Ursi
Prickly Ash	Shepherd's Purse	Vervain
Red Raspberry	Smartweed	White Oak Bark
Rhubarb	Solomon's Seal	Wild Cherry
Rosemary	Squaw Vine	Witch Hazel
Sage	Stoneroot	Yarrow
St. John's Wort	Tea (Black & Green)	Yellow Dock

Conditions aided by Astringents: Astringents can be used to firm up tissues and to arrest excessive discharges anywhere in or on the body. They can be applied topically to correct varicose veins, hemorrhoids, sagging tissues, and to reduce fine lines and wrinkles, as well as to correct excessive or chronic tearing, and sinus, vaginal, or urinary discharges. Weeping ulcers and slow healing wounds are positively affected by astringents. Taken internally, loose, flaccid, or atonic conditions of the smooth muscles, heart, and connective tissue, as well as excessive discharges can be corrected by this class of herb.

BITTERS (D,R,S)

Herbs that, when tasted, promote the flow of digestive juices throughout the body, and stimulate the peristaltic action of the digestive tract. They are sometimes called Digestives or Stomachics.

Agrimony	Dandelion	Oregon Grape
Angelica	Gentian	Peach Bark
Angostura	Gold Thread	Rhubarb
Barberry	Hops	Rue
Blessed Thistle	Horehound	Wormwood
Bugle	Mugwort	Yellow Root
Chamomile		

Conditions aided by Bitters: Constipation, diarrhea, indigestion, reflux, poor assimilation, anemia, dry mouth, irritable bowel, liver congestion, jaundice, skin eruptions and diseases

BLOOD PURIFIERS (See Alteratives)

CARDIACS

Cardiacs are herbs that improve the power and regularity of the heartbeat.

Black Cohosh	Hawthorn Berries	Motherwort
Bugleweed	Lily-of-the-Valley	

Conditions aided by Cardiacs: Irregular heart beat, arrythmia, tachycardia, low blood pressure, high blood pressure, valvular prolapsus, weak heart

CARMINATIVES (See Aromatics)

CHOLAGOGUES (D,R,S)

Cholagogues stimulate the flow of bile.

Barberry	Gentian	Podophyllum
Beets	Goldenseal	Vervain
Blue Flag	Hops	Wild Yam
Boneset	Horseradish	Wormwood
Culver's Root	Hyssop	Yellow Dock
Dandelion	Oregon Grape	Yellow Root
Fennel		

Conditions aided by Cholagogues: Gallbladder problems, gall stones, sluggish liver, jaundice, poor digestion, constipation

DEMULCENTS (R,S)

Demulcents are herbs that, when taken internally, help to soften, relieve, and protect irritated or inflamed tissue, particularly the mucus membranes. When applied to the skin for the same purposes, they are called Emollients. Because they are usually mucilagenous in nature, they are also used in combination with other powders to bind them in making pills and lozenges.

Agar
Aloe Vera
Bugle
Chickweed
Coltsfoot
Comfrey Root
Cornsilk

Elder (stem pith)
Fenugreek
Flax Seeds
Hollyhock Flowers
Irish Moss
Kelp
Licorice Root

Lungwort
Marshmallow
Mullein
Peach Bark
Psyllium Seeds
Sassafras Leaf
Slippery Elm

Conditions aided by Demulcents: Canker sores, inflammation of the esophagus, gastric ulcers, intestinal inflammation, irritable bowel, constipation, anal fissures, skin lesions, burns, sunburn, contact dermatitis, diaper rash

DIAPHORETICS

These are herbs that increase perspiration. Diaphoretics influence the entire circulatory system. Sudoriphics are herbs that simply stimulate the sweat glands. There are three classes of diaphoretics:

STIMULATING – Used when the overall condition is sluggish or unresponsive.

Angelica
Blessed Thistle
Boneset
Buchu
Elder Flowers

Ephedra
Garlic
Ginger
Horseradish
Hyssop

Pennyroyal
Peppermint
Spearmint
Yarrow

NEUTRAL – Safe for general use.

Horehound
Safflower

Sarsaparilla

Sassafras

SEDATIVE – Used when the condition is acute, distressed, or when there is hypertension.

Blue Vervain
Burdock
Calendula
Catnip
Chamomile

Lemon Balm
Motherwort
Mugwort
Passion Flower
Pleurisy Root

Thyme
Vervain
White Willow
Wild Yam

Conditions aided by Diaphoretics: Fevers, colds, flu, edema and skin disorders respond well to diaphoretics.

DIGESTIVES (See Bitters)

DISCUTIENTS (D,S)

These are herbs that dissolve and remove tumors and abnormal growths. These agents are used externally in ointments, poultices, fomentations, or they may be taken internally as teas, tinctures, or capsules.

Birch Bark	Chaparral	Pau D'Arco
Black Walnut	Chickweed	Plantain
Burdock	Devil's Claw	Red Clover
Butcher's Broom	Garlic	White Pond Lily

Conditions aided by Discutients: Tumors, polyps, abnormal growths

DIURETICS (D,S)

Diuretics are herbs that increase the flow of urine. Herbal diuretics are usually rich sources of bio-available minerals, and do not deplete mineral stores like their drug counterparts. They are usually combined with demulcents to soothe any irritation from acids or gravel.

Black Cohosh	Gravel Root	Plantain
Blackberry Fruit	Hawthorn Berries	Pleurisy Root
Blue Cohosh	Heartsease	Rosemary
Buchu	Horseradish	St. John's Wort
Burdock	Horsetail	Sassafras
Celery Seeds	Hydrangea	Saw Palmetto
Chaparral	Juniper Berries	Shepherd's Purse
Chicory	Kava Kava	Sorrel
Cleavers	Kelp	Squaw Vine
Cornsilk	Lily-of-the-Valley	Stoneroot
Damiana	Marshmallow	Uva Ursi
Dandelion	Meadowsweet	Watermelon Seeds
Elecampane	Mullein	White Oak Bark
False Unicorn	Parsley	White Willow
Fennel	Pipsissewa	Woodruff

Conditions aided by Diuretics: Diuretic herbs can be used to treat backache, prostatitis, sciatica, kidney stones, bladder ache, lymphatic swelling, scalding urine, gonorrhea, skin eruptions, water retention, high blood pressure, and obesity.

EMETICS (D)

Emetics are substances used to induce vomiting, and to help the body clear obstructions and offensive material from the stomach. They are usually administered as a tincture or a tea, in closely repeated doses until emesis occurs.

Bayberry (large dose)	Ipecac	Podophyllum
Chaparral	Lobelia	Poke root
False Unicorn	Mescal	Stillingia

Conditions aided by Emetics: Food poisoning, stomach cramps, unresponsive fevers

EMMENAGOGUES (D,R,S)

These are herbs that promote and regulate the menstrual flow.

Angelica	Gentian	Prickly Ash
Black Cohosh	Goldenseal	Queen of the Meadow
Black Haw (anti-abortive)	Horsetail	Rue
Blessed Thistle	Mistletoe (American)	Safflower
Blue Cohosh	Motherwort	Squaw Vine
Chamomile	Mugwort	Tansy
Dong Quai	Myrrh	Trillium
False Unicorn	Pennyroyal	Wild Yam (anti-abortive)

Conditions aided by Emmenagogues: Delayed menses, irregular cycle

EMOLLIENTS (See Demulcents)

EXPECTORANTS (D,S)

Expectorants aid production and elimination of mucus from the throat and lungs.

They usually are combined with demulcents, which are soothing to the mucus membrane.

Benzoin	Heartsease	Nettles
Boneset	Horehound	Parsley
Coltsfoot	Horseradish	Pleurisy Root
Comfrey	Hyssop	Sassafras
Elder Flowers	Licorice Root	Thyme
Elecampane	Lobelia	Vervain
Ephedra	Lungwort	Wild Cherry
Fennel	Mullein	Yarrow
Garlic	Myrrh	Yerba Santa

Conditions aided by Expectorants: Bronchitis, colds, flu, respiratory congestion, emphysema, pleurisy, allergies

FEBRIFUGES (S)

These are herbs used to reduce fevers.

Boneset	Hyssop	Shepherd's Purse
Catnip	Joe Pye Weed	White Willow
Dandelion	Peppermint	Yarrow

Conditions aided by Febrifuges: Dangerously high or prolonged fevers

GALACTAGOGUES (R,S)

These herbs promote and enrich the production of milk from the nursing mother.

Anise Seeds	Dandelion	Red Raspberry
Blessed Thistle	Fennel	Vervain
Cumin	Fenugreek	

Conditions aided by Galactagogues: Insufficient milk production, weak or slow growth of infant

HEMOSTATICS (S)

These are herbs that arrest internal bleeding or hemorrhaging. Also see Astringents.

Alum Root	Cranesbill	Self Heal (lungs)
Bayberry (uterus)	False Unicorn (uterus)	Shepherd's Purse (strong)
Bistort (powerful)	Horsetail (lungs)	Tormentil Root (bowel)
Black Cohosh (lungs)	Lady's Mantle	Uva Ursi (uterus, urinary)
Blackberry Root (uterus)	Lungwort	White Oak Bark
Blood Root (lungs)	Mullein (bowel, general)	Witch Hazel
Bugle	Nettles	Yarrow
Capsicum (powerful)	Red Raspberry	Yellow Dock (lungs)

Conditions aided by Hemostatics: Internal hemorrhage, blood in urine or stools, spitting blood, heavy or hemorrhagic menstruation

HEPATICS—SEE ALSO BITTERS (D,R,S)

These are herbs that strengthen, tone and stimulate the metabolic and secretive functions of the liver.

Agrimony	Cleavers	Podophyllum
Angelica	Dandelion	Poke
Barberry	Fennel	Red Root
Bayberry	Gentian	Self Heal
Bitter Root	Hops	Wild Yam
Blessed Thistle	Hyssop	Wood Betony
Blue Flag	Liverwort	Wormwood
Carrot	Milk Thistle	Yarrow
Cascara Sagrada	Oregon Grape	Yellow Dock

Conditions aided by Hepatics: Hepatitis, jaundice, sluggish liver, indigestion, constipation, skin eruptions, chronic skin diseases

LAXATIVES—SEE ALSO APERIENTS (D, R, S)

Laxatives are herbs that promote prompt bowel action. Laxatives in this class can be habit forming, and should not have to be taken for extended periods.

Buckthorn Bark
Cascara Sagrada
Elder Berries

Motherwort
Peach Bark
Poke Root

Senna
Turkey Rhubarb

Conditions aided by Laxatives: Chronic or obstinate constipation

LITHOTRIPTICS (D)

Lithotriptics are agents that dissolve and discharge urinary and gall bladder stones and gravel. They are usually escorted by Demulcents to make the evacuation of particulates more comfortable. When taken to prevent the formation of stones, herbs in this class are called Antilithics.

Black Currants
Blackberry Fruit
Buchu
Butcher's Broom (gallstones)
Cascara Sagrada (gall)
Chaparral
Cornsilk (Kidney stones)

Dandelion
Devil's Claw
Gravel Root
Horsetail
Hydrangea Root
Hyssop
Juniper Berries

Marshmallow
Parsley
Sarsaparilla
Sorrel
Stone Root
Tormentil
Uva Ursi

Conditions aided by Lithotriptics: Kidney stones, gall stones, gall bladder infection, calcium deposits, bone spurs

LYMPHATICS (D,R)

These are herbs used to stimulate and cleanse the lymphatic system.

Black Walnut
Chaparral
Dandelion

Echinacea
Garlic
Mullein/Lobelia

Oregon Grape
Poke
Yellow Dock

Conditions aided by Lymphatics: Fever, chronic infection, swollen glands or nodes, recuperation from illness or surgery

NERVINES (R,S)

Nervines are herbs that support the health of the nervous system. They are used to relieve pain and regulate the nerve responses. In addition to these supporting herbs, the Nervous System needs ample stores of B-vitamins, essential fatty acids, and bio-available minerals. Nervines can be divided into three classes.

SEDATIVE

Black Cohosh	Kava Kava	Saw Palmetto
Black Haw (Crampbark)	Lady's Slipper	Scullcap
Blue Cohosh	Lemon Balm	Sorrel
Bugleweed	Mints (warm infusion)	Thyme
Catnip	Peach Bark	Valerian
Chamomile	Pennyroyal	Wild Cherry
Hops	Red Clover	Witch Hazel
Hyssop	Rue	Wood Betony

BUILDING (Tonic)

Boneset	Lady's Slipper	Pleurisy Root
Celery	Lobelia	St. John's Wort
Chamomile	Mistletoe (American)	Valerian
Garlic	Motherwort	Virginia Snake Root
Gravel Root (Joe Pye)	Oats	Wood Betony
Hawthorn Berries	Passion Flower	Wormwood
Hops		

STIMULANTS

Angelica	Ginger	Prickly Ash
Bayberry	Ginseng (panax)	Red Clover
Black Pepper	Gravel Root (Joe Pye)	Red Raspberry
Boneset	Guarana	Rhubarb
Capsicum	Horseradish	Rosemary
Cardamon	Hyssop	Rue
Celery	Juniper Berries	Sassafras
Cloves	Kola Nut	Shepherd's Purse
Coffee	Lobelia (small doses)	Siberian Ginseng
Devil's Claw	Mandrake	Spearmint (cold infusion)
Elder Flowers	Myrrh	Suma
Elecampane	Oats	Tansy
Ephedra	Onion	Tea (Black or Green)
False Unicorn	Pennyroyal	Yarrow
Fennel	Peppermint (EO)	Yerba Santa
Garlic		

Conditions aided by Nervines: The nervous system is the primary communication pathway in the body. Virtually every disorder has some root in this system. Stress, anxiety, fatigue, poor nutrition, and disordered lifestyles take a toll on the integrity of the system.

NUTRITIVES (R)

Nutritives are herbs which supply a substantial amount of nutrients and aid in building and maintaining the body.

Alfalfa	Kelp	Rose Hips
Algae	Marshmallow Root	Slippery Elm
Comfrey	Mullein (leaves & root)	Spirulina
Horsetail	Nettles	Watercress
Irish Moss	Red Clover	Yellow Dock

Conditions aided by Nutritives: All

PARASITICIDES (D)

These are herbs that kill and remove parasites from the skin.

Black Walnut	False Unicorn	Rue
Cassia Oil	Garlic	Tansy
Chaparral	Gentian	Tea Tree Oil
Cinnamon Oil	Pau D'Arco	Thyme
Echinacea	Paw Paw	Wood Betony

Conditions aided by Parasiticides: Head lice, crab lice, scabies, ring worm, tinea

PARTURIENTS (S)

These are herbs that assist labor and promote easy childbirth. Also called Oxytocics.

Angelica	Cotton Root	Red Raspberry
Black Cohosh	Dong Quai	Squaw Vine
Blue Cohosh	Juniper Berries	Vitex

Conditions aided by Parturients: Childbirth

REFRIGERANTS (S)

Refrigerants are herbs that are cooling to the system. They help lower the body's temperature and reduce thirst; also called Antipyretics.

Alfalfa	Cranberries	Licorice
Benzoin	Elder Flowers	Prickly Pear Cactus
Borage	Gotu Kola	Purslane
Camphor	Lemon Balm	Sorrel
Chickweed	Lemons, Limes, Oranges	Sumac Berries

Conditions aided by Refrigerants: Fevers, heat stroke, heat prostration

RUBEFACIENTS (R,S)

These are agents used as local external applications that stimulate and increase the blood flow to the surface. They are often used as counter-irritants.

Capsicum	Peppermint Oil	Rue
Mustard Seeds	Prickly Ash	Thyme oil
Nettles (fresh)	Rosemary oil	

Conditions aided by Rubifacients: Cold hands and feet, numbness in the extremities, muscle or joint pain, inflammation

SIALAGOGUES—SEE ALSO BITTERS (R,S)

These are agents that promote an increased flow of saliva.

Black Pepper	Echinacea	Licorice
Capsicum	Ginger	Prickly Ash

Conditions aided by Sialagogues: Dry mouth, Sjogren's syndrome, poor digestion of carbohydrates, hypoglycemia, diabetes

STOMACHICS (See Bitters)

STYPTICS (S)

These herbs arrest bleeding, hemorrhaging and draining wounds. They are usually strong astringents and applied externally. When taken internally, they are called Hemostatics.

Alum Root	Horsetail	Trillium
Bistort	Nettles	White Oak Bark
Blackberry Root	Plantain Leaves	Witch Hazel
Cranesbill	Tormentil	Yarrow

Conditions aided by Styptics: Bleeding wounds, hemorrhage, nose bleeds

SUDORIFICS (See Diaphoretics)

TONICS (R, S)

These are herbs which increase energy and strengthen the body. The effect of tonic herbs is to increase the strength of the muscular and nervous system while improving digestion and assimilation, resulting in a general sense of well-being. Tonic herbs are classified by the system for which they have the greatest affinity, and, therefore, affect it in the most positive way.

GALL BLADDER TONICS

Goldenseal	Parsley	Wild Yam
Oregon Grape		

HEART TONICS

Bugleweed	Hawthorn Berries	Motherwort
Ginseng (panax)	Lily-of-the-Valley	

INTESTINAL TONICS

- Barberry
- Blackberry (leaves)
- Cascara Sagrada
- Cranesbill
- Oregon Grape
- Rhubarb

KIDNEY TONICS

- Buchu
- Burdock
- Celery
- Cleavers
- Dandelion
- Fo-ti
- Horsetail
- Kava Kava
- Parsley
- Pipsissewa
- Saw Palmetto
- Uva Ursi

LIVER TONICS

- Barberry
- Buckthorn Bark
- Cascara Sagrada
- Dandelion
- Eyebright
- Goldenseal
- Oregon Grape
- Podophyllum
- Stoneroot
- Yellow Root

LUNG TONICS

- Comfrey
- Elecampane
- Fenugreek
- Garlic
- Irish Moss
- Lungwort
- Mullein
- Pleurisy Root
- Trillium
- Wild Cherry

NERVE TONICS

- Celery
- Chamomile
- Hops
- Lobelia
- Motherwort
- Oats
- Passion Flower
- Valerian
- Wood Betony

SEXUAL TONICS

- Black Cohosh
- Black Haw (female)
- Carline Thistle
- Damiana
- Dong Quai (female)
- False Unicorn (female)
- Ginseng
- Kava Kava
- Nutmeg
- Oat Grass
- Quaker Button
- Sage
- Sarsaparilla (male)
- Saw Palmetto
- Squaw Vine (female)
- True Unicorn (impotence)
- Vanilla Pods
- Yohimbe

STOMACH TONICS

Agrimony
Blessed Thistle
Elecampane
Gentian

Goldenseal
Mugwort
Oregon Grape

Red Raspberry
Wild Cherry
Wormwood

Conditions aided by Tonics: Recuperation from illness or trauma, general debility or impairment of function in any of the systems affected

VULNERARIES (R,S)

These are herbs that promote the healing of fractures, cuts, wounds, and burns by protecting against infection, and by stimulating cellular renewal. Vulneraries may be taken internally, and applied externally as a poultice, fomentation, ointment, or wash.

Aloe Vera
Apricot Seeds
Benzoin
Black Walnut
Bugle
Calendula
Chickweed
Comfrey

Fenugreek
Garlic
Hollyhock
Honey
Horsetail
Irish Moss
Lungwort
Marshmallow

Mullein
Myrrh
Plantain
Rosemary
St. John's Wort
Self Heal
Slippery Elm
Yarrow

Conditions aided by Vulneraries: Wounds, fractures, burns, trauma, surgery

CHAPTER 4

Nature's Apothecary

46 Ordinary Plants with Extraordinary Powers

Common herbs that are readily found or easily grown

Birch Bark *(Betula alba, Betula spp.)*
Black Cohosh *(Cimicifuga racemosa)*
Black Walnut *(Juglans nigra)*
Bugle *(Ajuga reptans)*
Burdock *(Arctium lappa)*
Calendula *(C. officinale)*
Capsicum *(Capsicum annum, Capsicum spp.)*
Catnip *(Nepeta cataria)*
Cleavers *(Galium aparine)*
Comfrey *(Symphytum spp.)*
Cornsilk *(Zea mays)*
Dandelion *(Taraxacum officinale)*
Dill *(Anethum vulgare)*
Echinacea *(Echinacea spp.)*
Elderberry *(Sambucus spp.)*
Fennel *(Foeniculum vulgare)*
Garlic *(Allium sativum)*
Gravel Root *(Eupatorium purpureum)*
Hawthorn *(Cratagéus spp.)*
Hops *(Humulus lupus)*
Horehound *(Marrubium vulgare)*
Horsetail *(Equisetum arvense)*
Jewelweed *(Impatiens capensis)*

Juniper Berries *(Juniperis communis)*
Lemon Balm *(Melissa officinalis)*
Lobelia *(Lobelia inflata)*
Marshmallow *(Althea officinalis)*
Mullein *(Verbascum thapsus)*
Nettles *(Urtica dioica)*
Oregon Grape *(Berberis aquifolium)*
Passion Flower *(Passiflora incarnata)*
Peppermint *(Mentha piperita)*
Plantain *(Plantago major, P. lanceolata)*
Pleurisy Root *(Asclepius tuberosa)*
Poke *(Phytolacca americana)*
Red Clover *(Trifolium pratense)*
Red Raspberry *(Rubus idaeus, Rubus spp.)*
Sage *(Salvia officinalis)*
St. John's Wort *(Hypericum perforatum)*
Sassafras *(S. officinale)*
Thyme *(Thymus vulgaris)*
Vitex *(Vitex agnus-castus)*
Wild Cherry *(Prunus serotina)*
Willow *(Salix spp.)*
Yarrow *(Achillea millefolium)*
Yellow Dock *(Rumex crispus)*

Birch Bark

Betula alba, Betula spp.
(Betulaceae)

Common Names: White Birch, Paper Birch, Black Birch, River Birch, Sweet Birch, Mountain Mahogany

Physical Features: The Birch trees prevalent in our range typically average 50 to 70 feet in height at maturity. The bark may peel in distinct multiple thin layers, as the Paper and River Birch varieties, or they may be fixed, smooth, and non-peeling with horizontal striations as the Sweet or Black Birch. The leaves are alternate, oval, toothed at the margin, and range from 3 to 6 inches in length. They are usually hairless, dark green on the top surface and yellowish beneath. In some species, the bark, and to a lesser extent, the leaves have a strong wintergreen fragrance when injured.

Historical Information: About the Birch, King's tells us, "The white birch is a favorite remedy in northern Europe, where it is abundant. A spiritous beverage is prepared from the sap (through the intervention of yeast) by the peasants, and the sap itself is esteemed valuable in cutaneous disorders, renal and genito-urinary affections, scurvy, gout, rheumatism, and intermittent febrile states. An infusion of the leaves has been employed in rheumatism, skin diseases, gout, and dropsy; while, for the rheumatic, a bed of fresh leaves is prepared, and is said to occasion profuse diaphoresis. A pulpy mass of the bark, with gunpowder, is employed for scabies. The oil has been used internally in gonorrhoea, and externally in skin eruptions, especially those of an eczematous type."

Later, Maude Grieve says, "Various parts of the tree have been applied to medicinal uses. The young shoots and leaves secrete a resinous substance having acid properties, which, combined with alkalies, is said to be a tonic laxative. The leaves have a peculiar, aromatic, agreeable odor and a bitter taste, and have been employed in the form of infusion (Birch Tea) in gout, rheumatism and dropsy, and recommended as a reliable solvent of stone in the kidneys. With the bark they resolve and resist putrefaction. A decoction of them is good for bathing skin eruptions, and is serviceable in dropsy. The inner bark is bitter and astringent, and has been used in intermittent fevers."

Extracts of the sap and bark have long been used in refreshing and medicinal beverages, and contribute their characteristic taste to root beer. Sweet Birch Bark yields a compound identical in chemical composition to Oil of Wintergreen, and has often been substituted for it, in part or in total, in commerce. The northern Paper Birch yields the readily peeled sheets of white bark from which native American shelters and canoes have been built for eons.

Of greatest interest, perhaps, is the 1995 discovery by researchers at the University of Illinois at Chicago that a simple extract of Birch Bark, betulinic acid, has profound benefits in the treatment and prevention of skin cancers. UIC was awarded a "Use Patent" for this purpose. Not surprisingly, drug companies have subsequently worked feverishly to alter this simple medicine into other patentable (and controllable) analogs that can be sold for much higher prices. In the meantime, little or no publicity has been given to the ready availability of this potentially life-saving discovery in its simplest form. Thousands of tons of Birch Bark, the primary source of natural betulinic acid, is burned or buried as an unwanted by-product of lumber mills and sawyers. (UIC researchers said that they scrounged enough Birch Bark from a yard where firewood was being sold to make more than 100 human doses of betulinic acid.)

Growing Range: Various species of Birch can be found throughout the Northern hemisphere in both the old and new world. The handsome and ornamental White, Paper, and River Birches are often cultivated in modern landscaping plans.

Parts Used: Inner bark, leaves, buds

Cultivation/Wildcrafting Tips: Bud tips can be gathered in the early spring. The leaves are collected in late spring or summer. The bark is collected while the tree is dormant. (It is important not to take off the bark all around the circumference of a living tree; otherwise, the tree will die.)

Primary Constituents: Flavonoids, mainly hyperoside, with luteolin and quercetin glycosides; betulin, from which is derived betulinic acid; tannins, and essential oil (methy salicylate—aka wintergreen oil)

Action: *Traditional*—diuretic, astringent, anti-inflammatory, antiseptic, aromatic, stimulant, tonic, anti-psoriatic

Modern (particularly in reference to betulinic acid)—anti-carcinomic, anti-flu, anti-HIV, anti-inflammatory, anti-malarial, anti-melanomic, anti-plasmodial, anti-tumor, anti-viral, cytotoxic, hypolipemic

Tissues, Organs & Body Systems Affected: Urinary System, Muscles, Joints and Connective Tissue, Skin

Preparations & Dosage: Birch Bark typically contains only 2 to 3% tannin, which is low as barks go. This makes it possible to combine in formulas with high alkaloid herbs.

INTERNAL	
Decoction (bark)	1 oz. bark to 1½ pints water, simmer down to 1 pint, strain & cool; take 1–2 oz.; 3–4 times daily
Infusion (leaves)	1–2 tsp finely crushed dried leaf or leaf buds to 1 cup of boiling water, cover tightly & steep for 20–30 minutes, strain; take 3–4 times daily
Powder (inner bark)	2–5 #0 capsules (750–2000mg.); 3–4 times daily
Tincture	20–30 drops; 3–4 times daily

EXTERNAL	
Bath (balneotherapy)	Simmer 4–5 lbs. of chopped fresh leaves, or 6–8 oz. of bark, in 2 gals. of water, covered, for 1 hour. Strain and add water to bath sufficient to reach the waist when seated. Drench upper body and soak until very relaxed.
Essential Oil	Add 5–15 drops to 1 oz. carrier oil; DO NOT APPLY NEAT (Undiluted)
Lotion	To 1 pint of strong decoction, add 6 oz. vegetable glycerin & 40–50 drops tincture of benzoin. Apply to skin daily & after sun exposure using cotton pads or atomizer
Strong Decoction (bark)	2 oz. pulverized bark to 1½ pints water, boil down to 1 pint, strain; use as rinse (diluted) or fomentation (hot)

Indicated Usages:

Condition	Appropriate Preparations	Combines Well With:
INTERNAL		
Bladder Infection	Infusion, Decoction, Tincture	Parsley, Uva Ursi, Cranberry, Cornsilk
Canker Sores	Decoction, Tincture	Lemon Balm, Oregon Grape
Diarrhea	Infusion, Decoction, Tincture, Powder	Marshmallow, White Oak, Bayberry
Gout	Infusion, Tincture	Dandelion, Black Cohosh, Nettles
HIV	Decoction, Tincture, Powder	Lemon Balm, Olive Leaf
Kidney Stones	Infusion, Decoction, Tincture	Gravel Root, Horsetail, Hydrangea, Parsley
Parasites	Infusion, Decoction, Tincture, Powder	Black Walnut, Pumpkin Seed, Wormwood
Rheumatic Pains	Infusion, Decoction, Tincture, Powder, Bath	Black Cohosh, Willow, Elder Flowers
EXTERNAL		
Alopecia, Hair Loss	Strong Decoction, Tincture	Sage, Horsetail
Boils, Indolent Ulcers	Strong Decoction, Lotion, Tincture	Chaparral, Comfrey
Eczema, Psoriasis	Strong Decoction, Lotion, Bath	Burdock, Calendula, Cleavers, Oregon Grape, Comfrey
Skin Cancer	Strong Decoction, Lotion, Bath (take regular decoction internally)	Chaparral, Pau D'Arco
Warts	Raw (inner bark), Strong Decoction	

Special Considerations: As Birch contains substantial amounts of salicylates, it is possible, though highly unlikely, that aspirin sensitive people might react to Birch preparations. Use caution and conservative doses to gauge response.

Notes: Betulin and betulinic acid, which can be extracted from Birch Bark by simple decoction, have been shown to be effective against active melanomas, and as reversing agents for pre-cancerous skin lesions caused by sun damage. People with a history of sun exposure, especially "sun worshippers," might be well advised to use a Birch preparation like the lotion above on a daily basis, several times when possible. Keeping it in a small misting bottle is a convenient way to apply it. The glycerin and the benzoin in the formula act as preservatives as well as humectant and vulnerary, but it would be wise to make the lotion in small amounts and protect it from heat and light as much as possible.

Energetics: In the Traditional Chinese model, Birch can be used to clear damp heat. It affects the Kidney, Bladder, and Liver meridians.

Black Cohosh

Cimicifuga racemosa
(Ranunculaceae)

Common Names: Black Snake Root, Rattle Root, Squaw Root, Bugbane, Rattleweed, Macrotys

Physical Features: It is a tall, herbaceous plant, with feathery racemes of white blossoms, 1 to 3 feet long, which being slender, sway gracefully in the slightest breeze above the 2 to 3 foot high greenery. The fruits are small, dry, hollow shells containing many seeds, and often persist on the dry flower stalks through the winter. This gives rise to the names Rattleweed and Rattle Root. The plant produces a stout, cylindrical, blackish rhizome, which bears the remains of the ascending branches of previous seasons. The dried root has a faint, disagreeable odor, and a particularly bitter and acrid taste.

Historical Information: Black Cohosh was brought to the attention and common use of both the botanical and allopathic medical communities in the mid-1800's, though it had long been valued by native Americans. Its strongest proponent was Dr. John King. King's American Dispensatory, considered the standard formulary of the Physio-medical and Eclectic medical movements, expounded at great length on the herb's many benefits. It was often referred to as "Macrotys" in the old medical texts.

In part, King's tells us,

> "This is a very active, powerful, and useful remedy, and appears to fulfil a great number of indications. It possesses an undoubted influence over the nervous system. In small doses the appetite and digestion are improved, and larger amounts augment the secretions of the gastro-intestinal tract. Excretions from the skin and kidneys are increased by it, the peculiar earthy odor of the drug being imparted to the urine; the secretions of the bronchial mucous surfaces are also augmented under its administration. The heart-beat is slowed and given increased power by it, while arterial tension is elevated. Upon the reproductive organs it exerts a specific influence, promoting the menstrual discharge, and by its power of increasing contractility of the unstriped fibres of the uterus, it acts as an efficient parturient. The venereal propensity in man is also said to be stimulated by Cimicifuga.
>
> Few of our remedies have acquired as great a reputation in the treatment of rheumatism and neuralgia. Indeed, few cases of rheumatism, or conditions depending upon a rheumatic basis, will present, which will not be influenced for the better by Cimicifuga. Rheumatism of the heart, diaphragm, psoas muscles, lumbago, stiff neck, in fact all cases characterized by that kind of pain known as 'rheumatic' - dull, tensive, intermittent; as if dependent upon a contracted state of muscular fiber - soreness in muscular tissue, especially over the abdomen and in the extensor and flexor muscles of the extremities, all yield readily to it. In eye strain, giving rise to headache, and associated with a sensation of stiffness in the ocular muscles, or a bruised feeling in the muscles of the frontal region, it will give marked benefit. In doses of 1 fluid drachm of the tincture, repeated every hour, it has effected thorough cures of acute conjunctivitis, without the aid of any local application."

"Cimicifuga plays a very important part in the therapeutics of gynecology. It is a remedy for atony of the reproductive tract. In the painful conditions incident to imperfect menstruation, its remedial action is fully displayed. By its special affinity for the female reproductive organs, it is an efficient agent for the restoration of suppressed menses. In dysmenorrhoea it is surpassed by no other drug, being of greatest utility in irritative and congestive conditions of the uterus and appendages, characterized by tensive, dragging pains, resembling the pains of rheumatism. When there is a disordered action or lack of functional power in the uterus, giving rise to sterility, Cimicifuga often corrects the impaired condition and cures. It is the best and safest agent known for the relief of the after-pains of birth, and is effectual in allaying the general excitement of the nervous system after labor.

Cimicifuga exerts, a powerful influence over the nervous system. Its action is slow, but its effects, are permanent. It has been used successfully as an anti-spasmodlc in hysteria, epilepsy when due to menstrual failures, asthma and kindred affections, periodical convulsions, nervous excitability, pertussis, delirium tremens and many other spasmodic affections. For headache, whether congestive or from cold, neuralgia, dysmenorrhoea, or from la grippe, it is promptly curative. As a remedy for pain, Cimicifuga is a very prompt agent, often relieving in a few hours, painful conditions that have existed for a long time. In all cases where acidity of the stomach is present, this should first be removed, or some mild alkaline preparation be administered in conjunction with the remedy, before any beneficial change will ensue."

The root is supposed to be an antidote against poison and the bite of the rattlesnake, when taken internally and applied as a poultice at the site of the bite.

Growing Range: A native of North America, where it grows freely in shady woods in Canada and the United States. It is called Black Snake Root to distinguish it from the Common Snake Root (Aristolochia serpentaria).

Parts Used: Root and rhizome; dried, not fresh. Even when stored under ideal conditions, the dried root should be no more than two seasons old if it is to be effective in preparations.

Cultivation/Wildcrafting Tips: The roots are unearthed with the rhizome in autumn after the fruits have ripened. They should be cut in slices or split lengthwise and dried carefully in the warm shade, or with the aid of a dehydrator.

Primary Constituents: Triterpene glycosides, including actein, cimigoside, cimifugin (=macrotin), cimigenol-xyloside, racemosin, Isoflavones such as formononetin, Isoferulic acid, Miscellaneous; volatile oil, tannin. Root is a significant source of thiamin.

The chief constituent of Black Cohosh root is the amorphous resinous substance known as Cimicifugin, of which it contains about 18 per cent. The bitter taste is due to a crystalline principle named Racemosin.

Action: astringent, emmenagogue, parturient, estrogenic, anti-spasmodic, anti-tussive, nervine, alterative, cardiac stimulant, anti-venom, diuretic, expectorant

Tissues, Organs & Body Systems Affected: Female Glandular System, Uterus, Nervous System, Musculature, Respiratory System (calming, antispasmodic), Circulatory System (hypotensive)

Preparations & Dosage:

INTERNAL	
Decoction	1 tbsp dried root to 1 cup water; simmer 10–15 min; strain and take 2–3 oz.; 3–4 times daily
Fluid Extract	5–30 drops three times daily
Powder	1–4 #0 capsules three times daily
Powder (parturient)	1–2 gms. in warm water every 15–20 min until contractions become strong
Syrup	Usually combined with other balancing herbs for Respiratory support; ½ –1 tsp; 3–4 times daily
Tincture	15–30 drops three times daily—alcohol best extracts the antispasmodic properties

Indicated Usages:

Condition	Appropriate Preparations	Combines Well With:
INTERNAL		
Amenorrhea, Dysmenorrhea	Decoction, Tincture, Capsules	Blue Cohosh, Vitex, Angelica
Arthritis Pain	Decoction, Tincture, Capsules	Bugle, Plantain
Asthma, Bronchial Spasms	Decoction, Tincture, Syrup	Lobelia, Wild Cherry, Yarrow
Bronchitis	Decoction, Tincture, Syrup	Lobelia, Wild Cherry, Comfrey
Chorea	Decoction, Tincture	Crampbark, Hops, Blood Root
Cough	Decoction, Syrup	Lobelia, Wild Cherry, Comfrey, Coltsfoot
Cramps	Decoction, Tincture	Crampbark
Headache	Decoction, Tincture	Lemon Balm, Catnip

Condition	Appropriate Preparations	Combines Well With:
High Blood Pressure	Decoction, Tincture, Capsules	Dandelion, Prickly Ash
Hot Flashes, Menopausal Discomfort	Decoction, Tincture, Capsules	Vitex, Wild Yam, Burdock, Dong Quai, Black Haw, Red Clover
Labor (first pains)	Tincture, Powder (in warm water)	Red Raspberry Leaf, False Unicorn
Neuralgia	Decoction, Tincture, Capsules	Hops, Chamomile, Sage, Peppermint
PMS	Decoction, Tincture	Vitex, Nettles, Burdock, Scullcap, Dong Quai
Rheumatic Pains	Decoction, Tincture	Burdock, Capsicum, Nettles, Elder Flowers, Willow
Tinnitus	Decoction, Tincture, Capsules	Ginkgo

Special Considerations: Black Cohosh is a powerful remedy. Excessive doses may result in nausea, vomiting, dizziness, headache, and a dramatic drop in blood pressure. Any use of the herb should probably be avoided during pregnancy until the final stages (last five weeks).

Notes: The traditional use of Black Cohosh as a primary balancing herb for menopausal conditions has not been generally upheld in recent times, at least not in the author's personal experience. Black Cohosh does contain estrogen-like compounds that do bind to estrogen receptors in the body. This may actually exacerbate hormonal irregularities, though, that are often due to an excess of xeno-estrogenic environmental pollutants that have infiltrated the body tissues. In these cases, better response may be gained by the use of Progesterone and Progesterone precursors such as may be found in Dong Quai (Angelica) and Vitex (Chaste Tree). In all cases, liver cleansing and regeneration will help.

Energetics: Black Cohosh assists with issues of constrained Chi, particularly of the Lungs, or where there is a Lung Yin deficiency with dry heat. It affects the Lung, Liver, Heart, Kidney, Chong and Ren meridians.

Black Walnut

Juglans nigra, Juglans regia, Juglans spp.
(Juglandaceae)

Physical Features: As now found, the tree grows to a height of 40 to 60 feet, with a large spreading top, and thick, massive trunk. Old specimens, though very rare, can top 100 feet, with trunks measuring four feet or more in diameter. Across the northern tiers of states and in the mountainous areas of the South, the trees grow vigorously and bear abundantly, though the population in the wild has been much reduced by timber cutters in search of the beautiful wood.

The flowers of separate sexes are borne on the same tree and appear in early spring before the leaves. The male flowers have a calyx of five or six scales, surrounding from 18 to 36 stamens; whilst the calyx of the female flowers closely envelops the ovary, which bears 2 or 3 fleshy stigmas. The deciduous leaves are pinnate. The large green fruits, often the size of a tennis ball, develop in midsummer, and mature to black in the autumn, typically falling before the leaves. The fleshy husk covering the nut has a rich peppery smell, especially when green, and when cut quickly oxidizes to a deep reddish brown. The iodine rich juice from these injured fruits will stain the skin with a reddish pigment that persists for many days.

Historical Information: Nut meats from the Black Walnut were long considered to be good "brain food," and were used by those afflicted with problems attributed to that area, i.e. headaches, mental disturbances, senility, etc. This was expounded on by William Cole, an exponent of the Doctrine of Signatures in his Adam in Eden, written in 1657:

> "Wall-nuts have the perfect Signature of the Head: The outer husk or green Covering, represent the Pericranium, or outward skin of the skull, whereon the hair groweth, and therefore salt made of those husks or barks, are exceeding good for wounds in the head. The inner wooddy shell hath the Signature of the Skull, and the little yellow skin, or Peel, that covereth the Kernell, of the hard Meninga and Pia-mater, which are the thin scarfes that envelope the brain. The Kernel hath the very figure of the Brain, and therefore it is very profitable for the Brain, and resists poysons; For if the Kernel be bruised, and moystned with the quintessence of Wine, and laid upon the Crown of the Head, it comforts the brain and head mightily."

Culpeper found other uses for Walnuts:

> "…if they' [the leaves] 'be taken with onions, salt, and honey, they help the biting of a mad dog, or the venom or infectious poison of any beast, etc. Caius Pompeius found in the treasury of Mithridates, King of Pontus, when he was overthrown, a scroll of his own handwriting, containing a medicine against any poison or infection; which is this: Take two dry walnuts, and as many good figs, and twenty leaves of rue, bruised and beaten together with two or three corns of salt and twenty Juniper Berries, which take every morning fasting, preserves from danger of poison, and infection that day it is taken. . . . The kernels, when they grow old, are more oily, and therefore not fit to be eaten, but are then used to heal the wounds of the sinews, gangrenes, and carbuncles. . . . The said kernels being burned, are very astringent being . . . . taken in red

wine, and stay the falling of the hair, and make it fair, being anointed with oil and wine. The green husks will do the like, being used in the same manner...
A piece of the green husks put into a hollow tooth, eases the pain."

In recent times, Black Walnut earned a great reputation as a vermifuge and antiparasitical remedy, particularly for those affecting the intestinal tract. As a rich source of organic iodine, Black Walnut (the hulls in particular) also gained much popularity as nourishment for the thyroid, especially in the interior parts of the country where sea vegetables were hard to come by.

Growing Range: Throughout the upper regions of the Northern hemisphere, and in higher elevations further south.

Parts Used: Leaves, bark, green husk of the nut

Cultivation/Wildcrafting Tips: Gather prime unblemished leaves in late spring and early summer, in good weather, and preferably in the morning after any dew has lifted. Leaves should be placed on screen frames and dried out-of-doors in warm weather in the shade to retain the best color. Care should be taken to toss and stir them regularly to insure even drying, and they should be taken indoors at night to avoid any chance of them becoming damp from rain or dew. If any mold or mildew develops, discard the batch and start over. Bark strips and nut hulls should be dried with low heat. Green hulls can be pared from the nuts with a sharp knife. Wear gloves when peeling the hulls, or expect to have stains on your hands that will take several days to wash and wear off. Tincture is best made from the hulls in the fresh green state.

Primary Constituents: The active principle of the whole Walnut tree, as well as of the nuts, is Nucin or Juglone. The kernels contain oil, mucilage, albumin, mineral matter, cellulose and water. Iodine is present in all usable parts of the Black Walnut, but the highest concentration is in the outer hulls of the nuts. Black Walnut is also a significant source of potassium, magnesium, manganese, sulfur, copper, and silica. The nut meats are a rich source of essential fatty acids.

Action: *Bark and leaves*—alterative, laxative, astringent, antiseptic, antifungal, and detergent; *hull of fruit*—same, plus sudorific, anti-scorbutic, and vermifuge

Tissues, Organs & Body Systems Affected: Nerves, Intestines, Lymphatic System, Skin

Preparations & Dosage:

INTERNAL

Decoction	Simmer 1 pint water and 2 oz. dried powdered bark in tightly covered pan for 15 minutes; set aside until cool. Strain. Take 3–4 oz. morning and evening.
Infusion	Pour 1 pint boiling water over 1 oz. dried bark or leaves (2 oz. if undried) and let stand for 6–8 hours; strain, take 3–4 oz. 3 times daily.
Powder (hulls)	750–1,000 mg. 3 times daily
Tincture (green hulls)	Put 4 oz. of green walnut hulls in blender with 8 oz. of 100 proof vodka. Blend until hulls are completely reduced. Pour into a pint jar. Seal and set on a sunny window sill. Shake daily for two weeks, then strain and bottle. Take 15–30 drops 3–4 times daily.

EXTERNAL

Infusion	Prepare as above.
Powder (leaves, bark, or hulls)	Ground fine and applied to moist eruptions, ulcerations, and wounds
Strong Infusion	Pour 1 pint boiling water over 2 oz. dried bark or leaves; let stand overnight.
Tincture (leaves & bark)	Combine 2 oz. crushed dried leaves, 2 oz. powdered bark and 16 oz. 10 proof vodka. Seal and proceed as above.

Indicated Usages:

Condition	Appropriate Preparations	Combines Well With:
INTERNAL		
Ballooned or Relaxed Colon	Infusion, Powder	Bayberry, Plantain, Yarrow Flowers
Constipation	Decoction	Yellow Dock, Rhubarb
Diarrhea	Decoction, Powder, Tincture	Slippery Elm, Yarrow
Parasites (intestinal worms)	Decoction (green hulls), Powder, Tincture	Pumpkin Seed, Wormwood, Hyssop
Sore Throat, Tonsillitis	Infusion (gargle)	Lemon Balm, Sage
Warts	Tincture (long term daily use)	
EXTERNAL		
Abscesses, Boils	Strong Infusion, Tincture	Honey, Garlic Oil, Comfrey
Acne	Strong Infusion, Tincture	Thyme, Peppermint, Oregon Grape
Conjunctivitis, Eye Disorders	Infusion (as eye wash)	Thyme, Black Cohosh
Eczema, Psoriasis, Shingles	Strong Infusion, Tincture	Lemon Balm, Oregon Grape, Comfrey
Hemorrhoids	Strong Infusion, Tincture (also as retention enema)	White Oak, Plantain, Alum Root

— continues on next page

— continued from previous page

Condition	Appropriate Preparations	Combines Well With:
Leukorrhea, Yeast Infection, Candida	Infusion, Tincture	Oregon Grape, Tea Tree Oil, Garlic
Nosebleed	Strong Infusion, Tincture	Yarrow, Alum Root
Ringworm (tinea)		Pau D'Arco, Thyme
Sore Throat, Tonsillitis	Infusion (gargle)	Lemon Balm, Oregon Grape, Sage

Special Considerations: Studies have shown that consuming Walnut meats significantly lowers serum cholesterol, and favorably alters lipoprotein profiles. Not only that, they taste great.

Notes: The fruit, when young and unripe (no bigger than a golf ball), can be used to make a wholesome, spicy, anti-scorbutic pickle. The vinegar in which the green fruit has been pickled becomes a first class gargle for sore and slightly ulcerated throats.

Maude Grieve (A Modern Herbal, 1929) also suggested preserving green Walnuts in syrup, and offered this recipe.

> "Take as many green Walnuts as you please, about the middle of July, try them all with a pin, if it goes easily through them they are fit for your purpose. Lay them in water for nine days, washing and shifting them morning and night; then boil them in water until they be a little soft. Lay them to drain, and wipe them with a coarse cloth to take off the thin green skin. Then pierce them through with a wooden (not metal) skewer. In the holes put a whole clove, and in some a bit of Cinnamon, and in some the rind of a Citron, candied. Then take the weight of your nuts in Sugar, or a little more; make it into a syrup, (with an equal volume of water) in which boil your nuts, skimming them till they be tender. Put them up in Gally potts (Mason jars), and cover them close."

Honey could certainly be used instead of sugar, and the syrup could be made with a combination of lemon juice or vinegar and water. The hot walnuts should be packed into sterilized Mason jars, covered with boiling syrup and sealed immediately.

Energetics: Black Walnut affects the Large Intestine, Spleen, and Kidney meridians. It is said to clear damp cold conditions, and to raise stagnant Chi.

Bugle

Ajuga reptans
(Labiatae)

Common Names: Middle Comfrey, Sicklewort, Carpenter's Herb, Ajuga

Physical Features: Low growing, creeping perennial, 6 to 8 inches in height. Erect flower stalks are square, pale green, and often purplish towards the top. Leaves are oblong and obtuse in form, occasionally toothed but usually entire at the edges. Leaves are crumpled in appearance, covered with hairs on both surfaces and at the edges. Leaf color ranges from dark green to reddish bronze, with ornamental forms selected for reddish color. Flowers open in early summer, and are purplish blue, crowded onto a 10 to 14 inch spike in multiple whorls, usually six flowers to a ring.

Historical Information: While not presently on the list of our most popular herbs, Bugle has been considered a wound herb of the highest order for centuries. Its strongly astringent nature is uniquely balanced by soothing demulcent and sedative characters, making it an ideal herb for internal bleeding, heavy menstruation, diarrhea, etc. Maude Grieve (A Modern Herbal, 1931) says of Bugle, "In its action, it rather resembles digitalis, lowering the pulse and lessening its frequency; it allays irritation and cough, and equalizes the circulation and has been termed one of the mildest and best narcotics in the world. It has also been considered good for the bad effects of excessive drinking." Culpeper also held Bugle in the highest esteem, and says, "If the virtues of it make you fall in love with it (as they will if you are wise), keep a syrup of it to take inwardly, and an ointment and plaister of it to use outwardly, always by you."

Growing Range: Wild Bugle is abundant throughout the United States except for arid zones. It can be cultivated practically anywhere if adequate moisture and some shade is provided.

Parts Used: Aerial parts, fresh or dried. Harvest throughout growing season for fresh use as first aid. For drying and storage, harvest whole plants in May or June when the leaves are in their best condition, and the plant is in full bloom.

Cultivation/Wildcrafting Tips: Hardy perennial. Bugle prefers moderately moist ground and semi-shade. It is commonly used as an ornamental ground cover, and can often be purchased at local nurseries. Plant multiplies by runners, rather like strawberries, and will form rather dense colonies. Bugle may be purposely spread by division and transplanting, which is best done in early spring as the new plants are just beginning to grow. Aerial portions may be harvested anytime during the growing season, though the herb is at its most potent while in flower. Dry in the shade, or with very low heat.

Primary Constituents: Iridoid glycosides and ajugols; ajugalactone; diterpine bitter principles; caffeic acid derivatives, including rosmarinic acid.

Action: analgesic, astringent, demulcent, nervine, vulnerary, hemostatic, expectorant, aromatic, bitter

Tissues, Organs & Body Systems Affected: Gastro-Intestinal Tract, Lungs, Skin, Mucus Membranes, Nervous System, Circulation

Preparations & Dosage:

INTERNAL

Infusion	3–4 oz.; every 2–3 hours with acute symptoms
Tincture	15–30 drops; 3–6 times daily

EXTERNAL

Fomentation	Prepared from strong tea; leave on for 1–2 hours changing as needed to keep warm; twice daily
Juice	Mix with water to bath wounds, sores and injuries.
Oil, Salve, or Ointment	As often as needed
Poultice	Crushed fresh herb or dried powdered herb mixed with Aloe Gel or honey —Apply to injury and hold in place with bandage; change daily.

Good choice for First Aid Kit—Medicine Cabinet.

Indicated Usages:

Condition	Appropriate Preparations	Combines Well With:
INTERNAL		
Broken Bones, Internal Bruising	Infusion, Tincture	Comfrey, Calendula
Cough, Respiratory Inflammation	Infusion, Tincture	Mullein
Diarrhea	Infusion, Tincture	Slippery Elm
Hemorrhage, Heavy Menstruation	Infusion, Tincture	Horsetail
Sore Throat, Laryngitis	Infusion (gargle)	Hawthorn Berry, Marshmallow
EXTERNAL		
Bruises, Varicosity	Fomentation, Poultice	Calendula
Burns, Abrasions	Fomentation, Salve	Calendula, Aloe
Fresh Wounds	Fomentation, Poultice, Salve	
Ulcers, Sores, Slow Healing Wounds	Fomentation, Infusion, Juice, Salve	Comfrey, Calendula, St. John's Wort

Special Considerations: Do not confuse by name with Bugleweed (*Lycopus virginiana*), as some plant nurseries may have the plants mislabeled by common name.

Notes: Bugle should be thought of much like Comfrey, and can be used for most of the same purposes when that plant is not available. Bugle is more effective than Comfrey at stopping the bleeding of fresh wounds, due to its greater astringency. Its traditional reputation for lowering the pulse and evening the circulation might prove beneficial in avoiding shock from trauma. It is one of the few effective analgesic herbs that we have readily available to us.

Energetics: Chinese medicine considers the herb particularly effective in conditions of toxic heat and Chi level heat. It affects the Liver, Heart, and Stomach meridians.

Burdock

Arctium lappa
(Compositae)

Common Names: Lappa; Fox's Clote; Thorny Burr; Beggar's Buttons; Cockle Buttons; Love Leaves; Philanthropium; Personata; Happy Major; Clot-Bur

Physical Features: A handsome biennial plant, with large, wavy leaves and round heads of purple flowers. The blossom is enclosed in a globe of long, stiff scales with hooked tips—the burr—which are sometimes interwoven with white, cottony fibers. The whole plant is a dull, pale green, standing about 3 to 4 feet or more, and many branched. The lower leaves are very large, on long, solid foot-stalks, furrowed above, frequently more than a foot long, and heart-shaped. The underside of the base leaves is covered with a mass of fine down, giving them a whitish or gray cast. The upper leaves are much smaller, more egg-shaped in form, with much less down on the underside.

Historical Information: Burdock was a staple in Culpeper's medicine chest. He recommends the following uses for it:

> "The Burdock leaves are cooling and moderately drying, thereby good for old ulcers and sores. The leaves applied to the places troubled with the shrinking in the sinews or arteries give much ease. A juice of the leaves or the roots given to drink with old wine, doth wonderfully help the biting of any serpents. The root beaten with a little salt and laid on the place suddenly easeth the pain thereof, and helpeth those that are bit by a mad dog. The seed being drunk in wine 40 days together doth wonderfully help the sciatica. The leaves, bruised with the white of an egg and applied to any place burnt with fire, taketh out the fire, gives sudden ease and heals it up afterwards. The root may be preserved with sugar for consumption, stone and the lax. The seed is much commended to break the stone, and is often used with other seeds and things for that purpose."

The Eclectics of the late 19th and early 20th centuries also held Burdock in high esteem. Priest & Priest considered that it is a good general alterative, influencing the skin, kidneys, mucus and serous membranes by removing accumulated waste products. They considered it specific for skin eruptions on the head, face, and neck, and for acute, irritable, and inflammatory conditions such as eczema, psoriasis, dermatitis, boils, carbuncles, styes, sores, rheumatism, gout, and sciatica. Ellingwood recommended it for the following pathologies: aphthous ulcerations, irritable coughs, psoriasis, and chronic cutaneous eruptions, chronic glandular enlargements, syphilitic, scrofulous, and gouty conditions.

King's spoke more highly of the seeds of Burdock than of the root, recommending them as a very efficient diuretic, particularly when taken as an alcoholic tincture. King's states:

> "They form a good diuretic alterative, and are used in diseases of the kidneys, and to remove boils and styes on the eyelids. The action of the seeds upon the urinary tract is direct, relieving irritation and increasing renal activity, assisting at the same time in eliminating morbid products. In chronic disorders Lappa may be used to remove worn-out tissues, where the saline diuretics are inadmissible. Dropsy and painful urination, due to renal obstruction, have been relieved by it. It is of marked value in catarrhal and aphthous ulcerations of the digestive tract. A favorable action is

obtained from it in dyspepsia. It relieves broncho-pulmonic irritation and cough. Rheumatism, both muscular and articular, are said to be benefited by the seeds. It has been particularly praised in psoriasis, its use being long-continued to produce good results. Chronic erysipelas, milk crust, and various forms of eczema have been cured with it."

Growing Range: On waste ground, disturbed soil, and around old buildings, by roadsides, and in fairly damp places throughout most of North America, in Europe, and parts of Asia. It is cultivated in Japan where the root is highly esteemed as a vegetable.

Parts Used: Root, herb, and seeds (fruits). The dried root from plants of the first year's growth was the once official drug, but the leaves and fruits (commonly, though erroneously, called seeds) which appear the second year are also used by traditional healers.

Cultivation/Wildcrafting Tips: It will grow in almost any soil, but the best roots are formed in light, well-drained soil. The seeds germinate readily, and may be sown directly in the field, either in autumn or early spring, in rows 2 to 3 feet apart. Sow one inch deep in autumn, less in spring. When well up, the young plants should be thinned out to six inches apart in the row. The roots should be dug in September or October of the first year, the seeds must wait for the second year to develop.

Primary Constituents: Lignans, including arctigenin, its glycoside arctiin, and matairesinol; polyacetylenes, in the root, mainly tridecadienetetraynes and tridecatrienetriynes, with the sulphur-containing arctic acid; amino acids, such as a-guanidino-n-butyric acid; inulin in the roots; miscellaneous organic acids, fatty acids and phenolic acids, including acetic, butyric, isovaleric, lauric, myristic, caffeic and chlorogenic acids; mucilage; sugar; a bitter, crystalline glucoside—Lappin; a little resin, fixed and volatile oils, and some tannic acid.

Burdock provides significant amounts of chromium, copper, iron, and magnesium. The root also contains trace amounts of organic mercury, making it a good choice for mercury detox formulas.

Action: *Root*—alterative, diuretic, diaphoretic, bitter, anti-psoriatic, and demulcent *Seeds*—same, plus nervine and tonic

Tissues, Organs & Body Systems Affected: Skin, Liver, Lungs, Digestive Tract

Preparations & Dosage:

INTERNAL	
Decoction (root)	1 tsp cut root in 1 cup of water; simmer 10–15 min.; strain and drink 3–4 times daily
Powder (root or seeds)	1,000–2,000 mg.; 3–4 times daily
Strong Decoction (seeds) - Preserved	2 oz. crushed seed in 1 qt. water, simmer 30 min.; strain and simmer until reduced to 1 pint liquid; cool and add 8 oz. vegetable glycerin. Take 1 tbsp in a little water 3–4 times daily for adults; 15 drops to 1 tsp for children.
Tincture	10–30 drops; 3–4 times daily

EXTERNAL	
Fomentation (root or seeds)	Saturate a compress with hot decoction and apply to affected area, change as it cools.
Ointment (leaves, root, and/or seeds)	Apply to ulcers, boils, cysts, or swollen glands several times a day.
Powder (seeds)	Apply fine powder to affected areas.
Tincture	Dilute with hot water and apply as fomentation.

Indicated Usages:

Condition	Appropriate Preparations	Combines Well With:
INTERNAL		
Acne, Dermatitis, Rashes	Decoction, Strong Decoction, Tincture, Powder	Oregon Grape, Yellow Dock, Cleavers
Boils, Indolent Ulcers, Lesions	Decoction, Strong Decoction, Tincture, Powder	Yellow Dock, Red Clover, Chaparral
Diabetes	Decoction, Tincture, Powder, Fresh Root	Prickly Pear, Flax Seed
Dropsy, Edema	Decoction, Tincture	Dandelion, Nettles
Eczema, Psoriasis	Decoction, Strong Decoction, Tincture, Powder	Cleavers, Oregon Grape, Comfrey
Fever	Decoction, Strong Decoction, Tincture	Elder Flowers, Sage
Fibroid Growths, Tumors	Decoction, Tincture, Powder (root)	Black Walnut, Butcher's Broom, Pau D'Arco
Gout, Arthritis	Decoction, Tincture, Powder	Dandelion, Nettles, Meadowsweet
HIV, AIDS	Decoction, Tincture, Powder	Lemon Balm
Hives, Shingles	Decoction, Strong Decoction, Tincture	Lemon Balm, Passion Flower
Inflamed Kidneys, Scalding Urine	Decoction, Strong Decoction, Tincture	Cornsilk, Calendula, Marshmallow
Kidney Stones	Decoction, Tincture	Catnip, Gravel Root
Lymphatic Congestion	Decoction, Tincture	Mullein, Echinacea
Respiratory Problems	Decoction, Tincture (root)	Mullein, Lobelia

Condition	Appropriate Preparations	Combines Well With:
Rheumatism, Sciatica	Decoction, Strong Decoction, Tincture, Powder	Angelica, Wild Yam, Yarrow, Willow
Syphilis, STD's	Decoction, Strong Decoction, Tincture, Powder	Sassafras, Garlic, Yellow Dock, Oregon Grape
EXTERNAL		
Burns, Scalds	Fomentation, Ointment	Flax Seed, Comfrey, Calendula
Rashes, Poison Ivy	Fomentation, Ointment	Plantain, Jewelweed
Swollen Glands	Fomentation	Mullein, Lobelia, Peppermint

Special Considerations: For its blood cleansing effects to be maximized, Burdock needs to be used consistently over an extended period. Even though relief from many toxic blood conditions is usually promptly seen and felt, the herb should be taken for at least three months to normalize the system.

Notes: The fresh root (called "Gobo" in Japan) can be used much like potatoes in recipes, and is considered a staple food item in much of the Orient.

Energetics: Burdock Root affects the Kidney, Bladder, Liver, Gallbladder, and Lung meridians. It is used to clear damp heat, and to raise the central Chi. The seed is used to clear wind heat, particularly of the respiratory system.

Calendula Blossom

Calendula officinalis
(Compositae)

Common Names: Pot Marigold

Physical Features: Erect and coarse many branched annual, 18 to 30 inches tall, sporting 1½ to 4 inch yellow to golden-orange daisy-like ray flowers in solitary terminal heads. Entire plant is covered with fine hairs. Leaves are oblong to oblong-obovate, edges smooth to faintly toothed. Lower leaves short stemmed, middle to upper leaves clasp the stalk. Flowers from late spring through fall.

Historical Information: Calendula is a remedy long used throughout Europe and the Americas for wound healing and ulcer treatments. Culpeper speaks of the flowers, either fresh or dried as being "much used in possets, broth, and drink as a comforter of the heart and spirits, and to expel any malignant or pestilential quality which might annoy them." Ellingwood recommends it for varicose veins, chronic ulcers, capillary engorgement, hepatic and splenic congestion, recent wounds and open sores, and severe burns. Calendula petals have often been used to add color and flavor to breads, soups, pickles, and salad oils.

Growing Range: As annual throughout United States, persists in mild climates.

Parts Used: Flower heads, petals

Cultivation/Wildcrafting Tips: Tender annual; plant in full sun; harvest flower heads when fully opened on dry day before the hottest hours. Dry on screens in the shade. Allow some flowers on healthiest plants to go to seed for next year's crop. Prefers slightly acid soil, well-drained and not too rich.

Primary Constituents: Triterpenes, pentacyclic alcohols such as faradol, brein, arnidiol, erythrodiol, Calenduladiol, heliantriol C and F, ursatriol, logispinogenine; the calendulosides A-D; a & b-amyrin, taraxasterol, gamma-taraxasterol, and lupeol Flavonoids; isorhamnetin glycosides including narcissin and quercitin glycosides including rutin; volatile oil; chlorogenic acid.

Action: anti-inflammatory, anti-spasmodic, astringent, vulnerary, anti-microbial, anti-fungal, lymphatic, emmenagogue, diaphoretic

Recent studies are showing significant anti-viral, anti-tumor, and cytogenic properties. (See Citations)

Tissues, Organs & Body Systems Affected: Blood, Mucus Membranes, Skin, Gastro-Intestinal Tract

Preparations & Dosage:

INTERNAL	
Fluid Extract	½–1 tsp; 3 times daily
Infusion	1–2 tbsp Each hour to 1 cup (8 oz.) daily
Powder	3–10 #0 capsules (15–60 grains); 3 times daily
Tincture	15–30 drops; 3–6 times daily

EXTERNAL	
Fomentation	Prepared from strong tea; leave on for 1–2 hours changing as needed to keep warm; twice daily
Oil, Salve, or Ointment	As often as needed

Good choice for First Aid Kit—Medicine Cabinet

Indicated Usages:

Condition	Appropriate Preparations	Combines Well With:
INTERNAL		
Bleeding, Hemorrhoids	Tincture, Fluid Extract, Infusion	Comfrey, Plantain
Cramps	Tincture, Fluid Extract	
Fever	Infusion	
Hemorrhage	Tincture, Fluid Extract, Infusion	Plantain
Measles	Infusion	
Skin Eruptions, Fungal Conditions	Tincture, Fluid Extract, Infusion	Comfrey, Plantain, Oregon Grape
Ulcers, Digestive Inflammation	Infusion	Comfrey
EXTERNAL		
Bee Stings, Insect Bites	Fomentation, Salve, Poultice	Plantain
Earache	Oil (drops in ear)	Mullein Flower Oil
Hemorrhoids	Strong Infusion (sitz bath)	Bugle
Sinus Lavage	Infusion, Tincture (diluted)	
Skin Diseases, Eczema, Psoriasis	Fomentation, Salve	Comfrey, Oregon Grape
Sunburn, Burns, Scalds	Fomentation, Salve, Oil	St. John's Wort, Comfrey
Ulcerations	Fomentation, Salve	Comfrey, Oregon Grape
Vaginal Discharge	Infusion (douche)	Juniper Berries
Varicose Veins	Fomentation	White Oak Bark, Bugle
Wash Wounds	Infusion, Tincture (diluted)	Oregon Grape, Myrrh
Wounds, Abrasions	Fomentation, Salve	Comfrey, Oregon Grape, Myrrh

Special Considerations: Do not confuse this plant with the more common garden Marigold, French Marigold, or Tagetes.

Notes: Calendula is one of the best herbs for treating local skin problems. It may be used safely wherever there is an inflammation on the skin, whether due to infection or physical damage. It may be used for any external bleeding or wounds, bruising, or strains. It will also be of benefit in slow-healing wounds and skin ulcers. A very useful anti-septic ointment can be made by combining it with Comfrey root, Oregon Grape Root, and Myrrh.

Energetics: Calendula addresses issues caused by liver Chi stagnation. It affects Liver, Heart, Lung, Chong and Ren meridians.

Capsicum

Capsicum frutescens, C. annum
(Solanaceae)

Common Names: Cayenne, Chili or Chili Pepper, Hot Pepper, Tabasco Pepper, African Pepper, Bird Pepper

Physical Features: So well known, it needs no description.

Historical Information: The pungent heat of red peppers has long added spice and character to culinary creations all over the world. The use of the fiery fruits as medicine—in any broad sense, at least—was first popularized by Samuel Thomson in the early 1800's. Thomson depended on Capsicum second only to Lobelia as a mainstay of his patented healing system that swept over rural America in the first half of the nineteenth century. Introducing hot pepper into medicinal practice brought another kind of heat on Thomson, though. In his 1833 "New Guide to Health," he states:

> "When I first began to use this article, it caused much talk among the people in Portsmouth and the adjoining towns. The doctors tried to frighten them by saying that I made use of Cayenne pepper as a medicine, and that it would burn up the stomach and lungs as bad as vitriol. The people, generally, however, became convinced by using it, that what the doctors said about it was false, and it only proved their ignorance of its medicinal virtues, and their malignity towards me. It soon came into general use, and the knowledge of its being useful in curing disease, was spread all through the country. I made use of it in curing the spotted fever, and where it was known, it was the only thing depended on for that disease. I have made use of Cayenne in all kinds of disease, and have given it to patients of all ages and under every circumstance that has come under my practice; and can assure the public that it is perfectly harmless, never having known it to produce any bad effects whatever. It is, no doubt, the most powerful stimulant known; but its power is entirely congenial to nature, being powerful only in raising and maintaining that heat on which life depends. It is extremely pungent, and when taken, sets the mouth, as it were, on fire. This lasts, however, but a few minutes, and I consider it essentially a benefit, for its effects on the glands causes the saliva to flow freely and leaves the mouth clean and moist."

As the Thomsonian movement evolved into the Physio-Medicalists and their successors, the Eclectics, Capsicum secured a revered and dependable place in their formularies. King's Dispensatory describes Capsicum as "a pure, energetic, permanent stimulant." It was used as a "catalyst" in a majority of the herbal formulas relied upon by the botanical practitioners of the 19th and 20th centuries, and, like its aromatic peer, Peppermint, was often found to promote healing "where all other measures had failed."

Capsicum is still found in many modern Western herbal formulas, much as Ginger is in Traditional Chinese and Ayurvedic preparations, but it also has many uses as a "Simple," especially where its powerful influence over the Circulatory System can bring benefit.

Capsicum has benefits for both young and old, but is particularly useful in the elderly and the debilitated, when the body-heat is low, vitality depressed, and reaction sluggish. This medicine possesses an extraordinary power in removing congestion by its action upon the nerves and circulation. Tired, painful muscles, stiffened joints, poor circulation, and relaxation of any part are common conditions in the elderly that can be improved by Capsicum. Externally, the infusion and tincture have been found valuable as a stimulating astringent gargle for sore throat. Powdered Capsicum, sprinkled inside the stockings, was a favorite prescription of the Eclectics for cold feet, a practical use no doubt derived from an old folk remedy.

Recent research into Capsicum and its constituents have validated the effects claimed by Thomson and his heirs, and have exposed an incredible array of medicinal uses that they never dreamed of.

Growing Range: Capsicum is a plant of tropical origin, but it can be cultivated as a tender annual in most temperate regions.

Parts Used: The fruit

Cultivation/Wildcrafting Tips: The fruit should be harvested when fully ripe, and has become a deep orange red. It can be dried in the shade on screen trays, or strung on "ropes." It benefits from a long hot growing season, where its medicinal strength has time to fully develop.

Primary Constituents: Capsaicin, Carotenoids; capsanthin, capsorubin, carotene, 1,8-cineole, 2-undecanone, alpha-carotene, alpha-linolenic-acid, alpha-phellandrene, alpha-terpinol, apiin, asparagine, benzaldehyde, beta-ionine, beta-pinene, betaine, caffeic-acid, camphor, carvone, caryophyllene, delta-3-carene, dihydrocapsaicin, hesperidin, limonene, lutein, myrcene, octanoic acid, oxalic acid, p-courmaric acid, pulegone, quercetin, scopoletin, solanidine, solanine, solasodine, terpinen-4-ol, thujone, toluene, and zeaxanthin. Capsicum is a significant source of beta-carotene, vitamin C, niacin, thiamin, riboflavin, vitamin B6, potassium, and molybdenum.

Action: stimulant, astringent, hemostatic, carminative, sialagogue, anti-tumor, anti-catarrhal, sialagogue, rubefacient, counter-irritant, analgesic, anti-ulcer, anti-arrhythmic, anti-microbial, thermogenic

Tissues, Organs & Body Systems Affected: Circulatory System (particularly the heart and peripheral vessels), Nervous System, Digestive System, Skin, Mucus Membranes

Preparations & Dosage:

INTERNAL

Infusion	Pour 1 cup boiling water over 1 tsp Capsicum powder; steep 10 minutes; strain. Take up to 1 tbsp of the resulting liquid in a little water 3–4 times daily.
Powder	500–1,000 mg.; 3 times daily
Tincture	10–30 drops; 3 times daily

EXTERNAL

Fomentation	1 tsp powder to 1 qt. boiling water; dip cloth and apply as hot as can be tolerated for 15–20 minutes.
Oil Extract	Mix 1 tbsp powder in 1 pint hot Olive Oil; set aside and let macerate 24 hours; apply to affected area once daily.

Indicated Usages:

Condition	Appropriate Preparations	Combines Well With:
INTERNAL		
Arteriosclerosis	Tincture, Powder	Garlic
Arthritis	Infusion, Tincture, Powder	Nettles, Willow
Asthma	Infusion, Tincture	Lobelia
Cold Extremities	Infusion, Tincture, Powder	Ginkgo, Garlic
Delirium Tremens	Tincture, Powder	Passion Flower
Depression	Infusion, Tincture, Powder	Lemon Balm
Dry Mouth	Infusion, Tincture	Dandelion
Heart Attack	Tincture, Powder (not capsules)	
Heart Disease (prevention)	Infusion, Tincture, Powder	Garlic, Ginger, Hawthorn Berries
Hemorrhage, Heavy Menstruation	Infusion, Tincture, Powder	Yarrow
Herpes, Shingles	Infusion, Tincture, Powder	Lemon Balm, Olive Leaf Extract
Pain	Infusion, Tincture, Powder	Bugle
Stroke, CVA	Tincture, Powder	Garlic, Ginkgo
Ulcers	Tincture, Powder	Aloe
EXTERNAL		
Arthritis, Muscle Pain	Tincture, Oil	Oil of Wintergreen
Bleeding Wounds (styptic)	Tincture, Powder	Yarrow Flowers
Cold Extremities	Oil, Powder	
Laryngitis	Tincture (diluted, as gargle)	Myrrh, Oregon Grape
Pleurisy, Lung Congestion	Fomentation	Mullein, Lobelia
Rheumatism	Fomentation, Oil	Black Cohosh
Sore Throat, Tonsillitis	Infusion, Tincture (diluted, as gargle)	Sage, Flax Seed

Special Considerations: The Physician's Desk Reference for Herbal Medicines warns that long-term topical applications can lead to blistering and skin ulceration, and that high doses taken internally over extended periods might bring about chronic gastritis, kidney and liver damage, and neurotoxic effects. Traditional herbalists strongly disagree, and the author's experience has never given the slightest indication of persistent irritation or injury from the use of Capsicum, topically or internally.

Notes: Topically applied, Capsicum relieves pain by depleting the activity of Substance P, the body's chemical pain messenger. While this might give relief from painful muscles and joints, it does not repair the damage that gave rise to the pain in the first place. Use good judgement when "pushing through" pain messengers, so as not to aggravate a deteriorating physical condition.

Energetics: Capsicum affects the Stomach, Kidney, Lung, and Spleen meridians. It is used to address stagnant Chi conditions, and Yang deficient, cold conditions, particularly of the digestive tract.

Catnip

Nepeta cataria
(Labiatae)

Common Names: Catnep, Catmint

Physical Features: A member of the Mint family, Catnip's root is perennial and sends up square, erect, and branched stems, 2 to 3 feet high, which are very leafy and covered with a coarse down. The heart shaped, toothed leaves are also covered with a soft, close down, especially on the under sides, which are quite white with it. The whole plant has a grayish appearance, as though it is covered with dust.

The flowers grow on short stalks in dense whorls. Towards the top of the stem, the flowers, which bloom from July to September, are so close that they appear to form a spike. The individual flowers are small, the corollas two-lipped, the upper lip straight, whitish or pale pink, and dotted with red spots. The anthers are deep red. The calyx tube has 15 ribs, a distinguishing feature of the genus Nepeta.

Historical Information: While the contemporary use of the flowering tops of Catnip is oriented towards its mild sedative qualities, the plant had quite a different reputation amongst the medieval herbalists. They held that when the root was chewed, it would make the most gentle person fierce and quarrelsome. There is an old English legend of a certain hangman who could never work up his courage to hang anybody until he had gotten a good dose of it.

Other old writers recommended a decoction of the herb (not the root), sweetened with honey for relieving a cough. Culpeper tells us that "the juice drunk in wine is good for bruises, and the green leaves bruised and made into an ointment is effectual for piles." He also observed that, "the head washed with a decoction taketh away scabs, scurf, etc."

Catnip is one of the traditional cold and flu remedies. It is an excellent diaphoretic, and its ability to induce sleep while producing perspiration without increasing the heat of the system makes it a valuable drink in every case of fever. As a carminative with antispasmodic properties, the herb also eases any stomach upsets, dyspepsia, flatulence, and colic. Its sedative action on the nerves adds to its generally relaxing properties.

Owing to its gentle nature, Catnip is highly prized in the treatment of children's ailments. It is good in colic, anxiety, and nervousness, and is used as a mild nervine. Catnip is an ideal remedy for the treatment of diarrhea in children.

The plant has an aromatic, peculiar odor, which is described as like that of Mint and Pennyroyal combined. It is this scent that provides its intoxicating fascination for cats, who will generally engage in the ecstatic destruction of any plant of it that may happen to be bruised.

Growing Range: Native to England and northern Europe where it is a fairly common wild plant, Catnip can now be found across most of North America as an escape from cultivation. It is easily grown wherever the mints can be grown, though it tends to like drier conditions than most of its botanical cousins.

Parts Used: Leaves, flowering tops

Cultivation/Wildcrafting Tips: A hardy perennial, Catnip is easy to grow in any garden soil, and does not require as much moisture as most of the other Mints. It makes a very attractive border plant, and blends well in the garden landscape with Hyssop and Lavender. It also grows well in the rock garden.

Catnip may be increased by dividing the plants in spring, or by sowing seeds at that same time. The choice of propagation methods might be determined by whether or not cats have access to your garden. There is an old saying about this plant: "If you set it, the cats will eat it. If you sow it, the cats don't know it."

It seems true that, unless protected, transplanted plants are almost always destroyed by cats, but they seldom meddle with plants raised from seed. They seem to be attracted to it when the scent of the plant is released by being bruised in gathering or transplanting. Barring feline intervention, Catnip plants require little or no attention, and will last for several years if the ground is kept free from weeds.

The flowering tops are the part utilized in medicine. They should be harvested in late summer when the plant is in full bloom, and dried in the shade. The flowering stems can be tied in loose bundles and hung upside-down to dry, well away from any cat's reach.

Primary Constituents: Volatile oil, carvacrol, citronellal, nerol, geraniol, citral, pulegone, thymol, camphor, rosmarinic acid, and nepetalic acid; Iridoids, including epideoxyloganic acid and 7-deoxyloganic acid; caryophyllene, myrcene, nepetalactone, piperitone, and tannins. Catnip is a significant source of cobalt, manganese, and selenium.

Action: carminative, diaphoretic, antispasmodic, refrigerant, emmenagogue, anodyne, sedative, antacid, astringent, nervine

Tissues, Organs & Body Systems Affected: Nervous System, Glandular System (particularly Pituitary and Adrenals), Disgestive and Intestinal Systems, Lungs, Liver

Preparations & Dosage: Catnip should never be boiled. When making a tea, it should be covered while it is infusing.

INTERNAL	
Infusion	1 oz. herb to 1 pint boiling water, cover tightly and steep 10–15 minutes; strain. May be taken freely by adults; 1 tbsp to 2 oz. up to hourly for children.
Injection (rectal)	Use infusion; 1 pint for adults; 2–4 oz. for children.
Juice	1 tbsp; 3 times daily
Tincture	30–60 drops up to 4 times daily

EXTERNAL	
Fomentation	Use a strong infusion; apply hot.

Indicated Usages:

Condition	Appropriate Preparations	Combines Well With:
INTERNAL		
Anxiety, Nervousness	Infusion, Tincture	Chamomile, Lemon Balm, Passion Flower
Bronchitis	Infusion, Tincture	Mullein, Lobelia
Colds, Flu	Infusion, Tincture	Capsicum, Echinacea, Elder Flowers, Yarrow
Colic	Infusion, Tincture, Injection	Raspberry Leaf, Dill, Fennel, Peppermint
Diarrhea	Infusion, Tincture	Plantain, Yarrow
Fever	Infusion, Tincture, Injection	Elder Flowers, Boneset
Gas, Bloating	Infusion, Tincture	Peppermint
Headache	Infusion, Tincture, Injection	Meadowsweet
Indigestion	Infusion, Tincture	Peppermint, Marshmallow
Insomnia	Infusion, Tincture	Hops, Passion Flower, Chamomile, Valerian
Menstrual Difficulty	Infusion, Tincture, Juice	Angelica, Vitex, Hyssop
Morning Sickness	Infusion	Ginger
Stomach Cramps	Infusion, Tincture	Pennyroyal
Toothache	Fresh Herb (crushed)	Plantain
EXTERNAL		
Sore Eyes	Fomentation, Infusion (as eye wash)	
Swollen Glands	Fomentation	Mullein, Lobelia

Energetics: Catnip exerts its influence on the Large Intestine and Kidney meridians. It is said to be balancing for both wind heat and wind cold, and effective for releasing constrained Chi conditions.

Cleavers

Galium aparine
(Rubiaceae)

Common Names: Goose Grass, Bedstraw, Stick-a-back, Clivers

Physical Features: Long, brittle, procumbent or clinging stems, covered with small hooks that give the plant a sticky feeling even when dry. Leaves are small, lanceolate, and arranged in whorls of 6 or 8 radiating from axils often spaced several inches apart. Color is evenly light green, and stems are distinctly square. Plant frequently grows amongst other plants or grasses, using them for support.

Historical Information: Herbal healers in the Old World used the herb much as the Native Americans did, as a classic "spring tonic" herb, with a reputation for being an excellent blood purifier, long before they had contact with each other. As Culpeper noted, "It is a good remedy in the spring, to cleanse the blood and strengthen the liver, thereby to keep the body in health, and fitting for that change of season that is coming." Gerard writes of Cleavers as a marvelous remedy for the bites of snakes, spiders, and all venomous creatures, and quoting Pliny, says: "A pottage made of Cleavers, a little mutton and oatmeal is good to cause lankness and keepe from fatnesse." In more recent times, Cleavers has come to be used as an effective remedy for all nature of eruptive or wasting skin disorders, as a potent diuretic, and as an aid to clearing stones and sediment from the urinary system.

Growing Range: Throughout North America except desert Southwest

Parts Used: Aerial parts, fresh or dried, juice of fresh plant

Cultivation/Wildcrafting Tips: Gather in May and June just as inconspicuous flowers begin to open for fresh use. Dry in shade for later use. Does not domesticate well.

Primary Constituents: Glycoside asperuloside, gallotannic acid, citric acid.

Action: diuretic, alterative, anti-inflammatory, tonic, astringent, aperient, refrigerant, anti-scorbutic, lymphatic, laxative

Tissues, Organs & Body Systems Affected: Blood, Lymphatic System, Kidneys, Bladder, Skin, Glandular System

Preparations & Dosage:

INTERNAL	
Infusion	Best made with warm (not boiling) water, steep 2–3 hours. 3–4 oz.; 3–4 times daily
Juice	Extracted from fresh plant. 2–3 oz.; 3 times daily

EXTERNAL	
Fomentation	Prepared from strong tea; leave on for 1–2 hours, changing as needed to keep warm; twice daily
Infusion	As a skin wash
Salve or Ointment	As often as needed

Indicated Usages:

Condition	Appropriate Preparations	Combines Well With:
INTERNAL		
Blood Purifier	Infusion, Juice	Red Clover, Burdock
Edema, Swelling	Infusion	Cornsilk, Dandelion
Fever	Infusion	
Head Colds	Infusion	Thyme, Lemon Juice
Kidney-Bladder Inflammation	Infusion, Juice	Cornsilk, Marshmallow
Skin Eruptions and Disorders	Infusion	Oregon Grape (tincture or decoction)
EXTERNAL		
Eczema, Psoriasis	Fomentation, Salve	Comfrey, Calendula, Oregon Grape
Poison Ivy, Rashes	Infusion (skin wash), Fomentation, Salve, Juice	Jewelweed, Plantain

Notes: Cleavers is a good addition to spring tonic teas, particularly when blended with Dandelion, Red Clover Blossoms, Sassafras root (decoct separately and mix with infusions), Chickweed, or Raspberry leaf. Add a bit of Peppermint leaf for flavor.

It can also be steamed and eaten as a vegetable.

Energetics: Cleavers' refrigerant and detoxifying properties can be used to clear heat from intermittent fevers presenting Yin deficiency with empty heat. Kidney, Bladder, and Liver meridians are affected.

Comfrey

Symphytum officinale—(Common Comfrey),
S. uplandicum—(Russian Comfrey)
(Boraginaceae)

Common Names: Knitbone, Knitback, Consound

Physical Features: A stout and coarsely hairy plant, reaching as much as three feet in height. Leaves are large, oval to lance shaped, with hairy, brittle, and juicy stems with a strong central fiber that makes them difficult to break away from the plant. Leaves form large rosettes, and often lay upon the ground in thick mats. Flowers are small, bell shaped, range from purplish-blue to rosy or white, and stand well above the plant in curled or "scorpoid" clusters. Root is thick and spreading, often hollow, brownish black and wrinkled externally, white to tan on fracture, and slimy when bruised or broken.

Historical Information: Well known in ancient times, Culpeper says of this wonderful healer, "The great Comfrey helps those that spit blood, or make a bloody urine. The root boiled in water or wine, and the decoction drank, helps all inward hurts, bruises, wounds, and ulcers of the lungs, and causes the phlegm that oppresses them to be readily spit forth. It is said to be so powerful to knit together (wounds and broken bones), that if the root be boiled with dissevered pieces of flesh in a pot, it will join them together again." Priest & Priest tell us that it is a soothing demulcent, gently stimulating to the mucous membranes, allays irritation and encourages cell growth. It increases expectoration and tones the bronchi, especially suitable for conditions involving capillary hemorrhage or excessive mucous. They give the following specific indications: coughs and colds, gastric and duodenal ulcers, gastro-intestinal inflammation, congealed or stagnant blood, pruritus ani, chronic suppurative ulcerations, bruised and damaged joints, damaged muscles or pulled tendons, delayed union of fractures, and traumatic injury to the eye. Ellingwood recommends it for bronchial irritation, pneumonia, inflammation of the stomach, and as being useful in all hurts and bruises both internal and external.

Growing Range: Throughout North America as long as adequate moisture is available. Flourishes in moist ground and along stream banks.

Parts Used: Leaf or root, fresh or dried

Cultivation/Wildcrafting Tips: Comfrey is a strong perennial and very easily grown. It prefers moist conditions, such as along streams and ponds. It is readily self-sowing, and can be multiplied by root division. Be careful of your site choice, as it can be difficult to eradicate once established. (The smallest piece of root left in the ground will rapidly regenerate a new plant.) Leaves can be gathered at any time during the growing season, and should be dried quickly in the shade. The roots should be unearthed in the spring or autumn when the allantoin levels are the highest. Split the roots down the middle and dry in low temperatures of about 120–145°F.

Primary Constituents: Allantoin; Pyrrolizidine alkaloids, including echimidine, symphytine, lycopsamine, symlandine. (The alkaloids are found in the fresh young leaves and in the root, but in two separate investigations were found to be absent in the dried herb.); Phenolic acids including rosmarinic, chlorogenic, caffeic and lithospermic acids; Mucilage, about 29%, composed of a polysaccharide containing glucose & fructose; miscellaneous elements including choline, asparagine, volatile oil, tannins, steroidal saponins, and triterpenes

Action: mucilaginous, vulnerary, demulcent, anti-inflammatory, anti-psoriatic, astringent, expectorant, anti-tumor, anti-mutagenic, cell proliferant, nutritive, hemostatic

Tissues, Organs & Body Systems Affected: Structural System (bone and muscle), Respiratory System, Mucus Membranes, Stomach and Digestive System, Skin

Preparations & Dosage:

INTERNAL*	
Decoction (root)	Simmer 15–30 min. 3–4 oz. Frequently
Infusion (leaf)	Steep 20–30 min. 4–6 oz.; 3 times daily
Powder	5–10 #0 capsules (3–6 gm.); 3 times daily
Syrup	1 tsp; up to 6 times daily
Tincture	½–1 tsp In juice or water; 3–5 times daily

EXTERNAL	
Fomentation	Best with decoction; leave on for 1–2 hours, changing as needed to keep warm; twice daily
Ointment	Apply directly to large areas, as often as needed.
Poultice	Crushed or ground fresh leaf or root needs no binder, moisten dried herb with water or aloe juice
Powder	Sprinkle on clean wound to assuage bleeding.
Tincture	Apply directly to clean wound or pad of bandage.

Good choice for First Aid Kit—Medicine Cabinet

Indicated Usages:

Condition	Appropriate Preparations	Combines Well With:
INTERNAL		
Arthritis	Infusion, Decoction, Powder	Flax Seed, Gelatin
Asthma	Infusion, Decoction, Tincture	Lobelia, Mullein
Blood Purifier	Infusion, Decoction, Powder	Burdock, Red Clover
Broken Bones	Infusion, Decoction, Powder	Bugle, Horsetail
Bronchitis	Infusion, Decoction, Tincture, Syrup	Wild Cherry, Lobelia, Thyme, Mullein

Condition	Appropriate Preparations	Combines Well With:
Cough, Pertussis	Infusion, Decoction, Syrup	Wild Cherry, Ginger
Diarrhea, Dysentery	Decoction, Powder	Slippery Elm, Plantain, Raspberry
Emphysema	Infusion, Decoction, Powder, Syrup	Wild Cherry, Lobelia, Capsicum
Gall Bladder	Decoction, Powder	Dandelion
Hemorrhage	Infusion, Decoction, Powder	Plantain, Bugle
Inflamed Kidneys	Infusion, Decoction, Powder	Gravel Root, Cornsilk, Marshmallow
Inflammation	Infusion, Decoction	
Irritable Bowel, Colitis	Infusion, Decoction, Tincture, Powder	Aloe Juice, Plantain, Marshmallow
Osteoporosis, Calcium Deficiency	Infusion, Decoction, Powder	

EXTERNAL

Condition	Appropriate Preparations	Combines Well With:
Boils, Old Sores	Poultice, Ointment, Tincture	Oregon Grape, Calendula
Broken Bones	Fomentation, Poultice	Plantain
Bruises	Fomentation, Poultice	
Burns, Scalds	Fomentation, Ointment	Calendula
Diaper Rash	Powder, Ointment	Plantain, Calendula, Oregon Grape, Aloe
Eczema, Psoriasis	Fomentation, Poultice, Ointment, Tincture	Plantain, Calendula, Oregon Grape, Aloe
Sprains	Fomentation, Poultice	

Special Considerations: Care should be taken when using Comfrey with very deep wounds as its rapid healing power can lead to tissue forming over the wound before it is healed deeper down, possibly leading to abscesses. Make sure that wounds are thoroughly cleaned and protected from infection.

*The FDA advises against taking Comfrey internally, due to the presence of trace amounts of pyrrolizidine alkaloids (PA's). In contrast, data published in the journal, Science, by noted biochemist Bruce Ames, Ph.D., of U.C. Berkeley, would indicate that Comfrey taken internally is less toxic or carcinogenic than an equivalent amount of beer. It is probably wise NOT to make Comfrey, or beer, a significant part of your regular diet for an extended period of time.

Pre-bloom Comfrey plants are similar in appearance to the first year growth of Foxglove (Digitalis spp.), which is very toxic. The roots are decidedly different.

Notes: Comfrey tincture is best prepared using low alcohol (20%) or glycerine based menstruum, which effectively releases the active saccharides while minimizing the extraction of offensive alkaloids. Dried leaf and root can also be made into very effective infusion and decoction on an as-needed basis.

Energetics: Comfrey is an excellent choice for Yin and fluids deficiency of the lung, stomach, and intestines presenting dryness, and for blood deficiency with depletion. It affects the Lung, Large Intestine, Stomach, and Bladder meridians.

Cornsilk

Zea mays
(Graminaceae)

Physical Features: The corn plant itself needs no description. Cornsilk refers to the stigmas (fine soft, yellowish threads) from the female flowers of maize (the tassels atop the plant is the male flower). They envelop the developing ear, and protrude from the top of the husk wrapper. They may range from 4 to 8 inches long, and are typically of a light green, purplish red, yellow, or light brown color. As the ear matures, the exposed silk will dry and turn dark brown to black. Fresh or dried, Cornsilk is nearly odorless, and has a faintly sweet taste.

Historical Information: Native to the Americas, corn is now one of the world's most important food crops. Sadly, it has become one of the most pesticide drenched and genetically manipulated crops on the planet, as well. Nearly lost in the agribusiness and biotech crush has been the gentle and predictable medicine that can be found in the fine silk fibers that embrace immature ears of corn.

Cornsilk has been a popular remedy for kidney and urinary difficulties among botanical healers since early colonial times. No doubt such uses were shared by the Native Americans that gave the colonists their first tastes of maize.

Ultimately it came to be included in the Materia medica of the Eclectics. According to Ellingwood,

> "The agent is a diuretic and demulcent. It apparently has antiseptic properties, due probably to the presence of maizenic acid which has a desirable influence in neutralizing excessive alkalinity of the urine, and in the cure of phosphatic gravel. It is of value in catarrhal cystitis, soothing, and neutralizing the strong ammonia odor, and decreasing the mucous secretion. In lithemia (stones), it increases the flow of water, and decreases the excessive proportions of uric acid and the urates. It is specific in relieving bladder irritation in these cases. In painful urination from any cause, it is beneficial, and is a good auxiliary in the treatment of gonorrhea. It influences all catarrhal conditions of the urinary passages.
>
> Dupont advised its use in dropsy due to heart disease. He says it reduces the edema, and as the edema disappears there is a better regulation of the blood supply throughout the system; the pulse beats more regularly, the action of the heart is slower and the rhythm is improved. The agent is well tolerated by all patients."

Growing Range: Maize is cultivated in warm and temperate climates around the globe.

Parts Used: The 4 to 8 inches long fine soft threads (stigmas from the female flowers) from immature (milk stage or earlier) ears of corn.

Cultivation/Wildcrafting Tips: Ideally, the silk should be collected just before pollination occurs. The timing depends upon the variety of corn and the climate, but that stage will always be just as the corn tassels begin to unfurl. The silk from organically grown sweet corn can be collected as late as when the corn is ready for eating (milk stage), but before the kernels turn starchy. Cornsilk must be dried carefully, in the shade, and without auxiliary heat. It is best when used fresh, and if dried, should be used within a year of gathering.

Primary Constituents: Saponins; Allantoin; Sterols, especially b-sitosterol and stigmasterol; the alkaloid hordenine; Miscellaneous; Vitamins C & K, cryptoxanthin, anthocyanins, plant acids. Maizenic acid is present in the dried Cornsilk; also fixed oil, resin, chlorophyl, sugar-gum extractive albuminoids; phlobaphine salt, cellulose and water.

Action: diuretic, demulcent, anti-inflammatory, lithotriptic, mildly tonic

Tissues, Organs & Body Systems Affected: Urinary System, Kidneys, Bladder, Mucus Membranes

Preparations & Dosage:

INTERNAL	
Infusion	1 tbsp powdered silks to 1 cup boiling water; steep 10–15 minutes. Drink without straining 2–3 times daily.
Powder	1–3 gms.; 3–4 times daily with lots of water
Tincture	30–60 drops; 3–4 times daily

Indicated Usages:

Condition	Appropriate Preparations	Combines Well With:
INTERNAL		
Cystitis	Infusion, Tincture	Oregon Grape, Uva Ursi, Yarrow, Buchu
Edema	Infusion, Tincture, Powder	Dandelion, Horsetail
Enuresis, Bedwetting	Infusion, Tincture	Catnip, Valerian
Kidney Stones	Infusion, Tincture	Gravel Root, Hydrangea
Prostatitis	Infusion, Tincture, Powder	Saw Palmetto, Parsley, Birch Bark, Nettles
Uric Acid Excess	Infusion, Tincture	Nettles
Urinary Tract Infection	Infusion, Tincture	Cranberry, Cleavers, Juniper Berries, Thyme

Special Considerations: Be certain that the Cornsilk you use is from an organically grown source, preferably using "heirloom" (non-hybrid) varieties of corn. Never use commercially grown corn, and particularly not the field corn varieties where genetic engineering is pervasive.

Energetics: Cornsilk is a purely Western herb that has been received and incorporated into the Chinese herbal system. It influences the Bladder, Small Intestine, Gallbladder, and Liver meridians. It is used to clear damp heat, and reduce Kidney Chi stagnation.

Dandelion

Taraxacum officinale
(Compositae)

Common Names: Puff-ball, Lion's Tooth, Wild Succory, Gowan (anc.)

Physical Features: Dandelion is so well known, that for most it needs no description. It is that persistent weed that grows in millions of yards and pastures, seemingly invulnerable to every physical or chemical effort to eradicate it. The true Dandelion has a basal rosette of deeply toothed leaves laying close to the ground, from which arises bright yellow many-petaled singular flowers on a hollow stalk. The flower is soon followed by the familiar globe shaped "puff ball" that has delighted children and aggravated groundskeepers since time immemorial. The root is a slim, carrot-like tap root, often 8 to 14 inches long, that is milky white in color, and bitter to the taste.

Historical Information: Dandelion is commonly thought to be one of the "bitter herbs" recommended in the Bible. Its young leaves have been gathered and eaten as a pot herb or as an addition to salads for centuries. It has been used to aid digestion, relieve liver distress, and to treat all manner of ills from dropsy, jaundice, and kidney stones to warts and psoriasis. Culpeper states, "It is of an opening and cleansing quality, and, therefore, very effectual for the obstructions of the liver, gall, and spleen. It opens the passages of the urine, both in young and old, powerfully cleanses, and doth afterwards heal them."

Growing Range: Rampant weed throughout North America

Parts Used: Leaf, root and flowers, fresh or dried; root roasted as coffee substitute

Cultivation/Wildcrafting Tips: Dandelion can be readily found wild virtually everywhere. When grown in deep, well-cultivated soil, though, it produces the best quality roots and greens. Tender leaves should be harvested early in the spring for inclusion in salads and spring tonic tea. For medicinal use, roots are best harvested in mid-summer when their bitter principles are highest.

Primary Constituents: Sesquiterpene lactones; taraxacoside (an acylated g-butyrolactone glycoside) and at least four others of the eudesmanolide, germacranolide and tetragydroridentin types; Triterpenes; taraxol, taraxerol, y-tarazasterol, b-amyrin, stigmasterol, b-sitosterol; Phenolic acids; caffeic and r-hydroxyphenylacetic acids; Polysaccharides; glucans and mannans and inulin; Carotenoids such as lutein and violaxanthin. Flowers contain lecithin, helenin, choline, Vitamins A and B-2 (riboflavin). Roots contain therapeutic amounts of inulin.

Action: diuretic, hepatic, bitter, cholagogue, anti-rheumatic, anti-spasmodic, aperient, digestive, laxative, tonic, nutritive, galactagogue, lithotriptic

Tissues, Organs & Body Systems Affected: Urinary System, Circulatory System, Digestive System, Liver, Kidneys, Stomach, Spleen, Skin

Preparations & Dosage:

INTERNAL	
Decoction (root)	Simmer 30 mins.; 6 oz.; 3–4 times daily, hot or cold.
Infusion (leaf or flower)	Steep 30 mins.; 6 oz.; 3–4 times daily, hot or cold.
Powder	6–18 #0 capsules (2–6 gms.) daily
Tincture	½–1 tsp; 3–4 times daily

EXTERNAL—Dandelion is not commonly used for external purposes

Indicated Usages:

Condition	Appropriate Preparations	Combines Well With:
INTERNAL		
Acne, Skin Eruptions	Decoction, Tincture	Oregon Grape
Alzheimer's	Infusion, Tincture (flowers)	Gotu Kola, Ginkgo
Anemia	Decoction, Powder	Yellow Dock
Blood Purifier	Decoction, Infusion, Tincture, Powder	Yellow Dock, Burdock, Red Clover, Cleavers
Boils, Cysts	Decoction, Infusion, Tincture, Powder	Burdock, Oregon Grape
Constipation	Decoction, Infusion	Psyllium
Diabetes	Decoction, Powder (root)	Goldenseal
Edema, Swelling, Water Retention	Decoction, Infusion, Powder, Tincture	Cornsilk, Cleavers, Juniper Berries
Gall Stones	Decoction (root), Infusion (flowers)	
High Blood Pressure (due to Dropsy)	Decoction, Infusion, Powder, Tincture	Passion Flower, Linden
Indigestion	Infusion	Comfrey, Peppermint
Jaundice, Hepatitis	Decoction, Infusion	
Kidney Stones	Decoction	Hydrangea
Obstructions - Liver, Spleen, Pancreas	Decoction	
Skin Diseases, Psoriasis, Eczema	Decoction, Infusion, Tincture, Powder	Comfrey, Burdock

Special Considerations: Dandelion is an extremely effective diuretic, but without the common side effect of mineral depletion prevalent with diuretic drugs.

Notes: Dandelion is rich in many nutrients, particularly in bio-available minerals. It enriches breast milk in nursing mothers, benefiting both mother and child. The plant helps control blood pressure by reducing excess fluids in the body, as well as by the presence of mannitol, a substance commonly prescribed in Europe for hypertension.

The milky sap from the broken stems of leaves and flowers has been used to remove warts and fade "age spots."

Dandelion Wine: This may be one of the most fun ways to benefit from Dandelion blossoms. To make this "down home" remedy, you'll need:

    2 quarts fresh Dandelion flowers (make sure they haven't been sprayed.)
    2 quarts spring water
    1 orange
    1 lemon (wash fruit to remove any chemical residues.)
    3 cups brown sugar or turbinado
    ½ pack of yeast

Carefully remove any trace of stems from flowers. Place in some sort of large crock or non-metallic container. Thinly slice the orange and lemon, and add to the flowers, along with the sugar. Bring water to a boil, and pour over the flowers, fruit, and sugar. Cover loosely and let set two days, stirring occasionally. Strain liquid into another large crock, and add yeast. Cover loosely again, and allow to ferment in a warm place for two weeks. Skim off any foam, and carefully pour off wine, trying not to disturb any sediment. Use immediately, or store in the refrigerator in tightly sealed bottles. One cup of crushed fresh Red Raspberries may be used in place of the citrus.

Energetics: Dandelion is effective for those presenting Liver and Gall Bladder Chi stagnation with damp heat. It affects the Liver, Gall Bladder, Spleen, and Bladder meridians.

Dill

Anethum graveolens
(Umbelliferae)

Physical Features: The plant grows ordinarily from 2 to 2½ feet high and looks very much like Fennel, though smaller, having the same feathery leaves, which stand on sheathing foot-stalks, with linear and pointed leaflets. Unlike Fennel, however, it has seldom more than one stalk and its long, spindle-shaped root is only annual. It is of very upright growth, its stems smooth, shiny and hollow, and in midsummer bearing flat terminal umbels with numerous yellow flowers, whose small petals are rolled inwards. Dill fruits are oval, compressed, winged about $1/10^{th}$ inch wide, with three longitudinal ridges on the back and three dark lines or oil cells between them and two on the flat surface. The flat fruits, mistakenly referred to as seeds, are produced in great quantities. They are very pungent and slightly bitter in taste, and very light, an ounce containing over 25,000 seeds. The whole plant is aromatic, and on warm days the fragrance will pervade the growing area.

Historical Information: Dill is commonly regarded as the Anethon of Dioscorides. It was well known in Pliny's days and is often mentioned by writers in the Middle Ages. It has been in use as medicine from very early times. It occurs in the tenth-century vocabulary of Alfric, Archbishop of Canterbury. In the Middle Ages, Dill was also one of the herbs used by magicians in their spells, and charms against witchcraft.

Culpeper says of Dill:

> "Mercury has the dominion of this plant, and therefore to be sure it strengthens the brain. It stays the hiccough, being boiled in wine, and but smelled unto being tied in a cloth. The seed is of more use than the leaves, and more effectual to digest raw and vicious humours, and is used in medicines that serve to expel wind, and the pains proceeding therefrom."

In King's American Dispensatory, Dill is described as:

> "Carminative and stomachic and used in the preparation of Dill-water. The natives of India use the fruit largely in medicine and cookery. Flatulent colic and singultus, when due to disordered digestion, are relieved by the administration of Dill-water or the oil of Dill; the former in 1 or 2 drachm doses, the latter in from 2 to 5 drop doses on sugar."

The French use Dill seeds for flavoring cakes and pastry, as well as for sauces, but as a sweet herb, Dill is not much used in this country. It is used to flavor soups, and sauces, for which purpose the young leaves are generally used. By far, its greatest popularity in this country lies in pickling cucumbers, millions of tons of which are sliced and piled on hamburgers, and laid alongside sandwiches every year.

Growing Range: As a short season annual, Dill can be grown in gardens in every part of North America.

Parts Used: The feathery young leaves, often called Dill Weed, and the dried ripe fruit, erroneously referred to as seeds.

Cultivation/Wildcrafting Tips: Dill is very easy to grow in any average garden soil. Small plots should be planted every 2 to 3 weeks beginning in early spring and continuing until mid-summer, to provide a steady supply of fresh herb. One substantial planting can be made in early summer to provide a stock of ripe seeds. The seeds should be collected when fully ripe, plump, and dark brown in color. They should be rubbed off the flower heads and spread out to dry in the shade, without the use of artificial heat. The seeds can then be stored in air-tight dark containers in a cool, dry location, where they will remain viable for up to five years.

Primary Constituents: Volatile oil, consisting mainly of carvone with dihydrocarvone, limonene, a- and b-phellandrene, eugenol, anethole, myristicin, carveole, x-pinene; Flavonoids: kaempferol and its blucuronide, vicenin; Coumarins such as scopoletin, esculetin, bergapten, umbelliferone; Xanthone derivatives such as Dillanoside; Miscellaneous; triterpenes, phenolic acids, protein, fixed oil.

Action: carminative, aromatic, anti-spasmodic, anti-inflammatory, stomachic, galactogogue, emmenagogue

Tissues, Organs & Body Systems Affected: Digestive Tract, Stomach, Liver, Milk Glands

Preparations & Dosage:

INTERNAL	
Dill Water	1 tbsp whole seed in 1 qt. distilled water; cover and set in open sunshine for 12 hours; strain and keep refrigerated. Take 2–3 ounces as needed. Dispose of leftover after 1 week.
Essential Oil	2–5 drops on a sugar cube or in warm water; 3–4 times daily
Infusion	1–2 tsps crushed seed to 1 cup boiling water; cover and steep 10–15 minutes; strain and drink 1 cup before meals or as needed through the day
Tincture	15–30 drops; 3–4 times daily
Whole Seed	Chew a pinch (¼ tsp or so) several times daily.

Indicated Usages:

Condition	Appropriate Preparations	Combines Well With:
INTERNAL		
Amenorrhea	Strong Infusion, Tincture, Essential Oil, Whole Seed	Blue Cohosh, Celery Seed, Wild Carrot
Bad Breath	Essential Oil, Whole Seed	Fennel, Basil, Parsley
Bronchitis	Infusion, Tincture	Mullein, Thyme
Colic	Infusion, Dill Water, Tincture	Catnip, Fennel
Cough	Infusion, Tincture	Wild Cherry

Condition	Appropriate Preparations	Combines Well With:
Dyspepsia	Infusion, Tincture, Dill Water, Essential Oil	Fennel, Peppermint, Catnip
Flatulence, Gas	Infusion, Tincture, Essential Oil, Whole Seed	Peppermint, Savory
Insomnia	Infusion (try making it with warm white wine)	Catnip, Passion Flower
Lactation (to promote)	Infusion, Whole Seed	Anise, Coriander, Caraway, Fenugreek
Poor Appetite	Infusion, Dill Water, Whole Seed	

Special Considerations: Dill contains significant amounts of apiole, which, on its own, is a proven and powerful emmenagogue. It is probably wise to avoid therapeutic doses of Dill if you are pregnant or trying to get that way. While they are not the healthiest food for other reasons, a craving for Dill pickles is still a safe and pretty reliable indicator that you may well have succeeded.

Energetics: Dill exerts its spicy, warm influence over the Stomach, Spleen, and Liver meridians.

Echinacea

Echinacea angustifolia, E. purpurea, E. pallida
(Compositae)

Common Names: Purple Coneflower, Black Sampson, Prairie Coneflower, Rudbeckia, Brauneria pallida (Nutt.)

Physical Features: The flowers are a rich purple and the florets are seated round a high cone; seeds, four-sided achenes. Root tapering, cylindrical, entire, slightly spiral, longitudinally furrowed; fracture short, fibrous; bark thin; wood, thick, in alternate porous, yellowish and black transverse wedges, and the rhizome has a circular pith. It has a faint aromatic smell, with a sweetish taste, leaving a tingling sensation in the mouth not unlike Aconite, but without its lasting numbing effect.

Historical Information: The Dakota and Sioux Indians used the fresh scraped root of Echinacea to treat hydrophobia, snake bites, and blood poisoning from infected wounds, while the Kiowas and Cheyenne chewed the fresh root or made tea as a remedy for cough, sore throat, and ulcers of the mouth and gums. In fact, (according to ethnobotanist Melvin Gilmore, in 1917) the Plains tribes used Echinacea "for more ailments than any other plant." Unfortunately, by the time early white settlers reached the Great Plains, their relationship with the Native Americans was strained at best, and unlike the Eastern tribes, many of the Plains and Western Indians jealously guarded their medicinal lore (a condition which still, to some extent, exists to this day). It was not until after the Civil War that Echinacea was "discovered" by prairie doctors, and brought to the attention of the Eclectics. By that time the rift in medicine between the allopathic and botanical practitioners was so great, that the "regulars" refused to even entertain the powers of the "new drug." Eclectic Dr. John King (author of King's American Dispensatory) was so impressed with the tales of the uses of Echinacea by the legendary "root doctor" H.F.C. Meyer, of Pawnee City, Nebraska, though, that he embraced an extensive study of the plant. An associate recounted Dr. Meyer and Prof. King's initial communications.

"(Dr. Meyer) had, for many years (since 1870), been using the plant without knowing its botanical position. In a letter to Prof. King (see *Eclectic Medical Journal*, 1887), in 1886, he communicated to the latter his uses of the drug, as he had employed it for 16 years. His claims for the remedy were based upon the conclusion that it was "an antispasmodic and antidote for blood-poisoning." The enthusiastic doctor had been using it in a secret mixture with wormwood and Hops, which be had denominated "Meyer's Blood Purifier." Among his claims for it was its antidotal action upon the poison of various insects, and particularly that of the rattlesnake. Meyer stated that he even allowed a rattler to bite him, after which he bathed the parts with some of the tincture, took a drachm of it internally, and laid down and slept, and upon awakening all traces of swelling had disappeared! Prof. King wrote: 'He (Dr. Meyer) kindly offered to send me a rattler eight feet long, that the antidotal influence of the tincture upon dogs, rabbits, etc., bitten by said serpent, might be tested. But having no friendship for the reptile, and being unaccustomed to handling this poisonous ophidian, the generous offer was courteously declined.'"

Though a skeptic by nature, King's enthusiasm for Echinacea began to spill over in his reports. He wrote,

> "If any single statement were to be made concerning the virtues of Echinacea, it would read something like this: 'A corrector of the depravation of the body fluids,' and even this does not sufficiently cover the ground. Its extraordinary

powers—combining essentially that formerly included under the terms antiseptic, antifermentative, and antizymotic—are well shown in its power over changes produced in the fluids of the body, whether from internal causes or from external introductions. The changes may be manifested in a disturbed balance of the fluids resulting in such tissue alterations as are exhibited in boils, carbuncles, abscesses, or cellular glandular inflammations. They may be from the introduction of serpent or insect venom, or they may be due to such fearful poisons as give rise to malignant diphtheria, cerebro-spinal meningitis, or puerperal and other forms of septicaemia. Such changes, whether they be septic or of devitalized morbid accumulations, or alterations in the fluids themselves, appear to have met their antagonist in Echinacea. "Bad blood," so called, asthenia, and adynamia, and particularly a tendency to malignancy in acute and subacute disorders, seem to be special indicators for the use of Echinacea."

Years later, in 1915, Ellingwood also gave an extensive report on the Eclectics' research and experience with Echinacea as it had evolved by the early 20th century.

"The physiological effects are manifested by its action upon the blood, and upon the mucous surfaces. The natural secretions are at first augmented, the temperature is then lowered, the pulse is slowed, and the capillary circulation restored. It exerts a peculiar affinity over local debilitated inflammatory conditions, attended with blood dyscrasias. It has its greatest field in adynamic fevers, reducing the pulse and temperature and subduing delirium.

It promotes the flow of saliva in an active manner. The warmth and tingling attendant to oral administration extend down the esophagus to the stomach, but no further unpleasant influence is observed. In a short time diaphoresis is observed, and the continuation of the remedy stimulates the kidneys to increased action. All of the glandular organs seem to feel the stimulating influence, and their functional activity is increased. The stomach is improved in its function, the bowels operate better, and absorption, assimilation, and general nutrition are materially improved. It encourages secretion and excretion, preventing further auto-intoxication, and quickly correcting the influence in the system of any that has occurred. It influences the entire lymphatic system. Sallow, pallid, and dingy conditions of the skin of the face quickly disappear, and the rosy hue of health is apparent. Anemic conditions improve with increased nerve tone.

There are but few subjective symptoms from large doses of this agent. It is apparently non-toxic, and to any unpleasant extent non-irritant. This agent is markedly anesthetic in its local influence. Applied to open wounds and to painful swellings, while the alcohol may at first induce a burning sensation, this is quickly followed by entire relief from pain in many cases. So marked is this influence that it could well be used for an antiseptic local anesthetic.

I am convinced that success in certain cases depends upon the fact that the patient must have at times, a sufficiently large quantity of this remedy in order to produce full antitoxic effects on the virulent infections. I would therefore emphasize the statement which I have previously made that it is perfectly safe to give Echinacea in massive doses—from two drams to half an ounce every two or three hours—for a time at least, when the system is overwhelmed with these toxins. This applies to tetanus, anthrax, actinomycosis, pyemia, diphtheria, hydrophobia, and meningitis."

Growing Range: Echinacea angustifolia is native to the North American prairies, plains, and open woodland meadows west of Ohio. The Purple Coneflowers, particularly E. purpurea and E. pallida, were more common n the East. All are now cultivated in gardens across the United States.

Parts Used: E. angustifolia is the officinal species, of which the dried root is active. E. purpurea and E. pallida have similar properties to E. angustifolia, though they are generally considered to be somewhat weaker in action. The fresh or dried root of three year old plants, and the aerial parts of these are the parts used.

Cultivation/Wildcrafting Tips: Echinacea grows well in most garden soils. For medicinal use, the character of the soil should be neutral to slightly acidic, light and well drained. Moist or boggy soil will support Echinacea and yield attractive blooms, but the medicinal properties will be reduced.

Primary Constituents: Echinacoside, in E. angustifolia but not E. purpurea; Unsaturated isobutyl amides, echinacin and others, in E. angustifolia and E. pallida; Polysaccharides; a heteroxylan and an arabinorhamnogalactan; Polyacetylenes (At least 13 of which have been isolated. It has been postulated that these are artifacts formed during storage, since they are found in dried but not fresh roots of E. pallida.); Essential oil, containing humulene, caryophyllene and its epoxide; germacrene D and methyl-p-hydroxycinnamate; Miscellaneous; vanillin linolenic acid derivatives, a labdane derivative, alkanes and flavonoids and the alkaloids tussilagine and isotussilagine.

Note: Research suggests that the echinacoside glycosides appear to be the primary anti-microbial constituents in Echinacea. However, there are many other biologically active substances present, and there is evidence that they work synergistically. The polysaccharides, for example, possess the best immune stimulating properties and are also antiviral.

Action: anti-microbial, anti-viral, immuno-stimulant, anti-catarrhal, diaphoretic, sialagogue, alterative

Tissues, Organs & Body Systems Affected: Echinacea is one of the best general remedies for helping the body rid itself of microbial infections. In conjunction with other "guiding" herbs it may be used for any infection or inflammation anywhere in the body. (For example, in combination with Cornsilk and Uva Ursi, it will effectively stop cystitis and UTI's.) It is often effective against both bacterial and viral attacks, and may be used in conditions such as boils, septicemia and similar infections. The tincture or decoction may be used as a mouthwash in the treatment of pyorrhea and gingivitis. It may be used as an external lotion to help septic sores and cuts. It is especially useful for infections of the upper respiratory tract such as laryngitis, tonsillitis and for catarrhal conditions of the nose and sinus. In general, it may be used widely and safely.

Preparations & Dosage:

INTERNAL	
Decoction	Simmer 1 tbsp cut dried root in 1 pint water for 10 min.; set aside to cool for 30 min.; strain, take 1 tbsp frequently repeated.
Infusion	Only the aerial parts of E. purpurea or E. pallida.; 1 tsp cut dried herb to 1 cup boiling water; cover and steep 10–15 minutes. Sweeten with honey if desired, and drink 1 cup every 2–3 hours for acute conditions.
Powder	500–1500 mg.; 3–6 times daily
Tincture	15–30 drops; every 2–3 hours

EXTERNAL	
Decoction	Prepare as above; apply as fomentation or wash.

Indicated Usages:

Condition	Appropriate Preparations	Combines Well With:
INTERNAL		
Bites - Snake, Scorpion, Spider	Decoction, Tincture (also apply as fomentation), Fresh Root	Plantain, Black Cohosh

Condition	Appropriate Preparations	Combines Well With:
Blood Poisoning	Decoction, Tincture, Powder	Oregon Grape, Burdock, Yellow Dock, Colloidal Silver
Boils, Indolent Ulcers, Abscesses	Infusion, Decoction, Tincture, Powder	Myrrh, Oregon Grape, Comfrey, Blue Flag
Cancer	Decoction, Tincture, Powder	Chaparral, Pau D'Arco, Red Clover
Colds, Flu	Infusion, Decoction, Tincture	Garlic, Una de Gato, Zinc
Fever	Infusion, Decoction, Tincture	Elder Flowers, Boneset
Gangrene	Decoction, Tincture (also apply as fomentation)	Comfrey, Myrrh, Thyme, Juniper Berries, Colloidal Silver
Herpes, HIV	Decoction, Tincture, Powder	Lemon Balm, St. John's Wort, Oregon Grape
Infection	Decoction, Tincture, Powder	Myrrh, Oregon Grape, Thyme, Una de Gato
Inflammation	Infusion, Decoction, Tincture	Calendula, St. John's Wort, "guiding herbs" (See note under Tissues, Organs, Systems affected.)
Lymphatic Congestion	Decoction, Tincture, Powder	Mullein, Lobelia
Mastitis	Infusion, Decoction, Tincture	Garlic, Squaw Vine
Skin Diseases	Infusion, Decoction, Tincture	Burdock, Oregon Grape, Comfrey
Tuberculosis	Decoction, Tincture, Powder	Mullein, Lobelia
Vaccination Reaction	Decoction, Tincture	Red Clover
Yeast Infections	Decoction, Tincture	Garlic, Licorice, Ginger, Pau D'Arco
EXTERNAL		
Athlete's Foot, Tinea (Fungus)	Decoction (as wash)	Thyme, Tea Tree Oil, Pau D'Arco
Old Sores, Ulcers	Decoction (as fomentation, wash)	Comfrey, Myrrh
Sore Throat	Infusion, Decoction (as gargle)	Myrrh, Sage

Special Considerations: Echinacea is sometimes used as a prophylactic against infection, and this may be appropriate under extraordinary circumstances where exposure to pathogens is known or unavoidable. In general, though, it should not be taken for extended periods, or used as a "daily immune support." Echinacea's influence is best when there is a battle to be fought, and its power may be blunted when the body becomes accustomed to its stimulation. It is probably wisest to reserve it for times of need.

Notes: Much research has been focused on this plant since its introduction to contemporary medicine in the 1880's, and to this day still produces contradictory results. Taken as a whole (rather than as isolated constituents), it is the author's opinion that the primary benefits of Echinacea come from the detoxification and enhancement of the physiology of the person using it rather than from some direct action of the herb itself against pathogens. It is definitely a case where treating the person rather than the disease brings the greatest benefit.

Energetics: According to TCM tropism, Echinacea affects the Lung, Large Intestine, and Stomach meridians. It dispels external wind heat, and relieves Stomach and Kidney Chi stagnation.

Elderberry

Sambucus canadensis (America), S.nigra (Europe)
(Caprifoliaceae)

Common Names: Black Elder; Common Elder; Pipe Tree; Bore Tree; Ellhorn; Hollunder (*German*); Sureau (*French*)

Physical Features: Elder is a small shrubby tree, growing from 5 to 12 feet in height. It blooms in June and July with large flat-topped masses of ¼ inch creamy-white, star-shaped, fragrant blossoms. The blossom heads are followed by large drooping bunches of purplish-black, juicy berries. The branching stems are covered with rough, pitted gray bark, while the central stems are smooth. The stems are very lightweight, due to a central core filled with an easily removed pithy material. (It is this feature that made the stems popular as children's flutes and "pop-guns" in an earlier, simpler time.) The leaves are compound, consisting of 5 to 11 leaflets, but usually 7, which are pointed at the tips, toothed, mostly smooth on top, but somewhat hairy and lighter colored beneath.

Historical Information: From the days of Hippocrates through to the Middle Ages and into the 19th century, Elder has been famous for its medicinal properties. In 1644, a book entitled The Anatomie of the Elder, by Dr. Martin Blockwich, dedicated some 230 handcrafted pages to the medicinal virtues and uses of nearly every part of the Elder—its flowers, berries, leaves, 'middle bark,' pith, and roots. It sets forth that as every part of the tree was medicinal, so virtually every ailment of the body was curable by it, from toothache to the plague. It was used externally and internally, and in amulets (these were especially good for epilepsy, and in popular belief also for rheumatism), and in every kind of form—in rob and syrup, tincture, mixture, oil, spirit, water, liniment, extract, salt, conserve, vinegar, oxymel, sugar, decoction, bath, cataplasm, and powder. Some of these were prepared from one part of the plant only, others from several or from all. Their properties are summed up as "desiccating, conglutinating, and digesting," but are extended to include everything necessary to a universal remedy. The book prescribes in more or less detail for some seventy or more distinct diseases or classes of diseases. Blockwitch seems never at a loss for an authority, from Dioscorides to the Pharmacopeias of his own day. His examples of cures are drawn from all classes of people, from Emylia, Countess of Isinburg, to the tradesmen of Heyna and their children.

Of course in those early days, drastic purgatives and emetics were also considered a standard practice. These days, we look less kindly upon such strong measures, and the more benign actions of the Elder berries and particularly the flowers retain the greatest favor. The flowers were used by our forefathers in bronchial and pulmonary affections, and in scarlet fever, measles and other eruptive diseases. Of those, Priest & Priest tell us that they are:

> "a mild diffusive & relaxing diaphoretic with alterative properties, indicated for children subject to frequent febrile reactions. Relaxing to the eliminative organs, soothing to the nervous system and gently laxative." Preparations of Elder berries and flowers are indicated for: "Colds & flu with dry, hot skin; chronic nasal catarrh or sinusitis; dry coryza; spasmodic croup; weakening night sweats; skin eruptions from metabolic disturbance; eczema; and dermatitis."

King's describes the uses of Elder in more specific terms.

> "In warm infusion, Elder Flowers are diaphoretic & gently stimulant; in cold infusion they are diuretic, alterative & cooling, & may be used in all diseases requiring such action, as in hepatic derangements of children, and erysipelas. The expressed juice of the berries evaporated to the consistence of a syrup is a valuable aperient and alterative; one ounce of it will purge. An infusion of the young leaf-buds is likewise purgative, and sometimes acts with violence. The flowers and expressed juice of the berries have been beneficially employed in scrofula, cutaneous diseases, syphilis, and rheumatism."

Elder Berries provide a classic country remedy in the form of an excellent homemade wine. It is quite tasty, and improves with age. When taken hot with honey, just before going to bed, it is an old-fashioned and well-established cure for a cold.

Elder leaves are still occasionally used in the preparation of an ointment as a domestic remedy for bruises, sprains, chilblains, for use as an emollient, and for applying to all kinds of tumors, swellings, and wounds. (See the recipes under Notes.)

Growing Range: Throughout North America (except in the desert Southwest) from southern Florida to Canada, Elder prefers moist ground, but will grow in substantial thickets alongside railroads, and on other dry waste ground.

Parts Used: All parts of the tree—bark, leaves, flowers and berries—have long enjoyed a high reputation in domestic medicine. At present, though, only the flowers and berries are widely used. The bark, leaves, and especially the root are generally considered too drastic in their action.

Cultivation/Wildcrafting Tips: The flowers are collected by cutting the entire cluster when fully opened in the spring and early summer. If the clusters are piled on a canvas in the open sun for 2 or 3 hours, the flowers can be easily shaken from the stems. They must then be dried as rapidly as possible, using gentle heat. Gentle handling, and quickness in drying is essential to avoid discoloration and spoilage. The berries are best collected in August and September when they are fully ripe and sweet to the taste. When desired to make an ointment, Elder leaves are gathered fresh and processed promptly.

Primary Constituents: Flowers: Triterpenes including ursolic acid, 30-b-hydroxyursolic acid; oleanolic acid; a- and b-amyrin and free and esterified sterols;

Fixed oil, containing free fatty acids, mainly linoleic, linolenic and palmitic acids; alkanes; Flavonoids, including rutin, quercitin and kaempferol; Miscellaneous phenolic acids; pectin; sugars. Leaves: Triterpenes similar to those found in the flowers; Cyanogenetic glycosides, e.g. sambunigrin; Flavonoids including rutin and quercitin; Miscellaneous fatty acids; alkanes tannins.

Elder berries furnish Viburnic acid, with an odorous oil, combined with malates of potash and lime. The fresh, ripe fruits contain Tyrosin.

Action: *Bark:* purgative (drastic), emetic (drastic), diuretic; *Leaves:* emollient, vulnerary (topical), purgative (strong), expectorant, diuretic, diaphoretic; *Flowers:* diaphoretic, anti-catarrhal, anti-spasmodic, febrifuge, aperient, anti-inflammatory; *Berries:* diaphoretic, diuretic, laxative, aperient, anti-rheumatic

Tissues, Organs & Body Systems Affected: Respiratory System, Glandular System, Skin

Preparations & Dosage: Elder flowers are a time tested safe remedy. Measures and doses are not critical. They may be used liberally in quantities sufficient "to get the job done." All other parts of Elder, including fresh uncooked berries, should be used in conservative doses to gauge the body's response.

INTERNAL	
Infusion	2–3 tsp flowers in 1 cup boiling water; steep 10–15 min; drink hot 3–4 times daily
Juice (berries)	Simmer fresh berries with $\frac{1}{10}$ part water for 2–3 min.; express the juice and combine with $\frac{1}{10}$ part raw honey; return to boil then bottle and refrigerate. Mix 2–3 oz. with equal amount of hot water; take 2–3 times daily.
Strong Infusion	¼ cup flowers in 1 pint boiling water; cover and steep for 30 min.; strain, drink hot and freely
Tincture (flowers)	20–60 drops; 3–4 times daily
EXTERNAL	
Ointment (leaves)	Apply to affected area as needed.

Indicated Usages:

Condition	Appropriate Preparations	Combines Well With:
INTERNAL		
Allergies, Hay Fever	Infusion, Strong Infusion, Tincture	
Colds, Flu	Strong Infusion (at bedtime)	Peppermint, Yarrow
Constipation	Strong Infusion, Juice	Slippery Elm

Condition	Appropriate Preparations	Combines Well With:
Emphysema, Pleurisy	Strong Infusion, Tincture	Mullein, Pleurisy Root, Comfrey
Fever	Strong Infusion	Echinacea, Boneset
Rheumatism	Juice	Capsicum
Sinusitis	Strong Infusion, Tincture	Echinacea
Sore Throat	Strong Infusion, Tincture (as gargle)	Echinacea, Sage
Spring Tonic	Infusion (first fresh blossoms)	Cleavers, Chickweed
EXTERNAL		
Bruises	Ointment	Comfrey
Chilblains (frostbite)	Ointment	Comfrey, St. John's Wort, Calendula
Skin Blemishes, Discoloration	Infusion, Fresh Flowers (as wash)	Sour milk
Sprains	Ointment	Comfrey, Calendula
Tumors	Ointment	Butcher's Broom, Chickweed

Notes: Dr. Phil's Green Elder Ointment: (Using fresh—not dried—herbs)

> 8 oz. Elder leaves 4 oz. St. John's Wort
> 4 oz. Plantain leaves 4 oz. Wormwood

Cut the herbs into small pieces, and place in a large stainless steel or porcelain pot. Cover the herbs with 1 liter of good extra virgin olive oil. Simmer slowly in the oven or on a low burner, stirring frequently, until the leafy material becomes crisp. Strain and press out the oil. Return to gentle heat and add 4½ oz. of beeswax chips or beads. Heat and stir just until wax is melted. Stir in 60 drops of Tincture of Benzoin, and a little essential oil of your choice. Pour into small jars or tins and leave undisturbed until cool. Cap and share.

Here are some classic recipes worthy of trying, from Maude Grieve's "A Modern Herbal":

To make Elderberry Rob (medicinal syrup):

> 5 lb. of fresh ripe, crushed Elder berries are simmered with 1 lb. of loaf sugar, and the juice evaporated to the thickness of honey. It is cordial, aperient, and diuretic. One or two tablespoonsful mixed with a tumblerful of hot water, taken at night, promotes perspiration and is demulcent to the chest. The Rob when made can be bottled and stored for the winter.

Elderberry Wine:

"If two gallons of wine are to be made, get one gallon of Elderberries, and a quart of plums; boil them together in six quarts of water for half an hour, breaking the fruit with a mashing stick. Run off the juice, and squeeze the pulp through a sieve, or straining cloth. Boil the juice up again with six pounds of coarse sugar, two ounces of ginger, two ounces of bruised allspice, and one ounce of Hops; (the spice had better be loosely tied in a bit of muslin). Let this boil above half an hour; then remove it from the heat. When quite cool, stir in a teacupful of yeast, and cover it up to work. After two days, skim off the yeast, and put the wine into the barrel, and when it ceases to hiss, which will be in about a fortnight, paste a stiff brown paper over the bung-hole. After this, it will be fit for use in about eight weeks, but will keep eight years, if required. The bag of spice may be dropped in at the bung-hole, having a string fastened outside, which shall keep it from reaching the bottom of the barrel."

Energetics: Elder flowers affect the Lung and Bladder meridians. They are used to dispel wind heat, and relieve Kidney Chi stagnation. In Ayurveda, they are said to decrease Kapha, increase Vayu.

Fennel

Foeniculum vulgare
(Umbelliferae)

Common Names: Sweet Fennel

Physical Features: A tall and graceful plant, Fennel adds height, texture and fragrance to the herb garden. It has a thick, perennial root supporting strong bold stems, 4 to 5 feet or more in height. It is erect and cylindrical in form. The plant is bright green, sometimes bluish, and tends to be reddish brown at the tips in some varieties. The stems are very smooth, almost polished in appearance, heavily branched and terminating in feathery masses of very fine leaves. The flowers are golden, and produced in large, flat terminal umbels characteristic of the family. The whole plant has a light licorice or anise-like fragrance when bruised.

Historical Information: Fennel was cultivated by the ancient Romans for its aromatic fruits and succulent, edible shoots, and was well known to the ancient herbalists. Pliny had much faith in its medicinal properties, according no less than 22 remedies to it. He observed that serpents eat it "when they cast their old skins, and they sharpen their sight with the juice by rubbing against the plant." Many of the old herbals uphold this trait of its strengthening effect on the sight.

In medieval times, Fennel was employed, together with St. John's Wort, Elder, and other herbs, to ward off witchcraft and other evil influences. It was said to convey longevity, and to give strength and courage. Its primary use, however, was culinary, as its unique flavor and aroma helped overcome the taste and smell of tainted meats and fish, as well as their impact on the digestive system.

Culpeper says:

> "One good old custom is not yet left off, viz., to boil Fennel with fish, for it consumes the phlegmatic humour which fish most plentifully afford and annoy the body with, though few that use it know wherefore they do it. It benefits this way, because it is a herb of Mercury, and under Virgo, and therefore bears antipathy to Pisces. Fennel expels wind, provokes urine, and eases the pains of the stone, and helps to break it. The leaves or seed boiled in barley water and drunk, are good for nurses, to increase their milk and make it more wholesome for the child. The leaves, or rather the seeds, boiled in water, stayeth the hiccup and taketh away nausea or inclination to sickness. The seed and the roots much more help to open obstructions of the liver, spleen, and gall, and thereby relieve the painful and windy swellings of the spleen, and the yellow jaundice, as also the gout and cramp. The seed is of good use in medicines for shortness of breath and wheezing, by stoppings of the lungs. The roots are of most use in physic, drinks and broths, that are taken to cleanse the blood, to open obstructions of the liver, to provoke urine, and amend the ill colour of the face after sickness, and to cause a good habit through the body; both leaves, seeds, and roots thereof, are much used in drink, or broth, to make people more lean that are too fat. A decoction of the leaves and root is good for serpent bites, and to neutralize vegetable poison, as mushrooms, etc."

King's American Dispensatory describes it as carminative, stimulant, galactagogue, diuretic and diaphoretic, and suggested its use in flatulent colic, and as a corrigent of unpleasant medicines. May be used in amenorrhea and suppressed lactation.

Growing Range: A hardy perennial, Fennel grows wild as a garden escape in many parts of North America and Europe. It is generally considered indigenous to the coastal areas of the Mediterranean. It flourishes particularly on dry limestone soils near large bodies of water and streams. It can be readily grown in most any good garden soil.

Parts Used: Seeds (fruit), leaves, roots—the roots of Fennel were formerly employed in medicine, but are now used primarily as a vegetable. ("Let your food be your medicine, and your medicine be your food.") The fruit, generally but incorrectly called the seeds, and the essential oil are now the only parts commonly used medicinally.

Fennel seed is fragrant, and anise-like in character. Its taste is warm, sweet and agreeable to most people. It yields its virtues to hot water, but more freely to alcohol. The essential oil may be separated by distillation.

Cultivation/Wildcrafting Tips: Fennel will thrive anywhere, and a planting will last for years. It is easily grown from seed, sown in early spring in ordinary soil. It likes plenty of sun and is adapted to dry and sunny situations, not needing heavily manured ground, though it will yield more on rich soil. The seeds should be harvested when ripe and split in the autumn. The brown umbel should be cut off, and the seeds combed or rubbed to free them. Spread out in the shade, and allow to dry a little more.

Primary Constituents: Volatile oil, up to about 8%, consisting mainly of anethole; 80% in sweet Fennel and 60% in bitter Fennel. The other major component of the oil is fenchone, higher in bitter than sweet Fennel, 10–30%. Minor components include limonene; anisaldehyde; a- and b- pinene; a- phellandrene; myrcene; ocimene; a- and b- terpinene; apiole; and the polymers of anethole, dianethole & photoanethole. Flavonoids, mainly rutin, quercitin and kaempferol glycossides; Coumarins: bergapten, imperatorin, xanthotoxin, and marmesin; Miscellaneous sterols, fixed oils and sugars. There are also present in oil of Fennel, d-pinene, phellandrine, anisic acid and anisic aldehyde.

Action: carminative, aromatic, anti-spasmodic, anti-inflammatory, stomachic, galactogogue, hepatic

Tissues, Organs & Body Systems Affected: Stomach, Intestines, Nerves, Eyes

Preparations & Dosage:

INTERNAL

Essential Oil	1–5 drops on sugar cube, or in 1 cup warm water; up to 3 times daily
Infusion	1–2 tsp crushed seed to 1 cup boiling water; cover and allow to infuse for 10–15 minutes; drink with meals, or up to 3 times daily
Tincture	15–30 drops up to 3 times daily

EXTERNAL

Essential Oil	Add 5–15 drops to 1 oz. carrier oil; apply to affected area.
Strong Infusion	1 tbsp crushed seed to 1 cup boiling water; cover and infuse for 15–20 minutes

Indicated Usages:

Condition	Appropriate Preparations	Combines Well With:
INTERNAL		
Colic	Infusion (small doses, frequently repeated)	Catnip
Cramps	Infusion, Tincture	Black Cohosh
Dysmenorrhea	Infusion, Tincture	Vitex
Gas, Flatulence	Infusion, Tincture, Essential Oil	Peppermint
Gout	Infusion, Tincture	
Indigestion	Infusion, Tincture, Essential Oil	Papaya, Peppermint
Intestinal Griping	Infusion, Tincture, Whole Seed	Anise, Coriander
Lactation (to promote)	Infusion, Tincture, Whole Seed	Dandelion, Fenugreek, Blessed Thistle
EXTERNAL		
Blepharitis, Conjunctivitis	Infusion (as eye wash)	Sage
Joint, Muscle Pain	Essential Oil (in carrier as muscle rub)	Capsicum, Wintergreen
Laryngitis, Hoarseness	Infusion, Tincture (as gargle)	

Special Considerations: One of Fennel's greatest attributes is its ability to make the unpleasant taste of many herbs more tolerable, particularly to children's taste buds. Its aromatic quality also gives it some activity as a "catalyst" for other herbs.

On account of its aromatic and carminative properties, Fennel fruit is used in many purgative and laxative formulas to offset their tendency to intestinal griping. Fennel water has properties similar to those of Anise and Dill water, and mixed with sodium bicarbonate (baking soda) and simple syrup, these waters constitute the classic 'Gripe Water,' used to correct the colic and flatulence of infants.

Notes: People who do not like the smell or taste of Licorice might be better using Fennel's close cousin, Dill, for many of the same purposes. Fennel is one of the plants that is said to be disliked by fleas, and the powdered herb has the effect of driving away fleas from kennels and stables. The plant gives off substantial amounts of ozone.

Energetics: Fennel affects the Kidney, Bladder, Spleen, Chong, and Ren meridians. It is said to tonify and relieve Chi stagnation, particularly of the kidneys, bladder, and stomach.

Garlic

Allium sativum
(Liliaceae)

Common Names: Poor Man's Treacle

Physical Features: A member of the onion family, Garlic has a clustered bulb made up of several segments enclosed in a papery shroud. The entire plant has a strong odor when bruised. It has a single stem, with long, grass like flat leaves topped with a cluster (umbil) of edible flowers that occasionally become sterile bulbils. In some varieties of Garlic, the flowering stem curls back on itself to form a complete circle near the top.

Historical Information: Probably because of the strong sulphury odor associated with it, Garlic was given mixed reviews by historical herbalists. There is even a Mohammedan legend that: "when Satan stepped out from the Garden of Eden after the fall of man, Garlick sprang up from the spot where he placed his left foot, and Onion from that where his right foot touched." According to Maud Grieve, "Many of the old writers praise Garlic as a medicine, though others, including Gerard, are sceptical as to its powers. Pliny gives an exceedingly long list of complaints, in which it was considered beneficial, and Galen eulogizes it as the rustics' Theriac, or Heal-All." Garlic was an important ingredient in the famous "Vinegar of Four Thieves" that protected looters that plundered the bodies and homes of Plague victims. In more recent times, Garlic has gained the status of one of the few herbs universally recognized as a beneficial healer. Prior to the advent of antibiotics, and during wars when they have been in short supply, Garlic preparations were used on wounds to prevent infection. Practical experience and scientific research alike has confirmed its abilities to strengthen immune function, improve circulation, lower blood pressure and cholesterol, quell infections and lower fevers. In laboratory studies, Garlic has been shown to have direct anti-microbial actions equivalent to many anti-biotic drugs, but without those drugs' tendency to create resistant strains of pathogens.

Growing Range: Widely cultivated throughout the world

Parts Used: Segments of the bulb, called cloves

Cultivation/Wildcrafting Tips: Plant individual cloves early in the spring, or in the fall in mild climates. Harvest bulbs when tops begin to wither. Store in mesh bags or in braids.

Primary Constituents: Volatile oil, consisting of sulphur-containing compounds, including allicin (=S-allyl-2-propenthiosulphinate), allyl-methyltrisulphide, diallyldisulphide, diallyltrisulphide, diallyltetrasulphide, allylpropyldisulphide, ajoene, 2-vinyl-4H-l,3 dithiin, and alliin, which breaks down enzymatically to allicin; with citral, geraniol linalool and a- and b-phellandrene; miscellaneous; enzymes including allinase; B vitamins, minerals and flavonoids.

Action: anti-microbial, antibiotic, anti-fungal, immuno-stimulant, anti-oxidant, diaphoretic, cholagogue, hypotensive, anti-spasmodic, anthelmintic, expectorant, anti-thrombotic, anti-diabetic

Tissues, Organs & Body Systems Affected: all systems (especially Circulatory, Respiratory, Intestinal, and Immune)

Preparations & Dosage: Garlic can be taken raw, or used in cooking. When cooking with fresh Garlic, it is best to crush the cloves and allow them to stand a while before heating to allow the enzymes to convert as much alliin to allicin as possible.

INTERNAL	
Juice	½–1 tsp; 3–4 times daily
Oil	½–1 tsp; 3–4 times daily; every hour for acute conditions. Excellent for cooking.
Powder	4–8 #0 capsules (1–4 gm.); 3–4 times daily
Raw	1–3 cloves daily
Syrup	1–2 tsp; 3–4 times daily
Tincture	½–1 tsp; 3–4 times daily

EXTERNAL	
Enema (retention)	½–1 tsp Oil or 1 tbsp Decoction in 1 pint warm water
Oil	2–3 drops; 2–3 times daily (ears); as much as needed for wounds
Poultice	Crush raw cloves wrapped in gauze or flannel. Change daily.

Indicated Usages:

Condition	Appropriate Preparations	Combines Well With:
INTERNAL		
Arthritis, Joint Issues	Oil, Powder, Raw	Cat's Claw, Flax Seed
Cholesterol, Arteriosclerosis	Oil, Powder, Raw	Flax Seed, Oat Bran, Evening Primrose Oil
Colds, Flu, Other Contagions	Oil, Powder, Raw, Syrup, Tincture	Echinacea, Cat's Claw, Goldenseal
Cough	Syrup	Comfrey, Wild Cherry
Emphysema	Powder, Raw, Syrup, Tincture	Comfrey, Lobelia, Wild Cherry
Flatulence	Oil, Powder	Peppermint
Indigestion	Oil, Powder, Raw	Ginger, Peppermint, Fennel
Irritable Bowel	Oil, Powder, Raw	Comfrey, Marshmallow
Liver Congestion	Powder, Raw	Barberry, Dandelion
Parasites	Oil, Powder, Raw	Black Walnut, Pumpkin
Sinus, Respiratory Problems	Juice, Oil, Raw	Fenugreek, Thyme
Ulcers	Juice, Oil, Syrup	Capsicum, Marshmallow
EXTERNAL		
Burns, Scalds	Oil, Juice (diluted in water)	Echinacea, St. John's Wort, Comfrey

Condition	Appropriate Preparations	Combines Well With:
Fever, Infection	Enema	
Intestinal Parasites	Enema (double strength)	Black Walnut
Lice, Skin Parasites	Oil, Poultice	Tea Tree Oil
Ringworm, Fungal Infections	Oil, Poultice	Tea Tree Oil, Pau D'Arco
Toothache	Poultice (mix with a little peanut butter and press against tooth)	Clove Oil
Tumors	Oil, Poultice	
Warts	Oil, Raw slice, Tincture	
Yeast Infections	Douche (dilute as for enema)	Pau D'Arco

Special Considerations: Garlic, much like aspirin, has a reputation as a blood thinner. It has been shown to inhibit blood platelet aggregation (reduce the clotting ability of blood). While that makes it a powerful aid if you are at risk for stroke or heart attack, it has also been suggested that it is probably unwise to consume it in large amounts in advance of any anticipated surgical procedure, or if you are taking other anti-coagulant medications. Garlic's actual effect on blood viscosity could better be classified as a "normalizing agent," and it has never been shown that it will make the blood "too thin," as some chemical agents do.

Notes: Garlic's power and value as a healing agent cannot be overstated. John Heinerman (Heinerman's Encyclopedia of Healing Herbs & Spices) states, "The role of Garlic as an antiviral and anti-bacterial agent is unsurpassed. There are no…repeat, NO…modern antibiotic drugs in the entire arsenal of medical science that even come close to doing what Garlic can do."

To reduce the odor associated with consuming Garlic, take it with fresh or dried Parsley, or chew a few caraway or Fennel seeds. To reduce the feeling of nausea that occasionally accompanies large doses, a bit of fresh or crystallized Ginger can be added. To remove Garlic odor from hands, rub with fresh lemon juice before washing.

The entire onion (Allium spp.) family contains to a lesser or greater degree many of Garlic's constituents and properties.

Energetics: Garlic is useful in dispelling cold, damp conditions. In Traditional Chinese Medicine, it is a specific for syndromes such as Heart Yang deficiency and wind/damp/cold obstructions such as Spleen damp and food stagnation. It affects Spleen, Lung, Heart, and Liver meridians.

In Ayurvedic medicine, Garlic increases Pitta and Vayu, and decreases Kapha.

Gravel Root

Eupatorium purpureum
(Asteraceae)

Common Names: Gravelweed, Joe-Pye Weed, Queen-of-the-Meadow, Purple Boneset

Physical Features: Tall and graceful, Gravel Root varies greatly in form and foliage. Usually standing 5 to 6 feet, it can reach 12 feet tall. The central stalk is rigid and erect, covered in purplish lines or spots above each leaf node. Leaves are oblong to lanceolate, coarsely toothed, rough and prominently veined on top, downy underneath, and usually circle the stalk at the nodes in whorl-like clusters from four to six. Dense, large clusters of flower heads top the stalk. Flowers range from flesh colored, to pink and purple, with a distinct and pleasant fragrance.

Historical Information: Traditionally, Gravel Root is used primarily for kidney stones or calculous in the body. Its ability to help resolve and balance minerals in the body account for its historical use in the treatment of rheumatism and gout. Ellingwood recommends it in the following conditions: dropsy, strangury, gravel, blood in the urine, disease of the kidney and bladder from an excess of uric acid, chronic endometriosis, leucorrhoea, chronic uterine disease, threatened abortion, ovarian and uterine atony, dysmenorrhea, dysuria, constant desire to urinate, intermittent fever, and severe bone pains. The name Joe-Pye comes from a Native American who is credited with saving countless early American colonists from the ravages of typhus by teaching them how to use the plant to break fevers.

Growing Range: Throughout the United States in swampy or rich, low ground

Parts Used: Root, fresh or dried

Cultivation/Wildcrafting Tips: Common along ditches, road sides, and low pasture boundaries. Commonly grown in bog gardens as an ornamental. Select moist ground (as for Lobelia and Marshmallow), scatter seed in the fall, and mulch lightly. The root and rhizome should be dug up in the autumn after the plant has stopped flowering. Wash thoroughly, slice ⅜ inch thick, and dry with low to moderate heat.

Primary Constituents: Volatile oil; Flavonoids, including euparin; Resin

Action: diuretic, lithotriptic, anti-rheumatic, febrifuge, nervine, tonic, astringent

Tissues, Organs & Body Systems Affected: Kidney, Bladder, Bones and Connective Tissue, Female Reproductive System, Nerves

Preparations & Dosage:

INTERNAL	
Decoction	Simmer 10–15 mins.; 1–2 oz. at a time; up to 12 oz. daily.
Powder	2–5 #0 capsules (600–2,000 mg.); 3–4 times daily
Tincture	½ –1 tsp; 3–4 times daily

Indicated Usages:

Condition	Appropriate Preparations	Combines Well With:
INTERNAL		
Arthritis, Gout	Decoction, Powder, Tincture	Dandelion, Cat's Claw
Edema, Water Retention	Decoction, Powder, Tincture	Dandelion, Cleavers
Endometriosis	Decoction, Powder, Tincture	Burdock, Dong Quai, Yellow Dock, Vitex
Fever	Decoction	Sage, Boneset, Yarrow
Kidney, Bladder Troubles	Decoction, Powder, Tincture	Dandelion, Uva Ursi, Cornsilk
Kidney Stones	Decoction, Powder, Tincture	Hydrangea
Menstrual Pain, PMS	Decoction, Powder, Tincture	Dong Quai, Vitex, Lady's Mantle
Prostate Issues	Decoction, Powder, Tincture	Saw Palmetto, Juniper Berries, Pygeum
Uterine Tonic	Decoction, Powder, Tincture	Red Raspberry, Lady's Mantle, Plantain

Special Considerations: Many members of the Eupatorium family have been found to contain trace amounts of pyrrolizidine alkaloids (PA's), the same alkaloids that the FDA warns against in Comfrey. It is probably wise to limit the internal use of Eupatorium spp. to short duration, and to be aware when combining it with other PA containing plants.

Notes: Queen-of-the-Meadow earned its name as an remedy for a wide variety of female issues including endometriosis, endometritis, leukorrhea, labor pains, threatened miscarriage, and menstrual problems. It is often effective when used as a simple, but it combines well with most other female herbs.

Energetics: The decoction of Gravel Root is considered good for increasing Kidney Chi where there is fluid congestion. It affects the Kidney, Liver, Bladder, Chong, and Ren meridians.

Hawthorn Berries

Crataegus spp.
(Rosaceae)

Common Names: Haw, Whitethorn, Mayflower

Physical Features: A thorny, deciduous, tree-like shrub with 3 to 5 lobed leaves, bearing white dense clusters of flowers followed by deep red false fruits containing 1 or 2 seeds. The flowers appear in early summer, and the fruits or "Haws" in late August or September.

Historical Information: The tree was formerly regarded as sacred, probably from a tradition that it furnished the Crown of Thorns. It is the plant that gave the pilgrim's ship, the Mayflower, its name. The Hawthorn is called Crataegus Oxyacantha from the Greek kratos, meaning hardness (of the wood), oxcus (sharp), and akantha (a thorn). Culpeper regarded the flowers and berries as beneficial for stones and dropsy, and noted that it could be used as a remedy for its own thorny offenses. "If cloths or sponges be wet with the distilled water, and applied to any place wherein thorns and splinters, or the like, do abide in the flesh, it will notably draw them out. And thus you see the thorn gives a medicine for its own pricking, and so doth almost everything else."

Due to the enormous increase in the incidence of coronary heart disease in the last century, Hawthorn's long standing reputation as a heart tonic gained it much attention in the research community. Research has validated this herb's historical uses, and shown it to be especially useful in treating congestive heart failure, preventing heart attack, normalizing blood pressure, regulating heart beat, and protecting the heart from oxidative stress. In China, Hawthorn is used to treat stomach and ovarian cancer.

Growing Range: Woodlands and hedges throughout North America.

Parts Used: Berries, flowers

Cultivation/Wildcrafting Tips: Widely grown as a barrier hedge plant, and as a showy ornamental specimen, sometimes attaining a height of 30 feet. Flowers are considered by many herbalists to be even more active than fruits. Flowers should be harvested when 30% to 40% open and dried in shade. Berries should be harvested when fully ripe, dark red, and may be dried with low heat. Dried flowers and berries should be protected from light in well-sealed containers.

Primary Constituents: Amines—phenethylamine, tyramine; Flavonoids - flavonoglycosyls, hyperoside, hesperidin, rutin, Vitexin, quercitin; Oligomeric procyanidines (OPC's), 1-epicatechol; Phenolic acids, Tannins, Ascorbic acid.

Action: cardio-tonic, diuretic, astringent, hypotensive, anti-sclerotic

Tissues, Organs & Body Systems Affected: Cardio-Vascular System, Heart

Preparations & Dosage:

INTERNAL	
Decoction (berries)	Simmer 5–15 minutes; 6 oz.; 2–3 times daily.
Infusion (flowers)	Steep 5–15 minutes; 1 cup; 2–3 times daily.
Powder	4–10 #0 capsules (1–4 gm.); 3 times daily
Tincture	½–1 tsp; 3 times daily

Indicated Usages:

Condition	Appropriate Preparations	Combines Well With:
INTERNAL		
Acidosis	Decoction, Powder	Dandelion
Arrhythmia, Palpitations	Decoction, Tincture	CoQ10, Garlic, Magnesium
Arteriosclerosis	Decoction, Infusion, Tincture, Powder	Garlic, Flax Seed
Arthritis	Decoction, Tincture, Powder	Dandelion, Flax Seed
Blood Pressure (high or low)	Decoction, Infusion, Tincture, Powder	Garlic, Passion Flower, Linden Blossom (high)
Dropsy (congestive heart failure)	Decoction, Infusion, Tincture, Powder	Garlic, Dandelion, Lily-of-the-Valley
Heart Tonic (valve problems)	Decoction, Infusion, Tincture, Powder	CoQ10, Garlic, Capsicum
Insomnia	Infusion	Passion Flower, Hops
Vertigo	Infusion, Decoction, Tincture	Ginkgo, Gotu Kola
EXTERNAL		
Sore Throat	Decoction, Syrup	Marshmallow
Splinters	Fomentation, Poultice	

Special Considerations: Seek the advice of a competent health practitioner when dealing with heart-related issues. It is unrealistic to expect an herb, even one with the proven ability of Hawthorn, to correct cardio-vascular problems if diet and lifestyle issues are not addressed. To reduce the risk of heart disease, get plenty of exercise, drink pure water, eat whole natural foods, and get adequate rest. Avoid unnecessary risk factors like smoking, pollutants, and excessive stress.

Standardized extracts of Hawthorn are gaining popularity, and may be indicated when medically diagnosed conditions exist. Historically, though, carefully prepared infusions, decoctions, and tinctures of Hawthorn have been used very effectively to prevent and control many heart-related problems.

Notes: Hawthorn needs to be used consistently and long-term to achieve optimum results. It is not known to interfere with medications (though many medications may blunt the effectiveness of Hawthorn), so it can be taken by anyone with known or suspected cardio-vascular issues, unless otherwise directed by a medical doctor. Hawthorn extracts are, in fact, amongst the most widely prescribed heart medications in Europe.

Energetics: Hawthorn Berries nourish the Heart Yin, tonify the Heart Chi, and calm the spirit. It affects the Pericardeum, Heart, Spleen, Stomach, Liver, and Yin Wei meridians.

In Ayurveda, Hawthorn is said to increase Vayu, and decrease Pita and Kapha.

Hops

Humulus lupulus
(Cannabinacece)

Physical Features: Hops is a twining vine, with rough, angular and flexible stems, growing to 20 feet in length (and, with adequate support, height). The leaves are deep green to golden, heart shaped, very rough—almost sandpapery—deeply veined, toothed at the margins, and with 3 to 5 lobes. The plants are dioecious, having separate male and female forms. Female plants produce the medicinal "fruit" called strobiles, which are oval, very light, and about 1 to 1¼ inches long, layered with yellow green membranous scales that curve over each other. The odor when fresh is strong, somewhat disagreeable, and, upon aging, reminiscent of Valerian. Lupulin, a grainy resinous material, forms in the scales of the strobiles as they ripen. It is easily separated by sifting, and is considered to be more active than the whole fruit.

Historical Information: Pliny speaks of the Hops as a garden plant grown by the Romans, who ate the young shoots in spring prepared much the same way as we do asparagus. The young tops, steamed, do make a pleasantly bitter potherb. Hops appear to have been first used in the breweries of the Netherlands in the beginning of the fourteenth century. It took nearly two more centuries, though, before the taste caught on, and spread to the brew masters of Bavaria and England. After the introduction of Hops, the fermented malt liquor flavored in the old manner retained the Anglo-Saxon name of Ale, while the name of German and Dutch origin, Bier or Beer, was given only to that made with the newly-introduced bitter catkins.

Old tastes did not change any more easily than now, it seems. The prejudice against the use of Hops was strong at first. Henry VIII forbade brewers to put Hops or sulfur into ale, Parliament having been petitioned against the Hops as "a wicked weed that would spoil the taste of the drink and endanger the people." Deriding the new brew's character, John Evelyn wrote in 1670, "The use of Hops has transmuted our wholesome ale into beer, which doubtless much alters its constitution. This one ingredient, by some suspected, not unworthily, preserves the drink indeed, but repays the pleasure in tormenting diseases and a shorter life."

Medicinally, Hops was received with more enthusiasm. Culpeper wrote:

> "It is under the dominion of Mars. This, in physical operations, is to open obstructions of the liver and spleen, to cleanse the blood, to loosen the belly, to cleanse the reins from gravel, and provoke urine. The decoction of the tops of Hops, as well of the tame as the wild, works the same effects. In cleansing the blood they help to cure the French diseases, and all manner of scabs, itch, and other breakings-out of the body; as also all tetters, ringworms, and spreading sores, the morphew and all discolouring of the skin. The decoction of the flowers and Hops, do help to expel poison that any one hath drank. Half a dram of the seed in powder taken in drink, kills worms in the body, brings down women's courses, and expels urine. A syrup made of the juice and sugar, cures the yellow jaundice, eases the head-ache that comes of heat, and tempers the heat of the liver and stomach, and is profitably given in long and hot agues that rise in choler and blood. Both the wild and the manured are of one property, and alike effectual in all the aforesaid diseases. By all these testimonies beer appears to be better than ale.
>
> Mars owns the plant, and then Dr. Reason will tell you how it performs these actions."

Mars notwithstanding, most of the actions attributed to Hops by Culpeper are a result of its bitter principles. The sedating aspect of the herb on the nervous system was not lost on early practitioners, either. Though Hops were at first thought to engender melancholy, Ellingwood considered it specific for marked cases of nerve irritation and wakefulness where anxiety and worry are the cause. He recommended it for the following pathologies: hysteria, insomnia, acute local inflammations, facial neuralgia, delirium tremens, and sexual excitement. King's went on to add:

> "They are principally used for their sedative or hypnotic action—producing sleep, removing restlessness, and abating pain, but which they often fail to accomplish. A pillow stuffed with Hops has long been a popular remedy for procuring sleep. Hops, as well as lupulin, are useful in delirium tremens to allay the morbid excitement and vigilance, while at the same time it exerts its stomachic effects. It is extremely efficient in dyspepsia where restlessness and a brooding disposition are prominent features. Fermentative dyspepsia, with consequent eructations, often yields to Hops or lupulin. Externally, in the form of a fomentation alone, or combined with Boneset or other bitter herbs, Hops have proved beneficial in pneumonia, pleurisy, gastritis, enteritis; also as an application to painful swellings or tumors. An ointment made by boiling two parts of Stramonium leaves and one of Hops, in lard, has proved an effectual application in eczema, ulcers, and painful tumors."

Hops has and is being used in China primarily as a disinfectant antibiotic to treat various forms of leprosy, tuberculosis, bacterial dysentery, and, most recently, antibiotic resistant staph infections.

Growing Range: Native to Europe, parts of Asia and North America, and extensively cultivated.

Parts Used: The strobiles, collected and dried as described, and the Lupulin, separated from the strobiles by sifting.

Cultivation/Wildcrafting Tips: Hops require deep, rich soil, and the plants prefer a south or southwest exposure with free circulation of air. Plants are usually set in the fall, spaced 6 feet apart each way. Very little growth takes place the first year, but by the second a sturdy trellis or pole frame must be provided to support the plants. The Hops cones are gathered just before they are fully ripe in August and September. They are fit to gather when they have turned a honey-amber color, and still retain a firm body.

When picked, the Hops must be quickly spread on screens in dry air—or a heated shed—to cure. They will spoil very quickly if allowed to stand in heaps or bags for even a few hours, especially if they are picked when moist. Store the dried herb in dark, air-tight containers away from heat.

Primary Constituents: Volatile oil, composed mainly of humulene (= x-caryophyllene), with b-caryophyllene, myrcene, farnesene, 2-methylbut-3-ene-2-ol, 3-methylbut-2-ene-l-al, 2,3,5-trithiahexane and similar compounds; with traces of acids such as 2-methylpropanoic and 3-methylbutanoic (which increases significantly in concentration in stored extracts); Flavonols; mainly glycosides of kaempferol and quercitin: Resin, composed of x-bitter acids such as humulone, cohumulone, adhumulone and b-bitter acids such as lupulene, colupulone, adlupulone; Estrogenic substances of undetermined structure; Miscellaneous tannins, lipids, and the chalcone xanthohumol.

Action: bitter, digestive, sedative, nervine, hypnotic, anti-microbial, diuretic, lithotriptic, anti-spasmodic, astringent, anodyne, aperient, anaphrodisiac

Tissues, Organs & Body Systems Affected: Nerves, Stomach, Liver, Gallbladder, Blood

Preparations & Dosage:

INTERNAL	
Infusion	1–2 tsp dried strobiles to 1 cup boiling water; steep 10–15 min.; take up to 3 times daily
Powder (herb)	350–1200 mg; at bedtime, or 3–4 times daily
Powder (lupulin)	100–350 mg; at bedtime, or 3–4 times daily
Tincture	15–30 drops; 3–4 times daily

EXTERNAL	
Pillow	Stuff a small pillow with Hops and Flax Seed; warm gently in the oven and place near the head.
Strong Infusion	1 tbsp per cup of boiling water; steep 10–15 minutes; apply as fomentation

Indicated Usages:

Condition	Appropriate Preparations	Combines Well With:
INTERNAL		
Alcohol Withdrawal, Delirium Tremens	Infusion, Tincture, Powder, Pillow	Kudzu Root, Capsicum
Anxiety, Stress	Infusion, Tincture, Powder, Pillow	Lemon Balm
Bladder Irritability	Infusion, Tincture	Cornsilk

Condition	Appropriate Preparations	Combines Well With:
Bronchitis	Infusion, Tincture	Lobelia, Mullein
Indigestion	Infusion, Tincture (MUST TASTE)	Angelica, Gentian, Blessed Thistle
Insomnia	Infusion, Tincture, Powder, Pillow	Valerian, Scullcap, Passion Flower
Liver Problems, Jaundice	Infusion, Tincture, Powder (herb)	Barberry, Oregon Grape
Neuralgia	Infusion, Tincture, Powder (also apply fomentation)	Black Cohosh, Yarrow, Sage, Peppermint
Restless Leg	Infusion, Tincture, Powder	Crampbark, Black Cohosh
EXTERNAL		
Earache, Toothache	Pillow	
Inflammation	Strong Infusion, Tincture	Calendula
Rheumatism	Strong Infusion, Tincture	Chamomile, Poppy, Bugle
Wounds, Ulcers, Suppurations	Tincture	Oregon Grape

Special Considerations: Persons with cases of marked depression should avoid the use of Hops. It can further exaggerate that symptom.

Notes: Hops is one of our most efficacious vegetable bitters. HOP BITTERS, to be taken in tablespoonful doses in a little water before eating, may be made as follows: Combine 1 oz. Hops, 1 oz. Angelica Herb, and 1 oz. blessed Thistle. Pour 1 pint of boiling water on them, and let stand until cold. Strain and store in the refrigerator. (Use within 1 week, or discard.)

The same herbs steeped in Sherry wine can be used the same way, and has a substantially better shelf life.

Energetics: Hops influences the Heart (pericardeum), Kidney, and Liver meridians. It is said to circulate constrained Chi, relieve nerve excess with internal wind, and balance Heart and Kidney Yin deficiency.

Horehound

Marrubium vulgare
(Labiatae)

Common Names: White Horehound

Physical Features: The plant is bushy, and like most members of the Mint family, produces numerous annual, quadrangular and branching stems. It stands a foot or more in height, and bears whitish or cream-colored flowers in crowded, woolly whorls at the topmost 3 or 4 leaf axils. The leaves are much wrinkled, opposite, petiolate, about one inch long, and covered with white, fine hairs, which give them a woolly appearance. The whole plant, when fresh, has a curious, musky smell, which is diminished by drying and lost in storage. Horehound typically flowers from June to September.

Historical Information: The Romans esteemed Horehound for its medicinal properties, and its Latin name of *Marrubium* is said to be derived from *Maria urbs*, an ancient town of Italy. Other sources attribute its name to the Hebrew word *marrob* (a bitter juice), and state that it was one of the bitter herbs which the Jews were admonished to take for the Feast of Passover.

Gerard recommends Horehound to "those that have drunk poyson or have been bitten of serpents," and it was also administered for "mad dogge's biting." He also states,

> "Syrup made of the greene fresh leaves and sugar is a most singular remedie against the cough and wheezing of the lungs . . . and doth wonderfully and above credit ease such as have been long sicke of any consumption of the lungs, as hath beene often proved by the learned physitions of our London College."

Later, Culpeper says:

> "It helpeth to expectorate tough phlegm from the chest, being taken with the roots of Irris or Orris (i.e. Blue Flag, ed.). There is a syrup made of this plant which I would recommend as an excellent help to evacuate tough phlegm and cold rheum from the lungs of aged persons, especially those who are asthmatic and short winded."

The Eclectics, Priest & Priest, considered Horehound to be a "gently diffusive tonic expectorant," and recommended it to relieve "hyperaemia" and congestion, and to "decrease discharge where secretion is too free." They give the following indications for its use: colds, bronchitis, catarrh; asthma with moist expectoration, aphonia, dyspnea and catarrhal dyspepsia.

King's American Dispensatory describes this valuable remedy in the following terms:

> "Horehound is a stimulant tonic, expectorant, and diuretic. Its stimulant action upon the laryngeal and bronchial mucous membranes is pronounced, and it, undoubtedly, also influences the respiratory function. It is used in the form of a syrup, in coughs, colds, chronic catarrh, asthma and all pulmonary affections. The warm infusion will produce diaphoresis, and sometimes diuresis, and has been used with benefit in jaundice, asthma, hoarseness,

amenorrhea, and hysteria; the cold infusion is an excellent tonic in some forms of dyspepsia, acts as a vermifuge."

Growing Range: White Horehound is a perennial herbaceous plant, and is often found in the wild over much of the northern and southeastern United States. It flourishes in waste places and by roadsides, and, due to its popularity in the 19th and early 20th centuries, it can often be found as an escape around old homesteads. It can be easily cultivated throughout the country in most any ordinary garden soil.

Parts Used: Flowering tops

Cultivation/Wildcrafting Tips: White Horehound is a hardy perennial plant that flourishes best in a relatively dry, not too rich soil. Seeds should be sown in the spring, or it can be propagated from cuttings, or by dividing the roots (the most dependable method). Little care will be needed other than weeding. The plants usually do not bloom until two years old. The tops should be gathered while the plant is in early bloom stage. The stems are tied in loose bundles, and hung to dry in the shade.

Primary Constituents: Marrubiin, a diterpene lactone, with premarrubiin; Diterpene alcohols, namely marruciol, marrubenol, sclareol, peregrinin, and dihydroperegrinin; Volatile oil, containing a-pinene, sabinene, limonene, camphene, p-cymol, a-terpinolene; Alkaloids; traces of betonicine and its isomer turicine; Miscellaneous alkanes, choline, phytosterols, tannins resin, wax, fat, sugar, etc. The chief constituent is a bitter principle known as Marrubium.

Action: expectorant, anti-spasmodic, anti-tussive, bitter, hepatic, vulnerary, vermifuge, diuretic, mild emmenagogue

Tissues, Organs & Body Systems Affected: Lungs, Liver, Gallbladder, Skin

Preparations & Dosage:

INTERNAL	
Decoction	Simmer 2 oz. dried herb in 1½ pint water till reduced to 1 pint. Strain and keep refrigerated. Take 1 or 2 tsp as needed, cold or in a little hot water.
Infusion	1 tsp dried herb (1 tbsp fresh) to 1 cup boiling water; cover and steep 10–15 min,; strain, sweeten with honey if desired, and drink to 4 times a day
Powder	1–4 gms.; as needed
Syrup	Add 1 lb. raw sugar (or honey) to hot strained decoction prepared as above (add Marshmallow root, Comfrey Root, and/or Licorice Root, if desired); return to heat and simmer until completely dissolved. Cool and bottle. Take 1 tbsp as needed.
Tincture	15–60 drops; 3–4 times daily

EXTERNAL		
Ointment	Apply frequently to affected areas.	

Indicated Usages:

Condition	Appropriate Preparations	Combines Well With:
INTERNAL		
Amenorrhea	Infusion, Decoction, Tincture	Ginger, Black Cohosh
Asthma	Infusion, Decoction, Syrup, Tincture	Lobelia
Bronchitis	Infusion, Decoction, Syrup, Tincture	Mullein, Lobelia, Comfrey Root
Colds, Flu	Infusion, Decoction, Syrup, Tincture	Lemon Balm, Sage, Echinacea
Colic	Infusion, Syrup	Catnip
Cough	Infusion, Decoction, Syrup	Comfrey Root, Wild Cherry, Elecampane
Heart Palpitations	Infusion, Decoction, Syrup	Hawthorn Berries, Motherwort
Hepatitis	Infusion, Decoction, Tincture, Powder	Dandelion, Garlic, Acerola, Rose Hips
Indigestion	Infusion (cold), Decoction (cold), Tincture	Peppermint
Jaundice, Liver Difficulties	Infusion (cold), Decoction (cold)	Dandelion, Sweet Flag, Oregon Grape
Parasites (worms)	Decoction (cold), Powder	Black Walnut Hulls
Shortness of Breath, Emphysema	Infusion, Decoction, Syrup	Comfrey Root, Pleurisy Root, Marshmallow
Sore Throat	Infusion, Decoction (in warm water, as gargle), Syrup	Comfrey, Hyssop, Sage
Stomachache	Infusion	Catnip, Fennel, Pennyroyal (adults)
EXTERNAL		
Burns, Wounds	Ointment	Comfrey, Bugle, St. John's Wort

Special Considerations: Due to its mild emmenagogue nature, large or prolonged doses of Horehound should probably be avoided in early pregnancy.

Notes: Once very popular as a treat, a digestive, and a treatment for persistent cough, real Horehound candies are now a little difficult to find. You can make your own using the basic decoction outlined above.

In a large, heavy (NOT aluminum) saucepan, combine 3½ cups of sugar (raw or white) with 1 cup of Horehound decoction. Gradually bring the mixture to a rolling boil over medium high heat, stirring constantly until the sugar is completely dissolved. Reduce heat to a moderate simmer, and cook without stirring until the mixture reaches the hard crack stage (300° F). Pour the candy into a large, shallow baking pan that has been well buttered or sprayed with a good cooking release spray. When the candy is still pliable but cool enough to hold the marks, score it into narrow strips of cough drop size segments with a buttered knife (a pizza wheel makes short work of it). When completely cool, break apart and store in an air-tight container.

You can vary the recipe by adding Comfrey Root (for soothing, healing power) and/or Licorice Root (for flavor, and as anti-inflammatory) to the decoction when it is made. You may use other herbs, too, of course, but remember that most aromatics are too volatile to survive the long cooking of this recipe. A few drops of an essential oil, like Peppermint, might be stirred in at the last minute before pouring the candy.

Energetics: Horehound exerts its influence over the Lung, Liver, and Spleen meridians. It is a cool bitter that is said to resolve lung phlegm heat/damp, and to circulate stagnant Chi of the Heart, Stomach, and Kidney.

Horsetail

Equisetum arvense, E. hyemale
(Equisetaceae)

Common Names: Shavegrass, Scouring Rush

Physical Features: The Horsetail are a distinct class of plants with its roots in the age of dinosaurs. They appear as hollow, reed-like shoots, brittle and prominently grooved, without true leaves, and growing 2 to 3 feet in height. They are light green in color, difficult to tear, and are sometimes adorned with whorls of slender branchlets that give the plant the appearance of a bottle brush. The stems spring from a rapidly creeping rhizome, and on favorable ground will form large colonies.

Historical Information: Horsetail has found many uses through the ages, most of which can be traced in some way to its very high silica content. Maud Grieve writes that, "the epidermis contains so much silica that bunches of the stem have been sold for polishing metal and used to be imported from Holland for the purpose, hence the popular name of Scouring Rushes." Its high mineral content, astringency and effect on the urinary and circulatory systems gained it high regard among the old herbalists as a wound healing herb. Culpeper says, "It is very powerful to staunch bleeding, either inward or outward. It also stays all sorts of lasks and fluxes in man or woman, and bloody urine, and heals also not only the inward ulcers, but all other sorts of foul, moist, and running sores, and soon solders together the tops of green wounds." Horsetail's diuretic properties were also valued by 19th century practitioners. Ellingwood suggests of Horsetail the following uses: dropsy, lithemia, hematuria, gonorrhea, gleet, irritable bladder, enuresis in children, prostatitis, and its ashes for acid dyspepsia.

Growing Range: Common to moist loamy or sandy waste ground throughout North America.

Parts Used: Aerial parts, generally dried

Cultivation/Wildcrafting Tips: Be very selective where you plant Horsetail, for once it is established it is virtually impossible to eradicate. Select moist ground, in the sun or part shade. Sandy soil indicates availability of the desired silica. Cut shoots close to the ground in the early summer, tie in bundles, and hang up to dry in the shade.

Primary Constituents: Alkaloids, including nicotine, palustrine and palustrinine; Flavonoids such as isoquercitrin and equicetrin; Sterols including cholesterol, isofucosterol, campesterol; Silicic acid; a saponin equisitonin, dimethylsulphone, thiaminase and aconitic acid.

Action: astringent, diuretic, vulnerary, nutritive, lithotriptic

Tissues, Organs & Body Systems Affected: Kidneys, Blood, Bones, Heart, Lungs, Skin, Hair, and Nails

Preparations & Dosage:

INTERNAL

Decoction	Simmer up to 1 hour. 2–3 oz.; 3–4 times daily.
Infusion (not highly recommended)	Steep 45 minutes to 1 hour. 2–3 oz.; 4 times daily.
Powder	2–8 #0 capsules (600–2,000 mg.); 3 times daily
Tincture	5 drops to 1 tsp; 3–4 times daily

EXTERNAL

Fomentation	Prepare with decoction; change as needed.

Indicated Usages:

Condition	Appropriate Preparations	Combines Well With:
INTERNAL		
Bedwetting, Enuresis	Decoction, Tincture, Powder	
Blood in Urine	Decoction, Tincture, Powder	
Bursitis, Tendonitis	Decoction, Tincture, Powder	Willow, Ginger, Nettle, Turmeric, Licorice
Cystitis, Urethritis	Decoction, Tincture, Powder	Cornsilk, Goldenseal
Dropsy, Edema	Decoction, Tincture, Powder	Hawthorn, Dandelion
Hair, Skin, Nail Maintenance	Decoction, Infusion, Tincture, Powder	Irish Moss, Cleavers
Heavy Menstruation	Decoction, Tincture, Powder	Gravel Root
Osteoporosis	Decoction, Tincture, Powder	Dandelion, Flax Seed, Parsley, Turmeric
Prostate Problems	Decoction, Tincture, Powder	Hydrangea, Saw Palmetto
Stones, Calcium Deposits	Decoction, Tincture, Powder	Gravel Root, Hydrangea
Trauma, Injury	Decoction, Tincture, Powder	Calendula, Comfrey
EXTERNAL		
Fresh Wounds	Fomentation	Comfrey, Calendula
Profuse Bleeding	Powder	Bugle, Alum Root, Yarrow
Ulcers, Old Sores	Fomentation	Comfrey, Bugle, Oregon Grape

Special Considerations: When taking a course of Horsetail, be sure to drink plenty of pure water to avoid the possibility of kidney irritation. Some herbalists have noted that Horsetail favors the breakdown of B vitamins. It is probably wise to include a

B-vitamin source with your regimen. B vitamins are important to the production of healthy nerve and skin cells anyway, so it can only help.

Notes: Silicon is an essential element in the manufacture of collagen, the matrix material that holds the body together. It gives elasticity and suppleness to the skin, and contributes flexibility and strength to the bones, hair, and nails. Horsetail can be thought of as an "internal cosmetic," building beauty from the inside out.

Adding a spoon of sugar <u>while</u> <u>making</u> a decoction of Horsetail pulls more of the silicon from the plant matter.

Energetics: Horsetail is an important herb for the clearing of damp heat. It tonifies Kidney and Bladder Chi, and affects the Kidney, Bladder, Liver, Lung, and Large Intestine meridians.

Jewelweed

Impatiens capensis, I. pallida, I. biflora
(Balsaminaceae)

Common Names: Spotted-Touch-Me-Not, Wild Balsam, Balsam-weed, Impatiens, Pale-Touch-Me-Not, Slipperweed, Silverweed, Wild Lady's Slipper, Speckled Jewels, Wild Celandine, Quick-in-the-hand

Physical Features: The plants are 2 to 3 feet, tall, sparsely branching, tender and delicate succulent annuals, with swollen joints. They are smooth and somewhat glaucous. The stems are very succulent and somewhat translucent. The roots are very shallow and easily dislodged. The leaves are thin, ovate oval, usually lightly toothed, and of a tender green color, sometimes tending to be bluish. The leaves show a brilliant silvery surface when immersed in water, but water will not cling to the foliage, even after being fully submerged for some time. The foliage wilts very easily at the first exposure to direct sun if the conditions are dry, but it recovers just as easily when shade returns.

The 1½ to 2 inch long cornucopia-shaped flowers, in bloom from July to September, have long recurved tails. Spotted-touch-me-not has bright orange-yellow blossoms, crowded with dark reddish-brown spots. Pale-touch-me-not has flowers of a uniform pale lemon-yellow, without spots or markings. When ripe, the oblong seed capsules of both species explode at the slightest disturbance, scattering the seeds widely. Several of the common names of this species refer to this peculiarity, others to the shape or color of the flowers.

Historical Information: Historical references to the use of Jewelweed appear mostly as folklore, and extensions of the observations of its use by Native Americans. It was, for awhile at least, included in the repertories of the Physio-Medicals and the Eclectics, but even there its internal applications were considered, as Maude Grieve put it, "wholly questionable." External applications of Jewelweed held the highest esteem, and today, are the only uses recommended, except as homeopathic or flower essence preparations. (Impatiens was one of the first two flower essences that Dr. Edward Bach discovered and used in his practice.)

William Cook, in the 1869 Physiomedical Dispensatory, wrote:

> "This plant is a relaxant, with a full share of stimulating properties, an infusion acting somewhat promptly. It influences the kidneys, gall-ducts, and bowels; and has been well spoken of by Rafinesque and Bigelow in jaundice and dropsy, but is probably too feeble to effect much. Its outward application is most valuable; and is suitable to foul ulcers, ring-worm and other forms of tetter, and to piles. It may be used as a wash, or made into a strong ointment. D. H. Stafford, M. D., of Newcastle, Ind., informs me that, when a young man, he was bitten on the leg by a venomous snake; the limb swelled up enormously, became purplish-green through nearly its entire length; and he became delirious, and sank till his life was wholly despaired of. He was effectually cured by large masses of jewel-weed, bruised and applied to the entire limb, and changed as the mass became warm. Relief was obtained almost at once, and the recovery was rapid. The facts in this case suggest that this plant may be found valuable in arresting mortification under other circumstances."

King's says of the Jewelweeds:

> "They are aperient and diuretic; a decoction is recommended in jaundice, hepatitis, and dropsy. The juice is said to remove warts, cure ringworms, salt-rheum, etc., and to cleanse foul ulcers; or it may be applied for these purposes in the form of a poultice boiled in milk. The bruised plants or the juice applied to parts poisoned by rhus, give prompt relief. It also gives relief from the effects of stinging nettle. The recent plant boiled in lard, forms an excellent ointment for piles."

The 1922 Eclectic Materia Medica calls Jewelweed,

> "refrigerant and sedative. The fresh juice of the crushed Impatiens gives prompt relief in the dermatitis of rhus poisoning if used early. It also quickly relieves the intolerable stinging produced by Nettles. As these plants usually grow contiguously, the balsam can be procured and applied at once. The relief is almost magical. The bruised plants may also be used to relieve the pain of acute engorged hemorrhoids."

Growing Range: Jewelweed can be found in large colonies across southern Canada, and over the northern and southeastern United States. It prefers moist (but not wet) woods, shady ditches, and stream sides. It does not tolerate full sun, and does best in northern or eastern exposures. It is cold sensitive, and will disappear at the first frost.

Parts Used: Leaves, Flowering tops

Cultivation/Wildcrafting Tips: Jewelweed is more easily found than grown, though if the conditions are right, it will rapidly establish a large colony. Seed should be scattered in the fall, and allowed to respond to natural chilling cycles through the winter to emerge in the spring. The top 10 to 15 inches of the plant should be cut when it comes into bloom in mid-summer, and either used fresh or immediately processed as a tincture or oil extract. It does not dry well, and most, if not all, of its medicinal virtues are lost on drying.

Primary Constituents: Little is known of the chemistry of this neglected plant. Science has only recently uncovered a few of its antihistamine and anti-inflammatory compounds, i.e. kaempferol 3-rutinoside; 2-hydroxy-1, 4-naphthoquinone; and lawsone. For the most part, though, the secrets of Jewelweed's nearly magical mode of action remain a mystery.

Action: anti-inflammatory, antihistamine, antipruritic

Tissues, Organs & Body Systems Affected: Skin

Preparations & Dosage:

INTERNAL—*Not Recommended*

EXTERNAL

Decoction	Simmer 1 lb. of fresh plant in 1 qt. of water for 15–20 min.; strain; add 1 pt. of vegetable glycerin; store in the refrigerator until needed.
Juice	Crush stems and express the juice; apply as needed.
Oil Extract	Make hot oil extract with Extra Virgin Olive Oil; apply as needed.
Ointment	Prepare oil extract as ointment; apply as needed.
Poultice	Crush leaves and flowers; apply as a mass to affected area.
Tincture	Apply directly or dilute for wash.

Indicated Usages:

Condition	Appropriate Preparations	Combines Well With:
INTERNAL—*Not Recommended*		
EXTERNAL		
Dermatitis	All of the preparations listed above can be used to resolve these conditions. Decide which is the most appropriate based on seasonal availability, area and method of application, and severity of the problem.	Comfrey, Calendula, Oregon Grape
Diaper Rash		Comfrey, Calendula, Oregon Grape
Eczema, Psoriasis		Comfrey, Calendula, Oregon Grape
Hemorrhoids		Plantain, Yarrow
Hives		Lemon Balm
Insect Bites, Stings		Plantain, Houndstongue, Solomon's Seal
Poison Ivy, Nettle Rash (urticaria)		Plantain, Houndstongue, Solomon's Seal
Ringworm, Tinea		Pau D'Arco
Warts	Juice (stem)	Sassafras (oil)

Special Considerations: While several of the older herbals refer to internal use of Jewelweed for jaundice, liver problems, and as a diuretic, it should not be considered the herb of choice for those purposes. There are many better, more effective, and safer herbs to fill those internal needs. It would be wise to restrict your use of Jewelweed to outward applications.

Notes: The decoction of Jewelweed (see above) without the glycerin, can be frozen as ice cubes and stored for future use. These are especially useful when there is inflammation at the site of application.

Energetics: Various species of Jewelweed have been used in well-balanced Chinese herbal formulas to influence the Liver and Stomach meridians.

Juniper Berries

Juniperis communis
(Cupressaceae)

Common Names: Ginepro, Enebro, Gin Berry

Physical Features: Evergreen shrub or small tree with a wide variety of forms.

Historical Information: Much of our historical information about Juniper Berries centers around the essential oil extracted from its berries, which was originally a by-product of the manufacture of Gin. For those who did not have access to or know how to produce the oil, Culpeper says, "they may content themselves by eating ten or a dozen of the ripe berries every morning fasting. They are admirably good for a cough, shortness of breath, and consumption, pains in the belly, ruptures, cramps, and convulsions. They give safe and speedy delivery to women with child, they strengthen the brain exceedingly, help the memory, and fortify the sight. They are excellently good in all sorts of agues, help the gout and sciatica, strengthen the limbs of the body, kill worms in children, and are as great a resister of pestilence as any that grows. The berries break the stone, procure appetite when it is lost, and are excellently good for all palsies, and falling-sickness."

With such accolades and a ready supply of Juniper Berries handy, you might be forgiven for wondering why the great herbalist needed any other remedy.

Growing Range: Throughout most of North America

Parts Used: Berries, fresh or dried

Cultivation/Wildcrafting Tips: Juniper prefers a somewhat chalky or alkaline soil. The berries take as much as three years to ripen, so there are usually green and ripe berries on the bush at the same time. The berries are ripe in the fall of the year that they turn from greenish-blue to blue-black, after which they drop from the bush. The ripe, unshrivelled berries should be collected in the autumn and dried slowly in the shade, to avoid losing the oil present.

Primary Constituents: Volatile oil, containing mainly myrcene, sabinene and x-pinene, with 4-cineole, p-cymene, camphene, limonene, b-pinene, terpin-4--ol, y-terpinene, x-thujene; Condensed tannins; ()-afzelechin, (-)-epiafzelechin, ()-catechin, (-)-epicatechin, ()-gallocatechin and ()-epigallocatechin; 1,4-dimethyl-3-cyclohexen-l-yl, methyl ketone; Diterpene acids; myreocommunic, communic, sandaracopimaric, isopimaric, torulosic acids and other diterpenes such as geijerone; Miscellaneous sugars, resin, vitamin C; and an anti-viral compound called deoxypodophyllotoxin.

Action: diuretic, anti-microbial, carminative, anti-rheumatic, antiseptic, anti-diabetic, aperient, anti-inflammatory, anodyne, anti-spasmodic, anti-viral, hypotensive

Tissues, Organs & Body Systems Affected: Kidneys, Urinary System, Stomach, Female Reproductive System, Prostate, Skin

Preparations & Dosage:

INTERNAL	
Decoction	Simmer 5–15 minutes; ½–3 oz.; 2–3 times daily.
Infusion	Steep 5–15 minutes; 2–3 oz.; 1–3 times daily.
Oil (essential oil)	1–3 drops; 2–3 times daily
Powder	3–12 #0 capsules (1–5 gm.) per day
Tincture	5–30 drops; 2–3 times daily

EXTERNAL	
Oil (extract)	Macerate crushed berries in cold-pressed vegetable oil, or add 5–10 drops essential oil to 1 tbsp carrier oil.
Ointment	As often as needed

Indicated Usages:

Condition	Appropriate Preparations	Combines Well With:
INTERNAL		
Allergies, Hay Fever	Decoction, Infusion, Powder	Ephedra, Boneset, Fenugreek, Lobelia
Amenorrhea	Decoction, Infusion, Powder, Tincture	Vitex, Black Cohosh, Dill Seed, Gravel Root
Arthritis, Joint Problems	Decoction, Infusion, Powder, Tincture	Comfrey, Flax Seed, Willow Bark
Bedwetting, Enuresis	Decoction, Infusion, Powder, Oil, Tincture	Horsetail, Dandelion, Gravel Root, Uva Ursi
Bladder Infection	Decoction, Infusion, Powder, Oil, Tincture	Cornsilk, Cranberry, Horsetail, Dandelion
Colds, Flu	Decoction, Infusion, Powder, Tincture	Echinacea, Lemon Balm, Olive Leaf
Cough	Decoction, Infusion, Tincture	Comfrey, Wild Cherry, Lobelia, Ginger
Cystitis	Decoction, Infusion, Powder, Oil, Tincture	Cornsilk, Parsley, Uva Ursi, Goldenseal
Diabetes	Decoction, Infusion, Powder, Tincture	Dandelion, Life Root, Bilberry
Gas, Flatulence	Decoction, Infusion	Peppermint
Leukorrhea	Decoction, Infusion, Powder, Oil, Tincture	
Nephritis	Decoction, Infusion, Powder, Oil, Tincture	Comfrey, Cornsilk, Marshmallow
Parasites	Decoction, Infusion, Powder, Oil	Black Walnut

Condition	Appropriate Preparations	Combines Well With:
EXTERNAL		
Burns, Scalds	Oil Extract	Lavender Essential Oil
Leukorrhea, Vaginal Discharge	Douche (use infusion, diluted decoction or essential oil in water)	
Psoriasis, Eczema	Oil Extract, Ointment	Comfrey, Calendula, Oregon Grape
Skin Parasites	Oil Extract, Ointment	Garlic, Tea Tree Oil
Wounds, Abrasions	Oil Extract, Ointment	Comfrey, Calendula

Special Considerations: Exercise caution with large does of Juniper Berries, or when taking them for a protracted period. They can be irritating to the urinary tract under these conditions. Juniper Berries should be avoided during early pregnancy, or while nursing. The essential oil, like most essential oils, should be avoided at any stage of pregnancy.

Notes: A decoction of Juniper Berries can be used as a disinfectant spray for sick rooms. Chewing a few berries can help protect from pathogenic substances that may be inhaled.

Energetics: Juniper Berry is used to dispel cold and damp obstructions, and treat Spleen and Kidney Yang deficiency. It affects the Spleen, Kidney, Chong, and Ren meridians. In Ayurveda, Juniper Berry is said to increase Pita and Vayu, and decrease Kapha.

Lemon Balm

Melissa officinalis
(Labiatae)

Common Names: Balm, Melissa, Sweet Balm

Physical Features: Lemon Balm in all outward appearances looks like Mint, a close cousin. The stems are square and branching, somewhat floppy, growing 1 to 2 feet high. They have at each joint pairs of broadly ovate or heart-shaped, coarsely textured and toothed leaves, which emit a strong lemon fragrance when bruised. They also have a distinct lemon taste. The flowers, white or yellowish, are in loose, small bunches from the axils of the leaves and bloom from June to October. The plant dies down in winter, but the root is perennial.

Historical Information: Lemon Balm has been prized by bee keepers since earliest times (Melissa means "bee plant"). It was credited with the ability to attract and nurture swarms of bees, and as a remedy for their stings. By herbalists, it has long been favored for use in all complaints that were supposed to "proceed from a disordered state of the nervous system." The London Dispensary (1696) says, "An essence of Balm, given in Canary wine, every morning will renew youth, strengthen the brain, relieve languishing nature and prevent baldness." John Evelyn wrote, "Balm is sovereign for the brain, strengthening the memory and powerfully chasing away melancholy." Gerard tells us, "The juice of Balm glueth together greene wounds," and shares the opinion of Pliny and Dioscorides that "Balm leaves, being steeped in wine, and the wine drunk, and the leaves applied externally, are considered to be a certain cure for the bites of venomous beasts and the stings of scorpions." According to King's Dispensatory, "Lemon Balm is moderately stimulant, diaphoretic, and antisipasmodic. A warm infusion, drank freely, has been a serviceable diaphoretic in febrile diseases and painful menstruation, and to assist the operation of other diaphoretic medicines."

Growing Range: Throughout North America, except in the desert regions, hardy to Zone 4.

Parts Used: Aerial parts, fresh or dried

Cultivation/Wildcrafting Tips: Lemon Balm is easy to grow, and deserves a place in every herb garden. It likes well-drained average soil in sun or light shade. It is not common in the wild, though it can be found as an escape around old homesteads. The leaves may be harvested two or three times a year between June and September. They are gathered by cutting off the young shoots when they are approximately 30cm (12 inches) long, preferably just as the flower buds become well-formed, but before they open. They should be dried in the shade at a temperature not above 90°F. Propagates readily by cutting or division.

Primary Constituents: Volatile oil, 0.1-0.2%, consisting mainly of citral a & b (= neral and geranial); caryophyllene oxide; various terpenes such as linalool, citronellal, b-caryophyllene, nerol, geraniol, traces of eugenyl acetate, beta-ocimene, copaene and a-cubebene; Flavonoids in low concentrations; luteolin-7-glucoside and rhamnazin;

Polyphenolics, including protocatechuic acid, caffeic acid, rosmarinic acid & tannins; Triterpenic acids such as ursolic and pomolic

Action: carminative, nervine, anti-spasmodic, anti-depressive, hypotensive, diaphoretic, anti-microbial, hepatic, anti-viral

Tissues, Organs & Body Systems Affected: Nervous System, Immune System, Liver, Circulation

Preparations & Dosage:

INTERNAL	
Infusion	Steep 5–15 minutes; 1 cup as often as desired.
Powder	3–10 #0 capsules (1–4 gm.); 3–4 times daily
Tincture	½–1 tsp; as often as desired

Indicated Usages:

Condition	Appropriate Preparations	Combines Well With:
INTERNAL		
Anxiety	Infusion, Powder, Tincture	Kava, Passion Flower, Scullcap
Depression, Melancholy	Infusion, Powder, Tincture	St. John's Wort, Borage
Fever	Infusion, Powder, Tincture	Sage, Ginger, Elder Flowers
Grave's Disease, Hyperthyroidism	Infusion, Powder, Tincture	Bugleweed *
High Blood Pressure	Infusion, Powder, Tincture	Hawthorn, Linden Flowers
HIV, AIDS	Infusion, Powder, Tincture	Olive Leaf
Hyperactivity (children)	Infusion, Powder, Tincture	Catnip
Indigestion (stress related)	Infusion	Comfrey, Marshmallow
Insomnia	Infusion, Tincture	Passion Flower, Hops
Migraine	Infusion, Powder, Tincture	Feverfew
Shingles	Infusion, Powder, Tincture	Licorice, Dong Quai, Passion Flower
Viral Infections		Juniper Berries, Olive Leaf

* Bugleweed (Lycopus virginiana) is NOT Bugle (Ajuga reptans).

Notes: Taking a cup of hot water to the herb garden on a sunny afternoon, and crushing a few fresh picked leaves of Melissa into it, makes an instant and wonderful afternoon tea break.

Energetics: Lemon Balm circulates Chi, and is used to treat Heart Chi constraint and Heart Yin deficiency. It has tonifying effects on the Heart, Pericardeum, Triple Heater, Lung, Liver, Kidney, Bladder, Chong and Ren meridians.

Lobelia

Lobelia inflata
(Campanulaceae)

Common Names: Indian Tobacco, Pukeweed, Emetic Weed, Asthma Weed, Gagroot, Vomitwort, Bladderpod, Eyebright

Physical Features: It is an erect annual or biennial herb, standing six inches to two feet high. The lower leaves as well as the flower are stalked, the latter being pale violet-blue in color, tinted pale yellow within. The leaves are oval to lanceolate, toothed, and somewhat hairy on the underside. The flowers form in the axils of the small upper leaves from June through October, and are followed by the balloon shaped, two-celled inflated seed pods from which this species derives its name.

Historical Information: Few herbs native to the Americas have had such an impact on the field of botanical medicine as Lobelia. Central to the Thomsonian healing system that swept America in the early 1800's, the "Emetic Weed" was claimed to have been "discovered" by Samuel Thomson, himself. While there is little doubt that the plant was in use by the Penobscot Indians and other eastern tribes well before Thomson's time, it is also true that it had never before been applied to so many conditions and uses as Thomson outlined. It was highly valued for its power as an emetic—a key form of therapy in those days—as well as a dependable anti-spasmodic and near panacea for respiratory complaints.

As Lobelia was, in the beginning, at least, unique to his system, it almost immediately became the target of the same virulent criticism and aggressive attacks by allopathic "regulars" as were heaped on Dr. Thomson himself. Thomson contended, "There is no vegetable which the earth produces more harmless in its effect on the human system, and none more powerful in removing disease and promoting health than Lobelia." The controversy surrounding Lobelia has never subsided. As recently as the mid-1990's, it was once again withheld from the market in a flurry of bad press until its detractors once again failed to prove the slightest harm from its use.

The broad range of uses for Lobelia as prescribed by the Eclectics is barely touched upon in this partial description by King:

> "Perhaps the most important use for this drug will be in the treatment of respiratory affections. For this class of diseases no remedy is more highly valued by physicians of our school. Lobelia is an admirable pectoral remedy. As a nauseant expectorant it has no equal. When an emetic is desired in pulmonary complaints it is one of the most efficient that can be employed. It has come to be the first of remedies for spasmodic asthma, and is not without utility in whooping cough. It improves innervation and the circulation, and is one of the best remedies to employ in congestive conditions. It is frequently indicated in pleurisy and pleuro-pneumonia. As a sedative it ranks between veratrum and aconite. Acute pneumonia, with, tendency to congestion, the breathing being oppressed, is quickly relieved by Lobelia. All chronic forms of sore throat, especially when ulcerated, are benefited by it. Chronic pneumonia, bronchitis, and laryngitis are all conditions in which Lobelia will be of great service. In asthenic laryngitis of children it is exceedingly useful. It is a remedy of great value in chronic catarrh, dry, hard, or barking coughs,

colds, and all forms of irritation of the respiratory tract, with oppression. It relaxes the tissues, favors expectoration when a large quantity of mucus is secreted and there is want of power to remove it. The indications for this drug are the full, oppressed, or small, feeble pulse, praecordial oppression, with difficult respiration, oppression anywhere in the chest, with accumulation of the bronchial secretions, cough with loud mucous rattles within the chest."

Ellingwood recommended Lobelia for the following pathologies:
"spasmodic asthma, whooping cough, spasmodic croup, membranous croup, infantile convulsions, puerperal eclampsia, epilepsy, tetanus, hysterical paroxysms, hysterical convulsions, rigid os uteri, diptheria, tonsillitis, pneumonia," among others.

So much has been written about Lobelia in the two centuries of its recognized life in domestic medicine that the interested student might focus on a dedicated study for some months. One of the better contemporary summaries available may be found in Dr. John Christopher's "School of Natural Healing." Lobelia is the only herb in this substantial tome to which he dedicates an entire chapter.

Growing Range: Dry fields, open woods, roadsides, and waste places in the northern and eastern United States and Canada.

Parts Used: The dried flowering herb, and the seeds

Cultivation/Wildcrafting Tips: The entire plant above ground should be collected when the plant is in flowering time, and after some of the inflated seed pods have formed in the lower axils, usually between August and September. The seed pods should be collected as well. The plant should be well dried in the shade, and then stored as whole as possible in dark, air-tight containers until ready for use.

Primary Constituents: Piperidine alkaloids, mainly lobeline, with lobelanidine, lobelanine, and minor amounts of norlobelanine (=isolobelanine), lelobanidine, lovinine, isolobinine, lobinanidine and others; Chelidonic acid; Miscellaneous resins, gums, fats etc. The seeds contain a much higher percentage of lobeline than the rest of the plant.

Action: anti-asthmatic, anti-spasmodic, expectorant, emetic, nervine—stimulant (small doses) and relaxant (large doses), diaphoretic, diuretic, cathartic, astringent

Tissues, Organs & Body Systems Affected: Nerves, Stomach, Respiratory System, "Pneumo-gastric Nervous System," Heart, Circulation, Musclature

Preparations & Dosage:

INTERNAL	
Infusion (cold)	½–1 tsp of dried herb to 1 cup WARM water; allow to infuse for 1 hour or more; strain, and drink 3 times daily
Powder	300–1200 mg., 3–4 times daily or as needed
Tincture (vinegar is preferred or aqueous alcohol)	15–30 drops as needed; 1 tbsp repeated at close intervals for emesis

EXTERNAL	
Infusion	As a wash
Poultice	1 part of fresh or dried herb combined with 3 parts of Mullein leaf; apply and allow to remain until resolution

Indicated Usages:

Condition	Appropriate Preparations	Combines Well With:
INTERNAL		
Arthritis	Infusion, Tincture, Powder	Capsicum, Licorice
Asthma	Infusion, Tincture, Powder	Capsicum
Bronchitis	Infusion, Tincture, Powder	Capsicum, Mullein, Comfrey
Convulsions, Seizure	Tincture	Capsicum
Cough	Infusion, Tincture	Capsicum, Wild Cherry
Fever	Infusion, Tincture, Powder	Capsicum, Boneset
Food Poisoning	Tincture, Powder	Capsicum
Headache	Infusion, Tincture, Powder	Peppermint, Scullcap
Irregular Heartbeat	Infusion, Tincture, Powder	Capsicum, Hawthorn Berries
Jaundice	Infusion, Tincture, Powder	Capsicum, Barberry
Lock Jaw	Tincture (sublingual)	Capsicum
Muscle Spasms, Cramps	Infusion, Tincture, Powder	Capsicum, Passion Flower
Pleurisy, Emphysema	Infusion, Tincture, Powder	Capsicum, Comfrey, Wild Cherry
Smoking Cessation	Infusion, Tincture, Powder	Lemon Balm, Scullcap, Passion Flower
Teething, Toothache	Tincture (rub on gums)	Meadowsweet
Whooping Cough	Infusion, Tincture	Mullein, Oregon Grape

Condition	Appropriate Preparations	Combines Well With:
EXTERNAL		
Abscesses	Infusion, Poultice	Mullein, Oregon Grape
Erysipelas, Skin Diseases	Infusion, Poultice	Calendula, Oregon Grape
Muscle Spasms, Cramps	Tincture	Capsicum
Poison Ivy, Rashes	Infusion, Poultice	Plantain, Jewelweed
Tumors	Poultice	Mullein, Peppermint

Special Considerations: Many herbalists contend that heat destroys much of the medicinal value of Lobelia, particularly the alkaloid Lobeline. On this issue, Samuel Thomson himself wrote, *"There is but one way in which this herb can be prepared that it will refuse its services, and that is when boiled or scalded; it is therefore important to bear in mind that there must never be any thing put to it warmer than a blood heat."* When combined in formulas that are to be made into hot infusions or decoctions, Lobelia should always be added after the extract has cooled.

Lobelia can be an aggressive emetic, even in relatively small doses if the system is highly toxic. While the resulting nausea and vomiting can be alarming, it has and will always be proven to be beneficial to the patient.

Notes: Lobeline, a primary active alkaloid in Lobelia is chemically and physiologically similar to nicotine, without nicotine's addictive properties. It has been used in "Stop Smoking" formulas for many years, as it reduces the cravings associated with nicotine withdrawal. It may even be smoked—alone or in combination with Mullein—to help repair the damage to lung tissues.

Energetics: Lobelia exerts its influence over the Lung, Liver, Heart, Kidney, and Bladder meridians. It is used to release constrained Chi, and relieve damp heat.

Marshmallow

Althea officinalis
(Malvaceae)

Common Names: Althea, Sweet Weed, Cheeses, Wymote, Mallards, Mauls, Schloss Tea, Mortification Root

Physical Features: Common Marshmallow has soft, hairy, white stalks standing three or four feet high. It is a rather bushy plant, having many branches. The leaves are soft and hairy, oblong and pointed, and generally deeply cut into three divisions. The many small flowers are white, or tending to a bluish color, and are held close to the axils of the stem, though occasionally forming a loose panicle. The flowers are in bloom during August and September, and are followed, as in other species of this order, by the flat, round seed pods popularly called "cheeses."

The roots are many and long, branching from a central tap the thickness of a thumb or finger. They are yellowish white outside, more white within, and very pliant, tough, and full of a slimy juice. When the roots are let to stand in water, it will thicken as if it were a jelly.

Historical Information: The generic name, *Althaea*, is derived from the Greek, *altho* (to cure), while the name of the order, Malvaceae, is derived from the Greek, *malake* (soft), from the special qualities of the Mallows in softening and healing.

Many of the Mallows have been used as food by various cultures. A dish of Marshmallow was considered a great delicacy by the Romans. Dioscorides extolled it as a remedy for many ailments, and Pliny the Elder said that, "Whosoever shall take a spoonful of the Mallows shall that day be free from all diseases that may come to him." Not only was Marshmallow valued as food and medicine, but it was used by both the Greeks and the Romans to decorate the graves of friends.

By Culpeper's time, Marshmallow had exposed many of its virtues. He said:

> "The roots boiled in wine or water, or in broth with Parsley or Fennel roots, do help to open the body, and are very convenient in hot agues, or other distempers of the body, to apply the leaves so boiled warm to the belly. It not only voids hot, choleric, and other offensive humours, but eases the pains and torments of the belly coming thereby; and are therefore used in all clysters conducing to those purposes. The same used by nurses procures them store of milk. The decoction of the seed of any of the common Mallows made in milk or wine, doth marvellously help excoriations, the phthisic pleurisy, and other diseases of the chest and lungs, that proceed of hot causes, if it be continued taking for some time together. The leaves and roots work the same effects. They help much also in the excoriations of the bowels, and hardness of the mother, and in all hot and sharp diseases thereof. The juice drank in wine, or the decoction of them therein, do help women to a speedy and easy delivery. The syrup also and conserve made of the flowers, are very effectual for the same diseases, and to open the body, being costive. The leaves bruised, and laid to the eyes with a little honey, take away the imposthumations of them. The leaves bruised or rubbed upon any place stung with bees, wasps, or the like, presently take away the pain, redness, and swelling that rise thereupon. A poultice made of the leaves boiled and bruised, with some bean or barley flower, and oil of Roses added, is an especial remedy against all hard

tumours and inflammations, or imposthumes, or swellings of the privities, and other parts, and eases the pains of them; as also against the hardness of the liver or spleen, being applied to the places. The juice of Mallows boiled in oil and applied, takes away all roughness of the skin, as also the scurf, dandriff, or dry scabs in the head, or other parts, if they be anointed therewith, or washed with the decoction, and preserves the hair from falling off. It is also effectual against scaldings and burnings, St. Anthony's fire, and all other hot, red, and painful swellings in any part of the body. The flowers boiled in oil or water (as every one is disposed) whereunto a little honey and allum is put, is an excellent gargle to wash, cleanse or heal any sore mouth or throat in a short space."

The Eclectics, Priest & Priest tell us that it is a soothing demulcent indicated for inflamed and irritated states of mucous membranes. They considered it particularly suitable for the elderly, when there were chronic inflammatory conditions effecting the gastro-intestinal system or genito-urinary tract. They give the following specific indications: acute respiratory disease, gastro-enteritis, peptic ulcer, cystitis, urethritis, inflammation of mouth and throat, inflamed hemorrhoids, inflamed wounds, burns, scalds, bedsores, abscesses, boils, and ulcers.

Ellingwood considered it as the most mucilaginous of the diuretics, recommending it to soothe irritation in the mucous membranes of the stomach and intestines as well as those of the urinary apparatus. In addition he recommends it for inflammation of the bowels, irritation of the bladder, and acute painful cystitis.

King said that Marshmallow…

"… will be found valuable, in the form of decoction, in diseases of the mucous tissues, as hoarseness, catarrh, pneumonia, gonorrhea, vesical catarrh, renal irritation, acute dysentery, and diarrhea. In strangury, inflammation of the bladder, hematuria, retention of urine, some forms of gravel, and indeed in nearly every affection of the kidney and bladder, their use will be found advantageous. Much use is made of them combined with equal parts of spearmint, in urinary derangements. They are likewise efficacious in gastro-intestinal irritation and inflammation. As the decoction soon decomposes, or becomes moldy or acid, it should always be made in small quantities, not more than 1 or 2 pints at a time, according to the temperature of the weather. Externally, Marshmallow root is very useful in the form of poultice, to discuss painful, inflammatory tumors, and swellings of every kind, whether the consequence of wounds, bruises, burns, scalds, or poisons; and has, when thus applied, had a happy effect in preventing the occurrence of gangrene. The infusion or decoction may be freely administered."

In his renowned "Advanced Treatise in Herbology," Dr. Edward Shook carried the exaltation of Marshmallow into the 20th century:

> "This is an excellent remedy for all inflamed surfaces and organs, either internal or external, stomach, intestines, lungs, bronchi, and skin. It is especially good for fire burns, or burns due to acid or strong alkali, inflamed or swollen joints or muscles, dry and hacking cough, inflammation of the chest, inflamed and swollen glands, and infected wounds. It is a fine builder of bone and flesh in rachitic and weakly children, and a most remarkable treatment for chronic constipation with hard, dry stools. It gives prompt relief in gravel, as in inflammation of the kidneys and bladder. In fact, there is scarcely any form of inflammation in any part of the organism for which it is not beneficial."

Though a confection and a sweet paste were once made of the root of the plant, commercial "Marshmallows" are a mixture of sugar, flour, gum, egg-albumin, etc., and contain no mallow.

Growing Range: Whether the plant was introduced or was native, it can now be found over most of the continent.

Parts Used: The root is the most in demand, but the leaves and flowers are also used.

Cultivation/Wildcrafting Tips: In the wild, Marshmallow can be found along streams, salt marshes, ditch rows, and low ground, particularly around old homesteads where it was very likely once a valued part of the garden. It can be cultivated in most any ordinary garden soil, though it grows to its greatest size and medicinal value when given ample water. It can be raised from spring sown seed, but cuttings will root easily, and root divisions can be made in the autumn after the plant has gone dormant.

The leaves should be collected in summer after flowering, and carefully dried in the shade. The root should be dug in late autumn, cleaned of dirt, fibers and cork, and dried immediately with the aid of low heat.

Primary Constituents: In the root: Mucilage, 18-35%; consisting of a number of polysaccharides; one is composed of L-rhamnose, D-galactose, D-galacturonic acid and D-glucuronic acid in the ratio 3:2:3:3, another a highly branched L-arabifurranan, another a trisaccharide structural unit and one with a high proportion of uronic acid units; about 35% pectin, 1-2% asparagine, tannins, oil, sugar, asparagin, phosphate of lime, glutinous matter and cellulose. The root is a significant source of oxygen, calcium, magnesium, and tin.

In the leaves: Mucilage; including a low molecular weight D-glucan; Flavanoids such a kaempferol, quercitin and diosmetin glucosides; Scopoletin, a coumarin; Polyphenolic acids, including syringic, caffeic, salicyclic, vanillic, p-coumaric, etc.

Action: demulcent, emollient, diuretic, anti-inflammatory, expectorant, nutritive, vulnerary, laxative

Tissues, Organs & Body Systems Affected: Respiratory System, Kidneys, Bladder, Mucus Membranes, GI Tract, Skin

Preparations & Dosage:

INTERNAL	
Decoction	1 oz. root in 1½ pints cold water; let stand 1–2 hours; bring to boil and simmer until reduced to 1 pint; strain and keep refrigerated. Mix 2–3 ounces in juice or water and take freely.
Infusion	1 tsp finely chopped or powder root to 1 cup boiling water; let stand until cool; drink 2–3 times daily
Powder	1–4 gms.; 3–4 times daily; take with ample fluid
Syrup	Add 2 lbs. raw sugar (or 1 lb. raw honey) to 1 pint decoction, simmer 5 minutes, cool and bottle. Adults: 1 tbsp every 2–3 hours; Children: 1–2 tsp based on age.
Tincture	½–2 tsps.; 3–4 times daily

EXTERNAL	
Decoction	Apply as fomentation or dilute as soak or wash.
Ointment	Simmer fresh leaves and/or root in Olive Oil until crisp; strain and thicken with beeswax; apply as needed.
Powder	Apply freely to moist lesions, or make into a poultice.

Indicated Usages:

Condition	Appropriate Preparations	Combines Well With:
INTERNAL		
Acne	Infusion, Decoction, Tincture, Powder	Oregon Grape, Calendula, Comfrey
Arthritis	Infusion, Decoction, Tincture, Powder	Dandelion, Nettles, Licorice, Wild Yam
Bronchitis	Infusion, Decoction, Syrup	Elder Flowers, Lobelia, Horehound, Mullein

— continues on next page

— continued from previous page

Condition	Appropriate Preparations	Combines Well With:
Colitis, Irritable Bowel	Infusion, Decoction, Tincture, Syrup	Fennel, Dandelion, Sweet Flag, Ginger
Constipation	Infusion, Decoction, Powder	Dandelion, Rhubarb, Psyllium Hulls
Cough	Decoction, Tincture, Syrup	Licorice, Elecampane, Wild Cherry
Diabetes	Infusion, Decoction, Tincture, Powder	Red Raspberry, Thyme, Uva Ursi, Gymnema
Diarrhea, Dysentery	Infusion, Decoction, Powder	Comfrey, Oregon Grape, Slippery Elm
Gout	Infusion, Decoction, Tincture, Powder	Capsicum, Nettles, Wood Betony
Kidney Stones	Infusion, Decoction, Tincture	Dandelion, Gravel Root, Hydrangea
Lactation (enrich)	Infusion, Decoction, Powder	Blessed Thistle, Fenugreek, Alfalfa
Laryngitis, Sore Throat	Infusion, Decoction, Syrup	Sage, Catnip, Capsicum
Neuralgia	Infusion, Decoction, Tincture, Powder	Black Cohosh, Hops, Capsicum, Wild Yam
Pneumonia	Infusion, Decoction, Tincture, Syrup	Capsicum, Lobelia, Thyme, Olive Leaf
Skin Diseases, Eczema, Psoriasis	Infusion, Decoction, Tincture, Powder	Burdock, Yellow Dock, Oregon Grape
Urinary Tract Infection	Infusion, Decoction, Tincture	Cornsilk, Dandelion, Juniper Berries
Whooping Cough	Decoction, Tincture, Syrup	Thyme, Garlic, Lobelia

EXTERNAL

Abscesses, Boils	Decoction (as hot fomentation), Powder (as poultice), Ointment	Mullein, Lobelia, Oregon Grape
Conjunctivitis, Sore Eyes	Infusion, Decoction (as eye wash)	Red Raspberry Leaf, Thyme, Lobelia
Mastitis	Ointment, Decoction (apply as hot fomentation)	Chamomile, Poppy Flowers
Slow Healing Wounds	Ointment, Poultice (applied hot)	Slippery Elm, Comfrey, Oregon Grape
Sore Nipples	Ointment	Calendula Flowers
Vaginitis	Decoction (diluted as douche)	Motherwort, Thyme

Notes: Marshmallow root powder is very absorbent, and binds together when moistened. It does not contain any constituents that interfere with the action of other herbs. This makes it an ideal medium for making pills and lozenges from other herbal extracts.

Energetics: Marshmallow Root affects the Lung, Stomach, Large Intestine, and Bladder meridians. It is used to nourish deficient Yin, and to clear damp heat.

Mullein

Verbascum thapsus
(Scrophulariaceae)

Common Names: Aaron's Rod, Aaron's Staff, Great Mullein, White Mullein, Torches, Mullein Dock, Our Lady's Flannel, Velvet Dock, Candlewick Plant, Lungwort, Jupiter's Staff, Jacob's Staff, Peter's Staff, Shepherd's Staff, Golden Rod, Adam's Flannel, Beggar's Blanket, Old Man's Flannel, Hag's Taper

Physical Features: Tall and stately, wild and woolly. Mullein is a biennial plant, presenting in its first year a large rosette of gray-green thick flannel-like leaves lying close to the ground. The outermost base leaves are oblong, often 8 to 12 inches long and 4 to 5 inches wide, smooth at the edges, though covered with thick, frosty-white velvety hairs. Leaves get progressively smaller towards the center of the plant. In its second year, the plant sends up a dramatic solitary stalk that is also covered with down, usually 5 to 6 feet though sometimes as much as 10 feet in height, occasionally branched near the top, and with alternate leaves that clasp the stalk at their base. The top of the stalk presents a thick coarse flower spike, with bright custard-yellow blossoms arranged over the topmost 12 to 20 inches. Over the mid-summer flowering season, the blossoms open in a random fashion throughout this area, appearing almost like yellow popcorn attached here and there up its length.

Historical Information: As might be discerned from the great number of popular names given to this plant, few herbs have held such broad regard with the common citizenry as the Great Mullein. While this might be partially attributed to the plant's attention grabbing appearance when in bloom, the fact that it is an effective remedy for some of the most debilitating health complaints of our forebears secured its position in the history of botanical medicine. As an aid for chronic lung and respiratory problems, it was universally recognized by European, Asian, and Native American herbalists. Oil extracts of the flowers were considered excellent in soothing and healing any inflamed surface, and for easing ear problems. A decoction of its roots was used to alleviate a toothache, and thought to be good for cramps and convulsions. An early morning draught of the distilled water of the flowers was often recommended for gout. The seeds were considered mildly narcotic, and were taken to allay fears and anxiety, giving Mullein a similar reputation among common people that St. John's Wort held—as a sure safeguard against evil spirits and magic. (The ancient classics tell us that it was this plant which Ulysses took to protect himself against the wiles of Circe.) Its use as a wound healer carried over to the American Civil War when, in the South, its leaves and extracts were used to bandage and protect wounds when other medical supplies were unavailable. Mullein leaf was also smoked to help alleviate the lung diseases that overtook besieged soldiers in the trenches.

Physio-medical and Eclectic physicians of the 19th century also held Mullein in high regard. King's American Dispensatory described the uses of Mullein at length, stating, "Mullein is demulcent, diuretic, anodyne, and antispasmodic. It is likewise said to possess marked anti-periodic virtues. Besides, it is mildly nervine, controlling irritation, and favoring sleep. Upon the upper portion of the respiratory tract its influence is pronounced, particularly where the larynx and trachea are involved. The infusion is useful in coughs, protracted colds, catarrh, hemoptysis, diarrhea, dysentery, and piles. It is applicable to dry, hoarse coughs, which occur chiefly at night, as well as to cough associated with an abundant catarrhal discharge. Its diuretic properties are rather weak, yet it is very useful in allaying the acridity of urine, which is present in many diseases. A fomentation of the leaves also forms an excellent local application for inflamed piles, ulcers, and tumors. The leaves and pith of the stalk form a valuable cataplasm in white swellings, and when infused in hot vinegar or water it makes an excellent poultice to be applied to the throat in tonsilitis, malignant sore throat, and mumps. The seeds, it is said, will rapidly pass through the intestines, and have been successfully used in intestinal obstructions. They are narcotic, and have been used in asthma, infantile convulsions, and to stupify fish. The infusion may be drunk freely. The flowers, placed in a well-corked bottle with Olive oil, and exposed to the action of the sun, are said to yield an excellent relaxing extract. This oil is also valuable in some cases of deafness, used locally for its effect upon the membrana tympani (ear drum), and upon the secretion of cerumen (ear wax). The oil, in doses of 1 to 10 drops, is said to give excellent results in nocturnal enuresis and in vesical irritation caused by alkaline urine; it is also reputed a good agent to control painful micturation, in lithemia, chronic cystitis, and urinary calculus. The leaves, dried and smoked like tobacco, are often useful in asthma and laryngeal affections."

In more recent times, one of Mullein's greatest advocates was Dr. John Christopher. He states, "It is the only herb known to man that has remarkable narcotic properties without being poisonous or harmful. It is a great herbal pain killer and nervous soporific, calming and quieting all inflamed and irritated nerves. In wasting diseases (such as tuberculosis or consumption), the weight steadily increases, expectoration becomes easy, cough calms, and the general condition is improved. Mullein soothes and strengthens the bowels and renal system, and is one of the most important for the glands and serous and mucous membranes. It stops the escape of fluids from ruptured vessels, and eliminates toxins."

Growing Range: Throughout the Northern tier and the Eastern half of the United States, along road sides, waste ground and pasture fences. Its dramatic flower stalks are an increasingly common mid-summer sight on untended ground along the Interstate highways (though this is certainly not the place to collect the herb).

Parts Used: Leaves, flowers, and root, fresh or dried

Cultivation/Wildcrafting Tips: Mullein is a strong self-sowing biennial that is relatively easy to grow, loves poor soil, and once established, thrives on neglect. Like the Mallows and Hollyhocks, the tall flowering stalks of Mullein act as sentinels in the herb garden. The leaves of the first year growth are said to be the most effective medicinally. They are collected in mid-summer before they turn brown, and should be dried in the shade. Freshly opened flowers can be gathered between late June and September during dry weather, and dried in the shade, or with heat no higher than 100°F. The flowers turn brown with moisture, and become ineffective.

Primary Constituents: Flavonoids such as rutin, verbascoside and herperidin; mucilage, saponins, tannins, volatile oil

Action: expectorant, demulcent, emollient, diuretic, anti-inflammatory, nervine, anti-spasmodic, vulnerary, alterative, astringent, pectoral, nutritive, anti-septic, hemostatic, anodyne, narcotic, anti-asthmatic, germicide, vermicide

Tissues, Organs & Body Systems Affected: Lungs and Respiratory System, Glands, Lymphatic System, Nervous System, Urinary System, Intestinal System, Skin

Preparations & Dosage:

INTERNAL	
Infusion	Steep 10–15 minutes; 3–4 oz. taken frequently.
Oil (flowers)	2–10 drops; 3–5 times daily
Powder	3–10 #0 capsules (1–3 gm.); 4–5 times daily
Smoke Inhalant (dried first year leaves)	Hand-roll a cigarette, or smoke in ordinary tobacco pipe. Don't over do. Any kind of smoke can irritate the lungs.
Syrup (flowers or flowering tops)	1 tsp–1 tbsp; as frequently as needed
Tincture (first year leaves)	½–1 tsp; 4–5 times daily

EXTERNAL	
Decoction (root)	Simmer to reduce water volume by half. Moisten a piece of gauze or flannel and lay on gums next to tooth.
Fomentation	Made with decoction of 1st year leaves. Apply as hot as can be tolerated, 1 hour at a time, 3–4 times daily.
Oil (flowers)	1–3 drops in ear, or applied to burns and abrasions
Poultice	Crushed fresh leaves, or dried leaves moistened with aloe juice or warm water

Indicated Usages:

Condition	Appropriate Preparations	Combines Well With:
INTERNAL		
Allergies, Hay Fever	Infusion, Powder, Smoke, Syrup, Tincture	Ephedra, Lobelia
Asthma	Infusion, Powder, Smoke, Syrup, Tincture	Lobelia, Sage, Plantain
Bronchitis, Emphysema	Infusion, Oil, Powder, Syrup	Comfrey, Capsicum, Licorice, Lobelia
Bruises	Infusion, Oil, Tincture	Comfrey, Plantain
Constipation	Infusion, Powder, Syrup	Cascara, Psyllium
Cough	Infusion, Oil, Powder, Syrup, Tincture	Wild Cherry, Comfrey
Diarrhea	Infusion, Powder, Syrup, Tincture	Plantain, Slippery Elm
Hemorrhage	Infusion, Powder, Syrup, Tincture	Comfrey, Plantain
Hemorrhoids	Infusion, Powder, Tincture	Yarrow, Plantain
Insomnia	Infusion, Powder, Tincture	Passion Flower, Hops, Lemon Balm
Nervous Distress	Infusion, Powder, Tincture	Passion Flower, St. John's Wort
Nicotine Withdrawal	Infusion, Powder, Smoke, Tincture	Lobelia, St. John's Wort
Sinus Congestion	Infusion, Powder, Smoke, Syrup, Tincture	Ephedra, Thyme
Swollen Glands, Lymphatics	Infusion, Powder, Syrup, Tincture	Echinacea, Lobelia
Tumors	Infusion, Powder, Tincture	Chickweed, Butcher's Broom
Whooping Cough	Infusion, Oil, Powder, Syrup, Tincture	Comfrey, Lemon Balm, Marshmallow
EXTERNAL		
Boils, Sores, Abscesses	Fomentation, Poultice	Calendula, Comfrey, Lobelia
Burns, Rashes	Fomentation, Oil, Poultice	Calendula, Comfrey, St. John's Wort
Conjunctivitis, Eye Irritation	Fomentation, Poultice	Eyebright
Ear Infection, Earache	Oil	
Swollen Glands	Fomentation, Poultice	Lobelia
Toothache	Decoction, Poultice (on gums)	Clove Oil, Myrrh, Plantain
Tumors	Fomentation, Poultice	Chickweed, Lobelia
Wounds	Fomentation, Poultice	Comfrey, Plantain, Lemon Balm, Myrrh

Special Considerations: Infusions that include Mullein leaves should be strained through cheese cloth or an unbleached coffee filter to remove the potentially irritating hairs. Do not use Mullein oil in the ear if the ear drum is perforated.

Notes: Mullein's gentle nature makes it one of the very best herbs for use with children's health problems. It combines wonderfully with Chamomile, Catnip, and Lemon Balm where appropriate, and can be used to address a wide variety of childhood diseases.

Energetics: Mullein is used to address Lung Yin deficiency. It affects the Lung, Stomach, Large Intestine, and Bladder meridians.

Nettles

Urtica dioica
(Urticaceae)

Common Names: Stinging Nettle, Common Nettle

Physical Features: Nettle is a perennial plant, ranging in height from 1 to 4 feet, though most usually in the center of that range. The leaves are mostly oval, with heart shaped bases, finely toothed margins, and, along with the stems, are covered with stiff, stinging hairs. (Culpeper, with sardonic wit, tells us that, "Nettles are so well known, that they need no description; they may be found by feeling, in the darkest night.") The flowers hang in more or less long clusters from the axils of the upper leaf stems. The male and female flowers are usually found on separate plants, which gives rise to the species name—dioica—which means "two houses." The roots are creeping, allowing it to multiply rapidly, and it usually forms loose colonies that can be difficult to eradicate. It prefers moist ground in low areas.

The stinging hairs that cover the plant consist of very sharp, polished spines, which are hollow and arise from a swollen base. In this base, which is composed of small cells, is contained the "venom," an acrid fluid, the active principle of which is said to be bicarbonate of ammonia. When contact is made with the plant, the spine pierces the skin, and the poison is instantly expressed, causing the resultant irritation and inflammation. (The irritating property of the juice is destroyed by heat and drying. For this reason, the cooked young shoots of the Nettle can safely be eaten as a "spring tonic," and the dried herb may be used in medicinal preparations without concern.)

Historical Information: Culpeper gave us an extensive view of the many uses for Nettles.

> "This is also an herb Mars claims dominion over. You know Mars is hot and dry, and you know as well that winter is cold and moist. Then you may know as well the reason why Nettle-tops eaten in the spring consume the phlegmatic superfluities in the body of man, that the coldness and moistness of winter hath left behind. The roots or leaves boiled, or the juice of either of them, or both, made into an electuary with honey and sugar, is a safe and sure medicine to open the pipes and passages of the lungs, which is the cause of wheezing and shortness of breath. It helps to expectorate tough phlegm, as also to raise the imposthumed pleurisy; and spend it by spitting. The same helps the swelling of the almonds of the throat, the mouth and throat being gargled therewith. The juice is also effectual to settle the palate of the mouth in its place, and to heal and temper the inflammations and soreness of the mouth and throat. The decoction of the leaves in wine, being drank, is singularly good to provoke women's courses, and settle the suffocation, strangling of the mother, and all other diseases thereof; it is also applied outwardly with a little myrrh. The same also, or the seed provokes urine, and expels the gravel and stone in the reins or bladder, often proved to be effectual in many that have taken it. The same kills the worms in children, eases pains in the sides, and dissolves the windiness in the spleen, as also in the body, although others think it only powerful to provoke venery. The juice of the leaves taken two or three days together, stays bleeding at the mouth. The seed being drank, is a

remedy against the stinging of venomous creatures, the biting of mad dogs, the poisonous qualities of Hemlock, Henbane, Nightshade, Mandrake, or other such like herbs that stupify or dull the senses. As also the lethargy, especially to use it outwardly, to rub the forehead or temples in the lethargy, and the places stung or bitten with beasts, with a little salt. The distilled water of the herb is also effectual (though not so powerful) for the diseases aforesaid; as for outward wounds and sores to wash them, and to cleanse the skin from morphew, leprosy, and other discolourings thereof. The seed or leaves bruised, and put into the nostrils, stays the bleeding of them, and takes away the flesh growing in them called polypus. The juice of the leaves, or the decoction of them, or of the root, is singularly good to wash either old, rotten, or stinking sores or fistulous, and gangrenes, and such as fretting, eating, or corroding scabs, manginess, and itch, in any part of the body. As also for green wounds, by washing them therewith, or applying the green herb bruised thereunto, yea, although the flesh were separated from the bones. The same applied to our wearied members, refresh them, or to place those that have been out of joint, being first set up again, strengthens, dries, and comforts them. As also those places troubled with aches and gouts, and the defluction of humors upon the joints or sinews; it eases the pains, and dries or dissolves the defluctions. An ointment made of the juice, oil, and a little wax, is singularly good to rub cold and benumbed members. An handful of the leaves of green Nettles, bruised and applied simply themselves to the gout, sciatica, or joint aches in any part, hath been found to be an admirable help thereunto."

Two hundred and fifty years later, King's Dispensatory gives these specific indications for the use of Nettles: diarrhea, dysentery, hemorrhoids, hemorrhages, febrile affections, gravel, nephritic complaints, chronic diseases of the colon, eczematous affections, eczema of the face, neck and ears, and chronic cystitis.

According to Ellingwood, "*Urtica* has been employed for the general purposes of an astringent, both internally and externally, in hemorrhages, ill-conditioned ulcers, and in chronic disease of the mucous membranes of the bronchi, bowels and urinary organs." He states that, "Its influence in small doses is reliable" for post-partum hemorrhage, suppression of the milk in nursing women, skin eruptions, urticaria, jaundice, dropsy, ague, and corpulency.

Nettles was once extensively grown for its fiber, which is very similar to that of Hemp or Flax. It was used for the same purposes as those, for making cloth of the finest texture down to the coarsest, such as sailcloth, sacking, cordage, etc. In Hans Andersen's fairy-tale of the Princess and the Eleven Swans, the coats she wove for them were made of Nettles.

It is one of the wild plants still gathered each spring in rural regions as a "spring tonic" and pot-herb. It makes a healthy and very nutritious vegetable, which is cleansing and easy to digest. An old country remedy for chronic rheumatism and arthritis is "Urtication" or flogging with Nettles. Some folks even keep a nettle plant growing on a sunny windowsill, so that the healing stings might be applied throughout the winter.

It is a strange fact that the juice of the Nettle proves an antidote for its own sting, and being applied will afford instant relief. The sting of a Nettle may also be cured by rubbing the part with Dock, Rosemary, Mint or Sage leaves, as well as those of Comfrey, Plantain, or Jewelweed, which can often be found growing alongside Nettles.

Growing Range: Throughout most of North America and Europe on waste places, low ground, stream sides, ditches, and marshy areas.

Parts Used: Flowering tops, and lately, the roots

Cultivation/Wildcrafting Tips: As a spring tonic and vegetable, the young tops should be gathered when they are 6 to 8 inches high. (Older plants can be hurtful to consume because of the crystals that form on the leaves.) Gloves and long sleeves should be worn as protection when picking them. They should be washed in running water with a stick or long spoon, and then put into a pot, dripping, without any added water. They are best when cooked with the lid on for about 20 minutes. They are delicious chopped, and served plain or with a little pepper vinegar.

For medicinal use, the herb should be collected when the flowers are in bloom. When the herb is to be dried, it should be gathered in the morning, after the sun has dried off the dew, but before the plants have wilted. Cut the plants just above the root, pull off any discolored or insect-eaten leaves, and tie in loose bunches, so that the air can penetrate freely to all parts. Hang the bunches in the shade. (Be sure to bring them indoors if there is any risk of damp from dew or rain.) If dried indoors, hang up the bunches in a warm, well-ventilated room. When the stems and leaves are quite dry and crisp, they should be stripped and culled, and packed away immediately in airtight containers.

Primary Constituents: Chlorophyll, in high yields; Indoles such as histamine and serotonin; Tannins; Formic acid; and Acetylcholine. Nettles are a significant source of Vitamin C and Vitamin A, bio-available minerals, including calcium, silicon, and potassium chloride; protein and dietary fiber.

Action: astringent, alterative, diuretic, tonic, hypotensive, nutritive, hemostatic

Tissues, Organs & Body Systems Affected: Lungs, Kidneys, Bladder, Blood, GI Tract, Skin

Preparations & Dosage:

INTERNAL

Infusion	1–3 tsp dried herb to 1 cup boiling water; steep 10–15 min.; strain and drink 3–4 times per day
Powder	500–2000 mg.; 3–4 times daily
Tincture	15–60 drops; 3–4 times daily

EXTERNAL

Infusion	Apply as wash.
Juice (or crushed fresh herb)	Apply to wounds, hemorrhages.
Tincture	Apply as needed.
Urtication (fresh herb)	Apply stings to painful joints 1–3 times daily.

Indicated Usages:

Condition	Appropriate Preparations	Combines Well With:
INTERNAL		
Alzheimer's	Infusion, Tincture, Powder	Ginkgo, Sage, Dandelion Flowers
Anemia	Infusion, Tincture, Powder	Dandelion, Yellow Dock
Arthritis, Bursitis, Rheumatism	Infusion, Tincture, Powder (also try urtication)	Turmeric, Capsicum, Oregano
Asthma, Hay Fever	Infusion, Tincture, Powder	Mullein, Lobelia, Horehound
Diarrhea	Infusion, Tincture	Yarrow, Alum Root, Slippery Elm
Dropsy	Infusion, Tincture, Powder	Dandelion
Eczema, Psoriasis	Infusion, Tincture, Powder	Burdock, Oregon Grape, Calendula
Gout	Infusion, Tincture, Powder	Celery Seed, Turmeric, Licorice
High Blood Pressure	Infusion, Tincture, Powder	Passion Flower, Hawthorn Berries
Hives	Infusion, Tincture, Powder (also add to bath, soak)	Jewelweed, Ginger, Burdock, Scullcap
Internal Bleeding, Hemorrhage	Infusion, Tincture, Powder	Capsicum, Yarrow, Alum Root

Condition	Appropriate Preparations	Combines Well With:
Kidney Stones	Infusion, Tincture	Horsetail, Cornsilk, Marshmallow
Menorrhagia, Heavy Bleeding	Infusion, Tincture, Powder	Capsicum, Dong Quai, Vitex
Night Sweats	Infusion, Tincture, Powder	Sage
Osteoporosis	Infusion, Tincture, Powder	Comfrey, Horsetail, Marshmallow
Prostate Enlargement	Infusion, Tincture, Powder	Saw Palmetto, Licorice, Dandelion
EXTERNAL		
Bleeding Wounds	Tincture, Juice	Yarrow Flowers, Alum Root, Cranesbill
Burns, Scalds	Infusion, Tincture	Comfrey, Marshmallow
Hair Loss	Infusion, Tincture	Rosemary, Sage, Chamomile
Nettle Rash, Urticaria	Juice	Jewelweed, Comfrey, Plantain
Nosebleed	Tincture, Juice (on compress)	Yarrow Blossoms

Notes: The homoeopathic tincture, *Urtica*, is frequently administered successfully for rheumatic gout, also for skin rashes and chickenpox. It is applied externally for bruises.

Nettle Beer

Many of our recreational beverages, both soft and hard, began life as medicinal brews. (The ancients were generally wise enough to drink water when they were thirsty.) This old recipe for Nettle Beer was often taken by country folk as a tonic refresher, and given to their elders as a remedy for gouty and rheumatic pains. Apart from these purposes it forms a pleasant drink. The recipe may be varied as other herbs are more available.

It may be made as follows:

In a large pot (NOT aluminum), combine 2 gallons of cold water and an equal volume of washed young Nettle tops. Add 3 or 4 large hands full of Dandelion, the same of Cleavers (Goosegrass), and 2 or 3 oz. of grated fresh Ginger root. Bring to a boil, and simmer gently for 40 minutes. Strain off the liquid and return to the pot. Stir in 1½ cups of raw sugar (turbinado or brown sugar will do). When the extract is lukewarm, combine 1 heaping tablespoon of active dry yeast with 1 teaspoon of sugar, and enough warm water to make a thin paste. Spread the yeast mixture on a slice of dry toast, and float it on top of the extract. Keep the pot fairly warm for 6 or 7 hours, while it works. Then remove the scum and stir in a tablespoonful of cream of tartar. Bottle and cork securely.

The result is an especially wholesome sort of ginger beer. The juice of two lemons may be substituted for the Dandelion or the Cleavers. Other herbs are often added to Nettles in the making of Herb Beer, such as Burdock, Sassafras, Meadowsweet, Wintergreen, Birch Sap, and Horehound.

Energetics: Nettles affect the Small Intestine, Bladder, Lung, Chong and Ren meridians. It is said to nourish the Liver Yin, and to relieve damp conditions of the Lungs and Bladder.

Oregon Grape

Mahonia aquifolia, Berberis aquifolium
(Berberidaceae)

Common Names: Rocky Mountain Grape, Mountain Grape, Holly-leaved Barberry

Physical Features: Oregon is a quickly-growing shrub about 4 to 6 feet high. The oddly compound leaves have no spine at the base. They resemble holly leaves in that they are leathery, evergreen, and shining, and have scalloped edges with spines. The small greenish-yellow flowers grow in terminal racemes, and are followed by the long clusters of 3 to 9 seeded purple berries that account for the plants common name.

The bark is brown on the surface and yellow beneath. The root is bright yellow in the interior, and ranges from ½ inch in diameter to 3 inches thick at the base of the stem. It has a very slight odor, and a decidedly bitter taste.

Historical Information: Oregon Grape is a native American member of the Barberry family. Its most active constituent is berberine, and it has been used for many of the same purposes as the other herbs that contain high levels of that element—notably Goldenseal, Barberry, and Yellow Root. Of these, Oregon Grape does seem to have a greater affinity for the skin, and is to be preferred where skin afflictions are the target.

Priest & Priest tell us that it is a mildly stimulating tonic hepatic and alterative. It influences the alimentary mucus membranes, stimulates glandular elements, and improves the uptake of nutrition. It promotes the elimination of catabolic residues and stimulates recuperation. They give the following specific indications for its use: "catarrhal disorders of stomach, intestines and urinary organs; hepatic torpor; bilious headache; eczema, herpes, psoriasis, acne, facial blotches and pimples."

Ellingwood says that the root is, "specific for scaly, pustular, and other skin diseases due to disordered conditions of the blood. It is the most reliable alterative when the influences of the dyscrasia is apparent in the skin. It is given freely during the treatment of skin diseases where an alterative is considered an essential part of the treatment." In addition he recommends it for the following pathologies: "pimples, roughness, eczema capitis, eczema genitalis, puritis, scaly eczema, psoriasis, pityriasis, chronic dermatosis, glandular indurations, ulcerations, and syphilis."

Maude Grieve tells us that the Mountain Grape is, "Tonic and alterative, recommended in psoriasis, syphilis, and impure blood-conditions. It may be used like colombo, berberis, etc., in dyspepsia and chronic mucous complaints. In constipation it is combined with Cascara Sagrada. It improves digestion and absorption."

Growing Range: Native to the upper parts of the Western United States, easily cultivated elsewhere.

Parts Used: Root

Cultivation/Wildcrafting Tips: The roots are best when collected in the autumn, carefully cleaned, cut into slices, and dried with the aid of some heat. If done carefully, a small number of root segments can be dug from around the living plant, and the soil replaced without significant injury to the plant. Avoid cutting into the main root that extends down from the trunk.

Primary Constituents: Alkaloids of the isoquinoline type; berberine, berbamine, hydrastine, oxycanthine

Action: alterative, cholagogue, hepatic, laxative, anti-emetic, anti-catarrhal, antiseptic, antibiotic, anti-viral, lymphatic, tonic

Tissues, Organs & Body Systems Affected: Skin, Liver, Gall Bladder, Stomach, Bowels, Blood

Preparations & Dosage:

INTERNAL	
Decoction	1–2 tsp cut herb to 1 cup water, simmer 10–15 min.; strain and drink up to 3 times daily
Powder	500–2000 mg.; 3–4 times daily
Tincture	15–60 drops; 3–4 times daily

EXTERNAL	
Oil Extract	Apply to affected area as needed.
Ointment	Apply to affected area as needed.
Tincture	Apply to affected area as needed.

Indicated Usages:

Condition	Appropriate Preparations	Combines Well With:
INTERNAL		
Acne, Eruptive Skin Issues	Decoction, Tincture, Powder	Burdock, Yellow Dock, Cleavers
Constipation	Decoction, Tincture, Powder	Cascara Sagrada, Marshmallow
Eczema, Psoriasis, Systemic Skin Issues	Decoction, Tincture, Powder	Burdock, Comfrey, Milk Thistle
Gall Bladder Problems, Stones	Decoction, Tincture, Powder	Fringe Tree Bark, Dandelion Flowers
Gas, Bloating, Flatulence	Decoction, Tincture, Powder	Lovage, Peppermint
Herpes, Shingles	Decoction, Tincture, Powder	Lemon Balm, Garlic, Una de Gato
Jaundice, Liver Problems	Decoction, Tincture, Powder	Dandelion, Milk Thistle, Beet Greens
Leukorrhea, Yeast Infection	Decoction, Tincture (also as douche), Powder	Garlic, Pau D'Arco, Sage
Weak Digestion	Decoction, Tincture, Powder	Angelica, Catnip, Sage, Balmony

Condition	Appropriate Preparations	Combines Well With:
EXTERNAL		
Abscesses, Ulcers	Tincture, Oil Extract, Ointment	Comfrey, Calendula
Acne	Tincture	Comfrey, Calendula
Dermatitis	Tincture, Oil Extract, Ointment	Jewelweed, Plantain, Bugle
Herpes, Shingles, Cold Sores	Tincture, Oil Extract, Ointment	Lemon Balm, Garlic, Colloidal Silver
Inflammation	Tincture, Oil Extract, Ointment	Calendula, Licorice Root, Wild Yam
Wounds	Tincture, Oil Extract, Ointment	Comfrey, Bugle, Thyme, Juniper Berries

Special Considerations: Oregon Grape is highly dependent on its alkaloids for its actions. It should not be combined in formulas with herbs that have a high tannin content (usually the stronger astringents, many barks), as tannins may bind with and neutralize the alkaloids.

Notes: Virtually every benefit that can be derived from the use of Goldenseal can be found in Oregon Grape. Due to over harvesting, Goldenseal is extremely challenged in the wild, facing extinction in some areas. As it has only recently been successfully cultivated, the demand still far outpaces the supply from farm grown sources. Avoid the use of Goldenseal, and opt for Oregon Grape (or Goldthread, Barberry, or Yellow Root) whenever possible.

Energetics: Oregon Grape root focuses its influence on the Liver and Gallbladder meridians. It is said to clear damp heat, and promote the circulation of stagnant Chi in the Liver and Stomach.

Passion Flower

Passiflora incarnata
(Passifloraceae)

Common Names: Passion Vine, Maypop, GranaDilla, Maracoc

Physical Features: Passion Flower derives its name from physical suggestions found in its blossoms that remind the observer of the crucifixion and Passion of Jesus. The finely-cut corona in the center of the blossoms represents the Crown of Thorns, and of the other parts of the flower suggest the cross and wounds.

The plant has a perennial root from which a trailing vine of up to 30 feet in length will grow each year. The vine has many coiled tendrils, and bear three-lobed, finely serrated leaves. The prominent showy blossoms are typically flesh colored or yellowish, tinged with purple, and have a delightfully sweet scent. They are followed by lemon sized fruits (actually a many-seeded berry) which turn yellow to light orange as it ripens. The pulp of the fruit is yellow, sweet, and quite edible.

Historical Information: Passiflora was introduced into medicine in 1839 or 1840 by Dr. L. Phares, of Mississippi, in the New Orleans Medical Journal, and was later brought to the attention of the Eclectics by Prof. I. J. M. Goss, M. D., of Georgia. King's American Dispensatory subsequently described the herb and its indications.

"Its force is exerted chiefly upon the nervous system, the remedy finding a wide application in spasmodic disorders and as a rest-producing agent. It is best adapted to debility, and does not act so well in asthenic conditions, although not contraindicated in such. It is specially useful to allay restlessness and overcome wakefulness, when these are the result of exhaustion, or the nervous excitement of debility. It proves specially useful in the insomnia of infants and old people. It gives sleep to those who are laboring under the effects of mental worry or from mental overwork. It relieves the nervous symptoms due to reflex sexual or menstrual disturbances, and the nervous irritability resulting from prolonged illness. The sleep induced by Passiflora is a peaceful, restful slumber, and the patient awakens quiet and refreshed. An atonic condition appears to be the keynote to its selection.

Passiflora is a remedy for convulsive movements. Passiflora is praised for its control over the spasms of childhood, whether from dentition, worms, or undigested aliment. Spasms, dependent upon meningeal inflammation, have been controlled with it. It appears not to be contraindicated in any form of spasm. The remedy has given good results in chorea, especially in girls approaching the menstrual age. When whooping-cough is associated with convulsions, passiflora has given relief, and in hysteria with spasmodic movements it is reputed equally successful.

Passiflora is a remedy for pain, particularly of the neuralgic type. Thus it has relieved neuralgic and spasmodic dysmenorrhea, rectal pain, cardiac pain, facial and other forms of neuralgia, many reflex painful conditions incident to pregnancy and the menopause, and other forms of pain accompanied or not with spasmodic action. Sick or nervous headache, the headache of debility, or from cerebral fullness are often relieved by passiflora. All such cases show marked atony of some part or function.

Specific Indications and Uses.—Irritation of brain and nervous system with atony; sleeplessness from overwork, worry, or from febrile excitement, and in the young and aged; neuralgic pains with debility; exhaustion from cerebral fullness, or from excitement; convulsive movements; infantile nervous irritation; nervous headache; tetanus; hysteria; oppressed breathing; cardiac palpitation from excitement or shock."

According to Ellingwood, Passion Flower is,
"specific for wakefulness, disturbed sleep from mental worry, and exhaustion from cerebral fullness and from excitement, especially with feebleness. Anemic patients are relieved by it, also the wakefulness of infants and the aged. It is not usually efficient if the wakefulness is caused by pain, nor when the patient is in full strength. Nervous excitement, and irritation with muscular twitchings, evidences of approaching convulsions in childhood, with marked cerebral fullness are indications, and it is given at any time preceding or during convulsive paroxysms if it can be swallowed. It is indicated in convulsions of any character."

In addition he recommends it for "convulsions of childhood, severe spasms, epilepsy, chorea, tetanus, hysteria, persistent hiccough, and the sleeplessness of tuberculosis."

Growing Range: Native to the Eastern and Central United States, Passion Flower is widely cultivated elsewhere.

Parts Used: The above ground parts, collected after some of the fruits have matured, and occasionally the roots.

Cultivation/Wildcrafting Tips: If cultivated, the plant prefers somewhat sandy, mellow soil. Ample compost encourages the top growth. The top half of the length of the vine, complete with fruit and flowers, may be gathered in mid to late summer. The fruit should be separated, sliced, and dried with the aid of some heat. The rest of the herb should be dried in the shade. Fruit and herb are returned together, and stored in dark air-tight containers.

Primary Constituents: Alkaloids: harmine, harman, harmol, harmaline, harmalol, and passaflorine; Flavonoids: apigenin and various glycosides, homoorientin, isoVitexin, kaempferol, luteolin, orientin, quercitin, rutin, saponaretin, saponarin and Vitexen.

Action: nervine, sedative, hypnotic, anti-spasmodic, mildly anodyne, hypotensive

Tissues, Organs & Body Systems Affected: Nerves, Heart, Liver

Preparations & Dosage:

INTERNAL

Infusion	1–2 tsp dried cut herb (or 2 tbsp chopped fresh herb) to 1 cup boiling water; cover and steep 20–30 minutes, drink at bedtime or 2–3 times daily
Powder	325–1200 mg.; 2–3 times daily
Tincture	15–60 drops at bedtime; or 2–3 times daily

EXTERNAL

Poultice	Pounded fresh root, apply and bind to affected area

Indicated Usages:

Condition	Appropriate Preparations	Combines Well With:
INTERNAL		
Anxiety	Infusion, Tincture, Powder	Lemon Balm, Kava
Convulsions	Infusion, Tincture, Powder	Lobelia, Black Cohosh
Cough	Infusion, Tincture	Thyme, Horehound, Elder Flowers
Headache	Infusion, Tincture, Powder	Lemon Balm
Hiccough	Infusion, Tincture	Peppermint
High Blood Pressure	Infusion, Tincture, Powder	Nettles, Prickly Ash, Hawthorn Berries
Hyperactivity	Infusion, Tincture, Powder	Lemon Balm, Ginkgo, Gotu Kola
Insomnia	Infusion, Tincture, Powder	Hops, Valerian, Scullcap
Muscle Tension, Spasms, Twitches	Infusion, Tincture, Powder	Lobelia, Black Cohosh
Neuralgia	Infusion, Tincture, Powder	Capsicum, Turmeric, Thyme, Wild Yam
Parkinson's	Infusion, Tincture, Powder	St. John's Wort, Sage, Peruvian Bark
Restlessness	Infusion, Tincture, Powder	Hops, Scullcap
Sciatica	Infusion, Tincture, Powder	Burdock, Garlic, Southernwood
Seizures	Infusion, Tincture, Powder	Lobelia, Black Cohosh
Stress	Infusion, Tincture, Powder	Scullcap, Kava Kava, Hops
Tachycardia	Infusion, Tincture, Powder	Hawthorn Berries
EXTERNAL		
Boils, Cuts, Bruises	Poultice	Comfrey, Thyme
Rheumatic Pains	Poultice	Black Cohosh

Energetics: Passion Flower is considered a bitter, cool herb that influences the Heart, Lung, and Liver meridians. It is said to tone Heart Yin, and dispel floating Yang.

Peppermint

Mentha piperita
(Labiatae)

Common Names: Mint, Balm mint, Brandy mint

Physical Features: Many members of the Mint family have a similar appearance, making exact identification a little difficult. Adding to this dilemma is the great number of cultivars of a popular species like Peppermint. Fortunately, the properties of mints are more or less the same, and little harm or loss of benefit can come from choosing one over another. Peppermint leaves are somewhat unique in that they have short, but distinct stalks, and their surfaces are smooth on top and bottom, with only occasional minute hairs along the lower ribs and veins. The leaves can be 2 inches or more in length, and ¾ to 1½ inches broad. Their edges are finely toothed. The stems, growing 1½ to 4 feet high, are, as all members of the Mint family, characteristically square, and often purplish. The whorled clusters of little reddish-violet flowers are in the axils of the upper leaves, forming loose, interrupted spikes, and only rarely forming seeds. The entire plant has a very characteristic odor when bruised, due to the volatile oil present in all its parts. Chewing a leaf produces a hot, aromatic taste at first, quickly changing to a sensation of cold in the mouth caused by the menthol it contains.

Historical Information: The Mints are amongst the oldest and most reliable of herbal remedies, especially for issues relating to digestion. Culpeper quotes an even more ancient herbal authority, Simeon Sethi, and says, "It helps a cold liver, strengthens the belly, causes digestion, stays vomit, and hiccough. It is good against the gnawing of the heart, provokes the appetite, takes away obstructions of the liver, and stirs up bodily lust." Apart from that last commendation, most modern herbals recite virtually the same litany. Ellingwood considered it specific for flatulent colic, gastrodynia, nausea, vomiting, spasmodic pain in the bowels, hiccups, palpitation from indigestion, griping, irritability of the stomach, diarrhea with abdominal pain, and nervous headache. In addition he recommends it for the following pathologies: fevers associated with nausea and vomiting, local pain relief in rheumatism (as the oil), symptomatic relief of asthma and chronic bronchitis, toothache, acute indigestion, painful gonorrhea, and pruritis ani. Contemporary research shows this and several other members of the Labiatae family as having significant antiseptic and anti-viral properties, as well. The essential oil, distilled from the fresh cut plant, has enjoyed a wide range of medicinal and culinary uses since the 18th century, and is one of the few that are safe to take internally or apply to the skin undiluted.

Growing Range: Throughout North America, where adequate moisture is available.

Parts Used: Aerial parts, fresh or dried; essential oil

Cultivation/Wildcrafting Tips: This hardy perennial is so easy to grow that it is hard to contain. A couple of plants, obtained from a reputable nursery for proper identification, will quickly form a dense colony. Peppermint prefers a deep, rich, well-drained soil with good moisture retention. Harvest above ground parts just before flowering, during the morning hours after the dew has lifted. Tie in small loose bundles, and hang to dry in the shade. The highest essential oil content is in plants grown in full sun in the North, and semi-shade in the South.

Primary Constituents: Essential oil, up to 1.5%, containing menthol, menthone and menthyl acetate as the major components, with isomenthone, menthofuran, isomenthol, neomenthol, piperitone, a- & b-pinene, limonene, cineole, pulegone, viridiflorol, ledol etc.; Flavonoids; menthoside, rutin and others; rosmarinic acid, azulenes, choline, carotenes etc.

Action: carminative, anti-inflammatory, anti-spasmodic, aromatic, diaphoretic, anti-emetic, nervine, anti-microbial, analgesic, stimulant, anodyne

Tissues, Organs & Body Systems Affected: Stomach, Intestines, Liver, Muscles, Nervous System, Circulation

Preparations & Dosage:

INTERNAL	
Essential Oil	1–5 drops in warm water; 3–5 times daily
Infusion	Steep 3–10 minutes, well covered; 6 oz.; 3 times daily.
Powder	2–8 #0 capsules (600–2,500 mg.); 3 times daily
Tincture	30–60 drops; 3–4 times daily
Vapor	Strong infusion or 4–5 drops Essential Oil in hot water. Cover head and source with towel, breath deeply.

EXTERNAL	
Essential Oil	May be applied to the skin "neat," or undiluted.
Fomentation	Use a strong infusion; apply as hot as can be tolerated.

Indicated Usages:

Condition	Appropriate Preparations	Combines Well With:
INTERNAL		
Bronchitis	Infusion	Mullein, Lemon Balm
Chills, Poor Circulation	Infusion, Essential Oil, Tincture, Powder	Ginkgo, Ginger
Colds and Flu	Infusion, Essential Oil, Tincture, Powder, Vapor	Mullein, Lemon Balm, Boneset
Colic	Infusion	Catnip, Fennel, Caraway Seed
Colitis, Diverticulitis	Infusion, Powder	Comfrey, Plantain
Dizziness, Vertigo	Infusion, Essential Oil, Tincture	Ginkgo, Gotu Kola
Fever	Infusion, Essential Oil, Tincture	Gravel Root, Garlic, Elder Flowers
Gas, Flatulence	Infusion, Essential Oil, Tincture, Powder	Fennel, Catnip

Condition	Appropriate Preparations	Combines Well With:
Heartburn	Infusion, Essential Oil, Tincture	Comfrey, Papaya, Marshmallow, Fennel
Herpes	Infusion, Tincture	Lemon Balm
Hiccups	Infusion, Essential Oil	
Menstrual Cramps, Dysmenorrhea	Infusion, Essential Oil, Tincture	Lemon Balm, Scullcap, Black Cohosh, Vitex
Migraine, Headache	Infusion, Essential Oil, Tincture, Powder, Vapor	Lemon Balm, Feverfew, Wood Betony
Morning Sickness, Nausea	Infusion, Essential Oil, Tincture, Vapor	Ginger, Catnip
Sore Throat, Laryngitis	Infusion, Essential Oil, Tincture	Lemon Balm, Mullein, Chamomile (gargle)

EXTERNAL		
Fatigue	Essential Oil	
Halitosis	Essential Oil, Infusion	
Headache	Essential Oil, Fomentation	
Itching	Fomentation	Plantain, Ginger
Muscle Pain, Cramps	Essential Oil, Fomentation	Plantain, Black Cohosh
Sinus Congestion	Essential Oil, Vapor	
Toothache	Essential Oil	Clove Oil

Special Considerations: Like Ginger and Capsicum, Peppermint is a helpful herbal "catalyst" or activator; drinking a cup of Peppermint tea before taking other herbs opens the circulation, and potentiates their action. It also helps make the disagreeable taste of many herbal formulas a little more palatable.

Aromatics with a high essential oil content like Peppermint are particularly susceptible to retaining petroleum based pesticide residues, and these can be concentrated in the distillation process. When possible, select only organically produced essential oil.

Notes: A few sprigs of Peppermint placed in picnic baskets or food cabinets makes an effective deterrent to ants.

As the list above indicates, a small bottle of Peppermint Oil can be thought of as a "medicine cabinet in your pocket," and can be used as an emergency remedy for a myriad of conditions. Never leave home without it.

Energetics: Peppermint is used to normalize wind cold and wind heat conditions, and to stimulate constrained Chi. It affects the Lungs, Spleen, and Liver meridians. In Ayurveda, it is said to increase Vayu and Pitta.

Plantain

Plantago lanceolata, P. major, P. ovata, P. psyllium
(Plantaginaceae)

Common Names: Ribwort, Longleaf Plantain (P. lanceolata); Broadleaf Plantain, Greater Plantain, Waybread, White Man's Foot, Englishman's Foot (P. major)

Physical Features: Longleaf Plantain is the most common form in the United States. It varies greatly in size, depending on the soil and conditions of its habitat, though its appearance is consistent, just a matter of scale. The leaves are dark green, long and slender, seldom more than an inch or so wide, and arranged in a rosette around a ground-hugging central crown. In tall grass or pasture edges it can reach

12 to 16 inches in height, while in lawns or dry, stony ground it will struggle to reach 3 or 4 inches. The leaves have pronounced longitudinal ribs that run from tip to stem. The flowerstalks are long and wiry, grooved and angular, stand prominently above the leaves, and terminate in bullet-shaped cones that are surrounded with a halo ring of tiny blossoms. The leaves are often slightly hairy, which gives them a silvery appearance, especially in plants growing along the roadsides. Broadleaf Plantain has oblong to roundish leaves, more crumpled in appearance, but with the same characteristic ribs, growing from the crown on stems that often equal the leaf in length. The seedhead of this variety is also tall and wiry, but with the top third of its length covered with a rope-like span of coarse, shiny brown seeds. These are the seeds, along with those of other varieties, that are famous as Psyllium seeds and hulls.

Historical Information: Plantain was used by the ancients to heal the bites of "mad dogs, snakes, and venomous creatures." Interestingly, Native Americans quickly learned to use Plantain in the same way, and the colonial assembly of South Carolina granted a handsome reward and freedom to an African slave who taught them how to use the plant to remedy the bite of rattlesnakes. Maud Grieve quotes Salmon's Herbal (1710), and gives the following list of other uses for Plantago: "The liquid juice clarified and drunk for several days helps distillation of rheum upon the throat, glands, lungs, etc. Doses, 3 to 8 spoonsful. An especial remedy against ulceration of the lungs and a vehement cough arising from same. It is said to be good against epilepsy, dropsy, jaundice and opens obstructions of the liver, spleen, and veins. It cools inflammations of the eyes and takes away the pin and web (so called) in them. Dropped into the ears, it eases their pains and restores hearing much decayed. Doses, 3 to 6 spoonsful more or less, either alone or with some fit vehicle morning and night. The powdered root mixed with equal parts of powder of Pellitory of Spain and put into a hollow tooth is said to ease the pain thereof. Powdered seeds stop vomiting, epilepsy, lethargy, convulsions, dropsy, jaundice, strangury, obstruction of the liver, etc. The liniment made with the juice and oil of Roses eases headache caused by heat, and is good for lunatics. It gives great ease, being applied in all hot gouts, whether in hands or feet, especially in the beginning, to cool the heat and repress the humors. The distilled water with a little alum and honey dissolved in it is of good use for cleansing and healing a sore ulcerated mouth or throat."

In more recent times, Plantain has been acclaimed for its ability to relieve bee stings, insect and spider bites, and rashes from an unfortunate encounter with Poison Ivy or Stinging Nettles. Dr. Christopher referred to Plantain, along with Jewelweed

(Impatiens biflora) and Hound's Tongue (Cynoglossum officinale) as "Nature's erasers." "Stand anywhere within sight of Poison Ivy, and look about," he said. "You will always see at least one of these plants, placed by the hand of God to come to your aid, if you should need it." Contemporary research has confirmed the anti-inflammatory properties of Plantain, and has discovered elements that protect the body against tumors and help resist damage to the liver from chemotherapy drugs. The fiber and mucilage from the seeds of the Plantago species have gained prominence as the primary fiber supplement of choice for millions of people around the world.

Growing Range: Native Americans noticed that Plantain grew wherever the white man set foot, which accounts for a couple of its common names. It can be found virtually everywhere in North America, and grows on every continent except Antarctica.

Parts Used: Leaves, aerial parts, whole herb (roots and tops), fresh or dried; seeds

Cultivation/Wildcrafting Tips: Billions of dollars are spent each year spraying poisons to eradicate this precious weed from the lawns of America. Its persistence is a testament to its healing power, and there is very little need to cultivate it. Gather the whole herb—from unsprayed areas—anytime during flowering throughout the summer. Dry it as fast as possible—a warm oven is fine - as the leaves will discolor and lose their effectiveness if dried improperly. Seed heads from P. major can be gathered in late summer, dried in the shade, and the seeds rubbed off for storage.

Primary Constituents: Iridoids; aucubin, 3,4-dihydroaucubin, 6-O-b-glucosylaucubin, catalpol; Flavonoids; apigenin, lutelin, scutellarin, baicalein, nepetin, hispidulin, plantagoside; tannin, oleanolic acid, plant acids such as chlorogenic, neochlorogenic, fumaric, hydroxycinnamic and benzoic acids and their esters. Seeds are covered in mucilage.

Action: vulnerary, expectorant, demulcent, anti-inflammatory, anodyne, astringent, styptic, alterative, anthelmintic, anti-venomous, diuretic, deobstruant, anti-microbial, anti-tumor, hepato-protective (herb), emollient, laxative, mucilaginous, anti-diabetic (seeds)

Tissues, Organs & Body Systems Affected: Kidneys, Lungs, Veins, Digestive System, Intestinal System, Skin

Preparations & Dosage:

INTERNAL	
Decoction (seeds)	Soak overnight then simmer 10–15 minutes. ½–1 oz.; 3–4 times daily. Sweeten with a little honey to taste.
Infusion (tops)	Steep 15–30 minutes. 2–4 cups daily for adults. 1–2 oz.; 3–4 times daily for children
Powder (seeds, hulls)	3–10 #0 capsules (1–4 gm.); 2–3 times daily with ample water
Powder (tops)	3–10 #0 capsules (1–3 gm.); 2–3 times daily
Tincture	2–30 drops; 3–4 times daily

EXTERNAL	
Enema Injection	Warm strong infusion; twice daily.
Fomentation	Prepare with strong infusion, apply as hot as tolerated.
Ointment	As often as needed
Poultice	Crushed fresh herb, or powdered dry herb/seed mix moistened with aloe juice or warm water
Tincture	Apply as styptic/antiseptic.

Indicated Usages:

Condition	Appropriate Preparations	Combines Well With:
INTERNAL		
Cholesterol	Decoction, Powder (seeds)	Garlic, Flax Seed
Constipation	Decoction, Powder (seeds)	Cascara
Diabetes	Decoction (seeds)	Goldenseal, Juniper Berries, Dandelion
Diarrhea	Infusion, Decoction (tops)	Bugle
Hemorrhoids	Infusion, Tincture, Injection Enema	Bugle
Indigestion	Infusion	Peppermint, Marshmallow
Irritable Bowel	Decoction, Powder (seeds)	Comfrey, Marshmallow
Kidney/Bladder Inflammation	Infusion, Tincture, Powder (tops)	Comfrey, Cornsilk, Marshmallow
Liver Problems	Infusion, Tincture, Powder (tops)	Barberry, Dandelion, Milk Thistle
Mouth Ulcers, Canker Sores	Infusion, Tincture, Powder	Lemon Balm, Sage, Licorice
Uterine Tonic	Infusion, Tincture, Powder	Gravel Root, Lady's Mantle, Raspberry
EXTERNAL		
Bites, Stings	Fomentation, Poultice, Ointment	Comfrey, Calendula
Cuts, Bleeding Wounds	Poultice, Ointment	Bugle, Comfrey, Yarrow

— continues on next page

— continued from previous page

Condition	Appropriate Preparations	Combines Well With:
Eczema, Psoriasis	Fomentation, Oil, Ointment	Comfrey, Cleavers, Burdock
Leukorrhea, Yeast	Douche (infusion)	Garlic, Pau D'Arco, Juniper Berries
Rashes, Contact Dermatitis	Fomentation, Oil, Ointment	Bugle, Calendula, Jewel Weed
Toothache	Poultice (on gums)	
Ulcers, Old Sores	Poultice, Ointment	Comfrey, Horsetail, St. John's Wort
Varicose Veins	Fomentation	Bugle

Special Considerations: To be effective, and to avoid complications, all high-fiber supplements like Plantain or Psyllium seed should be taken with ample water.

Notes: Plantain is a first rate "First Aid" plant that is usually close-at-hand, wherever you may be. A few fresh leaves, crushed or chewed, can be used to quickly stop the bleeding of an open wound, stop the pain and inflammation of bites and stings, and relieve the itching from poison ivy. A cup of strong Plantain tea will quell the worst indigestion, and a small wad of chewed leaf placed next to the gum will quiet a painful toothache until it can be attended to.

A simple ointment, made with an olive oil extract of fresh Plantain and a little beeswax is a very good general purpose remedy for many skin ailments, and is especially helpful with diaper rash.

Energetics: Plantain is used to clear toxic heat and damp heat conditions from the body. It affects the Lung, Large Intestine, and Bladder meridians. In Ayurveda, it is said to decrease Pitta and Kapha.

Pleurisy Root

Asclepius tuberosa
(Asclepiadaceae)

Common Names: Butterfly Weed, Silk Weed, Swallow-wort, Tuber Root, Wind Root, Colic Root, Orange Milkweed

Physical Features: Pleurisy Root is one of our most attractive wildflowers. It is a handsome, fleshy rooted, perennial plant, growing 1 to 3 feet high, and bearing corymbs of deep orange, occasionally yellow flowers from mid-summer to early autumn. The stems are coarse, erect, and mostly unbranched. The dark green, lance shaped leaves, 3 to 5 inches long, are alternately arranged around the stem, which they clasp at their base. The leaves are mostly smooth on top, somewhat velvety beneath.

An exception to the Milkweed clan, Pleurisy Root is practically devoid of any of the acrid milky latex that exudes from most of the Asclepias when injured. The rootstock, the part used medicinally, is thick, spindle-shaped, and has a knotty crown. It has shallow but distinct annular rings toward the top, while the rest is wrinkled longitudinally. The heart of the root is pale yellow, has little if any distinct odor, and is disagreeably bitter to the taste. The distinctive seed pods are 4 to 5 inches long, bulging in the center, and tapering at both ends, distally to a long sharp point. When the pods split open, they reveal numerous flat oval seeds attached to clusters of long pure white silken fibers that form a parasol.

Historical Information: Once a mainstay of the Physio-Medicals and the Eclectics, Pleurisy Root was official in the United States Pharmacopoeia and the National Formulary until 1935.

Priest & Priest give the following specific indications for its use: catarrhal complaints from cold and damp, hard dry cough, bronchitis, pleurisy, peritonitis, pneumonia, influenza, intercostal rheumatism and intercostal diseases.

Quoting King at length:

> "It was one of the most common medicines employed by the Eclectic fathers. It was favorably written upon by most of the earlier writers on American medicinal plants. The drug has fallen into unmerited neglect, and could profitably be employed at the present day for purposes for which much more powerful and sometimes dangerous, drugs are used. It has an extensive range of usefulness, being possessed of diaphoretic, diuretic, laxative, tonic, carminative, expectorant, and probably anti-spasmodic properties. Asclepias is one of the best diaphoretics of the Eclectic materia medica. It is not stimulating, and may be used to promote diaphoresis, no matter how high the degree of fever. Pleurisy Root has a deservedly good reputation in respiratory diseases. It acts upon the mucous membrane of the pulmonary tract, augmenting the secretions and favoring easy expectoration. Besides its action on the respiratory mucous surfaces, its action upon the skin as a true diaphoretic, establishing the insensible perspiration when the skin is dry and harsh, and correcting that weakness of the skin which allows the sweat to pour out too freely, renders it of value in the sweating of phthisis. As its popular name indicates, Pleurisy Root is of much value in treating pleurisy. Not only is its action on serous membranes marked, but it is very effectual in intercostal neuralgia and rheumatism, as well as in pericardial pains. The chief action of Asclepias is to lessen arterial tension, and acute diseases are

those in which it is of most value. It is a safe drug, for while it may not act as efficiently when not indicated, it may be said to never be contraindicated, so far as expecting any harm from its use is concerned. In pneumonia, as well as in bronchitis, it is best adapted to the acute stage, where the lesion seems to be extensive, taking in a large area of lung parenchyma and mucous tissues. It undoubtedly acts upon the general circulatory apparatus, lowering arterial tension. In the convalescing stage of pneumonia, and other respiratory lesions, when suppression of the expectoration and dyspnea threaten, small doses at frequent intervals will correct the trouble. It, as well as Euphrasia and Matricaria, is among our best drugs for snuffles, or acute nasal catarrh of infants. It is an excellent remedy for ordinary colds. It is, in fact one of our best drugs for catarrhal conditions, whether of the pulmonary or gastro-intestinal tract, especially when produced by recent colds. Stomach troubles, particularly those of children, are often markedly benefited by small doses. Diarrhea and dysentery, when of catarrhal character and due to cold are benefited by alternating with other indicated remedies. As a remedy for gastric disorders it is well adapted to children and weak individuals. Headache from disordered digestion has been cured with it, and for flatulent colic in young children. Dioscorea may also be administered with it in cases of flatus in adults and children. Asclepias is a remedy for nervous irritability of children, especially when due to gastric disturbances. The dry forms of cutaneous affections are benefited by it especially where it is necessary to establish the true dermal secretions. It is not an active agent yet on the whole, though apparently a feeble remedy, when indicated, it accomplishes a purpose which no other remedy in the materia medica fulfils."

As a result of the blockade of Southern ports during the Civil War, many basic products including medicine were in short supply. For the all-too-common respiratory complaints ranging from bronchitis to "consumption," Pleurisy Root was found to be an effective substitute for Antimony and Calomel (mercury subchloride), poisonous drugs in common use by "regular" physicians of the era. In the process, no doubt many of the Confederacy's citizens were not only relieved of their conditions, but were also spared the painful miseries associated with those drugs.

Growing Range: Common along dry roadsides throughout the eastern and central North America, it is generally more abundant in the South.

Parts Used: Dried (not fresh) Root (rhizome)

Cultivation/Wildcrafting Tips: Once recognized, the blazing floral flags of Pleurisy Root can easily be spotted in the summer amongst native grasses and roadside plants. The root may be dug when the plant is in flower, but is more potent in the early spring, just as the plant begins to emerge. Wild stands should be marked and noted when they are in bloom, and then checked again in March or April of the next spring. Pleurisy Root can also be transplanted from the wild to a garden site in the fall, after the seed pods have ripened and the plant has gone dormant. It does best in a dry humus-rich soil. Seeds and plants are often available at nurseries and garden centers—generally sold as "Butterfly Weed." (Check the botanical name to be sure of identity.)

Primary Constituents: Cardenolides, including asclepiadin; Flavonoids: rutin, kaempferol, quercitin and isorhamnetin; friedalin; a-and b-amyrin; lupeol; viburnitol; choline; misc. resins, fatty acids, sugars, and a trace of volatile oil.

Action: diaphoretic, diuretic, expectorant, anti-spasmodic, carminative, laxative, tonic, anti-inflammatory

Tissues, Organs & Body Systems Affected: Lungs, Respiratory Mucosa, Skin, Intestines

Preparations & Dosage:

INTERNAL	
Infusion	½–1 tsp ground dried root to 1 cup boiling water; let steep 20–25 minutes; take 2–3 oz. warm every hour, or 1 cup 3–4 times daily
Powder	1–3 gms.; 2–3 times daily
Tincture	15–30 drops; 3–4 times daily, or frequently in warm water

Indicated Usages:

Condition	Appropriate Preparations	Combines Well With:
INTERNAL		
Asthma	Infusion, Tincture, Powder	Lobelia
Bronchitis	Infusion, Tincture, Powder	Marshmallow, Oregon Grape
Colds, Flu	Infusion, Tincture, Powder	Echinacea, Lemon Balm, Horehound
Diarrhea, Dysentery	Tincture, Powder	Comfrey, Oregon Grape, Yarrow
Emphysema	Infusion, Tincture, Powder	Comfrey, Wild Cherry, Lobelia
Fever	Infusion, Tincture	Sassafras, Boneset, Elder Flowers

Condition	Appropriate Preparations	Combines Well With:
Pleurisy	Infusion, Tincture, Powder	Mullein, Lobelia
Respiratory Infection	Infusion, Tincture, Powder	Echinacea, Garlic
Rheumatism	Infusion, Tincture, Powder	Ginger, Chaparral, Bugle, Meadowsweet
Tuberculosis	Infusion, Tincture, Powder	Garlic, Comfrey

Energetics: Pleurisy Root influences the Lung, Spleen, Stomach and Large Intestine meridians. It is said to relieve lung heat conditions, and to circulate constrained Chi, particularly of the Lungs and Intestines.

Poke

Phytolacca americana
(Phytolaccaceae)

Common Names: Pokeweed, Poke Salat, Pigeon Berry, Bear's Grape, Red-ink Plant, Skoke, Crowberry, Jalap, Cancer-root, Coakum, Poke Berry

Physical Features: Poke is a tall, single stalked, tropical-looking plant, with broad heart shaped leaves. The main stalk, which usually stands from 4 to 6 feet at maturity, is thick, round, and smooth. It is hollow, with thick walls, and sometimes a little pithy inside. The stalk and leaf stems are green when young, turning purplish red as they age. Leaves are dark green, fleshy, and supple. The prominent fruits appear in large drooping clusters beginning in mid-summer. They are deep dark purple, and individually, have the shape of a somewhat flattened blueberry, though much more red and dark in color. The large tap roots are simple in form, rather like a parsnip, except that the wrinkles run lengthwise, and range from ½ to 1 inch or more in thickness, and from 8 to 20 inches in length. Large roots can be hollow or pithy in the interior.

Historical Information: Priest & Priest tell us that it is a stimulating and relaxing alterative, and that it promotes the removal of catabolic wastes and the products of fatty degeneration. Ellingwood considered its most direct actions in inflammation of glandular structures, especially of the lymphatic glands. Arthritis and rheumatic pains from deficient catabolism are relieved by it. It is directly indicated in irritation, inflammation, and ulceration of mucous membranes in rheumatic subjects, old ulcers, scabies, fungal infections of the skin, psoriasis, and all squamous skin diseases. In addition, he recommends it for the following pathologies: inflammations of the throat, forms of diphtheria, goiter, adenitis, mastitis, syphilitic disorders, varicose ulcers, dermal abscesses, fissures, boils, and carbuncles. Famed 20th century herbalist, Dr. John Christopher, tells us. "Poke root is one of the most powerful botanical alteratives, especially beneficial where the glands (especially the thyroid and spleen) are hard, swollen, or enlarged. Poke root is excellent for all skin problems, and especially useful for hardened liver and scanty flow of bile. It works almost magically on new abnormal growths, as well as bony enlargements from direct injury, even chronic conditions. It is healing to inflamed kidneys and enlarged lymphatic glands, and is an effective and rapid anti-cancer agent." In recent years, research on the species has uncovered both anti-tumor and anti-viral properties in the plant and its seeds. Poke anti-viral protein (PAP) has become the focus of excited attention of researchers in Europe, Asia, and the United States.

Growing Range: Throughout North America, especially prevalent in the Eastern half and the Southeast.

Parts Used: Roots, especially effective when fresh, but may be dried.

Cultivation/Wildcrafting Tips: Poke grows most rampantly on newly disturbed ground, and along roadsides and pasture edges. The root can be used anytime during the growing season, but for preserving, it should be collected in the fall as the tops begin to die back. It is best preserved as a tincture or fluid extract made while the root is fresh, but it can be dried with low heat after slicing or splitting lengthwise.

The dried root deteriorates rapidly, and should be stored in opaque containers with as little air and moisture as possible.

Primary Constituents: Triterpenoid saponins; the phytolaccosides A, B, C, D & E. Based on the aglycones phytolaccagenin and phytolaccicacid; Lectins; mixture known as Pokeweed mitogen, consisting of a series of glycoproteins, including variants of Poke anti-viral protein (PAP).

Action: anti-rheumatic, stimulant, anti-catarrhal, alterative, lymphatic, purgative, emetic, anti-psoriatic, anti-viral

Tissues, Organs & Body Systems Affected: Bowel, Blood, Lymph, Lungs

Preparations & Dosage:
CAUTIONARY NOTE: POKE PREPARATIONS ARE MADE WITH PROPORTIONS AND DOSAGES OUTSIDE THE NORMAL RANGE. DO NOT EXCEED THE RECOMMENDED LIMITS UNTIL EXPERIENCED WITH THE USE OF THIS HERB.

INTERNAL	
Infusion	Use ¼ tsp to 1 cup boiling water, steep 3–5 minutes for fresh root, 5–10 minutes for dried. ½–1 tsp; 3 times daily.
Powder	1 #0 capsule (250–300 mg.); 3–4 times daily
Tincture	16 oz. fresh root or 8 oz. dried root to 2 qts. menstruum Dosage: 3–15 drops every 4 hours

EXTERNAL	
Fomentation	Prepare with Infusion or diluted Tincture (1 tbsp to 1 pint warm water), apply warm.
Ointment	Macerate fresh ground root in sufficient oil to cover for 7–10 days. Strain and prepare ointment. Apply as needed. Best blended with supporting herbs.
Poultice	Use sufficient ground root moistened with Poke infusion to cover affected area. Wrap herb in cheesecloth or muslin and apply. Cover with plastic. Keep moist with additional infusion as needed. Change after three days.

Indicated Usages:

Condition	Appropriate Preparations	Combines Well With:
INTERNAL		
Arthritis, Rheumatism	Infusion, Tincture	Elder Berries, Sumac Berries, Bramble Root
Blood Toxicity	Infusion, Tincture	Burdock, Yellow Dock, Red Clover, Sassafras
Constipation	Infusion, Tincture	Slippery Elm

Condition	Appropriate Preparations	Combines Well With:
Glandular Swelling, Spleen and Thyroid	Infusion, Tincture	Dandelion, Yellow Dock, Black Walnut
Liver Congestion, Cirrhosis	Infusion, Tincture	Dandelion, Milk Thistle
Lymphatic Congestion	Infusion, Tincture, Powder	Echinacea, Cleavers, Blue Flag, Sassafras
Skin Disorders, Eczema, Psoriasis	Infusion, Tincture, Powder	Cleavers, Horsetail, Oregon Grape
Tumors	Infusion, Tincture, Powder	Dandelion, Gentian
EXTERNAL		
Fatty Tumors	Fomentation, Ointment, Poultice	Chickweed, Butcher's Broom
Goiter	Fomentation, Poultice	Black Walnut, Mullein
Mastitis, Swollen Breasts	Fomentation, Ointment, Poultice	Gravel Root, Lady's Mantle, Mullein
Skin Diseases	Fomentation, Ointment, Poultice	Comfrey, Calendula, Oregon Grape

Special Considerations: Poke root preparations are potent, and should NOT be used casually. Even small doses of Poke can be powerfully emetic and purgative. Exercise caution with initial doses to gauge response. Use very small amounts when preparing infusions or decoctions, i.e. ¼ tsp powdered or ½ tsp ground fresh root to 1 cup of water (Christopher recommends ½ oz. to 1½ pints), and give the resulting product in small doses.

Notes: Popular in the South and throughout Appalachia, Poke greens, commonly called Poke Salat, were at one time canned commercially. Their preparation needs to be undertaken with care, though, as the fresh greens can be strongly purgative. The berries, or more correctly, the seeds contained within, are considered to be highly toxic, and children should be taught not to ingest the inviting looking fruit.

Energetics: In Traditional Chinese Medicine, Poke is used to dispel wind damp and phlegm from the skin and channels. It affects the Liver, Kidney, and Bladder meridians.

Red Clover

Trifolium pratense
(Leguminosae)

Common Names: Trefoil, Wild Clover, Purple Clover

Physical Features: A short lived perennial, Red Clover is generally abundant on pasture and meadow land of a light sandy nature. It produces excellent forage, and is often grown as a hay crop. The plants stand as independent clumps of usually upright somewhat hairy branches, typically from 1 to 2 feet in height. The green leaves are stalked and each has three oval leaflets as is typical of the clovers. Each leaflet carries a distinctive V-shaped marking, usually whitish, but occasionally red. The characteristic globe-shaped flower heads, which form in great profusion, may range from rose-pink to purplish in color, and may expand to over an inch in diameter. The flowers usually appear from late spring to late summer, depending on weather and moisture conditions.

Historical Information: Little is known about how or when Red Clover was introduced into medical use. What is known is that, once recognized, it was highly esteemed by the botanical practitioners, and dismissed by the "regulars." In 1896, King said that,

> "Red Clover is an excellent alterative, and one of the few remedies which favorably influences pertussis. In earlier editions of this work it was stated that 'a strong infusion of the plant is said to afford prompt relief in whooping-cough, suspending the spasmodic cough entirely in 2 or 3 days; it is to be given in ½ fluid ounce, every 1 or 2 hours, throughout the day.' Since then the remedy has come into extensive use, but the statement should be modified, as it does not reach all classes of cases. When the proper case is found it acts promptly, but as yet the specific indications in this complaint have not been discovered. It is also a remedy in other spasmodic coughs, as those of measles, bronchitis, laryngitis, phthisis, etc. It is an excellent internal agent for those individuals disposed to tibial and other forms of ulcers, and it unquestionably retards the growth of carcinomata, and may be freely administered to those of a cancerous diathesis. The extract, spread on linen or soft leather, has long been said to be an excellent remedy for cancerous ulcers. This assertion, however, has not been so well verified as its action in retarding the growths when administered internally for a prolonged period. It is also highly recommended in ill-conditioned ulcers of every kind, and deep, ragged-edged, and otherwise badly-conditioned burns. It possesses a peculiar soothing property, proves an efficient detergent, and promotes a healthful granulation."

After another quarter century of experience with the herb, the Eclectic Materia Medica of 1922 recommended it for the specific indications of, "irritability of the respiratory passages, with dry, explosive cough; carcinomatous cachexia," and gave the following information:

> "Trifolium is alterative and antispasmodic. It relieves irritability of the respiratory tract, alleviating dry, irritable and spasmodic cough. Whooping cough is especially moderated by it, and it is frequently effective in lessening the distressing cough of measles. It also modifies cough in bronchitis and laryngitis.

> Its alterative powers are underrated, and it should be given where a general deobstruent effect is desired in chronic skin diseases, and unquestionably has a retarding effect upon malignant neoplasms."

Red Clover's prestige in the alternative health community in the last few decades has been based partly on its use as an anti-cancer agent. It is an ingredient in every famous cancer formula, including such as Jason Winter's Tea, the Hoxsey Cancer Formula, Essiac Tea, and Christopher's Anti-Cancer Remedy (Red Clover Blend). More recently, it has become a hot topic because of potential estrogenic effects of its isoflavone content. The jury is still out on that one, but most of its more traditional uses seem well justified.

Growing Range: Widely distributed throughout Europe including Britain, naturalized in North America and many other parts of the world.

Parts Used: Blossoms

Cultivation/Wildcrafting Tips: The flowers are gathered when fully formed, usually in late spring and early summer. They may be used fresh, or spread on screens to dry in the shade.

Primary Constituents: Isoflavones: biochanin A, daidzein, formononnetin, genistein, pratensein, trifoside; Other flavonoids including pectolinarin and trifoliin (=isoquercitrin); Volatile oil, containing furfural; Clovamides; L-Dopa-caffeic acid conjugates; Coumarins ; coumestrol, medicagol and coumarin; galactomannan; Miscellaneous resins, minerals vitamins, phytoalexins. Red Clover is a significant source of calcium, niacin, and tin.

Action: alterative, expectorant, anti-spasmodic, depurant, alkalizer, estrogenic*

(* The estrogenic activity of Red Clover is controversial—or maybe more correctly, disputable. The herb was never used for that effect by classical herbalists, and only in the past decade has it gained some notoriety in women's formulas. It does contain some isoflavones that have estrogenic potential, but no true phyto-estrogens have ever been identified in Red Clover. This author is inclined to believe that the primary benefit in female issues stems from its detoxifying (alterative) action. Still, its hormone balancing effects are a common enough claim that the herb deserves consideration in this area.)

Tissues, Organs & Body Systems Affected: Nerves, Lungs, Blood, Liver, Lymph

Preparations & Dosage:

INTERNAL	
Extract	1 cup of chopped blossoms in 1½ pints water; simmer slowly until reduced to 1 pint; strain and press; return to heat and reduce to 1 cup. Take 1–2 tbsp in warm water 4–6 times daily. Keep refrigerated.
Infusion	1 tbsp in 1 cup boiling water; steep 20–30 minutes; drink freely
Powder	500–2000 mg. (2–8 capsules); 4–6 times daily
Tincture	15–30 drops; frequently taken

EXTERNAL	
Decoction	¼ cup of blossoms in 1 pint of water; bring to boil and simmer 15–20 min.; strain and bathe affected areas; use as injection (vaginal, enema); use as fomentation
Ointment	Apply to affected area as needed.
Thomson's Plaster	See "Notes" below for preparation.

Indicated Usages:

Condition	Appropriate Preparations	Combines Well With:
INTERNAL		
Acne	Infusion, Tincture, Powder, Extract	Burdock, Cleavers, Oregon Grape
Asthma	Infusion, Tincture, Powder, Extract	Yerba Santa, Lobelia, Thyme, Capsicum
Blood Alkalizer	Infusion, Tincture, Powder, Extract	Nettles, Horse Tail, Alfalfa, Marshmallow
Blood Cleanser (esp. heavy metals)	Infusion, Tincture, Powder, Extract	Burdock, Mullein, Yellow Parilla
Blood Thinner	Infusion, Tincture, Powder, Extract	Ginkgo
Cancer	Infusion, Tincture, Powder, Extract	Poke Root, Stillingia, Chaparral, Sheep Sorrel, Cascara
Cradle Cap	Infusion (1–2 oz.; 3–4 times daily), also use as wash	Chamomile
Eczema, Psoriasis	Infusion, Tincture, Powder, Extract	Oregon Grape, Calendula, Comfrey
PMS, Menopausal Issues	Infusion, Tincture, Powder, Extract	Vitex, Dong Quai
Prostate Problems	Infusion, Tincture, Powder, Extract	Saw Palmetto
Purulent Ulcers	Infusion, Tincture, Powder, Extract	Burdock, Yellow Dock
Whooping Cough	Infusion, Tincture, Powder, Extract	Horehound, Mullein
EXTERNAL		
Abscesses, Ulcers, Boils	Decoction, Ointment, Thomson's Plaster	Burdock, Bloodroot, Oregon Grape

— continues on next page

Condition	Appropriate Preparations	Combines Well With:
Cancer	Decoction, Ointment, Thomson's Plaster	Violet, Burdock, Rock Rose, Oregon Grape
Tumors, Scrofula Swelling	Decoction, Ointment, Thomson's Plaster	Chickweed, Mullein, Bayberry, Blue Flag

Special Considerations: Many women—and some men—are beginning to take substantial amounts of Red Clover products with the expectation that the isoflavones will, like those from Soy, have beneficial effects on their hormone balances. It is important to remember that while Soy is a food, and can be eaten in substantial quantities, Red Clover is a medicinal herb with effects that could go well beyond its nutritive benefits, particularly if too much is consumed for too long. In addition to its isoflavones, Red Clover also provides high levels of coumarins, one of which has become the potent blood thinning drug (nee rat killer) warfarin, also known as coumadin. Attempting to use an herb for an isolated effect is a very UN-holistic and potentially unhealthy approach.

Notes: Samuel Thomson was seldom tenuous about any of his beliefs. His confidence that Red Clover was "good to cure cancers, sore lips and old sores" was no exception. Here is an updated recipe for his "Cancer Plaster."

Gather a good pressed gallon or so of Red Clover blossoms. If necessary, rinse them in a sink of cold water to remove any dust and grit. Drain on paper towels, and divide the pile into two equal quantities. Put one half of the blossoms into a stainless steel pot (NEVER aluminum), and add just enough distilled water to cover. Bring to a simmer over medium heat, and reduce the temperature to maintain a slow simmer for 1 hour. Strain out the spent blossoms, pressing to reclaim as much liquid as possible. Put the remaining half of the blossoms in the pot with the same liquid, and simmer them the same way for 1 hour. Strain and press as before. Return the liquid extract to the pot, place it over low heat, and simmer until it is reduced to the consistency of heavy syrup or molasses. Be very careful not to scorch it. It should be poured hot into small jars, sealed, and kept refrigerated. When needed, the plaster should be spread on muslin or flannel and secured over the lesion to be treated. It should be replaced daily until the desired result is achieved.

Energetics: Red Clover blossoms influence the Kidney, Bladder, Lung, and Large Intestine meridians. They are used to reduce damp conditions, hot and cold, and to relieve constraint of Lung and Bladder Chi.

Red Raspberry

Rubus idaeus, Rubus spp.
(Rosaceae)

Common Names: American Raspberry, Black Raspberry, Blackberry, Dewberry, Bramble Fruit, Thimble Berry

Physical Features: Red Raspberries, Black Raspberries, and Blackberries are all commonly cultivated in American gardens. While it is Red Raspberry that has captured the bulk of the notoriety in herbal literature, virtually all members of the bramble fruit (Rubus spp.) family can be used in similar fashion. Red Raspberry fruits range in color from deep pink to crimson red when ripe, though some varieties are actually golden yellow. Black Raspberries and Blackberries range from deep red to purplish black when ripe. All of the fruits are compound clusters of juicy segments that can form berries ranging in size from small globes the diameter of a dime to huge fruits larger than a man's thumb. Within the family, a distinction can be made between Raspberries and Blackberries based basically on the way the fruit separates from the plant. Raspberries, both red and black, separate cleanly from their core when picked, leaving the core and stem attached to the plant. Blackberries, even when fully ripe, cling tenaciously to their cores, and their stems will remain with the fruit when picked.

Leaves of the Rubus species are alternate, pinnately compound with 3 to 7 serrated leaflets, generally hairy, more or less deeply wrinkled, and finely toothed at the margins. All have medium to deep green upper leaf surfaces, with lighter colored undersides. The coloration difference is most pronounced amongst the Raspberries, with Red Raspberry having a silver, nearly white bottom surface. With few exceptions, all have arching, mostly hairless canes, 3 to 5 feet in height, that are generally well armed with downward hooking thorns. Blackberry and Black Raspberry cane tips will take root when they arch to the ground, and, if not controlled, will quickly form large, dense, virtually impenetrable thickets. Red Raspberry canes do not root from the tips, and propagate themselves exclusively by underground runners. The flowers, usually appearing in June and July, often hang in panicles or clusters, are greenish-white, with very small petals that fall away within a day or two, giving way to the developing fruit.

Historical Information: The fruit, leaves, and roots of the bramble fruits were well known to the ancient herbalists and our Native Americans as well. The Eclectics made great use of the strong astringency of Blackberry root, and it was officinal in the U.S.P. and National Formulary through the first third of the 20th century. Preparations of Red Raspberry leaves were the most cherished by folk practitioners, with whom they assumed powers of almost mythic proportions.

King's gave us an official view of the species in popular use.

> "These plants are useful as astringents. An infusion or decoction of the leaves of raspberry or the bark of the roots of the others has been found an excellent remedy in diarrhea, dysentery (chronic), cholera infantum, relaxed conditions of the intestines of children, passive hemorrhage from the stomach, bowels, or uterus, and in colliquative diarrhea. The decoction, used as an injection, is useful in gonorrhea, gleet, leucorrhea, and prolapsus uteri and ani. In prolapsus uteri, it may be used either alone or combined with the internal use of a decoction of equal parts of Black Cohosh and blackberry roots,

taken freely. Rubus villosus is especially adapted to children's diarrheas, the stools being copious, watery, and clay-colored. Such children are pale, fretful, without appetite, there is deficient glandular activity, and the gastro-intestinal tract shows evidence of enfeeblement and relaxation. The leaves of raspberry, in decoction with cream, will allay nausea and vomiting, and, combined with aromatics, have been found useful in diarrhea, cholera morbus, and cholera infantum. It is said that raspberry will, during labor, increase the activity of the uterine contractions when these are feeble, even in instances where ergot has failed, and that it has been found serviceable in after-pains. The fruit, especially that of the blackberry, makes an excellent syrup, which is of much service in dysentery, being pleasant to the taste, mitigating the accompanying tenesmus and sufferings of the patient, and ultimately effecting a cure. The fruit of the raspberry contains very little nourishment, (We have subsequently found differently. –Ed.) but is an agreeable acidulous article, rarely disturbing the stomach, and, when eaten freely, promotes the action of the bowels. Raspberry syrup, added to water, forms a refreshing and beneficial beverage for fever patients, and during convalescence."

The renowned Quaker herbalist, Henry Box, is quoted as saying,

"A tea made from Red Raspberry leaves is the best gift God ever gave to women. Its utility in travail is surprising. As a drink before and after confinement, it is unequaled by any other agent. If the pains of childbirth are premature, it will make all quiet. When timely, it will occasion a safe and easy parturition. If the mother is weak, it will abundantly strengthen her, cleanse her and enrich her milk. It is perfectly safe under all circumstances. Raspberry tea with a little Composition Powder (See "Notes" below. –Ed.) in it will effectually remove the afterpains, from which some suffer so severely. It is also most excellent in flooding, uterine hemorrhage, and to prevent miscarriage. For disorders of children, it is no less effectual. In thrush and its attendant disorders, during teething, bowel complaints, diarrhea, dysentery, urinary complaints, colds and fevers in all their stages, it is one of the most reliable remedies to which employment can be given."

Red Raspberry leaf tea has been taken freely during all phases of pregnancy, and particularly during the last trimester to tone the uterus, and prepare the body for delivery. Dr. Christopher summed it up thus:

"When taken regularly in pregnancy, the infusion will quiet inappropriate premature pains and produce a safe, speedy, and easy delivery. Raspberry leaves stimulate, tone, and regulate before and during childbearing, assisting contractions and checking hemorrhage during labor, relieving after-pains, then strengthening, cleansing, and enriching the milk of the mother in the post-delivery period."

Growing Range: Red Raspberry and its botanical cousins, Black Raspberry, Blackberry, Dewberry, etc., are widely cultivated and found in the wild in most of the country, and, indeed in most of the world. The Red Raspberry prefers the cooler regions, while the Black Raspberry and Blackberry is found more widely dispersed.

Parts Used: Leaves, fruit, root. Most species have similar medicinal value. Red Raspberry leaves are preferred as the most dependable and predictable general astringent tonic, and aid to female and children's issues. Blackberry Root is generally considered to be the most potent astringent of the group.

Cultivation/Wildcrafting Tips: The fruit should be gathered when fully ripe, and processed (or eaten) promptly, as they do not store well, even with refrigeration. They can, however, be washed and frozen for later use. The leaves may be collected throughout the growing season. To ensure proper preservation of their properties, they should be dried slowly in a well-ventilated area, turning and mixing frequently to avoid mold and discoloration. Roots should be dug when the plant is dormant, in the fall or early spring. They should be cleaned, and laid on screens to dry in a warm well ventilated room, or with the aid of some heat.

Primary Constituents: Polypeptides; Flavonoids, mainly glycosides of kaempferol and quercitin; Tannins; Fruit sugar; Volatile oil; Pectin; Citric acid; Malic acid; mineral salts; coloring matter, and water.

Blackberry Root bark contains up to 10% tannic acid, which can be readily extracted by boiling water or dilute alcohol. Rubus leaves and fruit are very rich in iron and calcium, and the fruits has large amounts of soluble fiber.

Action: astringent, tonic, alterative, anti-emetic, antiseptic, hemostatic, anti-abortive, parturient (leaves)

Tissues, Organs & Body Systems Affected: Genito-Urinary System, Mucus Membranes, Stomach, Intestines, Blood, all soft tissue

Preparations & Dosage:

INTERNAL	
Decoction (root bark)	1 tbsp chopped bark to 1 pint water; simmer 15–20 mins.; let stand until cool; strain; take 1 tbsp–2 oz., 3–4 times daily
Infusion (leaf)	2 tsp dried leaf to 1 cup boiling water; cover and let steep 10–15 min.; drink freely
Powder (leaf)	350–1500 mg.; 3–4 times daily
Tincture	15–60 drops in juice or water, frequently repeated as needed

EXTERNAL	
Decoction	Use hot as Fomentation; warm as wash or injection.
Infusion	Use warm as Injection, Douche, Gargle.
Ointment	Apply to affected area as needed.

Indicated Usages:

Condition	Appropriate Preparations	Combines Well With:
INTERNAL		
Amenorrhea, Dysmenorrhea	Infusion, Decoction, Tincture, Powder	Dandelion, Angelica
Canker Sores, Mouth Ulcers	Infusion, Tincture (also use as mouthwash, gargle)	Horsetail, Agrimony, Lemon Balm
Diabetes	Infusion, Decoction, Tincture, Powder	Thyme, Marshmallow, Capsicum, Gymnema
Diarrhea	Infusion, Decoction, Tincture, Powder	Slippery Elm, Bayberry, Plantain
Hemorrhoids	Decoction, Tincture, Powder	Cranesbill, Comfrey
Indigestion	Infusion, Tincture, Powder	Cleavers, Dandelion, Ginger
Leukorrhea	Infusion, Tincture (also as douche)	Trillium, Myrrh
Menorrhagia, Excessive Bleeding	Infusion, Decoction, Tincture, Powder	Capsicum, Prickly Ash, Wild Yam, Blue Cohosh
Miscarriage, Labor Pains (premature), Menstrual Cramps	Infusion, Tincture, Powder	Composition Powder
Morning Sickness	Infusion, Tincture, Powder	Ginger, Peppermint
Nausea (children)	Infusion, Tincture	Catnip, Fennel
Parturient	Infusion, Tincture, Powder	Capsicum, Composition Powder
Pregnancy	Infusion, Tincture, Powder	Alfalfa, Marshmallow, Peppermint
Thrush	Infusion, Tincture	Pau D'Arco
Urinary Tract Infection	Infusion, Tincture, Powder	Cornsilk, Thyme, Juniper Berries

Condition	Appropriate Preparations	Combines Well With:
EXTERNAL		
Bleeding Gums	Infusion, Tincture	White Oak, Bayberry
Eyewash	Infusion, Tincture	Sage, Eyebright
Hemorrhoids, Piles	Decoction, Ointment	Yarrow, Plantain
Sore Throat	Infusion, Tincture	Sage, Comfrey, Myrrh
Wounds, Burns	Decoction, Tincture, Ointment	Slippery Elm, Comfrey

Special Considerations: Rubus spp. root bark, particularly from the Blackberry, contains very high levels of tannins, and should not be combined in formulas with herbs that contain desirable active alkaloids. The leaves and fruit can generally be used without such a concern.

Those same tannins give Blackberry root bark the powerful astringency that is very useful for loose bowel conditions. Its use should be discontinued, though, as soon as the symptoms disappear, so that the opposite problem does not develop.

Notes: Composition Powder

This preparation originated with Samuel Thomson's practice, and became a mainstay of the Physio-Medical and Eclectic movements. Thomson's own guidance is still valid today. In his *New Guide to Health* (1841), he stated,

> "This composition is calculated for the first stages and in less violent attacks of disease. It is a medicine of much value, and may be safely used in all complaints of male or female, and for children. It is good for relax (i.e. diarrhea - Ed.), dysentery, pain in the stomach and bowels, and to remove all obstructions caused by cold, or loss of inward heat."

In addition to its specific applications, Composition Powder came to be used as a general tonic in all cases of debility, and was taken by many as a preventative measure against disease, particularly during outbreaks.

4 ounces	Bayberry Root bark powder
2 ounces	Ginger Root powder
1 ounce	Hemlock Spruce inner bark powder (Tsuga canadensis) (Dr. Christopher substituted White Pine bark powder)
1 teaspoon	Cloves, powdered
1 teaspoon	Capsicum powder

Mix the powders well, and pass through a sieve or sifter at least twice to thoroughly incorporate the herbs and remove any heavy particles. Usual dose is 1 teaspoon in a cup of boiling water, covered and infused for 10 to 15 minutes. Tea may be sweetened with raw sugar or honey, if desired, and taken several times a day.

Energetics: Raspberry Leaf exerts its influence over the Stomach, Lung, Bladder, Chong, Ren, and Dai meridians. It is used to balance deficient Chi conditions, and to relieve the damp heat of stomach Chi stagnation.

Sage

Salvia officinalis
(Labiateae)

Common Names: Common Sage, Garden Sage, Meadow Sage, Red Sage, Broad-leaved White Sage

Physical Features: Sage varies widely in size and leaf color. It generally grows to be a foot or more high, with wiry stems that are woody at the base. The leaves are set in pairs on the stem, and range from 1 to 2 inches long and ¾ to 1 inch broad. They are stalked, oblong, usually rounded at the ends, though some varieties are pointed, and are finely wrinkled by a strongly-marked network of veins on both sides. The leaves are usually grayish-green in color, though they can range from reddish green through pink and mottled with white. They are always softly hairy. The flowers are in whorls, purplish to red, and the corollas lipped. They blossom in late summer. All parts of the plant have a strong spicy fragrance when bruised, and a warm, slightly bitter, somewhat astringent taste.

Historical Information: Among the Ancients and throughout the Middle Ages Sage was held in high esteem. Hippocrates held that, "Cur moriatur homo cui Salvia crescit in horto?" ("Why should a man die while Sage grows in his garden?") In old England, another tradition maintained that the wife rules where Sage grows by the garden gate, but Gerard went on to credit it as being, "singularly good for the head and brain, it quickeneth the senses and memory, strengtheneth the sinews, restoreth health to those that have the palsy, and taketh away shakey trembling of the members." Culpeper says, "It is good for diseases of the liver and to make blood. A decoction of the leaves and branches of Sage made and drunk, saith Dioscorides, provokes urine and causeth the hair to become dark. It is profitable for all pains in the head coming of cold rheumatic humours, as also for all pains in the joints, whether inwardly or outwardly. The juice of Sage in warm water cureth hoarseness and cough. Sage is of excellent use to help the memory, warming and quickening the senses."

Later, Maud Grieve tells us, "Sage tea is a valuable agent in the delirium of fevers and in the nervous excitement frequently accompanying brain and nervous diseases, and has considerable reputation as a remedy, given in small and oft-repeated doses. It is highly serviceable as a stimulant tonic in debility of the stomach and nervous system and weakness of digestion generally. It was for this reason that the Chinese valued it, giving it the preference to their own tea. It is considered a useful medicine in typhoid fever and beneficial in biliousness and liver complaints, kidney troubles, hemorrhage from the lungs or stomach, for colds in the head as well as sore throat and quinsy and measles, for pains in the joints, lethargy and palsy. It will check excessive perspiration in phthisis cases, and is useful as an emmenagogue. A cup of the strong infusion will be found good to relieve nervous headache." She also relates that the fresh leaves, rubbed on the teeth, will cleanse them and strengthen the gums.

Among Native Americans, particularly in the Southwest, Sage is considered a sacred plant, with the whole herb and its tea being used in physical and spiritual purification rites. Contemporary herbalists have found Sage to be useful for all afflictions of the mouth and throat, and that when taken hot, it will provoke fever-breaking perspiration, but when taken cool or in capsules, that it will curb excessive sweating, dry up breast milk, and reduce mucous congestion. Recent scientific studies have shown anti-viral, anti-fungal, hypotensive, and anti-oxidant properties in the plant and its extracts.

Growing Range: Sage is a native to the Mediterranean states, and is cultivated worldwide. The plant is evergreen in the South, but needs to be protected, or grown as an annual in colder climates.

Parts Used: Leaves, fresh or dried; essential oil

Cultivation/Wildcrafting Tips: Sage grows best in sunny, relatively dry locations on sandy, slightly alkaline soil. The leaves should be gathered shortly before or just at the beginning of flowering in dry sunny weather starting in May or June and continuing through the summer. Dry in the shade or not above 100°F.

Primary Constituents: Volatile oil, containing a and b-thujone as the major components, with cineole, borneol, camphor, 2-methyl-3-methylene-5-heptene and others; Diterpene bitters, picrosalvin (= carnosol), carnosolic acid and others; Flavonoids, salvigenin, genkwanin, 6-methoxygendwanin, hispidulin, luteolin a; Phenolic acids, rosmarinic, caffeic, labiatic etc.; Salviatannin, a condensed catechin.

Action: aromatic, carminative, digestive, diaphoretic, stimulant, anti-spasmodic, anti-microbial, antioxidant, expectorant, hypotensive, astringent, anti-hydrotic, anti-inflammatory, anti-fungal, anti-viral, anti-thrombotic

Tissues, Organs & Body Systems Affected: Lungs, Sinuses, Mucus Membranes, Bowel, Bladder, Stomach, Brain, Heart, Nerves, Skin, Hair

Preparations & Dosage:

INTERNAL	
Infusion	Steep 10–30 minutes tightly covered. 6 oz.; 3–4 times daily, taken hot or cool as recommended.
Powder	2–4 #0 capsules (200–400 mg.), 3–4 times daily
Syrup	Mix tincture or strong decoction with equal parts sugar, glycerin or honey. 1 tsp to 1 tbsp; 3–4 times daily.
Tincture	½–1 tsp; 3–4 times daily in hot or cold water as recommended

EXTERNAL	
Fomentation	Prepare with decoction. Apply warm.
Skin Wash, Scalp Rinse	3 tbsp herb to 1 pint water. Simmer, tightly covered, 10 minutes, steep 20 minutes more. Strain.

Indicated Usages:

Condition	Appropriate Preparations	Combines Well With:
INTERNAL		
Alzheimer's, Dementia	Infusion, Tincture (cold), Powder	Ginkgo, Lemon Balm, Dandelion Flowers
Bronchitis, Emphysema	Infusion, Tincture (cold), Powder, Syrup	Wild Cherry, Comfrey
Excessive Sweating, Excessive Salivation	Infusion, Tincture (cold), Powder	Alfalfa, Yarrow
Fever	Infusion, Tincture (hot)	Ginger, Lemon Balm
Gum Disease	Infusion, Tincture (mouth rinse)	Cinnamon, Green Tea, Myrrh, Licorice
Hair Loss, Graying	Infusion, Tincture (cold), Powder	Horsetail, Dulse
Headache	Infusion, Tincture (hot)	Lemon Balm, Wood Betony
High Blood Pressure	Infusion, Tincture (cold), Powder	Garlic, Dandelion
Mouth Ulcers, Canker Sores	Infusion, Tincture (mouth rinse)	Lemon Balm, Plantain, Licorice
Nausea	Infusion, Tincture (warm)	Peppermint, Ginger
Nervous Exhaustion	Infusion, Tincture (hot), Powder	Suma, Ginseng
Night Sweats	Infusion, Tincture (cold), Powder	Alfalfa, Vitex (female), Sarsaparilla (male)
Sinus Congestion	Infusion, Tincture (cold), Powder	Ephedra, Thyme
Sore Throat, Tonsils Laryngitis	Infusion, Tincture (gargle), Powder, Syrup	Lemon Balm, Echinacea
Ulcers	Infusion, Tincture (cold), Powder	Capsicum, Garlic, Parsley
Weaning	Infusion, Tincture (cold), Powder	Parsley
EXTERNAL		
Bad Breath	Fresh Leaves, Infusion	Parsley, Peppermint
Itching, Pruritus	Fomentation	Plantain
Scalp Problems, Hair Loss, Graying	Scalp Rinse	Rosemary, Peppermint
Tumors	Fomentation	Chickweed
Wounds, Sores	Fomentation, Wash	Comfrey, Plantain

Special Considerations: Most herbals recommend against taking Sage while pregnant. It should not be taken in therapeutic does while nursing until weaning, as it can be used to dry up the flow of milk. Amounts used as a culinary seasoning do not have that effect.

Notes: The oils and components of Sage are extremely sensitive, and the dry herb should be stored with care. Leave as whole as possible, and protect from heat light and air. Powdered or ground herb should be discarded after 48 hours.

Energetics: Sage is used to balance deficient Chi and deficient Yin conditions. It affects the Spleen, Liver, Kidney, Lung, Chong, and Ren meridians. In Ayurveda, it is said to decrease Kapha, and regulate Vayu.

St. John's Wort

Hypericum perforatum
(Hypericaceae)

Common Names: Goat weed, Klamath Weed, Amber, Rosin rose, Witch's herb

Physical Features: St. John's Wort has woody stems, branched frequently to an ultimate height of 2 feet, and having an airy appearance overall. Leaves are small, dark green, oblong to oval, opposite in pairs or fours along the branches, and when individually held to the light, reveal a myriad of tiny transparent oil glands that appear as pin holes. The flowers appear close to the tips of the many branches, and have five bright yellow petals dotted with black along heir margins. The blossoms are crowned with a spray of prominent stamens that gives them an appearance that is hard to mistake.

Historical Information: The current popularity that St. John's Wort is enjoying as an anti-depressant and mood elevating remedy is reflected in its ancient roots. The very name Hypericum, is derived from the Greek, meaning "over the spectre," relating its almost magical ability to lift the darkness from the spirit. The herb's effect on the nervous system was recognized to be physical as well as spiritual, though, and it came into great use as a healing plant for conditions and injuries that affected the nerves as well as the flesh. Culpeper wrote that, "It is a singular wound herb. Boiled in wine and drank it heals inward hurts and bruises. Made into an ointment, it opens obstructions, dissolves swellings, and closes up the lips of wounds." Millspaugh (American Medicinal Plants, 1892) states that, "It is to the nervous system what Arnica is to the muscular," and reported that many cases of injury to the cranium and the spinal column have benefited by its use. Ellingwood also considered it specific for muscular bruises, deep soreness, and painful parts, and added that it should be used for a sensation of throbbing in the body without fever; burning pain, or deep soreness of the spine upon pressure, spinal irritation, circumscribed areas of intense soreness over the spinal cord or ganglia; concussion, shock or injury to the spine, and lacerated or punctured wounds in any location, accompanied with great pain. Priest & Priest tell us that it is a sedative nervine for muscular twitching and uncontrolled movements, being especially indicated for nerve injuries to the extremities and teeth/gums. They give the following specific indications: painful injuries to sacral spine and coccyx, traumatic shock, hemorrhoids with pain and bleeding, facial neuralgia after dental extractions and toothache, neurasthenia, chorea, and depression.

Modern herbalists have found that, taken internally, St. Johns Wort has a sedative and pain reducing effect, which gives it a place in the treatment of neuralgia, anxiety, tension, and similar disorders. It is especially well regarded as an herb to lift the burden of depression, and particularly useful where there are menopausal changes triggering depression, irritability and anxiety. In addition to neuralgic pain, it is used to ease fibrositis, sciatica and rheumatic pain. Externally it is a valuable healing and anti-inflammatory remedy. In an ointment it will speed the healing of wounds and bruises, varicose veins, and mild burns. The garnet-red oil extracted from the flowers is especially useful for the healing of sunburn.

Growing Range: Throughout North America, especially in the Northern tier, on dry ground, waste land and pastures.

Parts Used: Flowering tops

Cultivation/Wildcrafting Tips: The plant prefers sunny locations and relatively dry conditions. It is a rampant spreader, once established, and can become invasive. The entire plant above ground should be collected when in flower and dried as quickly as possible. Fresh flowers are best for making oil extract.

Primary Constituents: Essential oil, containing caryophyllene, methyl-2-octane, n-nonane, n-octanal, n-decanal, a- and b-pinene, and traces of limonene and myrcene; Hypericins, prenylated phloroglucin derivatives; hypericin, pseudohypericin and hyperforin; Miscellaneous flavonoids, () and (-) - epicatechin.

Action: anti-inflammatory, astringent, vulnerary, diuretic, alterative, nervine, sedative, anti-depressant, anti-microbial, anti-viral

Tissues, Organs & Body Systems Affected: Nervous System, Stomach, Bladder, Blood, Liver, Skin

Preparations & Dosage:

INTERNAL	
Infusion	Steep 5–15 minutes; 2–3 oz.; 3–4 times per day.
Powder	3–8 #0 capsules (1–3 gm.); 2–3 times daily
Tincture	10–30 drops; 3–4 times daily

EXTERNAL	
Fomentation	Prepare with strong infusion. Apply warm.
Oil (flowers or flowering tops)	As often as needed
Ointment	As often as needed

Indicated Usages:

Condition	Appropriate Preparations	Combines Well With:
INTERNAL		
Alcohol Withdrawal	Infusion, Tincture, Powder	Kudzu, Passion Flower
Bedwetting, Enuresis	Infusion, Tincture, Powder	Horsetail, Gravel Root
Bruises, Muscle Pain	Infusion, Tincture, Powder	Bugle, Comfrey, Plantain
Depression, Anxiety	Infusion, Tincture, Powder	Lemon Balm, Borage
Herpes	Infusion, Tincture, Powder	Lemon Balm, Echinacea

— continues on next page

— continued from previous page

Condition	Appropriate Preparations	Combines Well With:
HIV	Infusion, Tincture, Powder	Lemon Balm, Licorice, Hyssop, Astragalus
Neuropathy, Bell's Palsy	Infusion, Tincture, Powder	Gotu Kola, Siberian Ginseng, Suma
Parkinson's, BET, Restless Leg	Infusion, Tincture, Powder	Passion Flower, Evening Primrose Oil
Postpartum Pain & Depression	Infusion, Tincture, Powder	Gravel Root, Dong Quai, Red Raspberry
Smoking Cessation	Infusion, Tincture, Powder	Lobelia, Mullein
Spinal Injury/Pain	Infusion, Tincture, Powder, Homeopathic	Comfrey, Plantain, Evening Primrose Oil
Urinary Deficiency	Infusion, Tincture	Dandelion, Cornsilk
Uterine/Menstrual Pain	Infusion, Tincture, Powder	Dong Quai, Vitex
EXTERNAL		
Bruises	Fomentation, Oil, Ointment	Bugle, Plantain
Burns, Scalds, Sunburn	Fomentation, Oil, Ointment	Calendula, Aloe, Comfrey
Cuts, Abrasions	Fomentation, Oil, Ointment	Comfrey, Calendula, Myrrh
Spinal Injury	Fomentation, Oil	Comfrey, Evening Primrose
Swollen Glands	Fomentation	Mullein, Lobelia

Special Considerations: Concern has been expressed about the idea that long-term use of St. John's Wort may cause the skin to become more sensitive to sun exposure. Recent studies have shown that such use falls far short of producing the levels of hypericin in the skin that are considered to be photo-toxic. Nevertheless, it makes good sense to protect the skin from sun exposure, whether or not you are taking St. John's Wort preparations, and especially if you are fair-skinned to begin with.

Notes: Studies have suggested that St. John's Wort may be able to help protect the gastro-intestinal tract and the liver from the effects of radiation therapy.

Energetics: St. John's Wort is used to tonify Chi, and clear Kidney Chi constraint with damp cold. It affects the Lung, Liver, Kidney, and Bladder meridians.

Sassafras

Sassafras officinale, S. varifolium
(Lauraceae)

Common Names: Saxifrax, Saloop, Ague Tree, Cinnamon Wood

Physical Features: Sassafras is a shrubby tree in the North, but can grow to 30 feet in the South. The bark of new growth is glossy green with a slight orange tint, while mature bark is smooth orange brown. Leaves are 4 to 6 inches long, variable on the same plant, taking three distinct forms—single lobed oblong, two-lobed mitten shaped, and three-lobed with the center lobe more prominent than the outer two. Leaves are thick and leathery, smooth at the edges, and exude a moderately fragrant oil in hot weather, leaving their surface resiny to the touch. The whole plant has a distinct sweet spicy smell when injured, and even in the spring before leaves emerge, the identity of the plant can be confirmed by scraping the young bark with a fingernail and smelling. The roots are light rust orange when first dug, darkening with exposure, and have a strong "root beer" fragrance.

Historical Information: Discovered by the Spanish in Florida, Sassafras had long been used by Native Americans for its curative powers. It became a celebrated item of commerce throughout Europe, largely it seems, for its reputation as a cure for syphilis, or the "King's Evil" as it was known, and for its ability to relieve rheumatic conditions. Its fragrant oil and extracts were used in northern and central colonies as a curative and flavoring for tonics and fermented brews, and its characteristic smell and taste are still associated with Root Beer beverages, though in commercial use those characters are now synthesized. While it is still widely used as a blood purifier and "spring tonic" in rural America, Sassafras has fallen into disfavor with many herbal practitioners because of the controversy over its safrole content.

Growing Range: Eastern North America, from Canada to Florida

Parts Used: Root bark, root

Cultivation/Wildcrafting Tips: Roots should be gathered in the early spring, and washed thoroughly. Root bark should be peeled down to the white inner wood, and bark strips dried in the shade. Smaller roots may be chipped and dried in small pieces. Dried bark should be stored in dark, air-tight containers to preserve its aromatic qualities.

Primary Constituents: Volatile oil, containing safrole 80-90%, with 5-methoxy-eugenol, asarone, eugenol, A- and -phellandrene, -pinene, myristicin, thujone, caryophyllene, anethole, and others; Alkaloids, boldine, norboldine, isoboldine, norcinnamolaurine, reticuline, and others; Lignans, sesamin desmethoxy-aschantin; Tannin and phlobaphene, resin

Action: aromatic, alterative, stimulant, diaphoretic, diuretic, lithotriptic, tonic, antipsoriatic

Tissues, Organs & Body Systems Affected: Blood, Liver, Circulation, Intestines, Skin

Preparations & Dosage:

INTERNAL	
Decoction	Simmer 10 minutes in an uncovered pot, then steep for 15–20 minutes more. 4–6 oz.; 1–3 times daily for no more than 4 weeks.
Tincture	15–30 drops; 3–4 times daily for no more than 4 weeks

Indicated Usages:

Condition	Appropriate Preparations	Combines Well With:
INTERNAL		
Acne, Poison Ivy, Skin Eruptions	Decoction, Tincture	Burdock, Oregon Grape, Cleavers
Blood Purifier	Decoction, Tincture	Red Clover, Yellow Dock, Dandelion
Cramps, Dysmenorrhea	Decoction, Tincture	Gravel Root, Vitex, Dong Quai
Dysentery	Decoction, Tincture	Plantain, Marshmallow
Eczema, Psoriasis	Decoction, Tincture	Comfrey, Calendula
Fever	Decoction, Tincture (hot)	Sage, Dandelion
Rheumatism	Decoction, Tincture	Poke, Blackberry Root
Shingles	Decoction, Tincture	Licorice, Passion Flower
Skin Ulcers, Boils	Decoction, Tincture	Burdock, Comfrey, Lemon Balm
Stones, Calculi	Decoction	Hydrangea

Special Considerations: Sassafras should not be taken during pregnancy. Controversy over the use of Sassafras centers around the primary constituent of its volatile oil—safrole—which has been found to be carcinogenic. It is unwise to take Sassafras for extended periods (over 4 weeks), or in unlimited quantities. Commission E and FDA advise against taking it at all. (Safrole is also found in other common spices like Black Pepper, Anise, Cumin, Ginger, Bay Leaf, and Cinnamon. Research has shown that heating or cooking with these spices dramatically reduces the safrole content.)

Notes: Young Sassafras leaves may be gathered in spring, dried in shade, crumbled into small pieces, and stored in tight containers to be used as the Cajun culinary seasoning and thickening agent known as gumbo file.

Energetics: Sassafras is used to dispel wind/damp/cold in the systems, and in the Spleen in particular. It affects the Lung, Spleen, and Kidney meridians.

Thyme

Thymus vulgaris
(Labiatae)

Common Names: Garden Thyme, Mother-of-Thyme, Red Thyme, Lemon Thyme

Physical Features: Thyme is a perennial plant with a woody, fibrous root. The stems are numerous, round, hard, branched, and usually stand from 4 to 8 inches high. The whole plant is procumbent, forming dense low spreading mounds. The leaves are small, usually no more than about ⅛ inch long and 1/16 inch broad. They are narrow and elliptical, most commonly greenish-grey in color, pinched at the waist, and set in pairs upon very small foot-stalks. Leaves can vary greatly in color, ranging from reddish to dark green, with some variegated varieties available, and may be smooth or woolly. Tiny light lavender flowers terminate the branches in whorls. The plant has a very strong fragrance when bruised.

Historical Information: Maud Grieve tells us that most sources, "derive the name from the Greek word thumus, signifying courage, the plant being held in ancient and mediaeval days to be a great source of invigoration, its cordial qualities inspiring courage, and in the days of chivalry it was the custom for ladies to embroider a bee hovering over a sprig of Thyme on the scarves they presented to their knights." Though better known in modern times as a culinary herb, the ancients recognized it for its medicinal powers. According to Culpeper, Thyme is, "a noble strengthener of the lungs, as notable a one as grows, nor is there a better remedy growing for hooping cough. It purgeth the body of phlegm and is an excellent remedy for shortness of breath. It is so harmless you need not fear the use of it. An ointment made of it takes away hot swellings and warts, helps the sciatica and dullness of sight, and takes away any pains and hardness of the spleen. It is excellent for those that are troubled with the gout, and the herb taken anyway inwardly is of great comfort to the stomach."

The Eclectics were more specific. King's American Dispensatory describes Thyme as, "tonic, carminative, emmenagogue, and anti-spasmodic. The cold infusion is useful in dyspepsia, with weak and irritable stomach, and as a stimulating tonic in convalescence from exhausting diseases. The warm infusion is beneficial in hysteria, dysmenorrhea, flatulence, colic, headache, and to promote perspiration. Occasionally the leaves have been used externally, in fomentation. The oil is valuable as a local application to neuralgic and rheumatic pains; and, internally, to fulfil any of the indications for which the plant is used."

Modern herbalists value Thyme for its expectorant and antibacterial properties, and it is frequently used in preparations to support and protect the respiratory system. The essential oil is an effective disinfectant and natural preservative that is used in many skin preparations, not only for its therapeutic effect, but to protect the product itself from microbial contamination and spoilage. Recent studies have validated many of Thyme's broad range of actions, and have even recognized potent antioxidant properties that have anti-aging implications.

Growing Range: Thyme is native to the rocky slopes of the Mediterranean, and thrives in gardens wherever a similar habitat can be arranged.

Parts Used: Flowering tops, fresh or dried; essential oil

Cultivation/Wildcrafting Tips: Thyme prefers dry, sandy soil, and makes a first rate rock-garden plant. Some varieties have been grown between stepping stones on the garden path, and pleasantly scent the air when walked upon. It is fairly hardy, and does particularly well where winter temperatures do not fall below 10°F, or when given some winter protection. Plants should be thinned every spring, because it is a rampant self-sower, and the thinnings can be used to establish new sites. Its shallow root system rapidly depletes the soil in which it is growing, and so it is best to find new locations every 3 to 4 years. Shear the top third of the plant when in full flower, and use fresh, or dry carefully on screen wire in the shade to protect its volatile oils. Do not over water.

Primary Constituents: Volatile oil, of highly variable composition, the major constituent is thymol, with lesser amounts of carvacrol, with 1,8-cineole, borneol, geraniol, linalool, bornyl and linalyl acetate, thymol methyl ether and a-pinene; Flavonoids, apigenin, luteolin, thymonin, naringenin and others; labiatic acid, caffeic acid, tannins etc.

Action: aromatic, carminative, anti-septic, anti-viral, anti-spasmodic, expectorant, anti-tussive, astringent, anthelmintic, antioxidant, preservative

Tissues, Organs & Body Systems Affected: Lungs, Throat, Stomach, Intestines, Skin

Preparations & Dosage:

INTERNAL	
Essential Oil	1–3 drops; 3–4 times daily
Infusion	Steep, tightly covered, 15–30 minutes; 1–2 oz. frequently up to 16 oz. per day.
Powder	3–8 #0 capsules (750–2,000 mg.); 2–3 times daily
Tincture	15–60 drops; 3–4 times daily

EXTERNAL	
Body Oil	Add 4–5 drops essential oil to 1 oz. carrier oil.
Fomentation	Make with strong infusion. Apply hot.
Strong Infusion – Skin Wash, Scalp Rinse, etc.	Use 2 oz. fresh or dried herb to 1 Pint boiling water. Steep, tightly covered, 30–40 minutes. Strain.

Indicated Usages:

Condition	Appropriate Preparations	Combines Well With:
INTERNAL		
Asthma	Infusion, Tincture	Lobelia
Bronchitis	Infusion, Tincture, Essential Oil, Powder	Comfrey, Wild Cherry
Candidiasis	Infusion, Tincture, Essential Oil, Powder	Pau D'Arco
Colds, Flu	Infusion, Tincture, Essential Oil, Powder	Lemon Balm, Garlic, Echinacea
Cough	Infusion, Tincture, Syrup	Lobelia, Wild Cherry
E. Coli / Food Poisoning	Infusion, Tincture, Essential Oil, Powder	Activated Charcoal, Slippery Elm
Fever	Infusion (warm)	Sage, Hyssop
Migraine	Infusion, Tincture, Essential Oil, Powder	Lemon Balm, Feverfew
Mouth Ulcers, Canker Sores	Infusion, Tincture, Essential Oil (mouth rinse)	Sage, Lemon Balm
Nightmares	Infusion, Tincture	Passion Flower, Kava
Sore Throat, Laryngitis	Infusion, Tincture, Essential Oil (gargle)	Sage, Lemon Balm, Echinacea, Comfrey
Spastic Colon	Infusion, Tincture, Essential Oil, Powder	Marshmallow, Comfrey
Tuberculosis	Infusion, Tincture, Essential Oil, Powder	Lemon Balm, Comfrey
EXTERNAL		
Crabs, Lice	Strong Infusion (rinse), Oil	
Deodorant	Strong Infusion, Oil	Sage, Coriander
Fungal Infections	Fomentation, Strong Infusion, Oil	Tea Tree Oil
Muscle Spasms, Cramps	Fomentation, Oil	Lobelia, Capsicum
Skin Infections, Old Sores, Ulcers	Fomentation, Strong Infusion, Oil	Comfrey, Oregon Grape
Sty, Conjunctivitis	Fomentation	Eyebright

Special Considerations: Always use very small doses of Essential Oil of Thyme when using it internally. Thyme tea is perfectly safe for children, but it is best to give it in small but frequently repeated doses.

Notes: As an anti-septic and anti-viral agent, Essential Oil of Thyme makes an ideal disinfectant to diffuse in a sick room, or a crowded meeting place, especially when combined with Essential Oil of Lemon. Thymol, the main element of Thyme's volatile oil is a primary active ingredient in Listerine Antiseptic, which is made with essentially the same formula today as when it was originally formulated by Joseph Lister in 1874. Lister used Thyme and Eucalyptus disinfectants to revolutionize the practice of surgery by providing a sterile field and an antiseptic environment for surgery, a radical concept in its time.

Energetics: Thyme is used to address Lung Chi constraint, tonify general Chi, and restore balance to cold/damp conditions. It affects the Lung, Spleen, and Kidney meridians.

Vitex

Vitex agnus-castus
(Verbenaceae)

Common Names: Chaste Tree, Chaste Berries, Monk's Pepper

Physical Features: A deciduous shrubby tree of free spreading habit from 6 to 10 feet in height. The young shoots are covered with a fine gray down. Leaves are opposite, composed of a "hand" of 5 to 7 radiating leathery leaflets, ranging from 3 to 6 inches in length. Individual leaflets are linear, lance-shaped, toothed, dark green above, gray beneath with a very close downy surface. Flowers are pink or bluish-lavender, fragrant, produced in early fall, in whorls on slender racemes 3 to 6 inches long, and sometimes branched. The berries are about the same size and somewhat like peppercorns in appearance, dark purple or black, half covered by their Sage-green calyces, yellowish within, hard, having a very aromatic fragrance. The taste is warm and distinct.

Historical Information: Vitex has been used for thousands of years for its beneficial affect on the female glandular system, and its restraining effect on male hormones. Modern research has confirmed at least one of these uses, and the berries are now widely used to restore balance and function to the female reproductive system, by stimulating the natural production of progesterone. Some of the old herbals classify the berries as anaphrodisiac, accounting for the name Monk's Pepper, and the tradition of using the kernels to lessen the urges of the flesh. Other sources list the Vitex fruit as aphrodisiac, implying the opposite tendency. The truth is that Vitex, like many other herbs, exerts a normalizing influence on the body—restoring that which is absent, and constraining excessive tendencies. Vitex acts upon the pituitary gland, reducing the production of certain hormones and increasing the production of others, shifting the balance in favor of the gestagens, hormones that normally condition the body for pregnancy. It has found a wide following of users for imbalances of the female reproductive system, especially when they are related to excessive estrogen or xeno-estrogen influence, and has been used with great effect in restoring absent menstruation, regulating heavy periods, restoring fertility when caused by hormonal imbalance, relieving PMS tension, and easing the changes of menopause. A tincture of the berries has also been used externally for the relief of paralysis, pains in the limbs, and neuropathic muscular weakness.

Growing Range: Vitex is native to the Mediterranean, but it can be grown successfully in a wide variety of climates where winter temperatures do not drop below -10° F. It is also suitable for growing in large containers that can be protected in colder climates.

Parts Used: Dried berries

Cultivation/Wildcrafting Tips: Vitex thrives in full sun, warm temperatures, and moist ground. It seldom sets fruit in the North, unless planted against a sunny wall. The very dark berries should be picked when fully ripe, which is between October and November, just as the leaves begin to drop. They may be dried in sun or shade, and stored in dark, air-tight containers. Leave whole until use.

Primary Constituents: Iridoid glycosides including aucbin and agnoside; Flavonoids including casticin, isoVitexin and orientin; Essential oil.

Action: anaphrodisiac, aphrodisiac, diaphoretic, diuretic, febrifuge, infertility, ophthalmic, sedative, stomachic, galactogogue, women's complaints

Tissues, Organs & Body Systems Affected: Glandular System, Reproductive Organs, Nervous System

Preparations & Dosage:

INTERNAL	
Infusion	Steep 25–30 minutes; 3–4 oz.; 3–4 times daily.
Powder	2–3 #0 capsules (500–750 mg.); 3–4 times daily
Tincture	½ –1 tsp; 3–4 times daily

Indicated Usages:

Condition	Appropriate Preparations	Combines Well With:
INTERNAL		
Amenorrhea	Infusion, Tincture, Powder	Blue Cohosh, Dong Quai, Thyme
Infertility	Infusion, Tincture, Powder	False Unicorn
Menopausal Discomfort	Infusion, Tincture, Powder	Black Cohosh, Licorice, Red Clover, Flax Seed
Menstrual Cramps	Infusion, Tincture, Powder	Crampbark, Dong Quai, Squaw Vine
Nursing (to initiate; short term use only)	Infusion, Tincture, Powder	Raspberry, Blessed Thistle, Marshmallow
PMS	Infusion, Tincture, Powder	Burdock, Dong Quai, Evening Primrose Oil
EXTERNAL		
Nerve Deficiency	Tincture (liniment)	St. John's Wort

Special Considerations: Large doses of Vitex have been know to cause a nervous disorder known as formication, which manifests as a tingling sensation like insects crawling over the skin.

Notes: Vitex berries can be used as a mild substitute for black pepper, and can even be ground in a pepper mill. Not only will the safrole in the pepper be avoided, but the libido may get an attitude adjustment.

Energetics: In Traditional Chinese Medicine, Vitex is used to help balance Kidney Chi deficiency with damp cold. It affects the Liver, Kidney, Spleen, Lung, Chong, and Ren meridians.

Wild Cherry

Prunus serotina, P. virginiana
(Rosaceae)

Common Names: Black Cherry, Choke Cherry, Virginia Prune Bark, Rum Cherry

Physical Features: The Wild Cherry tree grows from 50 to 80 feet tall, and 2 to 4 feet in diameter, though larger specimens are rare because the wood is so desirable for furniture and cabinetry. The tree is usually unbranched for the first quarter of its height. The bark of young trees is shiny, silvery-gray, and banded. Mature bark is black and rough, and will often have hardened "tears" of resin where the bark has been injured. Leaves are long, usually 3 to 5 inches, and about ⅓ as wide, rather thick with short in-curved teeth at the edges, smooth and glossy on the upper surface, matte and silvery green on the bottom. The tree blooms in early spring, and are white, in erect long terminal racemes, with occasional solitary flowers in the axils of the leaves. Edible fruits ripen in late summer, are about the size of a small pea, purplish-black, and hang in loose clusters.

Historical Information: As a native American tree, Wild Cherry was unknown to the ancients, but its usefulness was quickly made evident to the colonists by the Indian tribal healers. The wood, extraordinarily strong and beautiful, was used in great quantities by craftsmen, which, in turn, also made ample stores of the medicinal bark readily available. Wild Cherry bark became one of the most popular and widely used medical herbs in America, becoming "officinale" in both Eclectic and Regular pharmacopeias, and to this day, many cough syrups and medicines still have the traditional "Wild Cherry" flavor—now artificially added, of course. From the Indians, colonists learned that the root bark and the aromatic inner bark of the Cherry trees have expectorant and mild sedative properties. A tea made from either of them had been used in the treatment of fevers, colds, sore throats, and diarrhea, and even used to ease pain in the early stages of labor. King's American Dispensatory reflects the uses learned from the Natives, as well as new applications that evolved from their own experiences. According to King, "Wild Cherry bark has a tonic and stimulating influence on the digestive apparatus, and a simultaneous sedative action on the nervous system and circulation. It is, therefore, valuable in all those cases where it is desirable to give tone and strength to the system, without, at the same time, causing too great an action of the heart and blood vessels, as, during convalescence from pleurisy, pneumonia, acute hepatitis, and other inflammatory and febrile diseases. Its chief property is its power of relieving irritation of the mucous surfaces, making it an admirable remedy in many gastro-intestinal, pulmonic, and urinary troubles." The Eclectics considered Wild Cherry specific for rapid, weak circulation; continual irritative cough, with profuse muco-purulent expectoration; cardiac palpitation, from debility; dyspnea; pyrexia; loss of appetite; and cardiac pain.

Growing Range: North America, Nova Scotia to Minnesota, south to Florida and Texas; also in Arizona and New Mexico

Parts Used: Inner bark

Cultivation/Wildcrafting Tips: Wild Cherry trees can be found in almost any wooded area in the Eastern half of the U.S., and in deciduous stands of the Southwest. The tree prefers moist fertile conditions on north or east facing slopes. The bark should be harvested in autumn when the active constituents are at their peak. It is best when taken from 4 to 6 inch thick branches or trunks of trees being thinned.

The bark layers can be easily peeled, one at a time. Remove the outer gray bark and discard it. Lift the fawn-red under bark away in strips, and dry in the shade, or with low heat. This bark must be freshly collected each season as its properties deteriorate rapidly, and it should not be kept for longer than a year. Tinctures last much longer, and represent the best way to preserve your supply. The fresh bark has an odor like almonds, which almost disappears as it dries. If dried bark is still reasonably active, the smell should return almost as strong after it has been soaked for an infusion or tincture.

Primary Constituents: Prunasin, a cyanogenetic glycoside; Benzaldehyde; Miscellaneous others, including 3,4,5-trimethoxybenzoic acid (= eudesmic acid), p-coumaric acid, scopoletin (a coumarin derivative), tannins, sugars.

Action: astringent, tonic, pectoral, sedative, anti-tussive, stomachic

Tissues, Organs & Body Systems Affected: Lungs, Respiratory System, Stomach, Nervous System, Heart

Preparations & Dosage:
NOTE: Boiling destroys much of Cherry bark's medicinal properties. Unlike most other roots and barks, it should NOT be prepared by decoction.

INTERNAL	
Infusion	Pour 1 pint boiling water over 1 oz. ground bark. Cover and soak for 3–4 hours. Strain. 2–3 oz.; 3–4 times daily.
Powder	2–4 #0 capsules (600–1,200 mg.), 3 times daily
Syrup	Add tincture to equal part raw honey, vegetable glycerin, or simple syrup. 1–2 tsp; 3–4 times daily.
Tincture	½–1 tsp; 3–4 times daily

EXTERNAL	
Fomentation	Prepare with strong infusion. Apply warm.
Tincture	Equal parts with distilled water as wound wash

Indicated Usages:

Condition	Appropriate Preparations	Combines Well With:
INTERNAL		
Asthma	Infusion, Tincture, Powder	Lobelia, Mullein
Bronchitis	Infusion, Tincture, Syrup, Powder	Comfrey, Goldenseal
Colds, Flu	Infusion, Tincture, Syrup, Powder	Lemon Balm, Thyme

— continues on next page

— continued from previous page

Condition	Appropriate Preparations	Combines Well With:
Diarrhea	Infusion, Tincture, Powder	Marshmallow, Comfrey
Nervous Indigestion	Infusion, Tincture, Syrup, Powder	Comfrey, Peppermint
Palpitations, Arrhythmia	Infusion, Tincture, Powder	Hawthorn, Passion Flower
Persistent Cough	Infusion, Tincture, Syrup, Powder	Thyme, Comfrey, Mullein, Horehound
Tuberculosis	Infusion, Tincture, Syrup, Powder	Lemon Balm, Comfrey, Thyme
EXTERNAL		
Eye Inflammation	Fomentation	Eyebright
Indolent Ulcerations	Fomentation, Tincture (wash)	Comfrey, Sage, Thyme

Special Considerations: The primary active constituent in the bark is the glycoside prunasin, which is converted in the digestive tract to hydrocyanic acid.

In large doses, hydrocyanic acid is poisonous. In small amounts, this toxic compound stimulates respiration, improves digestion, relaxes the nervous system, and gives a general sense of well-being. Prunasin is at its highest level in the bark in the autumn, so the bark is harvested at this time and can be dried for later use.

Notes: Comfrey Root Tincture and Wild Cherry Tincture are extremely complimentary aids to the respiratory system. An excellent cough medicine can be made by combining 1 part of each of those tinctures with 1 part each of vegetable Glycerin and raw honey. A small amount of Tincture of Capsicum or Ginger Root and an equal amount of Tincture of Lobelia will "activate" the formula, and as much as ¼ part of Tincture of Thyme or Lemon Balm will enhance its anti-microbial properties.

Wild cherries are astringent, and their juice has been used to relieve diarrhea. Sweet cherries, on the other hand, can be laxative.

Energetics: Wild Cherry treats conditions presenting Yin deficiency with empty heat, and constrained Lung Chi. It affects the Lung, Heart, and Large Intestine meridians.

Willow

Salix alba, Salix spp.
(Salicaceae)

Common Names: European Willow, White Willow

Physical Features: While sometimes shrubby in stature, White Willow can also grow to a substantial size, sometimes reaching 60 feet or more in height. The bark is rough and deeply fissured, grayish in color. The leaves are long and slender being four or more inches in length and ¾ to 1 inch broad, light green in color, and softly fuzzy on both surfaces giving them a silvery appearance, especially on the underside. Outer branches are slender, swaying easily in the breeze, and twiggy growth is very brittle at the base, breaking easily away from the trunk and main branches. Willows hybridize easily between species, and so may be widely variable. The tree flowers in early spring, after the leaves have developed, producing soft, elongated catkins with yellow anthers. All of the Willows, including the Pussy Willow and the Weeping Willow, have similar medicinal properties.

Historical Information: Willow is the source of Salicin, only the second specific chemical drug isolated from botanical sources (the first was Coniine, a powerful nerve sedative from the Water Hemlock). Salicin, discovered in 1828, is the precursor to modern aspirin—which is synthesized as acetylsalicylic acid. The ability of Willow bark to reduce fevers and alleviate pain has been known for centuries, though the ancients found many other virtues in the tree. Culpeper tells us that, "Both the leaves, bark, and the seed, are used to staunch bleeding of wounds, and at the mouth and nose, spitting of blood, and other fluxes of blood in man or woman, and to stay vomiting, if the decoction of them in wine be drank." He also reports, or perhaps warns of, an attribute somewhat less popular in these times. "The leaves bruised and boiled in wine, and drank, stays the heat of lust in man or woman, and quite extinguishes it, if it long be used." Later, Eclectics recommended Willow for, "atonic conditions of the gastro-intestinal tract, especially where there is increased mucous secretion, passive hemorrhage, chronic diarrhea and dysentery, and diarrhea in children."

Modern herbalists often use Willow bark as a mild analgesic in structural pain, and for many of the other purposes for which people take aspirin. Master Herbalist and USDA pharmacognacist, James Duke, includes Willow bark in his herbal recommendations for everything from anti-aging to warts.

Growing Range: On moist ground, throughout North America

Parts Used: Inner bark

Cultivation/Wildcrafting Tips: Willow can be found growing alongside streams, ponds, ditches, and roadsides, wherever the ample water can be reached. (Salix comes from the Celtic sal-lis, meaning "near water.") Large branches can be gathered throughout the summer when the tree is in leaf, and the bark easily separated from the wood. Inner and outer bark layers are then separated, and the inner bark may be dried in strips in the shade or with low heat.

Primary Constituents: Phenolic glycosides including, salicin, picein and triandrin, with esters of salicylic acid and salicyl alcohol, acetylated salicin, salicortin and salireposide; plus miscellaneous tannins, catechin, p-coumaric acid and flavonoids.

Action: analgesic, anti-inflammatory, tonic, bitter, astringent, anti-periodic, anodyne, diaphoretic, antiseptic, diuretic, anti-thrombotic

Tissues, Organs & Body Systems Affected: Stomach, Kidney, Bowels, Nerves, Circulation

Preparations & Dosage:

INTERNAL	
Decoction	1 tbsp bark to 1 cup water. Soak 4–5 hours, bring to boil, simmer 10 minutes, cover and let stand till cool. 2–3 oz.; 3–4 times daily.
Powder	3–9 #0 capsules (1,000–3,000 mg.); 3–4 times daily
Tincture	½–1 tsp; as needed

Indicated Usages:

Condition	Appropriate Preparations	Combines Well With:
INTERNAL		
Arthritis, Muscle/Joint Pain	Decoction, Tincture, Powder	Bugle, Licorice, Turmeric
Dysentery, Diarrhea	Decoction, Tincture, Powder	Slippery Elm, Black Walnut, Pau D'Arco
Fever	Decoction, Tincture, Powder	Gravel Root
Hangover	Decoction, Tincture, Powder	Wintergreen, Ginger, Gotu Kola
Headache	Decoction, Tincture, Powder	Lemon Balm
Heart Protection	Decoction, Tincture, Powder	Garlic, Hawthorn
Internal Bleeding	Decoction, Tincture, Powder	Bugle, Plantain
Kidney Infections	Decoction, Tincture, Powder	Juniper Berries, Uva Ursi, Cornsilk
Mouth Ulcers, Canker Sores	Decoction, Tincture, Powder	Lemon Balm, Thyme
Neuralgia	Decoction, Tincture, Powder	St. John's Wort
Prostatitis	Decoction, Tincture, Powder	Saw Palmetto, Pygeum
Urine Retention	Decoction, Tincture	Dandelion
EXTERNAL		
Foot Odor	Decoction (soak)	Pau D'Arco
Mouth Sores, Gingivitis	Decoction (rinse)	Lemon Balm, Thyme
Tonsillitis	Decoction (gargle)	Sage, Thyme

Special Considerations: Allergy to aspirin might provoke a similar response to Willow preparations. Exercise caution when first using Willow when an aspirin allergy is present.

Notes: Activated Charcoal is made from kiln-burned White Willow logs.

A chip of Willow bark, soaked overnight in Castor oil, can be taped onto a wart to effect its removal. Apply a freshly prepared chip each day for five days.

Energetics: Willow is used to treat the empty heat of Yin deficient conditions, particularly of the Heart and Kidney. It affects the Bladder, Kidney, Heart, and Stomach meridians.

Yarrow

Achillea millefolium
(Compositae)

Common Names: Milfoil, Millefolium, Soldier's Woundwort, Knight's Milfoil, Nose Bleed, Carpenter's Weed, Bloodwort, Staunchweed

Physical Features: The stem is angular and rough. The dark green leaves are alternate, 3 to 4 inches long and 1 inch broad. They are bipinnate—deeply divided—which gives them a feathery, fern-like appearance. The plant stands from 12 to 30 inches tall; is more or less hairy overall, and is topped in mid-summer to early fall with flattened, loose cymes of densely packed white to pale lilac flowers.

Historical Information: Yarrow was formerly much esteemed as a vulnerary, and its old names of Soldier's Wound Wort and Knight's Milfoil testify to this. Gerard tells us it is the same plant with which Achilles stanched the bleeding wounds of his soldiers, hence the name of the genus, *Achillea*. By the Ancients themselves, it was called Herba Militaris, the military herb. Its ability to quickly stop nosebleeds gave it another of it popular names. The species name, *millefolium*, is derived from the many feathery segments of its foliage.

In Sweden it is called Field Hop, and has been used in the brewing of beer. Linnaeus, who also recommended the bruised herb, fresh, as an excellent vulnerary and styptic, considered beer thus brewed more intoxicating than when Hops were used.

King tells us that,

> "Its use in chronic diseases of the urinary apparatus, is especially recommended by Prof. J. M. Scudder. It exerts a tonic influence upon the venous system, as well as upon mucous membranes. It has been efficacious in sore throat, hemoptysis, hematuria and other forms of hemorrhage where the bleeding is small in amount; incontinence of urine, diabetes, hemorrhoids with bloody or mucoid discharges, and dysentery. Also in amenorrhea, flatulency and spasmodic diseases, and in the form of injection in leucorrhea with relaxed vaginal walls. It will be found to be one of our best agents for the relief of menorrhagia."

Priest & Priest tell us that it is a mild, slow, and stimulating diaphoretic that is best used for the first stage of acute fevers, and for atonic and relaxed tissues where there is free discharge or passive hemorrhage of bright red blood. They recommend cold preparations to stimulate the appetite and tone the digestive organs, and give the following specific indications: Acute stage of colds; influenza and respiratory catarrhs; chronic diarrhea and dysentery; epistaxis; intestinal hemorrhage, bleeding hemorrhoids; uterine hemorrhage; profuse or protracted menstruation; and leucorrhea.

Ellingwood considered it specific for hot, dry burning skin, at the beginning of acute asthenic fevers, with suppressed secretion; deficient renal action, with renal or urethral irritation; acute or chronic Brights disease in its incipient stage; leucorrhea with relaxed vaginal walls; menorrhagia and amenorrhea; hemorrhoids with bloody discharge; atonic gastric and intestinal dyspepsia; and passive hemorrhages. He also considered it useful for these pathologies: hematuria, uterine hemorrhage, intestinal irritation, leucorrhea, fevers, uremia, edema, tonsillitis, and epididymitis.

More recently, Dr. Christopher explained why he favored the herb.

"Yarrow, when administered hot and copiously, will raise the heat of the body, equalize the circulation, and produce perspiration. It opens the pores freely by relaxing the skin, and it purifies the blood of toxins. Yarrow regulates the liver and the secretions of the entire alimentary canal; it tones the mucus membranes of the stomach and bowels, and is healing to the glandular system. Yarrow will never weaken a patient, because of its tonic action."

Yarrow has a long history as a magical herb in both Eastern and Western cultures. Stems of Yarrow are used to divine the Chinese "I Ching."

Growing Range: Yarrow grows everywhere, in the grass, in meadows, pastures, and by the roadside. As it creeps greatly by its perennial roots and multiplies by seeds, some gardeners consider it a troublesome weed. Others flock to nurseries to buy it to plant for its delicate foliage, dense and enduring blossoms, and its carefree nature.

Parts Used: The above ground parts; the stems, leaves and flowers

Cultivation/Wildcrafting Tips: The whole of the plant above ground should be gathered when in full flower between June and September. It can be tied in loose bundles, and hung to dry in the shade.

Primary Constituents: Volatile oil, containing a- and b-pinenes, borneol, bornyl acetate, camphor, caryophyllene, eugenol, farnesene, myrcene, sabinene, salicylic acid, terpineol, thujone and many others, and including the sesquiterpene lactones. (Many samples contain high concentrations of azulenes—potent anti-inflammatory and skin healing agents—up to about 50%, including chamazulene and guajazulene.); flavones as 5-hydroxy- 3,6,7,4'-tetramethoxyflavone, artemetin, and casticin; Sesquiterpene lactones: achillin, achillicin, hydroxyachillin, balchanolide, leucodin, millifin, millifolide and others; Flavonoids: apigenin, luteolin, quercitin and their glycosides, artemetin, casticin, rutin, and others; Alkaloids and bases: betonicine (= achilleine), stachydrine, achiceine, moschatine, trigonelline and others; Miscellaneous acetylenes, aldehydes, cyclitols, plant acids, resin, tannin, gum and ash. Yarrow provides significant amounts of Potassium, Calcium, Magnesium, Iron, Phosphorus, Silicon, and vitamin C.

Action: diaphoretic, hypotensive, astringent, hemostatic, anti-inflammatory, diuretic, anti-microbial, anti-viral, bitter, hepatic, vulnerary, emmenagogue

Tissues, Organs & Body Systems Affected: Circulation, Lungs, Skin, Mucus Membranes, Urinary System

Preparations & Dosage:

INTERNAL	
Decoction	1 oz. dried herb to 1 qt. water; simmer down to 1 pint; strain, keep refrigerated; take ½ cup 3–4 times daily
Infusion	1–3 tsp finely chopped herb to 1 cup boiling water; cover and infuse for 10–15 min; drink hot 3–4 times daily, hourly for fevers
Tincture	15–60 drops; 3–4 times daily, hourly in hot water for fevers

EXTERNAL	
Oil Extract	Apply to affected area as needed.
Ointment	Apply to affected area as needed.

Indicated Usages:

Condition	Appropriate Preparations	Combines Well With:
INTERNAL		
Arthritis	Infusion, Tincture, Decoction	Turmeric, Wild Yam, Devil's Claw
Bedwetting	Infusion, Tincture	Dandelion, Cornsilk
Colds, Flu	Infusion, Tincture (in hot water)	Elder Flowers, Echinacea
Diarrhea (adults)	Tincture, Decoction	Blackberry Root, Slippery Elm
Diarrhea (infants)	Infusion (also give 2-4 oz. as rectal injection)	Catnip, Chamomile
Fever	Infusion, Tincture, Decoction	Boneset, Capsicum
Gout	Infusion, Tincture, Decoction	Sage, Dandelion, Celery Seed
Hemorrhage	Infusion, Tincture, Decoction	Plantain, Capsicum, Red Raspberry
Hemorrhoids	Infusion, Tincture, Decoction	Blackberry Root, Bugle
High Blood Pressure	Infusion, Tincture, Decoction	Nettles, Prickly Ash, Linden Flowers
Jaundice	Infusion, Tincture, Decoction	Dandelion, Barberry
Measles	Infusion, Tincture	Lemon Balm, Oregon Grape, Lobelia
Menorrhagia, Heavy Bleeding	Infusion, Tincture, Decoction	Red Raspberry, Blue Cohosh, Capsicum
Rheumatism	Infusion, Tincture, Decoction	Black Cohosh, Nettles
Skin Eruptions	Infusion, Tincture	Red Clover, Comfrey, Calendula, Cleavers
Urinary Discharges	Infusion, Tincture	Dandelion, Juniper Berries, Cornsilk

Condition	Appropriate Preparations	Combines Well With:
EXTERNAL		
Bleeding, Hemorrhage	Tincture, Fresh Herb	Nettles, Alum Root, Cranesbill, Capsicum
Hair Loss	Infusion, Tincture, Decoction, Oil Extract	Sage, Capsicum, Horsetail
Hemorrhoids	Decoction (as retention enema), Ointment	Blackberry Root, Alum Root, Bugle, Comfrey
Nosebleed	Tincture (on cotton wadding), Fresh Herb (crushed)	
Sore Nipples	Oil Extract, Ointment	Marshmallow, Calendula Flowers
Wounds, Burns	Tincture, Oil Extract, Ointment, Poultice (fresh herb)	Comfrey, Oregon Grape, Chickweed

Notes: Yarrow is difficult to reduce to a powder, even when fully dried. It is best used to make liquid extracts.

Energetics: Yarrow has influence over the Liver, Kidney, Bladder, Spleen, Heart, Chong, and Ren meridians. It is said to vitalize the blood, relieve and tonify stagnant Chi, and dispel wind cold/heat conditions.

Yellow Dock

Rumex crispus
(Polygonaceae)

Common Names: Curly Dock

Physical Features: Yellow Dock is a coarse perennial plant, growing from 2 to 4 feet in height. Leaves are thick and leathery, long and lance shaped, and decidedly curled or "crisped" at the edges. The leaves stand on long thick stems around the crown of its tap root. The flower and seed stalk is prominent, round and thick, standing well above the leaf tips, and when mature, is topped by masses of reddish-brown, papery, 3-angled seed cells, each approximately ⅜ inch across. The root is thick, spindle shaped, often 10 to 14 inches long, infrequently branched, and yellow inside. Taste is bitter.

Historical Information: Yellow Dock has been used extensively since ancient times in the treatment of "bad blood," especially as related to chronic skin complaints such as psoriasis. The anthraquinones present have a markedly cathartic action on the bowel, but in this herb they act in a mild way, possibly tempered by the tannin content. Thus it makes a valuable remedy for constipation, working as it does in a much wider way than simply stimulating the intestinal muscles. It promotes the flow of bile, and its action on the gall-bladder has given it a role in the treatment of jaundice when this is due to congestion. Priest & Priest tell us that it is a general tonic alterative with special influence upon skin eruptions. They give the following specific indications: simple deficiency anemias, eczema, psoriasis, urticaria, prurigo, and itching hemorrhoids. Ellingwood considered that its alterative properties are underestimated, saying that, "It is a renal depurant and general alterative of much value when ulceration of mucous surfaces or disease of the skin resulting from impure blood. It acts directly in its restorative influence, purifying the blood, removing morbidic material and quickly cures the disease conditions." In addition he recommends it for the following pathologies: ulcerative stomatitis, nursing sore mouth, syphilis, scrofula, cancer, and tuberculosis. King's American Dispensatory describes its specific indications as being, "bad blood with chronic skin disease; bubonic swellings; low deposits in glands and cellular tissues, and tendency to indolent ulcers; feeble recuperative power; irritative, dry laryngo-tracheal cough; stubborn, dry, summer cough; chronic sore throat, with glandular enlargements and hypersecretion; nervous dyspepsia, with epigastric fullness and pain extending through left half of chest; and cough, with dyspnea." The root is highly prized by modern herbalists as one of the richest sources of iron, and is used in most "blood cleansing" formulas.

Growing Range: Yellow Dock and its close cousins grow on every continent except Antarctica. It can be found in every state in the United States.

Parts Used: Root

Cultivation/Wildcrafting Tips: The plant is so prevalent in pastures and cultivated ground, along roadsides and ditches, and even in lawns, that it seldom needs to be cultivated. The roots may be dug at anytime after the seed heads have matured and the tops begin to die, until the early spring before new growth starts. Roots should be well cleaned, and split lengthways or sliced before drying in the shade or with low heat.

Yellow Dock

Primary Constituents: Anthraquinone glycosides, about 3-4%, including nepodin, and others based on chrysophanol, physcion and emodin; Flavonoids including quercitin; Rumicin; Tannins, and oxalates.

Action: alterative, astringent, laxative, hepatic, cholagogue, tonic, nutritive

Tissues, Organs & Body Systems Affected: Blood, Liver, Spleen, Gall Bladder, Skin

Preparations & Dosage:

INTERNAL	
Decoction	Simmer 5–15 minutes. ½–1 tbsp in water; 3–4 times daily.
Powder	3–8 #0 capsules (1–3 gm.); 3 times daily
Syrup	1 tsp; 3–4 times daily
Tincture	5–30 drops; 3–4 times daily

EXTERNAL	
Fomentation	Prepare with decoction. Apply hot as tolerated.
Ointment	As needed
Poultice	Simmer fresh or dried root in cider vinegar until fiber softens. Pound and apply in gauze or flannel.

Indicated Usages:

Condition	Appropriate Preparations	Combines Well With:
INTERNAL		
Acne, Skin Eruptions	Decoction, Tincture, Powder	Cleavers, Horsetail, Burdock
Anemia	Decoction, Tincture, Powder	Dandelion, Safflowers
Constipation	Decoction, Tincture, Syrup, Powder	Dandelion, Slippery Elm, Marshmallow
Eczema, Psoriasis	Decoction, Tincture, Syrup, Powder	Comfrey, Oregon Grape, Burdock
Emphysema, Bronchitis	Decoction, Tincture, Syrup, Powder	Comfrey, Mullein, Wild Cherry
Hemorrhoids	Decoction, Tincture, Powder	Bugle, Comfrey, Bayberry Bark
Jaundice, Liver Congestion	Decoction, Tincture, Syrup, Powder	Dandelion, Red Beet, Barberry
Lymphatic Congestion	Decoction, Tincture, Syrup, Powder	Echinacea, Mullein, Poke
Tonic (digestive)	Decoction, Tincture, Syrup, Powder	Dandelion, Peppermint
Vaginitis, Leukorrhea	Decoction, Tincture, Powder	Echinacea, Goldenseal, Siberian Ginseng

Condition	Appropriate Preparations	Combines Well With:
EXTERNAL		
Boils, Ulcers, Skin Disorders	Fomentation, Poultice, Ointment	Comfrey, Calendula, St. John's Wort
Hemorrhoids	Retention Enema	Bugle, Comfrey, Bayberry Bark
Itching, Pruritus	Fomentation, Ointment, Wash	Plantain, Ginger
Tumors	Decoction, Tincture, Syrup, Powder	Mullein, Lobelia, Chickweed

Special Considerations: The Docks, like Rhubarb, harbor high levels of toxic oxalates in the leaves, and that part of the plant is seldom consumed. The root also contains some oxalates, and should not be consumed in large quantities, or for very long periods. Black tea or coffee should not be consumed while taking Yellow Dock, or other strong iron tonics.

Notes: At various stages of growth, Yellow Dock can be confused with Horseradish—that is, until the roots are tasted.

Yellow Dock is a "combination friendly" herb that is synergistic with many other plants. It is particularly good as a "blood cleanser" when combined with Red Clover, Burdock, Cleavers, and Barberry.

Energetics: Yellow Dock releases wind damp and heat in the skin. It is used to reduce Chi stagnation of the Liver, Gall Bladder, and Intestines. It affects the Liver, Kidney, and Large Intestine meridians.

APPENDIX A

Glossary of Terms for the Herbal Practitioner

A

Abortifacient: substance that induces abortion or miscarriage.

Abscess: a localized collection of pus and liquefied tissue in a cavity.

Absolute: a highly concentrated viscous, semi-solid or solid perfume material, usually obtained by alcohol extraction from the concrete.

Absorbent: stimulating resorption of exudates or diseased tissue.

Acetylcholine: a neurotransmitter.

Achlorhydria: absence of hydrochloric acid in the stomach.

Acid: a compound producing hydrogen ions in aqueous solution. Acidic refers to a pH number below 7.0.

Acidosis: abnormal state of reduced alkalinity of blood and tissues.

Acrid: leaving a burning sensation in the mouth.

ACTH: adrenocorticotropic hormone.

Acupressure: manual application of pressure at points along the meridians where acupuncture needles would be inserted.

Acupuncture: Traditional Chinese Medicine practice that involves insertion of needles into body at specific points along energy meridians to treat disease and reduce pain.

Acute: designating disease with rapid onset, severe symptoms, and brief duration, opposite of chronic.

Acute abdomen: emergency condition caused by damage to one or more abdominal organs that results in intense pain and shock.

Adaptogen: herbs that increase resistance and resilience to stress, enabling the body to avoid reaching functional collapse because it can adapt around the problem.

Addison's disease: condition marked by weakness, low blood pressure, and dark pigmentation due to inadequate hormone secretion by adrenal glands.

Adenitis: regional inflammation of gland or lymph node.

Adenocarcinoma: malignant epithelial tumor in glandular tissue.

ADH: antidiuretic hormone.

Adhesion: union by abnormal fibrous connective tissue of two normally separate parts.

Adipose: fat in connective tissue.

Adrenaline: hormone secreted by the adrenal gland which produces the 'fight or flight' response. Also called epinephrine.

Adrenergic: compound that acts like epinephrine or norepinephrine.

Adrenocorticotropic hormone: ACTH; polypeptide secreted by anterior pituitary that stimulates adrenal cortex to secrete cortisol.

Aerophagy: swallowing of air.

Agar: polysaccharide derived from seaweed, used as culture medium for microorganisms; gelatinous natural laxative.

Agglutinin: substance, esp. Antibody, that causes bacteria, blood cells, and antigens to clump together.

Agranulocytosis: acute illness caused by chemicals or drug reaction in which certain white blood cells disappear, causing rapid, massive infection.

Ague: malaria; general malaise marked by fever.

AIDS: acquired immune deficiency syndrome; severe weakening or destruction of body's immune system by human immunodeficiency virus.

Aids related complex: ARC; chronic enlargement of lymph nodes and persistent fever caused by aids virus.

Albumin: most abundant protein found in blood plasma.

Albuminuria: presence of protein albumin in urine.

Aldosterone: a hormone secreted by the adrenal gland which causes the retention of sodium and water.

Algae: unicellular organism distinguished from plants by having no true root stem.

Alkaline: solution or material having a pH above 7.0.

Alkaloid: a large and varied group of nitrogen-containing compounds found in plants. Often alkaline, they react with acids to form soluble salts, many of which are physiologically active.

Alkalosis: abnormal state of increased alkalinity of blood and tissues.

Allergen: any substance which comes into contact with body tissue (by skin absorption, ingestion, or inhalation) and causes a specific reaction within the bloodstream.

Allergy: hypersensitivity to particular substance or antigen, such as pollens, furs, feathers, mold, dust, drugs, dyes, cosmetics, or foods, causing characteristic symptoms when encountered, ingested, or inhaled.

Alliaceous: Garlic or onion like.

Allopathy: a term that describes the conventional method of medicine which combats disease by using substances and techniques specifically against the symptoms of disease.

Alopecia: absence of hair from area where it normally grows esp. Progressive hair loss in men; baldness.

Alterative: herbs that gradually restore proper functioning of the body, increasing health and vitality by reducing toxicity in the tissues; blood cleanser.

Alzheimer's disease: progressive dementia and brain degeneration.

Amebiasis: infection with or disease caused by amebas.

Amebic dysentery: severe dysentery caused by protozoan amebas.

Amenorrhea: absence or cessation of menstruation due to congenital defect, hormonal deficiency, hypothalamus disorder, or emotional problem.

Amino acid: any of twenty-five organic acids containing an amino group that link together into polypeptide chains to form proteins.

Amoebicidal: a substance that kills amoebae.

Amphoteric: having the ability to act either as an acid or a base.

Amylase: enzyme that breaks down starch into saccharides.

Anabolism: constructive metabolism in which food is changed into living tissue.

Analgesic: a substance which reduces the sensation of pain.

Anaphrodisiac: a substance that reduces sexual desire.

Anaphylaxis: acute, allergic reaction to substance to which person has been previously sensitized, resulting in faintness, palpitations, loss of color, difficulty in breathing, and shock.

Androgen: male sex hormone.

Anemia: reduced hemoglobin in blood, causing fatigue, breathlessness, and pallor.

Anesthetic: agent that diminishes or abolishes sensation and can produce unconsciousness.

Aneurysm: balloon like swelling of arterial wall.

Angina: feeling of suffocation; chest pain.

Angina pectoris: pain in center of chest that spreads to jaws and arms, due to insufficient blood supply to heart.

Angiosperm: flowering plant.

Annual: plant with life cycle of one year or season.

Anodyne: substance that soothes or relieves pain.

Anodynia: absence of pain.

Anorexia: the medical term for toss of appetite.

Anorexia nervosa: extreme loss of appetite, occurring most frequently in adolescent females, and causing severe weight loss and starvation.

Anoxia: condition in which body tissues receive inadequate oxygen.

Antacid: substance that neutralizes acid.

Anthelmintic: a vermifuge, destroying or expelling intestinal worms.

Anther: part of stamen that produces and releases pollen.

Anthocyanidin: a particular class of flavonoids which gives plants, fruits and flowers colors ranging from red to blue.

Anthraquinones: glycoside compounds that produce dyes and purgatives.

Anti-abortive: substance that helps counteract to abort or miscarry.

Anti-anemic: an agent which combats anemia.

Anti-arthritic: an agent which combats arthritis.

Anti-asthmatic: substance that relieves asthma symptoms.

Anti-bilious: substance that relieves biliary or jaundice condition in the body.

Antibiotic: Drug or substance that kills microorganisms.

Antibody: protein manufactured by B-cell lymphocytes that reacts with specific antigen to fight invasion as principal component of immunity.

Anti-catarrhal: a substance that helps the body remove excess catarrh from various parts of the body.

Anticoagulant: agent that prevents blood from clotting; platelet aggregation inhibitor.

Anti-convulsant: substance that helps arrest or prevent convulsions.

Anti-depressant: substance that helps alleviate depression.

Anti-diarrheal: substance that helps control diarrhea.

Antidiuretic hormone: ADH; peptide hormone synthesized in hypothalamus and released from posterior pituitary, causing retention of more water in body.

Antidote: a substance which counteracts the effects of a poison.

Anti-emetic: an agent which reduces the incidence and severity of nausea or vomiting.

Antifungal: a substance that inhibits the growth or multiplication of fungi.

Antigen: any substance or microorganism that, when introduced into the body, causes the formation of antibodies against it.

Anti-hemorrhagic: an agent which prevents or combats hemorrhage or bleeding.

Anti-hepatotoxic: substance that protects liver cells from chemical damage.

Antihistamine: chemical that blocks action of histamine.

Anti-hydropic: substance that reduces excess body fluids or dropsy.

Anti-hypertensive: blood-pressure lowering effect; hypotensive.

Anti-inflammatory: substance that soothes inflammations or reduces the inflammatory response of the tissue directly.

Anti-lithic: prevents the formation of a calculus or stone.

Anti-microbial: substance that helps the body destroy or resist pathogenic microorganisms, including bacteria, fungi, and viruses.

Anti-neuralgic: relieves or reduces nerve pain.

Antioxidant: a compound which prevents free radical stressor oxidative damage.

Anti-periodic: substance that relieves malarial type fevers and chills.

Anti-phlogistic: checks or counteracts inflammation.

Anti-pruritic: relieves sensation of itching or prevents its occurrence.

Anti-putrescent: preservative; an agent which prevents and combats decay or putrefaction.

Anti-pyretic: reduces fever; see febrifuge.

Anti-rheumatic: helps prevent and relieve rheumatism.

Anti-sclerotic: helps prevent the hardening of tissue.

Anti-scorbutic: prevention or remedy for scurvy.

Anti-scrofulous: substance that helps heal tubercular condition of the lymph nodes.

Anti-seborrheic: helps control the production of sebum, the oily secretion from skin follicles.

Antiseptic: destroys and prevents the development of microbes.

Anti-spasmodic: substance that relieves smooth muscle spasms.

Anti-syphilitic: substance used to cure syphilis and other sexually transmitted diseases.

Anti-toxic: an antidote or treatment that counteracts the effects of poison.

Anti-tumor: a substance which prevents or is effective against tumors.

Anti-tussive: substance that reduces coughing, esp. one that affects activity in the brain's cough center and depresses respiration.

Anti-venomous: substances used to counteract, animal and insect poisons.

Anti-viral: substance which inhibits the growth of a virus.

Anti-zymotic: substances used to arrest the action of bacterial organisms.

Anxiety: an unpleasant emotional state ranging from mild unease to intense fear.

Aperient: a mild laxative.

Aperitif: aperitive; a stimulant of the appetite.

Aphonia: loss of voice.

Aphrodisiac: substance that increases or stimulates sexual desire.

Apnea: temporary cessation of breathing.

Apoplexy: sudden loss of consciousness, especially resulting from a stroke or sudden severe hemorrhage.

Appendicitis: acute inflammation of appendix.

Application: medication, herbal remedy, or antiseptic placed externally on body part, as in wash, fomentation, compress, or poultice.

Arbovirus: RNA-containing virus that can cause disease when transmitted from animals to humans by insects.

ARC: Aids-related complex.

Aril: the husk or membrane covering the seed of a plant.

Aromatherapy: the therapeutic use of essential oils.

Aromatic: a substance with a strong aroma or smell; or with high volatile oil content.

Arrhythmia: irregularity or deviation from normal rhythm or force of heartbeat.

Arteriosclerosis: deposit of cholesterol/calcium plaque on artery walls, hardening of the arteries.

Artery: a blood vessel which carries oxygen-rich blood away from the heart.

Arthritis: inflammation of joints, resulting in pain and swelling.

Asbestosis: lung disease caused by inhalation of asbestos fibers, increasing risk of lung cancer.

Asepsis: condition of complete absence of disease-causing bacteria, viruses, fungi, or other micro-organisms; sterile.

Asthenia: see debility.

Asthma: paroxysmal attacks of bronchial spasms that cause difficulty in breathing.

Astigmatism: distortion of visual images due to failure of retina to focus light.

Astringent: substance that has a tightening or contracting effect on tissue, and a drying effect on fluid secretions, usually because of high tannin content.

Asymptomatic: showing no symptoms or evidence of a disease.

Ataxia: shaky movements and unsteady gait when brain fails to regulate posture or direction of limb movements.

Atheroma: point of degeneration of artery walls due to fatty plaques and scar tissue.

Atherosclerosis; a process in which fatty substances (cholesterol and triglycerides) are deposited on the walls of medium to large arteries, eventually leading to a blockage.

Athlete's foot: contagious fungal infection of skin between toes.

Atony: lack of muscular tone or strength.

Atopy: a predisposition to various allergic conditions including eczema and asthma.

Atresia: congenital absence or abnormal narrowing of body opening.

Atrophy: wasting away of normally developed organ or tissue due to degeneration of cells.

Atropine: belladonna extract that inhibits activity of autonomic nervous system and relaxes smooth muscle.

Attrition: gradual wearing away, as in surface of teeth.

Auto-immune: a disorder of body's defense mechanisms in which antibodies are produced against the body's own tissue, treating them as foreign substances.

Autologous: derived from same individual or organism.

Autonomic: occurring involuntarily or without conscious will, controlled by autonomic nervous system.

Axil: upper angle between a stem and leaf or bract.

Ayurveda: A highly developed system of therapeutics developed in the Hindu and Buddhist cultures of the Indian subcontinent.

B

Bacteremia: presence of bacteria in blood, indicating infection.

Bactericidal: an agent that destroys bacteria (a type of microbe or organism).

Bacteriostat: substance that retards growth of bacteria.

Balm: fragrant ointment or aromatic oil with medicinal value.

Balsam: a resinous semi-solid mass or viscous liquid exuded from a plant.

Balsamic: substance that soothe and heal inflamed tissues.

Baroreceptor: neural receptor sensitive to pressure and rate of change in pressure; stretch receptor.

Basal cell carcinoma: common, usually curable, slow-growing malignant tumor on skin.

Basal metabolic rate: the rate of metabolism when the body is at rest.

Basal rosette: leaves radiating directly from the crown of the root.

Basophil: a type of white blood cell which is involved in allergic reactions.

Bechic: anything which relieves or cures coughs; or referring to cough.

Bedwetting: enuresis.

Bell's palsy: paralysis of muscles on one side of face and inability to close eye, sometimes with loss of taste and excess sensitivity to noise.

Benign: consisting of localized mass of non-malignant specialized cells within connective tissue that do not invade or destroy tissue or spread throughout body.

Berry: small, fleshy fruit or dry seed or kernel of various plants.

Beta blocker: drug that decreases heart activity by affecting receptors of sympathetic nervous system.

Beta cells: the cells in the pancreas which manufacture insulin.

Beta-carotene: vitamin a precursor; a plant substance which can be converted into vitamin a molecules.

Biennial: plant with two-year life cycle, in which the vegetative first-year growth is followed by fruiting and dying during second year.

Bile: greenish liver secretion that is stored in gallbladder until released to emulsify fats in small intestine.

Bile salts: steroid molecules in bile that emulsify and aid digestion of fats.

Bilirubin: the breakdown product of the hemoglobin molecule of red blood cells.

Bilirubinemia: excess bile pigment in blood that causes jaundice.

Binomial: standard scientific name for organism in Latin.

Biopsy: a diagnostic test in which tissue or cells are removed from the body for laboratory analysis.

Bipinnate: doubly pinnate; when the divisions of a pinnate leaf are themselves pinnate.

Bitters: herbs with a bitter taste, that promote secretion of digestive juices.

Blade: broad, expanded part of leaf.

Bleeding time: the time required for the cessation of bleeding from a small skin puncture as a result of platelet aggregation and blood vessel constriction.

Blennorrhagia: heavy discharge of mucus, especially from urethra.

Blepharitis: inflammation, scaling, and crusting of eyelids.

Blister: external swelling that contains watery fluid and blood or pus, caused by heat, chemical reaction, or friction.

Blocking antibody: antibody whose production is induced by cancer cells or tissue transplants and that blocks the killing of those cells by cytotoxic t cells.

Blood poisoning: prolonged invasion of bloodstream by pathogenic bacteria due to infectious disease or skin lesions; aka. bacteremia; septicemia; toxemia.

Blood pressure: the force exerted by blood as it is pumped by the heart through the circulatory system.

Blood-brain barrier: group of anatomical barriers and transport systems that tightly controls types of substances entering extracellular space of brain.

Boil: tender, inflamed, pustulant area of skin, usually due to staphylococcus infection; furuncle.

Bolus: single, compact mass of substance.

Botany: branch of biology dealing with structure, growth, and classification of plants.

Bract: leaf-like structure growing below or encircling flower cluster or flower.

Bradycardia: slowing of heart rate to under fifty beats per minute.

Bradykinin: peptide vasodilator that increases capillary permeability and probably stimulates pain receptors.

Bromeliad: member of the pineapple family of plants, usually with stiff, semi-succulent or leathery leaves and spikes of bright flowers.

Bronchial asthma: asthma.

Bronchitis: inflammation of walls of bronchi in lungs due to virus or bacteria, causing coughing and prolific production of mucous.

Bronchodilator: drug that relaxes bronchial muscle to open air passages to lungs.

Bronchospasm: muscular contraction that narrows bronchi and causes breathing difficulty, especially in exhalation.

Bruit: any abnormal sound or murmur heard with a stethoscope.

Bryophyte: any member of the division of nonvascular plants, including mosses and liverworts.

Bubo: swollen and inflamed lymph node in armpit or groin.

Bulb: dormant, underground bud and food storage stage of some plants.

Bulimia: binge purge syndrome; syndrome of overeating followed by vomiting, usually psychogenic, but caused by hypothalamus lesion.

Bunion: swelling of joint between big toe and first metatarsal.

Bursa: a sac or pouch which contains a special fluid which lubricates joints.

Bursitis: inflammation of a bursa.

C

Cachexia: weight loss, weakness, and debility associated with chronic disease.

Calcinosis: abnormal deposit of calcium salts in tissue.

Calcitonin: peptide hormone secreted by thyroid that reduces excess of calcium in blood by depositing it in bone.

Calculus: calcium rich pebble-like mass, such as gallstone or kidney stone, formed within body, or hardened deposit like bone spur or hard tartar layer formed on teeth by plaque.

Callus: hard thickening of area of skin on hands or feet—usually resulting from frequent friction or irritation; mass of tissue forming around fractured bone ends.

Calmative: a sedative.

Calorie: a unit of heat energy. A calorie is the amount of energy necessary to raise 1 liter of water 1°C.

Calyx: the sepals or outer layer of floral leaves.

Cambium: layer of formative cells beneath bark of tree.

Cancer: uncontrolled cell division, causing disruption of metabolism and invasion and destruction of neighboring tissue.

Cancrum: ulceration of lip or mouth; canker; chancre.

Candidiasis: yeast-like fungus infection in mouth and moist areas of body; thrush.

Canker: cancrum.

Capsule: small gelatin container for medicine powders that control taste and make swallowing easier; a dry fruit, opening when ripe, composed of more than one carpel.

Carbohydrate: sugars and starches.

Carbuncle: staphylococcus infection of skin that causes boils with multiple drainage channels.

Carcinogen: any agent or substance capable of causing cancer.

Carcinogenesis: the development of cancer caused by the actions of certain chemicals, viruses and unknown factors on primarily normal cells.

Carcinoma: cancer in epithelium lining skin or internal organs.

Cardiac arrest: heart attack; abrupt cessation of heartbeat, causing loss of pulse, consciousness, and breathing.

Cardiac depressant: substance that are sedative to the heart's action.

Cardiac output: volume of blood pumped by either ventricle per minute.

Cardiac remedies: herbal remedies that have a beneficial action on the heart.

Cardiac stenosis: abnormal narrowing of heart valve.

Cardiac stimulant: substance that increase and give greater power to the heart's action.

Cardiomyopathy: chronic viral, congenital, or other disorder that affects heart muscle and causes heart failure, arrhythmias, or embolisms.

Cardiopulmonary: pertaining to the heart and lungs.

Cardiotonic: a compound which tones and strengthens the heart.

Carditis: inflammation of heart.

Caries: decay of bone tissue, esp. tooth; cavity.

Carminative: substances that ease griping pains in the bowel, and aid the removal of gas from the digestive tract.

Carotenes: fat-soluble plant pigments, some of which can be converted into Vitamin A by the body.

Cartilage: a type of connective tissue which acts as a shock absorber at joint interfaces.

Carpal tunnel syndrome: compression of median nerve entering palm of hand that causes pain and numbing in middle and index fingers.

Castor oil: oil extract of Castor beans; irritant laxative and cathartic.

Catalyst: a chemical which increases the rate of a chemical reaction without itself being consumed.

Cataract: opaque deposit on lens of eye that causes blurred vision, especially in elderly.

Catarrh: excessive secretion of thick phlegm or mucus by mucous membranes; deposit of hardened mucus or secretions anywhere in tissues.

Catecholamines: chemically similar neurotransmitters including dopamine, epinephrine, and norepinephrine.

Cathartic: a substance which aggressively stimulates the movement of the bowels, more powerful than a laxative.

Catkin: a pendulous inflorescence, made up of tiny stalked flowers.

Caustic: substance that burns or destroys living tissue.

Cavity: hollow place, especially in tooth produced by caries.

Cell-mediated immunity: specific immune response mediated by cytotoxic T-lymphocytes.

Cell proliferant: substance that promotes accelerated regeneration and repair of damaged tissue.

Cephalalgia: headache.

Cephalic: remedy for disorders of the head; referring or directed towards the head.

Cerebral: pertaining to the largest part of the brain, the cerebrum.

Cerebral hemorrhage: bleeding from cerebral artery, or blood vessels of the head, into brain tissue.

Cervicitis: inflammation of cervix.

Chancre: painless ulcer on lips, genitals, urethra, or eyelid; cancrum.

Chelating agents: organic compounds capable of binding metals or minerals.

Chemotype: the same botanical species occurring in other forms due to different conditions of growth, such as climate, soil, altitude, etc.; variation.

Cheyne Stokes respiration: cyclical slowing of breathing to cessation, then speeding up to peak.

Chilblain: red, round, itchy swelling of skin on fingers or toes due to exposure to cold; frostbite.

Chiropractic: treatment method using manipulation of muscular and skeletal system, especially the spine, to restore nervous system integrity.

Chlamydia: sexually transmitted, virus-like microorganism causing conjunctivitis, urethritis, and cervicitis.

Chlorophyll: pigment in chloroplast, needed for photosynthesis.

Chloroplast: structure within plant cell that is site of photosynthesis.

Cholagogue: a compound which stimulates the contraction of the gallbladder.

Cholecystitis: inflammation of the gallbladder.

Cholecystokinetic: agent which stimulates the contraction of the gallbladder.

Cholecystokinin: CCK, peptide hormone secreted by small intestine.

Cholelithiasis: presence of gallstones.

Choleretic: aids excretion of bile by the liver, so there is a greater flow of bile.

Cholestasis: the stagnation of bile within the liver.

Cholesterol: fatty molecule that is precursor of steroid hormones and bile salts, component of plasma membranes, and present in fat and blood.

Cholinergic: pertaining to the release of acetylcholine as a transmitter substance in the parasympathetic portion of the autonomic nervous system.

Chromatography: separation of chemical compounds by their refracted light signature.

Chronic: long-term or frequently recurring.

Chronic fatigue syndrome: CFS, persistent, extreme exhaustion and weakness due to medically unknown causes.

Chyme: the partially digested food in lumen of stomach and small intestine.

Cicatrisant: an agent which promotes healing by the formation of scar tissue.

Cicatrix: scar.

Cirrhosis: progressive degeneration of the liver from various sources of chronic toxicity.

Claudication: cramping pain from inadequate blood supply to muscle.

Climacteric: physical and emotional changes associated with menopause in female, and adropause in male.

Clot: soft, thickened lump formed in liquid, especially blood.

Club moss: any of various small, nonseed-bearing vascular plants with conelike, spore-bearing structures on top of stems.

Clubbing: thickening of tissue at base of fingernail or toenail, esp. enlargement of fingertip.

CNS: central nervous system.

Coccus: spherical bacterium.

Coenzyme: nonprotein organic molecule that temporarily joins with enzyme during reaction, serves as a carrier molecule, is not consumed in reaction, and can be reused until degraded; cofactor, vitamin.

Cofactor: coenzyme.

Cold sore: viral eruption of skin around lips that dries to leave crusty patch; fever blister.

Colic: pain due to contraction of the involuntary muscle of the abdominal organs.

Colitis: any inflammation of colon, causing diarrhea and lower abdominal pain.

Collagen: extremely strong fibrous protein that functions as sub-structural element in connective tissue, tendons, ligaments, and skin.

Collagen diseases: various diseases characterized by changes in makeup of connective tissue; lupus, rheumatic fever, rheumatoid adhritis, and scleroderma.

Collodion: solution of nitrocellulose in alcohol or ether, applied to skin for protection of minor wounds.

Colloid: an extremely fine insoluble particle suspended in a surrounding medium.

Collyrium: medicated solution used to bathe eyes.

Coma: prolonged state of deep unconsciousness from which patient cannot be roused.

Comedo: blackhead.

Complement: set of enzymes in bloodstream that work with antibodies to attack invading cells and bacteria.

Compositae: one of a large family of herbaceous plants with daisy-like flower heads of dense clusters of small florets surrounded by ring of small leaves or bracts.

Compound: leaf or flower cluster with branched main axis; combination of complementary herbs or substances targeted to a common therapeutic use.

Compress: moistened pad of folded cloth, often medicated, applied with heat, cold, or pressure to soothe body part.

Concrete: a concentrated, waxy, solid or semi-solid resinous material prepared from previously live plant matter, usually using a hydrocarbon type of solvent.

Cone: reproductive structure of certain non-flowering plants with overlapping scales or bracts containing pollen, ovules, or spores.

Congestion: accumulation of fluid within an organ; clogging of upper respiratory system with mucus.

Congestive heart failure: inability of heart to adequately supply blood to body tissue, often due to weakening of cardiac muscle, causing body swelling and shortness of breath.

Conifer: cone-bearing gymnosperm, usually with narrow, needle-like or small, scale-like leaves.

Conjunctivitis: inflammation of mucous membrane covering front of eye, often with discharge of pus; pinkeye.

Connective tissue: the type of tissue which performs the function of providing support, structure, and cellular cement to the body.

Constipation: infrequent, difficult, often painful bowel movements with hard feces; irregularity.

Contagious: a disease which can be transferred from one person to another by direct contact.

Contraceptive: medication or device to prevent conception.

Contusion: surface injury in which skin is not broken; bruise.

Convulsion: involuntary muscle contraction that causes contorted movements of body and limbs.

Cordial: substance combining the properties of a stimulant and a warming tonic.

Corm: underground stem base that acts as reproductive structure.

Corn: area of hard or thickened skin on or between toes.

Corolla: the petals of a flower considered as a whole.

Coronary: of or pertaining to arteries of heart.

Coronary heart disease: serious condition affecting coronary artery.

Corpus luteum: lining of uterus that nourished fertilized egg.

Corrective: substance used to alter or mitigate the severity of action of other herbs.

Cortical: involving external layers of brain.

Corticosteroid: hormones a group of hormones produced by the adrenal glands that control the body's use of nutrients and the excretion of salts and water in the urine.

Corticosteroid drugs: a group of drugs similar to natural corticosteroid hormones which are used predominantly in the treatment of inflammation and to suppress the immune system.

Cortisol: steroid hormone secreted by adrenal cortex that regulates organic metabolism by converting fats and proteins to glucose.

Cortisone: steroid hormone secreted by adrenal cortex that counteracts pain and swelling.

Corymb: flat-topped or convex cluster of flowers in which outer flowers open first.

Coryza: catarrhal inflammation of mucous membrane in nose.

Cosmetic: substance used to improve the complexion and beautify the skin.

Cotyledon: first or second leaf of seedling.

Cough: violent exhalation of irritant particles or congestive mucus from respiratory system; tussis.

Coumarins: glycoside compounds that are sensed as the "new mown hay" smell of many grasses.

Counter-irritant: applications to the skin which relieve deep-seated pain, usually applied in the form of heat; rubefacient.

Crab louse: crab-like louse that infests pubic regions, transmitted by sexual contact.

Cramp: prolonged painful contraction or spasm of muscle.

Crepitation: soft crackling sound heard in lungs through stethoscope; rattle.

Crepitus: crackling sound made by grating of bone on bone or cartilage, as in arthritic joints.

CRH: corticotropin releasing hormone.

Crick: painful muscle spasm or cramp in neck or upper back.

Crohn's disease: condition marked by chronic inflammation and thickening of intestinal tract.

Croup: inflammation and obstruction of larynx in young children due to viral respiratory infections, characterized by harsh cough.

Cushing's Disease: syndrome due to excess corticosteroid hormone, causing weight gain, excess body hair, and high blood pressure.

Cutaneous: pertaining to the skin.

Cuticle: waxy layer on outer surface of plants.

Cyanosis: bluish discoloration of skin and mucous membrane due to poor oxygenation of blood.

Cycad: any of the order of gymnosperms intermediate between ferns and palms, often with thick, columnar trunk crowned by large, tough, pinnate leaves.

Cyme: inflorescence in which primary axis bears single central or terminal flower that blooms first.

Cyst: an abnormal lump or swelling, filled with fluid or semisolid material, in any organ or tissue.

Cystic fibrosis: hereditary disease of exocrine glands that produces respiratory infections, malabsorption, and sweat with high salt content.

Cystitis: inflammation of the inner lining of the bladder. It is usually caused by a bacterial infection.

Cytokinin: plant hormone that promotes cell division.

Cytomegalovirus: a virus in herpes family that causes enlargement of epithelial cells and mononucleosis-like disease.

Cytophylactic: increasing the activity of leukocytes in defense of the body against infection.

Cytotoxic: toxic to all cells.

Cytotoxin: substance that has toxic effect on certain cells, used against some tumors.

D

Debility: weakness, lack of tone.

Deciduous: designating any plant that sheds all its leaves once each year.

Decoction: a herbal preparation, where the plant material (usually hard or woody) is boiled in water and reduced to make a concentrated extract.

Decongestant: substance used to reduce nasal mucus production and swelling.

Deficiency disease: any disease, such as beriberi, caused by nutritional deficiency.

Dehiscence: splitting open of a wound.

Dehydration: deficiency or loss of water in body tissues marked by thirst, nausea, and exhaustion.

Delirium: acute mental disorder due to organic brain disease, causing hallucinations, disorientation, and extreme excitation.

Dementia: senility, loss of mental function.

Demineralization: loss of minerals from the bone.

Demulcent: herbs rich in mucilage that soothe and protect irritated or inflamed tissue.

Deobstruant: substance that removes obstructions from the alimentary canal and other areas of the body.

Deodorant: an agent which corrects, masks or removes unpleasant odors.

Depressant: drug that lowers nervous or functional activity; sedative.

Depurant: depurative.

Depurative: helps combat impurity in the blood and organs; detoxifying.

Dermal: pertaining to the skin.

Dermatitis: skin inflammation.

Dessicant: substance which is able to dry surfaces by absorbing moisture.

Detergent: substance which is cleansing to wounds, ulcers, or the skin itself.

Detumescence: reduction or subsidence of swelling.

Diabetes: deficient production of pancreatic hormone insulin, resulting in improper carbohydrate metabolism and uncontrolled sugar levels in the blood.

Dialysis: a technique using mechanical means to remove waste products from the blood and excess fluid from the body in the treatment of kidney failure.

Diaphoretic: substance that promotes perspiration, helping the skin eliminate waste from the body, and to help reduce fever.

Diarrhea: frequent bowel evacuation of soft or liquid feces.

Diastole: relaxation period of cardiac cycle.

Diastolic pressure: minimum blood pressure during cardiac cycle.

Dicot: dicotyledon.

Dicotyledon: angiosperm having two seed leaves or cotyledons; dicot.

Digestant: substance that aids in the digestion of food.

Digestion: process of breaking down large particles, especially food substances, into small molecules suitable for absorption into bloodstream.

Digestive: substance which promotes or aids the digestion of food.

Dioecious: having male and female flowers on different individuals.

Diphtheria: acute, highly contagious bacterial infection of the throat that can cause death from respiratory obstruction or carditis.

Disaccharide: a sugar composed of two monosaccharide units.

Discutient: substance that dispel or resolve tumors and abnormal growths.

Disinfectant: agent that destroys bacteria and other microorganisms.

Disk floret: small, tubular, central florets of a daisy-like (composite) flower.

Dissected leaf: leaf with deeply cut margins.

Diuretic: substance that increases the production and elimination of urine.

Diverticuli: sack-like protrusions of the wall of the colon.

Diverticulitis: inflammatory response to diverticuli.

Diverticulosis: presence of diverticular sacs at weak points in walls of large intestine.

Dizziness: feeling off-balance, unstable, confused, as though whirling in place.

Dopamine: catecholamine neurotransmitter, precursor of epinephrine and norepinephrine.

Dormancy: period of time in which growth ceases.

Double-blind study: a control against experimental bias by ensuring that neither the researcher nor the subject know when an active agent or placebo is being used.

Douche: introduction of water and/or a cleansing agent into the vagina.

Drastic: strong cathartic producing violent peristalsis, watery stools, and much griping pain.

Dressing: protective or healing material applied externally to wound or diseased body part.

Dropsy: excess of fluid in the tissues; edema associated with congestive heart failure.

Drug: substance, usually chemical, that directly affects the functional processes of an organ, the condition of tissue, or the response to a stimulus.

Drupe: a soft fleshy fruit, with one or more seeds, each surrounded by a stony layer.

Duodenal ulcer: most common kind of digestive ulcer, occurring in lining of duodenum, most often caused by irritation from helicobacter pylori bacteria, and occasionally by excess stomach acid.

Dysentery: infection of intestinal tract that causes severe diarrhea mixed with blood and mucus.

Dysfunction: abnormal function.

Dysmenorrhea: painful, difficult, irregular menstruation.

Dyspepsia: indigestion; digestive disorder with abdominal pain and gas after eating, burning sensation in esophagus, and sometimes with nausea and vomiting.

Dysplasia: any abnormality of growth.

Dyspnea: labored or difficult breathing; breathlessness.

Dystrophy: organ or muscle degeneration.

E

Ecchymosis: bluish black mark on skin from release of blood into tissues, usually due to injury; hematoma.

ECG: Electrocardiogram; measurements by machine which records the activity of the heart.

Eclampsia: convulsions, especially due to toxemia during pregnancy.

Ectopic pregnancy: state in which fertilized egg implants at a site other than uterus.

Edema: excessive accumulation of fluid in tissues; dropsy.

EEG: Electroencephalogram; measurements by machine which records brain waves.

EFA: Essential Fatty Acid.

Electrolyte: substance that ionizes in solution and conducts electrical current.

Electuary: medication mixed with honey or syrup to make it more palatable.

Elimination diet: a diet which eliminates suspected allergenic foods.

Elixir: substance that contains alcohol or glycerin, used as solution for bitter or nauseating herbs.

Elliptic: an oval leaf, pointed at both ends.

Elliptical: shaped like an ellipse, or regular curve.

Embolism: obstruction of artery by stationary blood clot, fat, air, or foreign body.

Embolus: mass of matter that obstructs blood flow.

Emesis: vomiting; vomited matter.

Emetic: substance that induces vomiting.

Emmenagogue: substance that stimulates menstrual flow and activity.

Emollient: medicinal preparation that soothes and softens external tissue.

Emphysema: pulmonary disorder, characterized by destruction of the walls of the air sacs of the lungs, resulting in chronic shortness of breath, especially on exertion.

Empyema: accumulation of pus, especially in pleural cavity.

Emulsification: homogenous mixture of fatty and aqueous substances.

Emulsify: using an agent or special process to combine two or more normally incompatible fluids, i.e. oil and water, into a stabile mixture.

Encephalitis: sleeping sickness; inflammation of brain, caused by viral or bacterial infection or allergic reaction.

Endemic: disease that is constantly present in particular region, but generally under control.

Endocarditis: inflammation and damage to heart cavity lining due to bacterial infection or rheumatic fever.

Endocrine gland: ductless organ that synthesizes hormones and releases them directly into bloodstream.

Endocrine system: all ductless glands in body.

Endocrinology: study of endocrine glands and their hormones.

Endometriosis: a condition in which tissue similar to that normally lining the uterus is found outside of the uterus, usually around the ovaries, fallopian tubes and other pelvic structures.

Endometrium: the mucus membrane lining the uterus.

Endorphin: neurotransmitter that exhibits painkilling activity.

Enervation: weakness, lack of energy.

Enfleurage: extraction of perfumes by exposure of odorless fats to aromatic parts of flowers.

Engorgement: congestion of a part of the tissues, or excessive fullness, as in the breasts.

ENT: ear, nose, and throat; treatment of diseases of these parts; otorhinolaryngology.

Enteric-coated: an enzyme activated coating on a capsule or tablet that ensures that it does not dissolve until it passes through the stomach, and reaches the intestinal tract.

Enteritis: viral or bacterial inflammation of small intestine, causing diarrhea.

Enuresis: involuntary urination, especially at night; bedwetting.

Enzyme: complex proteins that are produced by living cells, and catalyze specific biochemical reactions.

EPA: Eicosapentaenoic acid; a fatty acid found primarily in cold-water fish and flax seed.

Ephedrine: widely used stimulant and antihistamine drug based on extract of Ephedra sinensis.

Epidemiology: study of causes and control of epidemics.

Epilepsy: one of various brain disorders that cause recurrent, sudden convulsive seizures.

Epinephrine: hormone released by adrenal medulla that elevates blood sugar, and initiates the fight-or-flight response; adrenaline.

Epiphyte: non-parasitic plant growing upon another plant for support.

Epistaxis: attack of bleeding from the nose.

Epithelium: cells that cover the entire surface of the body, and the lining of the alimentary tract.

Epstein-barr syndrome: infectious mononucleosis caused by herpes-like virus; sometimes referred to as chronic fatigue syndrome.

Errhine: substance that increases secretions from the sinuses.

Erysipelas: skin infection from streptococcus bacteria that causes inflammation, swelling, and fever.

Erythema: a superficial redness of the skin due to excess of blood.

Erythrocyte: red blood cell, lacking a nucleus, that transports oxygen to body tissues.

Erythropoiesis: formation of erythrocytes.

Erythropoietin: hormone secreted mainly by kidney that stimulates erythrocyte production.

Essential fatty acid: fatty acids which the body cannot manufacture - linoleic and linolenic acids.

Essential Oil: EO; a highly concentrated volatile oil obtained by distillation from the leaves, stems, flowers, other parts of plants, usually carrying the odor characteristic of the plant.

Estrogen: a class of hormones, produced by the ovaries and fatty tissue of the body, that in concert with other hormones, stimulates and regulates changes in the female organs.

Etiology: science of causes and origins of diseases.

Evergreen: plant that maintains functional green foliage throughout year.

Exanthematous: substance that is healing to eruptive skin conditions.

Excito-motor: substance that increases motor reflex and spinal activity.

Excretion: the elimination of waste products from a cell, tissue or the entire body.

Exfoliant: a product or ingredient whose purpose is to remove unwanted tissue or waste products from the skin and other body surfaces.

Exocrine gland: gland that secretes through a duct.

Exophthalmic goiter: enlargement of thyroid gland accompanied by protrusion of eyeballs.

Expectorant: substance that soothes bronchial spasm, loosens mucus secretions, and aids in their elimination through a productive cough.

Extracellular: the space outside the cell, filled with fluid.

Exudate: fluid or semi-fluid material, containing serum, pus, oils and cellular debris, that is released by glands or follicles.

Eyewash: medicinal solution used to flush and soothe the eyes.

F

Fatty acid: organic compound whose carbon chain ends in a carboxyl group.

Febrifuge: substance that relieves or reduces fever.

Feces: digestive waste products found in, and excreted through the colon.

Fern: non-flowering, vascular plant having roots, stems, and fronds, and reproducing by spores instead of seeds.

Fever: elevation in body temperature above normal 98.6° F.

Fibrillation: rapid, uncontrolled irregular twitching of heart muscle.

Fibroma: generally benign tumorous mass composed mainly of fibrous or connective tissue.

Fibrocystic breast disease: formation of benign cysts of various sizes in the breast.

Fibrosarcoma: malignant tumor of connective tissue, especially in legs.

Fibrosis: thickening and scarring of connective tissue due to injury or inflammation.

Filament: the stalk of a stamen, or any thread-like part of a plant.

First-degree burn: reddening of outer layer of skin.

Fissure: crack in membrane lining.

Fistula: abnormal passage that leads from an abscess or cavity to the skin or to another abscess or cavity.

Fixative: a material which slows down the rate of evaporation of the more volatile components in an aromatic preparation.

Fixed oil: a name given to vegetable oils obtained from plants which, unlike essential oils, are fatty, dense, and non-volatile, such as olive or sweet almond oil.

Flatulence: expulsion of intestinal gas.

Flatus: intestinal gas.

Flavonoid: one of many plant pigments which exert a wide variety of physiological effects in the human body.

Floret: small flower; one of many individual flowers comprising the head of a composite plant.

Flower head: compact terminal cluster of stalkless flowers.

Flowering plant: any angiosperm that produces flowers, fruit, and seeds in an enclosed ovary.

Foliage: leaves of plant or tree.

Follicle: sac-like structure that forms inside an ovary when an egg is produced.

Free radical: highly reactive oxygen molecule that can bind to and destroy cellular compounds.

Frond: fern or palm foliage.

Fructose: yellowish to white, crystalline, water-soluble sugar found in many fruits.

Fruit: mature ovary of flowering plant, sometimes edible.

Fruit body: above ground or visible spore-producing part of a fungus.

Functional cyst: a benign cyst that forms on an ovary and usually resolves on its own without treatment.

Functional disorder: condition for which no physical cause can be found.

Fungicide: substance that destroys fungi, and prevents and combats fungal infection.

Fungus: unicellular or filamentous organism, having no chlorophyll, formerly classified with plants.

Furuncle: boil.

G

Galactagogue: substance that increases secretion or nutritional quality of milk.

Galactophygic: substance that arrests or dries up the flow of milk.

Gallstone: sedimentary mass of bile pigments, cholesterol, and calcium salts in gallbladder that causes pain, or passes into and obstructs bile duct.

Gamma globulin: part of blood serum that contains anti-bodies, used in temporary prevention of infectious diseases.

Garble: the process of separating unwanted material, i.e. stems, foreign matter, from herbs gathered for preservation; usually done by hand.

Gargle: liquid used to rinse mouth and throat, often medicated or antiseptic; mouthwash.

Gastric ulcer: stomach ulcer caused by action of acid on stomach lining.

Gastrin: digestive system hormone that stimulates hydrochloric acid release by stomach and secretion of digestive enzymes by pancreas.

Gastritis: inflammation of stomach lining.

Gastroenteritis: inflammation of stomach and intestine, due to virus, bacteria, or food poisoning, that causes vomiting, diarrhea.

Genital herpes: infection of genital area by herpes simplex virus resulting in recurrent sores.

Genus: category of closely related species ranking below family and above species.

German measles: rubella.

Germicidal: substance which destroys germs or micro-organisms such as bacteria, etc.

Germinate: sprout and start to grow from spore, seed, a bud.

Gingivitis: inflammation of gums, sometimes with bleeding.

Glaucoma: abnormally high fluid pressure in the eye, often leading to loss of vision.

Glaucous: covered with a fine, white, often waxy film, which rubs off.

Glioma: cancer of nerve tissue.

Glomerular filtration rate: GFR; volume of plasma per minute filtered through kidney.

Glomerulonephritis: potentially fatal streptococcal infection of kidney.

Glucagon: pancreatic hormone that increases blood glucose levels.

Glucocorticoid: adrenal cortex hormone that effects salt and water metabolism and stimulates conversion of noncarbohydrates to carbohydrates.

Glucose: a monosaccharide found in the blood and is one of the body's primary energy sources.

Glutamic acid: glutamine; amino acid that may be brain neurotransmitter.

Gluten: one of the proteins in wheat and certain other grains that gives dough its tough, elastic character.

Glycerin: a fatty sugar; glycerol.

Glycerol: syrupy liquid prepared by hydrolysis of fats and oils for use as skin lotion.

Glycine: simplest amino acid, present in most proteins.

Glycogen: white polysaccharide sugar, derived from glucose, that is principal form in which carbohydrate is stored in tissue.

Glycoprotein: carbohydrate-protein complex.

Glycosides: these common plant chemicals consist of molecules made up of two sections, one of which is a sugar.

Glycosuria: excretion of excess sugar in urine, as in diabetes.

Goblet cell: a goblet-shaped cell which secretes mucus.

Goiter: swelling of the throat due to enlarged thyroid gland.

Gonorrhea: sexually transmitted bacterial disease that affects mucous membranes in genital tract, pharynx, or rectum.

Gout: accumulation of excess uric acid in bloodstream and joints that causes joint destruction, kidney stones, and arthritis.

Grand mal: generalized epileptic seizure with flexion and extension of extremities and loss of consciousness.

Granuloma: nodule of connective tissue and capillaries associated with tuberculosis, syphilis, or nonorganic foreign bodies.

Grave's Disease: disease characterized by enlarged thyroid and increased basal metabolism, due to excessive thyroid secretion; hyperthyroidism.

Grippe: influenza.

Ground substance: the thick, gel-like material in which the cells, fibers and blood capillaries of cartilage, bone and connective tissue are embedded.

Gum: a class of carbohydrates which swell in the presence of water and increase the thickness of water-based products.

Gymnosperm: member of the division of seed plants having ovules on open scales, as cones.

H

Half-hardy: plant that may not survive extremely cold weather.

Halitosis: foul breath, especially from diseases of gums, teeth throat, or lungs, or from poor primary elimination.

Hallucinogen: substance that causes visions or delusions.

Hardy: plant capable of surviving normal winter weather without protection.

Hay fever: common, seasonal allergy to plant pollens that results in sneezing, runny nose, and watery eyes.

HDL: high-density lipoprotein; "good" cholesterol.

Headache: pain within skull, commonly due to stress or fatigue; cephalalgia.

Heart attack: myocardial infarction.

Heart failure: inadequate pumping of heart ventricle due to coronary thrombosis, hypertension, or arrhythmia; congestive heart failure.

Heart murmur: blowing or swishing noise produced by blood passing through defective heart valve.

Heartburn: burning sensation rising from abdomen to throat, often accompanied by bitter fluid in mouth; pyrosis.

Heartwood: the central portion of the wood of a tree trunk.

Helper T-cell: white blood cells which help in the immune response.

Hematoma: clotted accumulation of blood in tissue forming solid swelling.

Hematuria: blood in the urine.

Hemetic: blood builder; substance, rich in iron and manganese, which augment and enrich the red corpuscles of the blood.

Hemophilia: hereditary deficiency of one blood coagulant that causes slowness in clotting and prolonged or spontaneous bleeding.

Hemorrhage: uncontrolled bleeding from ruptured blood vessel, especially internal bleeding.

Hemorrhoids: weakened and enlarged veins in anus walls, due to prolonged constipation or diarrhea, characterized by painful swelling, itching, and bleeding; piles.

Hemostatic: a substance which checks bleeding.

Heparin: natural anticoagulant produced by liver cells as a polysaccharide.

Hepatic: pertaining to the liver; an aid to liver function.

Hepatitis: inflammation of liver, causing fever and jaundice, due to pathogen transmitted by food or drink (infectious hepatitis), or blood on needle or in transfusion (serum hepatitis).

Hepatomegaly: enlargement of the liver.

Herbaceous: non-woody.

Hernia: protrusion of tissue or organ outside of the cavity or membrane it normally occupies.

Herniated disk: "slipped" or distended cushion between vertebrae.

Herpatic: substance that heal skin eruptions, viral sores, and scaling diseases.

Herpes: outbreak of herpes simplex; small viral blisters on skin.

Herpes simplex: virus in herpes family; non-venereal blisters on mucous membrane that can cause conjunctivitis, vaginal inflammation, or cold sores.

Herpes zoster: shingles; virus in herpes family characterized by vesicles, often with severe pain along nerve pathways.

Hiccup: hiccough; characteristic sound made by abrupt involuntary lowering of diaphragm and closing of upper end of trachea.

High density lipoprotein: HDL; small lipid-protein molecule with low proportion of lipid or cholesterol that removes excess cholesterol from arteries; "good" cholesterol.

Histamine: amine derived from amino acid histidine that is released in allergic reaction, causing dilation of blood vessels, and activation of various defense mechanisms.

HIV: human immunodeficiency virus; virus associated with AIDS.

Hives: round, red, itching welts up to several inches across on skin, caused by acute or chronic allergic reaction, or stress responses; urticaria.

Hodgkin's disease: condition marked by malignancy in lymphatic tissue that causes enlarged lymph nodes, fever, and profuse sweating.

Holistic: a philosophy of healing that considers the whole person, including diet, lifestyle, and emotional state, as contributing factors to health, not just the part or parts in which symptoms occur.

Homeostasis: maintenance of constant and balanced internal environment.

Hormone: a secretion of an endocrine gland that controls and regulates functions in other parts of the body.

Housemaid's knee: fluid-filled swelling of bursa in front of kneecap, often caused by prolonged kneeling.

Human immunodeficiency virus: HIV; virus that causes AIDS.

Hybrid: a plant originating by cross-fertilization of one species or subspecies by another.

Hydrocarbon: compounds containing only hydrogen and carbon.

Hydrocele: accumulation of watery fluid, especially about testes.

Hydrocephalus: excess of cerebrospinal fluid in brain ventricles that causes enlargement of head in children and pressure and drowsiness in adults.

Hydrochloric acid: HCl; acid secreted by stomach during digestion.

Hyperglycemia: high blood sugar level; diabetes.

Hyperhidrosis: copious or excessive sweating.

Hyperinsulinism: overproduction of insulin, due to glandular disturbance or poor nutrition, producing symptoms of hypoglycemia.

Hyperlipidemic: elevation of cholesterol and triglycerides in the blood.

Hyperplasia: increase in number of fat cells, causing obesity.

Hypersecretion: excessive secretion.

Hypersensitivity: allergic reaction hypertrophy increase in size of cells; tissues, or organ.

Hypertension: high blood pressure.

Hypertensive: a substance that causes a raise in blood pressure.

Hyperthermia: high body temperature of 105°F or above; fever induced as treatment.

Hyperthyroidism: over-activity of thyroid gland that causes rapid heartbeat, sweating, tremors, weight loss, and anxiety.

Hypertrophy: increase in size of tissue or organ due to enlargement of cells.

Hyperventilation: abnormally rapid breathing that lowers carbon dioxide concentration in blood.

Hypnotic: substances that are powerful relaxants and sedatives, and induce sleep.

Hypochlorhydria: insufficient gastric acid output.

Hypochondria: obsession with real and imagined physical ailments.

Hypoglycemia: low blood sugar.

Hypoglycemic: substance that lowers abnormally elevated blood sugar.

Hypopraxia: listlessness, enfeeblement, or lack of interest in activity.

Hypotension: low blood pressure.

Hypotensive: substance that lowers abnormally elevated blood pressure.

Hypothermia: dropping of body temperature below normal range.

Hypothyroidism: subnormal thyroid gland activity that can lead to cretinism.

Hypoxia: an inadequate supply of oxygen.

Hysterectomy: surgical removal of the uterus.

Hysteria: extreme emotional excitation, sensory and motor disturbances, and outbursts of uncontrolled feeling.

I

Iatrogenic: meaning literally 'physician produced', the term can be applied to any medical condition, disease or other adverse occurrence that results from medical treatment.

Idiopathic: of unknown cause.

IG: immunoglobulin.

Ileitis: inflammation of ileum in small intestine.

Immune responses: body's defense reaction through dual modes of antibody and cellular response.

Immunity: ability of body to recognize and neutralize pathogens and foreign matter, either natural or acquired.

Immunoglobulin: IG; any of five classes of antibodies: Igg, Igm, Iga, and Igf.

Immunomodulator: substance that effects immune system functioning in some positive way.

Immunostimulant: substance that stimulates some aspect of immune system function.

Impairment: damage to or weakening of body part or function.

Impetigo: contagious skin infection from streptococcal or staphylococcal bacteria, usually in children, causing crusty yellow blisters.

Inborn immunity: congenital resistance to specific disease.

Incidence: the number of new cases of a disease that occurs during a given period in a defined population.

Incontinence: involuntary or uncontrollable passage or leakage of urine.

Incubation period: time between entry of disease organisms into body and onset of symptoms.

Infarction: death of tissue due to oxygen deprivation.

Infestation: attack on body by parasitic microorganism.

Inflorescence: flowering structure above the last stem leaves (including bracts and flowers).

Influenza: highly contagious viral infection of respiratory system, transmitted by coughing or sneezing, that causes headache, fever, general aches and pains; flu; grippe.

Infusion: a herbal remedy prepared by steeping the plant material in water.

Inorganic: in chemistry, refers to compounds which do not contain carbon; in Natural Health, refers to materials that are not, and have never been, alive.

Insecticide: substance used to destroy insects.

Insomnia: inability to fall asleep or remain asleep .

Insulin: pancreatic hormone that regulates blood sugar level.

Interferon: substance produced by infected cells that inhibits specific viral growth.

Intramuscular: situated in or administered by entering a muscle, as in injections.

Irreversible: impossible to halt or reverse by treatment.

Irritable bowel syndrome: IBS; recurrent chronic abdominal pain with constipation and/or diarrhea caused by abnormal contractions of colon muscles; spastic colon.

Irritant: a substance which produces redness, itching, swelling or blisters on the skin.

Ischemia: reduced blood supply resulting in destruction to organ or tissue.

J

Jaundice: a condition caused by elevation of bilirubin in the body and characterized by yellowing of the skin.

K

Keratin: an insoluble protein found in hair, skin and nails.

Ketone: product of lipid metabolism.

Kidney stone: hard, pebble like mass in kidney that causes pain and blood in urine; nephrolithiasis; renal calculus.

Kinin: vasodilatory polypeptide.

L

Laceration: tear in flesh, especially with irregular edges.

Lactase: an enzyme which breaks down lactose into the monosaccharides glucose and galactose.

Lactose: a disaccharide sugar present in milk.

Lacuna: an opening or separation in the fibers of the eye; a lesion.

Lanceolate: lance-shaped leaf, elongated oval and wider at the base.

Laparoscopy: a surgical procedure in which a slender, fiber optic viewing instrument, the laparoscope, is used to view internal organs.

Larvicidal: an agent with the ability to prevent or kill larvae.

Laryngitis: inflammation of larynx and vocal cords, infection, causing coughing, husky voice, or complete voice loss.

Laxative: a substance that stimulates bowel movements, either by increasing the flow of bile, or by increasing the peristaltic action of the colon muscle.

LDL: low-density lipoprotein; "bad" cholesterol.

Lecithin: a phospholipid found in nerve tissue and blood.

Legume: a fruit consisting of one carpel, opening on one side, such as a pea.

Lenticel: spongy area of bark on woody plant that allows exchange of gases between stem and atmosphere.

Lesion: any localized, abnormal change in tissue formation; in iridology, a lacuna.

Lethargy: a feeling of tiredness, drowsiness or lack of energy.

Leucocytosis: an increase in the number of white blood cells above the normal range, used as an indicator of active infection.

Leukemia: overproduction of abnormal white blood cells by bone marrow and other blood-forming organs, usually causing life-threatening systemic malignancy.

Leukocyte: white blood cells responsible for fighting disease.

Leukocytosis: abnormal level in number of white blood cells, used as an indicator of active infection.

Leukopenia: reduction in number of white blood cells to below normal level.

Leukoplakia: a precancerous lesion usually seen in the mouth that is characterized by a white colored patch.

Leukotrienes: inflammatory compounds produced when oxygen interacts with polyunsaturated fatty acids.

Lichen: fungus in symbiotic union with an algae.

Lignin: organic substance that serves as binder for cellulose fibers in wood and certain plants.

Ligulet: a narrow projection from the top of a leaf sheath in grasses.

Liniment: aromatic-alcohol preparation rubbed into skin to increase circulation to area.

Lipase: fat-splitting enzyme.

Lipid: fat, phospholipid, steroid or prostaglandin.

Lipolytic: substance that causes lipolysis, the chemical disintegration or splitting of fats.

Lipoprotein: molecule combining protein and lipid.

Lipotropic: promoting the flow of lipids to and from the liver.

Lithotriptic: substance used to dissolve and discharge urinary and biliary stones.

Liverwort: any of various small, flat bryophytes, usually found on logs, rocks, or soil in moist areas.

Lobed: Leaves that are slightly divided, with each division being rounded.

Lotion: an emollient emulsion, usually of the water in oil type.

Low density lipoprotein: LDL; large molecule protein-lipid aggregate; "bad" cholesterol.

Lozenge: medicated slow-release tablet that is dissolved in the mouth to soothe throat.

Lubricant: greasy substance applied to reduce friction on body surface.

Lumbago: lower back pain due to injury or sciatica.

Lumen: cavity within tubular structure.

Lung cancer: malignancy in epithelium of air passages or lung, usually due to chronic irritation by smoke or other outside agents.

Lupus erythematosus: chronic inflammation of connective tissue that causes red scaly rash on face, arthritis, and organ damage.

Lycopod: club moss.

Lyme disease: spirochetal infection transmitted by a tick that causes skin rash, headache, fever, and sometimes arthritis and heart damage.

Lymph: colorless fluid derived from blood and carried in special ducts of lymphatic vessels.

Lymphatic: pertaining to the lymph system; substance that enhances flow of lymph.

Lymphocyte: a type of white blood cell found primarily in lymph nodes.

Lymphoid tissue: connective tissue containing lymphocytes.

Lymphoma: malignant tumor of lymph nodes that is not Hodgkin's disease.

M

Macerate: soak until softened or until active constituents are extracted.

Macula: discoloration or thickening of skin in contrast to surrounding area.

Malabsorption: impaired absorption of nutrients, most often due to diarrhea.

Malaise: general sense of being unwell, often accompanied by physical discomfort and weakness.

Malignant: a term used to describe a condition that tends to worsen and eventually causes death.

Malnutrition: insufficient food consumption or absorption to satisfy bodily needs over prolonged period.

Mammogram: a diagnostic X-ray of the breast, used to detect breast cancer.

Mania: excessive activity and euphoria.

Manipulation: the skillful use of the hands to move a part of the body or a specific joint or muscle.

Mast cell: a cell found in many tissues of the body which contributes greatly to allergic and inflammatory processes by secreting histamine and other inflammatory chemicals.

Mastitis: inflammation of breasts, usually due to bacterial infection through damaged nipples.

Maturating: substances that promote the maturation or "ripening" of tumors, boils, ulcers, etc.

Measles: highly infectious viral disease, mainly in children, that causes high fever and an elevated pink rash; rubeola.

Melanoma: malignant tumor of melanin-forming cells in skin.

Meniere's syndrome: disease of labyrinth of inner ear, causing deafness and vertigo.

Meningitis: inflammation of membranes lining the skull and vertebral canal, due to viral or bacterial infection, causing fever, headache, muscular rigidity, convulsion, delirium, or death.

Menorrhagia: excessive loss of blood during menstruation.

Menstruation: the discharge of blood and tissue from the uterus that occurs when a fertilized egg does not implant.

Menstruum: liquid used to extract active constituents into a tincture, may be a combination of water and distilled spirits, wine, vinegar, or glycerin.

Metabolic rate: level of energy expenditure.

Metabolism: a collective term for all the chemical processes that take place in the body.

Metabolite: a product of a chemical reaction.

Metallo-enzyme: an enzyme which contains a metal at its active site.

Metastasis: spread of malignant cells far from site of origin.

Microflora: the microbial inhabitants of a particular region, e.g. colon.

Microorganism: any living organism too small to be viewed by unaided eye, including bacteria, viruses, and some algae and fungi.

Migraine: recurrent, intense headache, often accompanied by blurred vision and nausea.

Mineral oil: colorless, tasteless petroleum derivative used as laxative, and in skin preparations.

Mineralocorticoid steroid: salt-retaining hormone of adrenal cortex.

Miscible: a gas or liquid having the ability to mix uniformly with another gas or liquid.

Mitogenic: an agent that effects cell division.

Mold: multi-cellular filamentous fungus.

Mole: flat or raised growth demarcated by area of brown or colored pigment in skin.

Molecule: the smallest complete unit of a substance that can exist independently and still retain the characteristic properties of the substance.

Monoclonal antibodies: genetically engineered antibodies specific for one particular antigen.

Monocotyledon: angiosperm having only one seed leaf cotyledon.

Monocyte: large white blood cell with a horseshoe shaped nucleus.

Mononucleosis: infectious disease that manifests a high number of monocytes in blood, enlarged lymph nodes, prolonged fever, appetite loss, and malaise; glandular fever.

Monosaccharide: a simple one-unit sugar, like fructose and glucose.

Mordant: substance used to bind and fix plant based dye colors on fabrics.

Moss: any of various small bryophytes without true stems reproducing by spores, and growing in velvety clusters in moist areas on rocks, trees, and the ground.

Motion sickness: nausea, vomiting, dizziness, and headache caused by motion.

Motor neural: designating muscular activity stimulated by impulses from central nervous system.

Mouthwash: gargle.

Moxa: a dried herb (usually Mugwort) burnt on or above the skin to stimulate an acupuncture point or serve as a counterirritant.

Mucilage: a substance containing gelatinous constituents which are demulcent.

Mucilaginous: containing significant amounts of mucilage.

Mucin: protein that forms mucus when mixed with water.

Mucolytic: substance which dissolves or breaks down mucus.

Mucosa: another term for mucous membrane.

Mucous membrane: mucus-secreting membrane lining body cavities and canals connecting with external air.

Mucus: viscid watery lubricating solution secreted by mucous membranes.

Multiple sclerosis: MS; chronic nervous system disease with recurrent symptoms of unsteady gait, shaky limb movements, rapid involuntary eye movements, and speech defects.

Mumps: viral infection that causes fever and swelling of parotid salivary glands.

Muscle-relaxer: substance that acts to relieve tension in muscles.

Muscular dystrophy: inherited muscle disease marked by degeneration of muscle fiber.

Mutagen: external agent that increases mutation rate in cells.

Myasthenia gravis: muscular weakness that has its onset with repetitive activity and leads to paralysis.

Mycelium: mass of thread-like tubes forming the vegetative parts of a fungus.

Mycorrhiza: close symbiosis between mycelia of certain fungi and root cells of some vascular plants.

Mycosis: fungus infection.

Mycotoxins: toxins from yeast and fungi.

Mydriatic: herbs that cause dilation of the pupil of the eye.

Myelin sheath: a white fatty substance which surrounds and insulates nerve fibers, and which aids and protects nerve impulse transmission.

Myeloma: malignancy of bone marrow.

Myocardial infarction: death of portion of heart muscle due to interrupted blood supply.

Myocarditis: acute or chronic inflammation of heart muscle.

Myxedema: dry, firm, waxy swelling of skin and subcutaneous tissue, also characterized by labored speech and blunted senses.

N

Narcotic: a substance which induces sleep; intoxicating or poisonous in large doses.

Natural immunity: inborn lack of susceptibility to specific disease.

Naturopathy: healing art that uses only natural remedies and non-invasive therapies to stimulate the body's innate healing ability to prevent or overcome disease.

Nausea: feeling that one is about to vomit.

Nauseant: herbs that produce nausea or an inclination to vomit.

Necrosis: death of cells in organ or tissue.

Nectary: organ of plant that secretes nectar.

Neoplasia: a medical term for a tumor formation, characterized by a progressive, abnormal replication of cells.

Neoplasm: new tumor caused by uncontrolled reproduction of abnormal cells.

Nephralgia: pain in kidney and loin area.

Nephritic: herbs that influence the kidneys, and are healing in kidney complaints.

Nephritis: inflammation of kidney; Bright's disease.

Nephrosis: syndrome characterized by edema, excess albumin in urine, and cholesterol in blood.

Nervine: substance that supports the function of the nervous system; can be meaningfully subdivided into three groups, as follows:
- **Nervine relaxants:** substances that ease anxiety and tension by soothing both body and mind.
- **Nervine stimulants:** substances that directly stimulate nerve activity.
- **Nervine tonics:** substances that strengthen and restore the nervous system.

Neuralgia: a stabbing pain along a nerve pathway.

Neurasthenia: condition characterized by fatigue, irritability, headache, dizziness, anxiety, and intolerance to noise due to head injury or mental illness; nervous exhaustion.

Neuritis: inflammation of nerves.

Neurodermatitis: localized skin disease with itching and thickening of skin.

Neurofibrillary: tangles clusters of degenerated nerves.

Neurofibromatosis: congenital disease that causes the growth on fibrous nerve coverings of benign tumors that may become malignant.

Neuron: functional unit of a nerve, including cell body, axon, and dendrites.

Neuropathy: disorder or degeneration of nervous system.

Neurotransmitters: substances which modify or transmit nerve impulses.

Night sweats: copious perspiration while sleeping.

Nit: louse egg that attaches to body.

Nocturia: the disturbance of a person's sleep at night by the need to pass urine.

Node: place on stem from which leaves and shoot arise.

Nonvascular plant: bryophyte.

Norepinephrine: commercial form of neurotransmitter used for emergency treatment of lowered blood pressure.

Nut: dry, single-seeded fruit of various trees and shrubs consisting of kernel enclosed ill hard or tough shell.

Nutritive: herbs that contain rich stores of nutrients, and are building to body tissues.

O

Obovate: oval, but broader towards the apex; refers to leaf shape.

Occlusion: closing or obstruction of hollow organ or body part.

Ointment: medicated fatty substance used to soothe or heal skin; salve; unguent.

Oleo gum resin: a natural exudation from trees and plants that consists mainly of essential oil, gum and resin.

Oleoresin: a natural resinous exudation from plants, or an aromatic liquid preparation, extracted from botanical matter, consisting almost entirely of a mixture of essential oil and resin.

Olfaction: the sense of smell.

Opiate: one of several derivatives of opium that depresses central nervous system, relieves pain, and induces sleep.

Opium: resinous exudate from unripe opium poppy seed capsules; a narcotic.

Opportunistic: designating disease or infection occurring only under certain conditions, such as when immune system is impaired, or tissues are weakened.

Ophthalmic: herb that is healing to disorders and diseases of the eye.

Orchitis: inflammation of testis that causes pain, redness, and swelling of scrotum, usually due to infection such as mumps in adults.

Organ: collection of tissues joined in structural unit to serve a common function.

Organic: in chemistry, refers to all compounds containing carbon; in Natural Health refers to substances derived from living matter.

Organic disorder: disorder associated with physiological changes in structure of organ or tissue.

Osteoarthritis: joint cartilage disease that causes pain, swelling, and impaired joint function, due to overuse and breakdown of joint as a result of poor diet.

Osteomyelitis: inflammation of bone marrow and adjacent bone, mostly from infection after fractures.

Osteopathy: treatment of disease by manipulation and massage of musculoskeletal system.

Osteoporosis: loss of calcium in bone matrix resulting in weak and brittle bones.

Otalgia: earache; neuralgia in the ear.

OTC: over-the-counter; medication available without prescription.

Otitis: inflammation of ear canals, due to viral or bacterial infection, causing severe pain and high fever.

Otosclerosis: disease of bone surrounding inner ear, causing impaired hearing.

Ovate: egg-shaped.

Ovulation: the release of an egg from one of the ovaries.

Oxytocic: an agent that stimulates labor contractions.

P

Pack: medicated moist pad of cotton or cloth applied to body or inserted in cavity.

Painkiller: agent that relieves or inhibits pain, analgesic.

Palisade cell: chloroplast-containing cell just below surface of a leaf.

Palliative: medicine that relieves symptoms to make patient more comfortable, but has no direct effect on disease.

Palmate: with 3 or more leaflets, nerves, or lobes radiating from a central point.

Palpation: assessing the body's condition by means of touch.

Palpitation: abnormally rapid or violent heartbeat; arrhythmia.

Panacea: a cure-all.

Pancreatitis: inflammation of pancreas with sudden, severe pain.

Pandemic: epidemic disease that spreads to different countries over large region.

Panicle: loose, diversely branching cluster of stalked flowers.

Papain: the protein digesting enzyme of papaya.

Pappus: the calyx in a composite flower having feathery hairs, scales or bristles.

Papule: small, superficial bump or spot on skin, often part of rash.

Parahormone: chemical control agent that can be synthesized by more than one cell type.

Parasite: organism that lives in or on another living organism, stealing nutrients while contributing nothing to host's welfare, and often causing irritation or interfering with function.

Parasiticide: substance that prevents and destroys parasites.

Parathyroid hormone: PTH; hormone that promotes vitamin-D synthesis, and elevates blood calcium.

Paregoric: camphorated tincture of opium used to relieve diarrhea, formerly used as painkiller.

Parenchyma: soft tissue forming chief substance of leaves and roots, fruit pulp, and center of stems.

Parkinson's disease: neurological disorder of late middle age characterized by tremor, rigidity, and abrupt spontaneous movements.

Parkinsonism: Parkinson's disease.

Paroxysm: sudden, violent spasm or convulsion; abrupt worsening of symptom.

Parturient: substance that eases or facilitates childbirth.

Passive immunity: short-term resistance to disease from injection of another's antibodies.

Pathogen: any agent, particularly a microorganism, that causes disease.

Pathogenesis: the process by which a disease originates and develops.

Pathogenic: causing or producing disease.

Pectin: white, colloidal carbohydrate, found in certain ripe fruits, that has gelling properties.

Pectoral: herb that is healing to problems if the broncho-pulmonary area.

Pedicel: stalk of single flower, fruit, or leaf.

Pediculicide: an agent which destroys lice.

Pediculosis: infestation of body and/or scalp by lice, causing itching and sometimes bacterial infection with weeping lesions.

Peduncle: stalk supporting flower or flower cluster of an angiosperm or bearing the fruiting body of a fungus.

Pellagra: B-vitamin nutritional deficiency that causes scaly dermatitis, diarrhea, and depression.

Pepsin: stomach enzyme that breaks down proteins.

Peptic: referring to gastric secretions and areas affected by them.

Peptic ulcer: breach in lining of digestive tract due to excess acid or bacterial infection.

Peptide: compound of two or more amino acids

Perennial: herbaceous plant that develops new growth from the same root structure several years in a row.

Perfoliate: A leaf that appears to be perforated by the stem.

Perfusion: passage of fluid through tissue, especially blood through the lungs.

Pericarditis: acute or chronic inflammation of sac surrounding heart.

Periodontal disease: disease of gums, mouth lining, and bony structures supporting teeth, caused by plaque build-up and opportunistic bacteria; pyorrhea.

Peripheral resistance: opposition to flow of blood in vessels.

Peristalsis: successive muscular contractions of the intestines which move digesting material through the gastrointestinal tract.

Peristaltic: herb that stimulates or strengthens peristalsis.

Peristaltic waves: successive contractions of tubular muscles of the gastrointestinal tract.

Peritonitis: inflammation of abdominal cavity membrane, often due to perforation or rupture of abdominal organ.

Pertussis: whooping cough.

Pessary: medicated suppository intended for vaginal application.

Petal: one of the circle of flower parts inside the sepals.

Petiole: the stalk of a leaf.

Petit mal: lesser epileptic seizure characterized by brief spells of sleepiness or unconsciousness.

pH: measure of acid/alkaline character of solutions; on a scale from 0 to 14, pH 7.0 is considered neutral, below 7.0 is acid, above 7.0 is alkaline.

Pharmaceutical: manufactured drug or medication.

Pharmacognosy: science of plant-derived chemicals and drugs.

Pharmacology: medical science of drugs which deals with their properties and actions on bodily tissues.

Pharmacopoeia: an official publication of drugs in common use, in a given country.

Pharmacy: preparation and dispensing of drugs; place where this is done.

Pharyngitis: inflammation of pharynx that causes sore throat or tonsillitis.

Phenol: natural or synthetic aromatic compounds containing a hydroxide (OH) ring.

Phlebitis: inflammation of vein wall, especially in legs, as complication of varicose veins, causing extreme tenderness and pain.

Phlegm: sputum; expectorated mucus secretion of respiratory tract.

Phospholipid: fatty compound containing water-soluble phosphate group.

Photosynthesis: production of organic substances from carbon dioxide and water in green plant cells which chemically transform the energy of sunlight.

Physic: medicine or remedy, especially a laxative or cathartic.

Physiological: the natural functional biological processes of a living organism.

Physiology: the study of the functioning of the body, including the physical and chemical processes of its cells, tissues, organs and systems.

Physostigmine: a drug which blocks the breakdown of acetylcholine.

Phytoestrogen: plant compound which exerts estrogen-like effects.

Phytohormones: plant substances that mimic the action of animal hormones.

Phytotherapy: the treatment of disease by plants; herbal medicine.

Picolinic acid: an amino acid secreted by the pancreas that facilitates zinc and chromium absorption and transport.

Piles: hemorrhoids.

Pill: small ball or tablet of medicine to be swallowed whole; also commonly, an oral contraceptive.

Pinkeye: conjunctivitis.

Pinnate: a leaf composed of more than three leaflets arranged in two rows along a common stalk.

Placebo: a physically inactive substance taken by a patient in the belief that it will effect an improvement in condition.

Placebo effect: used to describe the power of the mind (by suggestion) alone to facilitate healing.

Plaque: sticky, colorless mixture of saliva, bacteria, and carbohydrates on surface of teeth that causes tartar and caries.

Plasma: fluid portion of blood and lymph.

Plaster: pasty medicinal dressing applied to body part on cloth as curative counterirritant; poultice.

Pleurisy: inflammation of pleura that cover lungs, causing difficult and painful breathing.

Pneumoconiosis: black lung.

Pneumonia: inflammation or infection of lungs in which the sacs fill with pus and fluid, causing coughing and chest pain.

Pneumothorax: collapsed lung.

Pod: vessel enclosing one or more seeds.

Podagra: gout of foot, especially the big toe.

Poliomyelitis: infectious viral disease of central nervous system, formerly epidemic, causing stiffness and paralysis of muscles, especially of the respiratory system; polio, infantile paralysis.

Pollen: fine, dust like grains containing plants' male sexual cells, produced in anthers or similar structures of seed plants.

Polymer: natural or synthetic macromolecules formed by the repetition of an identical small molecule.

Polyp: benign growth on mucous membrane, especially in the nose, ear, stomach or bowel.

Polypeptide: protein polymer of amino acid units.

Polysaccharide: a molecule composed of many sugar molecules linked together.

Pomade: a prepared perfume material obtained by the enfleurage process.

Poultice: the therapeutic application of a soft moist mass (such as fresh herbs) to the skin, to encourage local circulation, promote healing, and relieve pain.

Prednisone: synthetic steroid, administered orally, used to control inflammatory processes.

Press: device for; drying and flattening botanical specimens; extracting liquid residue from herbal preparations, i.e. tinctures, decoctions, etc.

Priapism: persistent erection of penis due to circulatory obstructions.

Progesterone: hormone that prepares uterus to receive and develop fertilized egg.

Prognosis: assessment of future course and outcome of patient's disease.

Prophylactic: substance or article used to prevent disease or infection.

Proptosis: outward displacement of an organ, especially the eyeball.

Prostaglandin: hormone-like compounds manufactured from essential fatty acids.

Prostate: muscular gland surrounding the base of the male urethra that secretes a milky fluid that transports sperm.

Prostatitis: inflammation of prostate gland, usually due to bacterial infection, and sometimes causing urinary obstruction.

Prostrate: lying flat; a plant growing flat along the ground.

Prostration: total exhaustion.

Protease: protein-splitting enzyme.

Protective: herb that serves as a protective covering to abraded, inflamed, or injured parts when applied topically.

Protein: any of a large class of organic nitrogenous substances built of amino acids.

Pruritus: itching.

Pruritus ani: painful itching of rectum or anus, often caused by parasites.

Psoriasis: condition characterized by chronic, itchy, scaly silvery patches of thickened skin, especially on elbows, forearms, knees, and scalp.

Psychomotor: relating to disorders of muscular activity affected by cerebral disturbances.

Puerperal fever: blood poisoning in mother shortly after childbirth due to infection of womb lining or vagina.

Pulmonary embolism: obstruction by blood clot of artery that conveys blood from heart to lungs.

Pungent: herb that causes sharply prickling, acrid, and penetrating sensation to the sensory organs.

Purgative: strong laxative or cathartic medication.

Purpura: skin rash due to bleeding into skin from defective capillaries or blood platelet deficiency.

Pus: thick yellow or green liquid containing blood cells and dead cells, formed at site of infection or inflammation.

Pustule: small, pus-containing blister.

Putrefy: to rot or decay as a result of anaerobic bacteria.

Putrescence: foul smell caused by decomposition of tissue.

Pyorrhea: periodontal disease.

Pyrexia: fever.

Pyrosis: heartburn; acid indigestion.

Q

Quinine: alkaloid extract of cinchona plant used to treat malaria and intermittent fevers.

Quinsy: pus-discharging inflammation of tonsils.

R

Raceme: un-branched flower clusters, usually pyramid shaped, with stalked flowers on a central axis.

Radiation sickness: acute disease caused by exposure to radioactive emissions, causing nausea, vomiting, diarrhea bleeding, hair loss, and death.

Raynaud's syndrome: disorder in which spasms of arteries to extremities cause fingertips and toes to turn pale, blue, and numb; more frequent in women.

Rays (ray flowers): outer ring of petals surrounding the flowerhead of a plant in the composite family.

Receptacle: the enlarged upper part of the stem from which the floral parts arise.

Rectification: the process of re-distillation applied to essential oils to rid them of certain constituents.

Referred pain: pain felt in part of body separate from its source.

Reflex: automatic, involuntary activity caused by stimulation of simple nervous circuits.

Refrigerant: cooling; herb that reduces fever, and relieves thirst.

Regurgitation: vomiting.

Rejection: immune reaction to transplanted organ or foreign substance.

REM sleep: deep sleep phase characterized by rapid eye movements.

Renal calculus: kidney stone.

Renal colic: severe pain in kidney.

Renin: enzyme produced by kidneys.

Resinoids: a perfumery material prepared from natural resinous matter, such as balsams, gum resins, etc.

Resins: a natural or prepared product, either solid or semi-solid in nature. Natural resins are exudations from trees, such as myrrh; prepared resins are oleoresins from which the essential oil has been removed.

Resolvent: an agent which disperses swelling, or effects resorption of a new growth.

Respiration: exchange of gases between body tissues and surrounding environment.

Respiratory arrest: cessation of breathing.

Restorative: an agent that helps strengthen and revive the body systems.

Reticulosis: abnormal malignant overgrowth of cells of lymphatic glands or immune system.

Retinitis pigmentosa: hereditary condition that causes progressive degeneration of retina of eye.

Revulsive: substance that relieves pain by means of the diversion of blood or disease from one part of the body to another.

Reye's syndrome: acute disorder primarily in children after viral infections such as chickenpox or influenza, associated with aspirin use, causing brain swelling and affecting organs.

Rheum: watery discharge from mucous membrane of mouth, eyes, or nose.

Rheumatic fever: delayed complication of upper respiratory streptococcus infection, especially in children.

Rheumatic heart disease: scarring and chronic heart inflammation from progressive state of rheumatic fever.

Rheumatism: any disorder causing aches and pains in muscles or joints.

Rheumatoid arthritis: common form of arthritis that affects extremities, digits, and hips.

Rhizome: creeping horizontal stem lying at or just beneath soil surface, which bears leaves at its tip and roots from its underside.

Rickettsiae: group of parasitic organisms similar to bacteria that infest body through ticks or mites.

Ringworm: highly contagious fungal infection of skin, especially the scalp, feet, or under the beard.

Root: underground part of plant that functions in nutrient absorption, aeration, food storage, and as a physical support system.

Rosacea: chronic acne characterized by red, pustular lesions and inflammation about nose, cheeks, and forehead.

Roseola: rubella.

Rosette: leaves which are closely arranged in a spiral.

Rubefacient: substance which generates a localized increase in blood flow when applied to the skin, promoting healing and relieving pain.

Rubella: highly contagious viral infection, primarily in children, causing enlarged lymph nodes in neck and an elevated pink rash; German measles; roseola.

Rubeola: measles.

S

Saccharide: a sugar molecule.

Saliva: watery, slightly acidic secretion of salivary glands that moistens food and initiates its breakdown.

Salmonella poisoning: food poisoning caused by ingestion of aerobic intestinal bacteria.

Salt: the chemical combination of an acid and a base yields a salt plus water.

Salve: medicinal ointment used to soothe or heal skin irritations, burns, or wounds; ointment; unguent.

Saponins: glycoside compounds that form a soap-like lather when shaken in water. There are two broad groups: the steroidal saponins, which seem to mimic the precursors of female sex hormones, and the tri-terpenoid saponins, which mimic the adrenal hormone ACTH.

Saprophyte: free-living organism that lives on dead or putrefying tissues.

Sarcoma: tumor of connective tissue.

Saturated fat: fat in which carbon chains are bonded by single bonds while simultaneously bound to as much hydrogen as possible; solid at room temperature, and often at body temperature.

Scab: hard crust of blood, serum, or pus over healing wound.

Scabies: skin infection from infestation of mites that causes severe itching, especially around groin, nipples, and between fingers.

Scar: mark left on skin by healing wound where connective tissues replace normal tissues; cicatrix.

Scarlatina: scarlet fever.

Scarlet fever: highly contagious childhood disease caused by streptococcus bacteria, characterized by sore throat and widespread rash; scarlatina.

Schistosomiasis: tropical disease of the intestines, due to infestation of blood flukes, that causes anemia, diarrhea, dysentery, and cirrhosis; snail fever.

Sciatica: condition marked by pain down back of thigh, due to displacement or disintegration of intervertebral disk, accompanied by numbness and stiff back.

Scleroderma: thickening and hardening of tissues beneath skin, causing rigidity of skin.

Sclerosis: hardening of tissue due to inflammation.

Scopolamine: belladonna derivative.

Scrofula: tuberculosis of the cervical lymph nodes, particularly with enlargement and degeneration of the lymphatic glands of the neck.

Scurvy: vitamin C deficiency from absence of fresh fruit and vegetables in diet that causes swollen, bleeding gums, subcutaneous bleeding, and death when prolonged.

Seborrhea: excessive secretion by sebaceous glands in face, often associated with hormonal changes.

Seborrheic dermatitis: skin eruption due to excess secretion of sebum, common on face at puberty.

Second-degree burn: blistering of surface skin and damage to underlying dermis.

Secretion: manufacture and release of substance by cell or organ; the substance released.

Sedative: an agent which reduces functional activity of the nervous system; calming.

Seed: fertilized plant ovule containing embryo, capable of germinating to produce a new plant.

Seizure: sudden attack of disease or condition, as in epilepsy.

Senescence: bodily degeneration after maturity.

Senile dementia: mental deterioration associated with aging.

Senility: loss of intellectual faculties in old age.

Sepal: leaf-like, usually green outer circle of calyx.

Sepsis: poisoning of blood by putrescent material containing pathogenic microorganisms.

Septic: putrefactive destruction of tissue by disease carrying bacteria or their toxins.

Septicemia: tissue destruction by bacteria or toxins absorbed from bloodstream; blood poisoning.

Serape: abrasion.

Serum: liquid portion of the blood.

Serum hepatitis: liver inflammation that causes fever and jaundice, transmitted by infected hypodermic needle or blood transfusion.

Sessile: lacking a stalk, such as a leaf or flower with no obvious stalk.

Shingles: painful skin disease with neuralgia, caused by herpes zoster virus.

Sialogogue: substance that stimulates the secretion of saliva.

SIDA: common name for AIDS outside English speaking countries; based on Spanish "sindrome inmuno-deficiencia adquirido" or French "syndrome immuno-deficitaire acquis."

Silique: the term applied to the peculiar seedpod structure of plants in the mustard family.

Sinusitis: inflammation or infection of sinus sacs behind and around nose, causing headache and discharge through nose.

Slipped disk: abnormal protrusion of disk between abutting vertebrae, causing painful pressure against spinal cord; herniated disk.

Soporific: herb that induces sleep.

Spadix: a thick, fleshy flower spike usually enveloped by a spathe.

Spasm: sustained involuntary muscular contraction.

Spasmolytic: anti-spasmodic.

Spastic colon: irritable bowel syndrome.

Spasticity: resistance to passive movement of limb; lack of motor coordination.

Spathe: a modified, leaf-like structure surrounding a spadix.

Species: basic unit of biological classification ranking below genus, including similar organisms capable of interbreeding.

Spike: inflorescence in which flowers bloom along entire length of single stalk.

Spinal meningitis: meningitis.

Spirillum: spiral bacterium.

Splenic: relating to the spleen, the largest endocrine gland.

Spondylosis: degeneration of inter-vertebral disks in back bone, causing pain and restricting movement.

Sprue: deficient absorption of food due to intestinal disease, that causes diarrhea, anemia, and inflamed tongue; psilosis.

Sputum: mucus coughed up from respiratory tract; phlegm.

Stamens: pollen-bearing floral organs consisting of filaments and pollen sacs.

Stenosis: abnormal narrowing of blood vessel or heart valve.

Sternutatory: herb that brings on sneezing.

Steroid: any of large family of chemical compounds including hormones produced by adrenal glands, ovaries, and testes; medication used for immuno-suppression and hormone replacement.

Stimulant: an agent which accelerates the physiological functions and responses of the body.

Stipule: appendages resembling small leaves at the base of the leaves of some plants.

Stitch: sudden, sharp pain, usually in muscle between ribs.

Stolon: stem that takes root at intervals along ground, forming new plants.

Stomachic: substance used as a digestive aid and tonic, and to improve appetite.

Strangury: painful urination in which the urine can only be released in droplets due to constriction of the urethra.

Strep throat: infection of throat by streptococcus bacteria.

Stridor: loud, harsh breathing noise due to partial obstruction of trachea or larynx.

Stroke: CVA, sudden weakness or paralysis, often on one side of body, due to interruption of blood flow to brain caused by a clot or hemorrhage; apoplexy; cerebrovascular accident.

Sty: acute bacterial infection of gland at base of eyelash.

Styptic: a strongly astringent agent which stops or reduces external bleeding.

Subclinical: designating suspected disease or injury that is not developed enough to produce definite signs and symptoms.

Submucosa: the tissue just below the mucous membrane.

Succulent: plant with thick, fleshy tissues that stores starchy juice.

Sudorific: substance that causes sweating when taken hot, and act as tonic when taken cold.

Suppressor T-cells: lymphocytes controlled by the thymus gland which suppress the immune response.

Suppuration: formation and discharge of pus.

Surfactant: wetting agent; a compound which reduces the surface tension in water, between water and another liquid, or between a liquid and a solid.

Sycosis: inflammation and itching of hair follicles.

Sympatholytic: substance that affects sympathetic nervous system.

Symptom: characteristic indication of disease or disorder.

Synapse: junction between two excitable nerve cells.

Syncope: fainting.

Syndrome: set of signs and symptoms characteristic of a particular disease or condition.

Syphilis: sexually transmitted bacterial disease that causes genital sore in the acute stage, and may lead to blindness or paralysis in chronic stage, and insanity in advanced stage.

Systemic: affecting the entire body, not just one part.

Systole: contraction of the heart muscle.

Systolic: the pressure in the arteries during the contraction phase of the heart beat; the first number in a blood pressure reading.

T

T-cell: a lymphocyte which is under the control of the thymus gland.

Tablet: small disk, made from compressed powders of one or more drugs, that is swallowed whole.

Tachycardia: abnormally increased heartbeat and pulse rate.

Tachypnea: rapid breathing.

Tampon: plug of absorbent material used to absorb blood or secretions, especially in vagina for menstrual discharge.

Tannin: astringent compound that reacts with protein to produce a leather-like coating on animal tissue, used to promote healing, reduce inflammation, and halt infection.

Taproot: deep main root from which lateral roots develop.

Tartar: calcareous deposit and encrustation on teeth.

Taxonomy: system of classifying organisms into natural related groups based on shared features or traits.

Tender: plant that is not frost hardy.

Tendonitis: inflammation of bands of connective tissue that join muscle to bones and joints.

Tendril: wiry, often spiral part of climbing plant which clings to or coils around objects for support.

Teratogen: substance that can cause birth defects.

Teratoma: tumor composed of tissues not normally found at site.

Testosterone: principal male sex hormone produced by testes.

Tetany: spasm and twitching of muscles of face, hands, and feet.

Thalassemia: genetic, anemic condition characterized by deficiency of hemoglobin in blood.

Thallus: nonvascular plant body without clear differentiation into stems, leaves, or roots.

Third-degree burn: total destruction of skin and damage to tissue beneath.

Thrombocytosis: condition marked by increase in number of platelets in blood.

Thromboembolism: condition in which blood clot forms at one point in circulation, dislodges, and moves to another point.

Thrombophlebitis: inflammation of a vein and formation of blood clot that adheres to its wall.

Thrombosis: formation of a thrombus or blood clot.

Thrush: whitish coating on tongue with spots and ulcers in mouth due to Candidiasis.

Thyroid hormone: TH; thyroxine.

Tic douloureux: neuralgia of facial nerves.

Tincture: a liquid extract of the active constituents of an herb or blend of herbs, prepared by maceration in a menstruum, usually aqueous-alcohol, but may be vinegar, glycerin, or wine.

Tinea: fungal infection of the skin, as in athlete's foot.

Tinnitus: ringing in the ears.

Tissue: group of similar cells that performs a particular function.

Tonic: a substance that strengthens and revitalizes.

Tonsillitis: inflammation of tonsils, due to bacterial or viral infection, causing sore throat and fever.

Topical: applied to the skin, not taken internally.

Torpor: sluggishness, unresponsiveness to stimuli.

Torsion: twisting of a bodily organ or mass.

Toxemia: accumulation of toxins in blood.

Toxic: poisonous.

Toxicosis: any disease condition caused by the toxic effect of a substance.

Toxin: poisonous substance.

Trifoliate: a plant having three distinct leaflets.

Triglyceride: neutral fat lipid molecule composed of glycerol and three fatty acids.

Troche: small, medicinal lozenge that soothes mouth and throat.

Tuber: fat underground stem from which some plants grow, similar to but shorter and thicker than a rhizome.

Tuberculosis: formation of small granular tumors within an organ, most often the lungs or lymph glands, resulting from bacterial infection of morbid or catarrhal matter.

Tularemia: disease transmitted to humans from rabbits by deer flies or direct contamination, characterized by infection with ulcers, fever, aches, and enlarged lymph nodes.

Tumescence: swelling due to accumulation of blood or other fluid in tissue.

Tumor: abnormal growth of tissue in or on a body part.

Tussis: cough.

Typhoid fever: bacterial infection of digestive system, transmitted through contaminated food or water, that causes high fever, red rash on stomach, chills, sweating, and sometimes intestinal hemorrhage.

Typhus: one of various infections caused by parasitic Rickettsiae that results in high fever, severe headache, widespread rash, and delirium.

U

Ulcer: open, inflamed, non-healing sore in skin or mucous membrane, especially in lining of gastrointestinal tract.

Ulcerative colitis: inflammation and ulceration of colon and rectum.

Ultrasound: a test in which sound waves are used to examine a fetus, or view the internal organs.

Umbel: umbrella-like; a flower where the petioles all arise from the top of the stem.

Unguent: fatty substance used to soothe and heal skin; ointment; salve.

Unsaturated fat: fat in which some carbons are linked by double bonds, usually liquid at room temperature.

Urea: nitrogenous waste product of kidneys.

Uremia: the retention of urine by the body and the presence of high levels of urine components in the blood.

Urethritis: inflammation of urethra, due to bacterial or viral infection or obstruction.

Urinalysis: the chemical analysis of urine.

Urticaria: hives; itchy rash.

Uterine: pertaining to the uterus.

V

Vaginitis: inflammation of vaginal tissue, due to irritation or infection, causing burning pain and discharge.

Varicella: chickenpox.

Varicose veins: bulging, distended, occasionally painful veins in legs, rectum, or scrotum due to poor vascular tone and obstruction of blood flow.

Variegated: leaves with secondary colorations or patterns.

Vascular plant: any plant, such as the angiosperms, gymnosperms, or ferns, in which the xylem and phloem conduct water and organic nutrients.

Vasoconstrictor: a substance which causes narrowing or tightening of blood vessels.

Vasodilator: a substance which dilates or relaxes the blood vessels.

Vector: carrier; any agent, such as a flea or tick, that transmits parasitic microorganisms and infectious diseases from host to host.

Veil: membrane on a mushroom that encloses the young fruit body.

Venereal disease: VD; any infectious disease transmitted by sexual contact, now usually called sexually transmitted disease or STD.

Vermicide: substance that kills parasitic worms in the intestine.

Vermifuge: substance that expels parasites from the intestine; anthelmintic.

Verruca: wart.

Vertigo: sense that the surroundings are in motion or spinning, due to a disorder of the inner ear or vestibular nerve.

Vesicant: causing blistering to the skin; a counter irritant.

Vesicle: a small blister or sac containing fluid.

Virulent: disease-producing; aggressive.

Vitamin: an essential compound necessary to act as a catalyst in normal processes of the body; co-enzyme.

Volatile: unstable, evaporates easily.

Volatile oil: complex chemical mixtures of hydrocarbons and alcohols in plants.

Vulnerary: substance that promotes wound healing or normalization of damaged tissue.

Wart: small, hard, usually benign growth in skin, caused by virus.

Welt: raised ridge on skin caused by physical blow.

Wheal: temporary, itching, red or pale raised area of skin resulting from abrasion or allergy.

Whooping cough: acute contagious bacterial infection of mucous membranes lining air passages, especially in children, causing fever and paroxysmal cough with bleeding from mouth and nose; pertussis.

Whorl: a circle of leaves around a node.

Xanthoma: skin condition characterized by raised patches.

Xerostomia: diminished secretion of saliva that causes abnormally dry mouth, especially as a drug reaction.

APPENDIX B

Citations for Herbal Section

General Bibliography

Referred to as:	Source:
Am. Family Phys.	The American Family Physician; or, Domestic Guide to Health, John King, M.D., Robert Douglas (Indianapolis, Ind.), Publisher, 1892
Christopher	School of Natural Healing, Dr. John R. Christopher, Christopher Publications, 1996
Culpeper	Culpeper's Complete Herbal
Duke	The Green Pharmacy, James A. Duke, Ph.D., Rodale Press, 1997
Ellingwood	Ellingwood's American Materia Medica, Therapeutics and Pharmacognosy (1919)
Grieve	A Modern Herbal, Mrs. M. Grieve, F.R.H.S.(1931), (Edited by Mrs. C.F. Leyel); Tiger Books Int'l., 1994
Heinerman	Heinerman's Encyclopedia of Healing Herbs & Spices, John Heinerman, Prentice Hall (Parker Publishing), 1996
Hoffman	The Herbal Handbook, David Hoffman; Healing Arts Press, 1988
Holmes	The Energetics of Western Herbs, Vols I & II, Rev. 3rd Ed., Peter Holmes, Snow Lotus Press, 1998
Hutchens	Indian Herbology of North America, Alma R. Hutchens, Shambhala Press, 1991
Kindscher	Medicinal Plants of the Prairie; An Ethnobotanical Guide, Kelly Kindscher, University Press of Kansas, 1992
King's	King's American Dispensatory (1898)
Kloss	Back to Eden (New Rev. Ed.), Jethro Kloss, Back to Eden Publishing Co., 1992

— continues on next page

— continued from previous page

Millspaugh	American Medicinal Plants, Charles F. Millspaugh (1892), Dover Publications, 1974
N. Am. Plants	Medicinal and Other Uses of North American Plants, Charlotte Erichsen-Brown, Dover Publications, 1979
PDR-HM	Physician's Desk Reference for Herbal Medicines, 1st Ed., Medical Economics Co., 1998
Peterson	Peterson Field Guide; Eastern/Central Medicinal Plants and Herbs 2nd Ed., Steven Foster & James Duke, Houghton Mifflin Company, 2000
Porcher	Resources of Souther Fields and Forests, Francis Peyre Porcher (1863), Norman Publishing, 1991
Potters	Potter's New Cyclopedia of Botanical Drugs & Preparations, R.C. Wren, FLS; C.W. Daniel Co., Ltd., (Essex, England) 1994
Santillo	Natural Healing With Herbs, Humbart Santillo, N.D., Hohm Press, 1993
Shook	Advanced Treatise in Herbology, Edward E Shook, N.D., D.C., Whitman Publications, 2000
Tierra	Planetary Herbology, Dr. Michael Tierra, C.A., N.D., O.M.D.,; Lotus Press, 1988

Citations from World Wide Web

Ellingwood's American Materia Medica, Therapeutics and Pharmacognosy (1919), Finley Ellingwood, M.D.
pdf version (abridged - botanicals only): http://www.swsbm.com/Ellingwoods/Ellingwoods.html
html version: http://www.ibiblio.org/herbmed/eclectic/ellingwood/main.html

King's American Dispensatory, by Harvey Wickes Felter, M.D., and John Uri Lloyd, Phr. M., Ph. D., 1898.
http://www.ibiblio.org/herbmed/eclectic/kings/main.html

Phytochemical and Ethnobotanical Databases
Agricultural Research Service, James Duke
http://www.ars-grin.gov/duke/

Birch Bark—Betula alba, Betula spp.

Bibliography

Duke; pp. 82,452
Grieve; pg. 104
Heinerman; pp. 63-65
Hoffman; pp. 31,33
Holmes; pp. 713-714
Hutchens; pp. 36-39
Kloss; pp. 208-209
PDR-HM; pg. 691

Potters; pg. 31
Tierra; pg. 235

Citations from the Medline database

Zuco V, et al.
Selective cytotoxicity of betulinic acid on tumor cell lines, but not on normal cells.
Cancer Lett. 2002 Jan 10;175(1):17-25.

Zhang Z, et al.
Natural products inhibiting Candida albicans secreted aspartic proteases from Tovomita krukovii.
Planta Med. 2002 Jan;68(1):49-54.

Salti GI, et al.
Betulinic acid reduces ultraviolet-C-induced DNA breakage in congenital melanocytic naeval cells: evidence for a potential role as a chemopreventive agent.
Melanoma Res. 2001 Apr;11(2):99-104.

Enwerem NM, et al.
Anthelmintic activity of the stem bark extracts of Berlina grandiflora and one of its active principles, Betulinic acid.
Phytomedicine. 2001 Mar;8(2):112-4.

Kanamoto T, et al.
Anti-human immunodeficiency virus activity of YK-FH312 (a betulinic acid derivative), a novel compound blocking viral maturation.
Antimicrob Agents Chemother. 2001 Apr;45(4):1225-30

Kouzi SA, et al.
Microbial transformations of the antimelanoma agent betulinic acid.
J Nat Prod. 2000 Dec;63(12):1653-7.

Fulda S, et al.
Betulinic acid induces apoptosis through a direct effect on mitochondria in neuroectodermal tumors.
Med Pediatr Oncol. 2000 Dec;35(6):616-8

Selzer E, et al.
Effects of betulinic acid alone and in combination with irradiation in human melanoma cells.
J Invest Dermatol. 2000 May;114(5):935-40.

Fulda S, et al.
Betulinic acid: a new chemotherapeutic agent in the treatment of neuroectodermal tumors.
Klin Padiatr. 1999 Jul-Aug;211(4):319-22.

Fulda S, et al.
Betulinic acid: a new cytotoxic agent against malignant brain-tumor cells.
Int J Cancer. 1999 Jul 30;82(3):435-41.

Steele JC, et al.
In vitro and in vivo evaluation of betulinic acid as an antimalarial.
Phytother Res. 1999 Mar;13(2):115-9.

Schmidt ML, Kuzmanoff KL, Ling-Indeck L, Pezzuto JM.
Betulinic acid induces apoptosis in human neuroblastoma cell lines.
Eur J Cancer. 1997 Oct;33(12):2007-10.

Pisha E, et al.
Discovery of betulinic acid as a selective inhibitor of human melanoma that functions by induction of apoptosis.
Nat Med. 1995 Oct;1(10):1046-51

BLACK COHOSH—Cimicifuga racemosa

Bibliography

Christopher; pp. 437-439
Duke; pp. 323-324, 422
Hoffman; pg. 88
Holmes; pg. 578
Hutchens; pg. 46
Millspaugh; pp. 37-40
PDR-HM; pg. 746
Porcher; pp. 19-21
Potters; pg. 83
Santillo; pp. 87-88

Citations from World Wide Web

Agricultural Research Service, James Duke
Phytochemical and Ethnobotanical Databases
http://www.ars-grin.gov/duke/ethnobot.html

Citations from the Medline database

Linde H
[Contents of Cimicifuga racemosa. 5. 27-desoxyacetylacteol]
Arch Pharm Ber Dtsch Pharm Ges 1968 May;301(5):335-41

Linde H
[Contents of Cimicifuga racemosa. 2. On the structure of actein]
Arch Pharm Ber Dtsch Pharm Ges 1967 Oct;300(10):885-92

Linde H
[Contents of Cimicifuga racemosa. 3. On the constitution of the rings A, B and C of actein]
Arch Pharm Ber Dtsch Pharm Ges 1967 Dec;300(12):982-92

Ito M Kondo Y Takemoto T
Spasmolytic substances from Cimicifuga dahurica maxim.
Chem Pharm Bull (Tokyo) 1976 Apr;24(4):580-3

Duker EM Kopanski L Jarry H Wuttke W
Effects of extracts from Cimicifuga racemosa on gonadotropin release in menopausal women and ovariectomized rats.
Planta Med 1991 Oct;57(5):420-4

Jarry H Harnischfeger G Duker E
[The endocrine effects of constituents of Cimicifuga racemosa. 2. In vitro binding of constituents to estrogen receptors]
Planta Med 1985 Aug(4):316-9 (Published in German)

Jarry H Harnischfeger G
[Endocrine effects of constituents of Cimicifuga racemosa. 1. The effect on serum levels of pituitary hormones in ovariectomized rats]
Planta Med 1985 Feb(1):46-9 (Published in German)

BLACK WALNUT—Juglans nigra

Bibliography

Christopher; pg. 200
Duke; pg. 203
Ellingwood; pg. 379
Heinerman; pp. 462-464
Holmes; pp. 724-727
Hutchens; pp. 52-53
King's; pg. 340
PDR-HM; pp. 917-918
Porcher; pg. 319
Potters; pg. 278
Santillo; pp. 89-90
Tierra; pg. 169

Citations from the Medline database

JDehon L, et al.
Involvement of peroxidases in the formation of the brown coloration of heartwood in Juglans nigra.
Exp Bot. 2002 Feb;53(367):303-11.

Bhargava UC, et al.
Preliminary pharmacology of ellagic acid from Juglans nigra (Black Walnut).
J Pharm Sci. 1968 Oct;57(10):1728-32.

BUGLE—Ajuga reptans

Bibliography

Culpeper; pg. 48
Grieve; pg. 140
Holmes
PDR-HM; pg. 620
Potters; pg. 47

Citations from World Wide Web

Agricultural Research Service, James Duke
Phytochemical and Ethnobotanical Databases
http://www.ars-grin.gov/duke/ethnobot.html

Citations from the Medline database

Elbrecht A, et al.
8-O-acetylharpagide is a nonsteroidal ecdysteroid agonist.
Insect Biochem Mol Biol. 1996 Jun;26(6):519-23.

Terahara N, et al.
Triacylated anthocyanins from Ajuga reptans flowers and cell cultures.
Phytochemistry. 1996 May;42(1):199-203.

Breschi MC; Martinotti E; Catalano S; Flamini G; Morelli I; Pagni
Vasoconstrictor activity of 8-O-acetylharpagide from Ajuga reptans
J Nat Prod 1992 Aug;55(8)
The traditional therapeutic indications for the use of Ajuga reptans (Labiatae) have been investigated. The H2O-soluble part of a crude and partially purified MeOH extract and two isolated iridoids (8-O- acetylharpagide and harpagide), were tested for a biological activity on isolated smooth muscle preparations from guinea pig.

BURDOCK—Arctium lappa

Bibliography

Christopher; pp. 70-77, 298-300
Duke; pp. 267, 269
Heinerman; pp. 103-106
Holmes; pp. 703-706
Hutchens; pp. 62-65
Kloss; pp. 100-101
Porcher; pg. 419
Potters; pg. 49
Santillo; pp. 95-96
Tierra; pp. 157-158, 267

Citations from the Medline database

Morita K Kada T Namiki M
A desmutagenic factor isolated from Burdock (Arctium lappa Linne).
Mutat Res (1984 Oct) 129(1):25-31

Yamaguchi S Takido M Sankawa U Shibata S
[On the constituents of the fruit of Arctium lappa (author's transl)]
Yakugaku Zasshi (1976 Dec) 96(12):1492-3

Saleh NA Bohm BA
Flavonoids of Arctium minus (Compositae).
Experientia (1971 Dec 15) 27(12):1494

Dombradi CA Foldeak S
Screening report on the antitumor activity of purified Arctium Lappa extracts.
Tumori (1966 May-Jun) 52(3):173-5

Kharlamov IA Khazanovich PL Khalmatov KhKh
[Pharmacognostic study of Arctium tomentosum Mill. and Arctium leiospermum Juz. et Serg. growing in Uzbekistan]
Farmatsiia (1968 May-Jun) 17(3):45-9

CALENDULA—C. officinalis

Bibliography

Culpeper; pg. 161
Ellingwood; pg. 389
Holmes; pg. 616
King's; pg. 401
Potters; pg. 184
Santillo; pg. 96

Citations from the Medline database

De Tommasi N Pizza C Conti C Orsi N Stein ML
Structure and in vitro antiviral activity of sesquiterpene glycosides from Calendula arvensis.
J Nat Prod (1990 Jul-Aug) 53(4):830-5
Previous research on the aerial parts of Calendula arvensis led to the isolation of the epicubebol glycoside 1 and of the sesquiterpene glycosides 2-5 based on the alloaromadendrane skeleton. A further investigation has revealed two new glycosides, 6 and 7, derived from the same sesquiterpene, the structures of which were elucidated by spectral studies. Furthermore a series of antiviral tests has been performed on glycosides 1-7 by examining their ability to interfere with rhinovirus 1B and vesicular stomatitis virus infection in vitro. Only glycoside 1 slightly reduced rhinovirus multiplication. All the compounds were able to inhibit vesicular stomatitis virus infection, 1 and 2 being the most effective.

Elias R De Meo M Vidal-Ollivier E Laget M Balansard G Dumenil G
Antimutagenic activity of some saponins isolated from Calendula officinalis L., C. arvensis L. and Hedera helix L.
Mutagenesis (1990 Jul) 5(4):327-31
Thirteen saponins were isolated and identified from Calendula officinalis, C. arvensis and Hedera helix. Mutagenic and antimutagenic activities of these products were investigated using a modified liquid incubation technique of the Salmonella/microsomal assay. The Salmonella tester strain TA98 +/- S9 mix was used. Screening of the antimutagenic activity was performed with a known promutagen: benzo-[a]pyrene (BaP) and a mutagenic urine concentrate from a smoker (SU). Antimutagenic activities were also compared with the activity of chlorophyllin. All the saponins were found to be non-toxic and non-mutagenic for doses of 400 micrograms. Chlorophyllin inhibited the mutagenic activities of BaP (1 microgram) and SU (5 microliters) in a dose-dependent manner. The four saponins from C. arvensis and the three saponins from H. helix showed antimutagenic activity against BaP (1 microgram) and SU (5 microliters) with a dose-response relationship. The possible mechanism of the antimutagenic activity of saponins is discussed.

Kartikeyan S Chaturvedi RM Narkar SV
Effect of Calendula on trophic ulcers [letter; comment]
Lepr Rev (1990 Dec) 61(4):399

De Tommasi N Conti C Stein ML Pizza C
Structure and in vitro antiviral activity of triterpenoid saponins from Calendula arvensis.
Planta Med (1991 Jun) 57(3):250-3
A reinvestigation of the aerial parts of Calendula arvensis afforded, in addition to the oleanolic acid glycosides 1-4 (4), the new glycoside 5 whose structure was elucidated by spectral and chemical studies and determined as 3-O-(beta-D-galactopyranosyl-(1----3) [beta-D-glucopyranosyl-(1----4)]-beta-D-glucopyranosyl) oleanolic acid (28----1)-beta-D-glucopyranosyl ester. Furthermore, some antiviral tests were performed on glycosides 1-5 and on 5a, the hydrolysis product of 5, towards vesicular stomatitis virus (VSV) and rhinovirus (HRV) infection in cell cultures. An inhibitory effect against VSV multiplication was observed for all the compounds tested while HRV replication was significantly affected only by compound 3.

Boucaud-Maitre Y Algernon O Raynaud J
Cytotoxic and antitumoral activity of Calendula officinalis extracts.
Pharmazie (1988 Mar) 43(3):220-1

Chemli R Toumi A Oueslati S Zouaghi H Boukef K Balansard G
[Calendula arvensis L. Impact of saponins on toxicity, hemolytic effect, and anti-inflammatory activity]
Calendula arvensis L. Impact des saponines sur la toxicite, le pouvoir hemolytique et l'activite anti-inflammatoire.
J Pharm Belg (1990 Jan-Feb) 45(1):12-6
The study of the chemical composition of Calendula arvensis var. eu arvensis Maire reveals the presence of saponins. These saponins confer a haemolytic property on the plant. In our work we have, first determined the saponin responsible for the haemolytic property; and then we have studied the impact of the saponins on the acute toxicity and the anti-inflammatory activity induced by carrhageenin oedema.

Klouchek-Popova E Popov A Pavlova N Krusteva S
Influence of the physiological regeneration and epithelialization using fractions isolated from Calendula officinalis.
Acta Physiol Pharmacol Bulg (1982) 8(4):63-7

Klouchek-Popova E Popov A Pavlova N Krusteva S
Influence of the physiological regeneration and epithelialization using fractions isolated from Calendula officinalis.
Acta Physiol Pharmacol Bulg (1982) 8(4):63-7
Standard skin wounds have been surgically induced in Wistar albino rats. The wounds were covered with 5% unguentum containing fractions C1 and C5, isolated from the flowers of Calendula officinalis belonging to fam. Compositae, in combination with allantoin.
Epithelization has been determined in dynamics as a percentage compared with the beginning of the experiment, using the formula (formula: see text), where t is the wound surface in mm2 and n is the respective day after the beginning of the experiment. The wound exudate has been studied cytologically using light- and fluorescent
microscopy on the 8th, 24th and 48th hour after inflicting the wounds. The histological changes in biopsy material taken from the edges of the wounds on the 10th day have also been investigated. The drug combination applied markedly stimulates physiological regeneration and epithelialization. This effect is assumed to be due to more intensive metabolism of glycoproteins, nucleoproteins and collagen proteins during the regenerative period in the tissues.

Chakurski I Matev M Koichev A Angelova I Stefanov G
[Treatment of chronic colitis with an herbal combination of Taraxacum officinale, Hipericum perforatum, Melissa officinaliss, Calendula officinalis and Foeniculum vulgare]
Vutr Boles (1981) 20(6):51-4
Twenty four patients with chronic non-specific colitis were treated with a herb combination. As a result from the treatment, the spontaneous and palpable pains along the large intestine disappeared in 95.83 per cent of the patients by the 15th day of their admission to the clinic. Defecation became daily in the patients with obstipation syndrome, but a combination of Rhamus frangula, Citrus aurantium, C. carvi was added to the herb combination already indicated. Defecation was normalized in patients with diarrhea syndrome. The pathological admixtures in feces disappeared.

Chakurski I Matev M Stefanov G Koichev A Angelova I
[Treatment of duodenal ulcers and gastroduodenitis with a herbal combination of Symphitum officinalis and Calendula officinalis with and without antacids]
Vutr Boles (1981) 20(6):44-7
A total of 170 patients were treated--137 only with the herb combination (78 with duodenal ulcer and 59 with gastroduodenitis), 33--with the herb combination together with antacid (21 with duodenal ulcer and 12 with gastroduodenitis). As a result from the treatment, the spontaneous pains disappeared in 90 per cent of the patients--in the group with and in the group without antacid, the dyspeptic complaints faded in over 85 per cent but in the patients, treated with herbs and antacid the mentioned complaints disappeared several days earlier. The palpitation pains, in both groups, disappeared in more than 90 per cent of the patients within the same time. Gastric acidity, in both groups, showed a statistically insignificant tendency to decrease prior and post treatment. The gastroscopically control revealed that the ulcer niche, in both groups, was healed in almost the same percentage of the patients.

CAPSICUM—C. annuum, C. frutescens

Bibliography

Duke; pp. 57-58, 175, 212-213, 347-348, 388
Ellingwood; pg. 168
Grieve; pp. 175-176
Holmes; pp. 381-383
King's; pg. 434
Kloss; pp. 106-115
PDR-HM; pp. 714-715
Potters; pg. 66
Santillo; pp. 99-100
Tierra; pg. 241

Citations from the Medline database

Visudhiphan S Poolsuppasit S Piboonnukarintr O Tumliang S
The relationship between high fibrinolytic activity and daily Capsicum ingestion in Thais.
Am J Clin Nutr 1982 Jun;35(6):1452-8

Nopanitaya W
Effects of capsaicin in combination with diets of varying protein content on the duodenal absorptive cells of the rat.
Am J Dig Dis 1974 May;19(5):439-48

Viranuvatti V Kalayasiri C Chearani O Plengvanit U
Effects of Capsicum solution on human gastric mucosa as observed gastroscopically.
Am J Gastroenterol 1972 Sep;58(3):225-32

Myers BM Smith JL Graham DY
Effect of red pepper and black pepper on the stomach.
Am J Gastroenterol 1987 Mar;82(3):211-4

Webb-Peploe MM Brender D Shepherd JT
Vascular responses to stimulation of receptors in muscle by capsaicin.
Am J Physiol 1972 Jan;222(1):189-95

Kumar N Vij JC Sarin SK Anand BS
Do chillies influence healing of duodenal ulcer?
Br Med J (Clin Res Ed) 1984 Jun 16;288(6433):1803-4

Winograd HL
Acute croup in an older child. An unusual toxic origin.
Clin Pediatr (Phila) 1977 Oct;16(10):884-7

Limlomwongse L Chaitauchawong C Tongyai S
Effect of capsaicin on gastric acid secretion and mucosal blood flow in the rat.
J Nutr 1979 May;109(5):773-7

Toda N Usui H Nishino N Fujiwara M
Cardiovascular effects of capsaicin in dogs and rabbits.
J Pharmacol Exp Ther 1972 Jun;181(3):512-21

Solanke TF
The effect of red pepper (Capsicum frutescens) on gastric acid secretion.
J Surg Res 1973 Dec;15(6):385-90

Jones LA Tandberg D Troutman WG
Household treatment for "chile burns" of the hands.
J Toxicol Clin Toxicol 1987;25(6):483-91

Henkin R
Cooling the burn from hot peppers.
JAMA 1991 Nov 20;266(19):2766

Collier HO McDonald-Gibson WJ Saeed SA
Letter: Stimulation of prostaglandin biosynthesis by capsaicin, ethanol, and tyramine.
Lancet 1975 Mar 22;1(7908):702

Wasantapruek S Poolsuppasit S Pibolnukarintr O
Letter: Enhanced fibriolytic activity after Capsicum ingestion.
N Engl J Med 1974 May 30;290(22):1259-60

Rubin HR Wu AW Tunis S
WARNING--inhaling tabasco products can be hazardous to your health [letter]
West J Med 1991 Nov;155(5):550

Makara GB Csalay L Frenkl R Somfai Z Szepeshazi K
Effect of capsaicin on experimental ulcer in the rat.
Acta Med Acad Sci Hung 1965;21(2):213-6

Halm I
[The capillary picture as a parameter for analyzing tinctures]
Acta Pharm Hung 1978 May;48(3):97-105

Baraz LA Khayutin VM Molnar J
Effects of capsaicin upon the stimulatory action of potassium chloride in the visceral branches of spinal afferents of cat.
Acta Physiol Acad Sci Hung 1968;33(2):237-46

Baraz LA Khayutin VM Molnar J
Analysis of the stimulatory action of capsaicin on receptors and sensory fibres of the small intestine in the cat. Further contribution to the problem of pain.
Acta Physiol Acad Sci Hung 1968;33(2):225-35

Osadchii LI Balueva TV Molnar J
Reflex changes in systemic vascular resistance following intracoronary injection of capsaicin and veratrine in the cat.
Acta Physiol Acad Sci Hung 1967;32(3):215-9

Molnar J
Effect of capsaicin on the cat's nictitating membrane.
Acta Physiol Acad Sci Hung 1966;30(2):183-92

Lembeck F
Columbus, Capsicum and capsaicin: past, present and future.
Acta Physiol Hung 1987;69(3-4):265-73

CATNIP—Nepeta cataria

Bibliography

Christopher; pp. 259-261
Duke; pp. 43, 126-129, 297
Ellingwood; pg. 346
Heinerman; pp. 122-124
Holmes; pp. 167-168
King's; pg. 465
Kloss; pp. 105-106
Potters; pg. 66
Santillo; pp. 98-99
Tierra; pp. 121, 157

Citations from the Medline database

Mathela CS Gupta A Upreti P Pant AK Olmstead MM Hope H Bottini AT
Coleon U 12-methyl ether from Nepeta leucophylla.
J Nat Prod (1991 May-Jun) 54(3):910-2

Murai F Tagawa M Damtoft S Jensen SR Nielsen BJ
(1R,5R,8S,9S)-Deoxyloganic acid from Nepeta cataria.
Chem Pharm Bull (Tokyo) (1984 Jul) 32(7):2809-14

Sherry CJ Hunter PS
The effect of an ethanol extract of Catnip (Nepeta cataria) on thebehavior of the young chick.
Experientia (1979 Feb 15) 35(2):237-8

CLEAVERS—Galium aparine

Bibliography

Culpeper; pg. 72
Grieve; pg. 206
Holmes; pg. 701
PDR-HM; pg. 859
Potters; pg. 79
Santillo; pg. 104

COMFREY—Symphytum spp.

Bibiography

Christopher; pg. 336
Culpeper; pg. 76
Duke; pp. 62, 241
Holmes; pg. 461
PDR-HM; pg. 1163
Potters; pg. 87
Santillo; pg. 106

Citations from Medline Database

Couet CE, et al.
Analysis, separation, and bioassay of pyrrolizidine alkaloids from Comfrey (Symphytum officinale).
Nat Toxins. 1996;4(4):163-7.
Pyrrolizidine alkaloids have been linked to liver and lung cancers and a range of other deleterious effects. As with many natural toxicants, major problems arise in determining the effects of the different members of the class and the importance of various forms of ingestion. In this study we have investigated the levels of pyrrolizidine alkaloids in Comfrey (Symphytum officinale), determined the levels in different parts of the plant and in herbal remedies, separated the alkaloids into two main groups--the principal parent alkaloids and the corresponding N-oxides--and, finally, carried out a simple bioassay based upon the mutagenic capability of the separated compounds in a human cell line. We conclude that the part of the plant ingested is important in terms of alkaloid challenge and that the effect of two of the major groups of alkaloids individually is different from that of alkaloids in the whole plant extract.

Olinescu A, et al.
Action of some proteic and carbohydrate components of Symphytum officinale upon normal and neoplastic cells.
Roum Arch Microbiol Immunol. 1993 Apr-Jun;52(2):73-80.

Behninger C, et al.
[Studies on the effect of an alkaloid extract of Symphytum officinale on human lymphocyte cultures].
Planta Med. 1989 Dec;55(6):518-22.

Dennis R, et al.
Studies on symphytum species--HPLC determination of allantoin.
Acta Pharm Hung. 1987 Nov;57(6):267-74.

Gracza L, et al.
[Biochemical-pharmacologic studies of medicinal plants. 1. Isolation of rosmarinic acid from Symphytum officinale L. and its anti-inflammatory activity in an in vitro model].
Arch Pharm (Weinheim). 1985 Dec;318(12):1090-5.

Shipochliev T.
[Uterotonic action of extracts from a group of medicinal plants].
Vet Med Nauki. 1981;18(4):94-8.

Shipochliev T, et al.
[Anti-inflammatory action of a group of plant extracts].
Vet Med Nauki. 1981;18(6):87-94.

Furuya T, et al.
Studies on constituents of crude drugs. I. Alkaloids of Symphytum officinale Linn.
Chem Pharm Bull (Tokyo). 1968 Dec;16(12):2512-6.

CORNSILK—Zea mays

Bibliography

Christopher; pg. 266
Duke; pp. 420-421
Heinerman; pp. 186-188, 340
Holmes; pp. 661-662
Kloss; pp. 122-123

Santillo; pg. 108
Tierra; pp. 118, 226

Citations from the Medline database

Poma A, Arrizza L, Picozzi P, Spano L.
Monitoring urban air particulate matter (fractions PM 2.5 and PM 10) genotoxicity by plant systems and human cells in vitro: a comparative analysis.
Teratog Carcinog Mutagen. 2002;22(4):271-84.

Xu X, Zhu W, Wang Z, Witkamp GJ.
Distributions of rare earths and heavy metals in field-grown maize after application of rare earth-containing fertilizer.
Sci Total Environ. 2002 Jul 3;293(1-3):97-105.

Goda Y, Kakihara Y, Akiyama H, Matsuoka T, Hino A, Toyoda M.
[Detection of unexpected recombinant DNA in maize grain]
Shokuhin Eiseigaku Zasshi. 2002 Apr;43(2):74-9. Japanese.

Martin-Orue SM, O'Donnell AG, Arino J, Netherwood T, Gilbert HJ, Mathers JC.
Degradation of transgenic DNA from genetically modified soya and maize in human intestinal simulations.
Br J Nutr. 2002 Jun;87(6):533-42.

Petsko GA.
Grain of truth.
Genome Biol. 2002;3(5):comment1007.

Brye KR, Andraski TW, Jarrell WM, Bundy LG, Norman JM.
Phosphorus leaching under a restored tallgrass prairie and corn agroecosystems.
J Environ Qual. 2002 May-Jun;31(3):769-81.

Shanker K, Srivastava MM.
Uptake and translocation of selenium by maize (Zea mays) from its environmentaly important forms.
J Environ Biol. 2001 Jul;22(3):225-8.

Moriyama TF.
Corn might prevent Parkinson's Disease.
Clin Nutr. 2001 Dec;20(6):559.

Butler D.
Alleged flaws in gene-transfer paper spark row over genetically modified maize.
Nature. 2002 Feb 28;415(6875):948-9.

Orlandi PA, Lampel KA, South PK, Assar SK, Carter L, Levy DD.
Analysis of flour and food samples for cry9C from bioengineered corn.
J Food Prot. 2002 Feb;65(2):426-31.

DANDELION—Taraxacum officinale

Bibliography

Culpeper; pg. 87
Duke; pp. 39, 310

Heinerman; pg. 200
Holmes; pp. 196, 677
PDR-HM; pg. 1174
Potters; pg. 100
Santillo; pg. 111

Citations from the Medline database

Takasaki M, et al.
Anti-carcinogenic activity of Taraxacum plant. I & II.
Biol Pharm Bull. 1999 Jun;22(6):606-10.
An extract of the roots of Taraxacum japonicum (Compositae) exhibited strong anti-tumor-promoting activities on the two-stage carcinogenesis of mouse skin tumor induced by dimethylbenz[a] anthracene (DMBA) as an initiator and 12-O-tetradecanoylphorbol-13-acetate (TPA) as a promoter, as well as on that induced by DMBA and fumonisin B1. Further, the extract exhibited anti-tumor-initiating activity on the two-stage carcinogenesis of mouse skin tumor induced by (+/-)-(E)-methyl-2-[(E)-hydroxyimino]-5-nitro-6-methoxy-3-hexen amide (NOR-1) as an initiator and TPA as a promoter. These results suggested that an extract of the roots of the Taraxacum plant could be a valuable chemopreventive agent against chemical carcinogenesis.
Eleven triterpenoids (1-11) from the roots of Taraxacum japonicum (Compositae) were examined for their inhibitory effects on Epstein-Barr virus early antigen (EBV-EA) induced by the tumor promoter, 12-O-tetrade-canoylphorbol-13-acetate (TPA), in Raji cells as a primary screening test for anti-tumor-promoters (cancer chemopreventive agents). Of these triterpenoids, taraxasterol (1) and taraxerol (7) exhibited significant inhibitory effects on EBV-EA induction, but the inhibitory effects of their acetates 2 and 8 were weaker than those of 1 and 7. Furthermore, 1 and 7 exhibited potent anti-tumor-promoting activity in the two-stage carcinogenesis tests of mouse skin using 7,12-dimethylbenz[a]anthracene (DMBA) as an initiator and TPA as a promoter, and 1 showed a remarkable inhibitory effect on mouse spontaneous mammary tumors using C3H/OuJ mouse. These results strongly suggested that taraxasterol (1) could be a valuable chemopreventive agent.

Williams CA, et al.
Flavonoids, cinnamic acids and coumarins from the different tissues and medicinal preparations of Taraxacum officinale.
Phytochemistry. 1996 May;42(1):121-7.

Grases F, et al.
Urolithiasis and phytotherapy.
Int Urol Nephrol. 1994;26(5):507-11.
The effects of seven plants with suspected application to prevent and treat stone kidney formation (Verbena officinalis, Lithospermum officinale, Taraxacum officinale, Equisetum arvense, Arctostaphylos uva-ursi, Arctium lappa and Silene saxifraga) have been studied using female Wistar rats. Variations of the main urolithiasis risk factors (citraturia, calciuria, phosphaturia, pH and diuresis) have been evaluated. It can be concluded that beneficial effects caused by these herb infusions on urolithiasis can be attributed to some disinfectant action, and tentatively to the presence of saponins. Specifically, some solvent action can be postulated with respect to uric stones or heterogeneous uric nucleus, due to the basifying capacity of some herb infusions.

Zheng M.
[Experimental study of 472 herbs with antiviral action against the herpes simplex virus].
Chung Hsi I Chieh Ho Tsa Chih. 1990 Jan;10(1):39-41, 6. Chinese.

Akhtar MS Khan QM Khaliq T
Effects of Portulaca oleracae (Kulfa) and Taraxacum officinale
(Dhudhal) in normoglycaemic and alloxan-treated hyperglycaemic rabbits.
JPMA J Pak Med Assoc 1985 Jul;35(7):207-10

Chakurski I Matev M Koichev A Angelova I Stefanov G
[Treatment of chronic colitis with an herbal combination of Taraxacum officinale, Hipericum perforatum, Melissa officinaliss, Calendula officinalis and Foeniculum vulgare]
Vutr Boles 1981;20(6):51-4

Baba K Abe S Mizuno D
[Antitumor activity of hot water extract of Dandelion, Taraxacum officinale-correlation between antitumor activity and timing of administration (author's transl)]
Yakugaku Zasshi (JOURNAL OF THE PHARMACEUTICAL SOCIETY OF JAPAN) 1981 Jun;101(6):538-43

Racz-Kotilla E Racz G Solomon A
The action of Taraxacum officinale extracts on the body weight and diuresis of laboratory animals.
Planta Med 1974 Nov;26(3):212-7

Rutherford PP Deacon AC
-Fructofuranosidases from roots of Dandelion (Taraxacum officinale Weber).
Biochem J 1972 Feb;126(3):569-73

DILL—Anethum graveolens

Bibliography

Duke; pp. 12, 43, 78, 240-241
Grieve; pp. 255-257
Heinerman; pp. 204-206
King's; pg. 203
Kloss; pg. 124
PDR-HM; pp. 646-647
Potters; pp. 102-103

Citations from the Medline database

[An investigation of benzine extract obtained from Dill fruits (Anethum graveolens L.)]
Ann Univ Mariae Curie Sklodowska [Med] (1982) 37:251-7

Szujko-Lacza J
Hypostase, embryonic sac and endosperm in Anethum graveolens L., and in various families.
Acta Biol Acad Sci Hung (1978) 29(3):255-71

Teuber H Herrmann K
[Flavonol glycosides of leaves and fruits of Dill (Anethum graveolens L.). II. Phenolics of spices (author's transl)]
Z Lebensm Unters Forsch (1978 Aug 30) 167(2):101-4

Suprunov NI Kurlianchik IA Deren'ko SA
[Dynamics of accumulation of essential oils in specimens of Anethum graveolens of different geographic origin]
Farm Zh (1976 Nov-Dec) (6):52-4

Shcherbanovsky LR Kapelev IG
[Volatile oil of Anethum Graveolens L. as an inhibitor of yeast and lactic acid bacteria]
Prikl Biokhim Mikrobiol (1975 May-Jun) 11(3):476-7

ECHINACEA—Echinacea spp.

Bibliography

Christopher; pp. 97-100
Duke; pp. 69, 91, 210, 449
Ellingwood; pg. 182
Heinerman; pp. 211-213
Holmes; 610-612
Hutchens; pp. 113-114
Kindscher; pp. 84-94
King's; pg. 671
Kloss; 124-125
Potters; pp. 105-106
Santillo; pp. 112-113

Citations from the Medline database

Binns SE, et al.
Light-mediated antifungal activity of Echinacea extracts.
Planta Med. 2000 Apr;66(3):241-4.

Luettig B Steinmuller C Gifford GE Wagner H Lohmann-Matthes ML
Macrophage activation by the polysaccharide arabinogalactan isolated from plant cell cultures of Echinacea purpurea.
J Natl Cancer Inst 1989 May 3;81(9):669-75
In this study, acidic arabinogalactan, a highly purified polysaccharide from plant cell cultures of Echinacea purpurea, with a molecular weight of 75,000, was effective in activating macrophages to cytotoxicity against tumor cells and micro-organisms (Leishmania enriettii). Furthermore, this polysaccharide induced macrophages to produce tumor necrosis factor (TNF-alpha), interleukin-1 (IL-1), and interferon-beta 2. Arabinogalactan did not activate B cells and did not induce T cells to produce interleukin-2, interferon-beta 2, or interferon-gamma, but it did induce a slight increase in T-cell proliferation. When injected ip, this agent stimulated macrophages, a finding that may have therapeutic implications in the defense against tumors and infectious diseases.

Lersch C Zeuner M Bauer A Siebenrock K Hart R Wagner F Fink U Dancygier H Classen M
Stimulation of the immune response in outpatients with hepatocellular carcinomas by low doses of cyclophosphamide (LDCY), Echinacea purpurea extracts (Echinacin) and thymostimulin.
Arch Geschwulstforsch 1990;60(5):379-83

Mengs U Clare CB Poiley JA
Toxicity of Echinacea purpurea. Acute, subacute and genotoxicity studies.
Arzneimittelforschung 1991 Oct;41(10):1076-81

Schumacher A Friedberg KD
[The effect of Echinacea angustifolia on non-specific cellular immunity in the mouse]
Arzneimittelforschung 1991 Feb;41(2):141-7 (Published in German)

Gaisbauer M Schleich T Stickl HA Wilczek I
[The effect of Echinacea purpurea Moench on phagocytosis in granulocytes measured by chemiluminescence]
Arzneimittelforschung 1990 May;40(5):594-8

Bauer VR Jurcic K Puhlmann J Wagner H
[Immunologic in vivo and in vitro studies on Echinacea extracts]
Arzneimittelforschung 1988 Feb;38(2):276-81 (Published in German)

Orinda D Diederich J Wacker A
[Antiviral activity of components of Echinacea purpurea]
Arzneimittelforschung 1973 Aug;23(8):1119-20 (Published in German)

Schulte KE Rucker G Perlick J
[The presence of polyacetylene compounds in Echinacea purpura Mnch and Echinacea angustifolia DC]
Arzneimittelforschung 1967 Jul;17(7):825-9 (Published in German)

Stimpel M Proksch A Wagner H Lohmann-Matthes ML
Macrophage activation and induction of macrophage cytotoxicity by purified polysaccharide fractions from the plant Echinacea purpurea.
Infect Immun 1984 Dec;46(3):845-9
Purified polysaccharides (EPS) prepared from the plant Echinacea purpurea are shown to strongly activate macrophages. Macrophages activated with these substances develop pronounced extracellular cytotoxicity against tumor targets. The activation is brought about by EPS alone and is independent of any cooperative effect with lymphocytes. Also the production and secretion of oxygen radicals and interleukin 1 by macrophages is increased after activation with EPS. Cells of the macrophages lineage seem to be the main target for the action of these polysaccharides.

Roesler J Emmendorffer A Steinmuller C Luettig B Wagner H Lohmann-Matthes ML
Application of purified polysaccharides from cell cultures of the plant Echinacea purpurea to test subjects mediates activation of the phagocyte system.
Int J Immunopharmacol 1991;13(7):931-41

Roesler J Steinmuller C Kiderlen A Emmendorffer A Wagner H Lohmann-Matthes ML
Application of purified polysaccharides from cell cultures of the plant Echinacea purpurea to mice mediates protection against systemic infections with Listeria monocytogenes and Candida albicans.
Int J Immunopharmacol 1991;13(1):27-37

Tubaro A Tragni E Del Negro P Galli CL Della Loggia R
Anti-inflammatory activity of a polysaccharidic fraction of Echinacea angustifolia.
J Pharm Pharmacol 1987 Jul;39(7):567-9

Jacobson M Redfern RE Mills GD Jr
Naturally occurring insect growth regulators. III. Echinolone, a highly active juvenile hormone mimic from Echinacea angustifolia roots.
Lloydia 1975 Nov-Dec;38(6):473-6

[Proceedings: Echinacea activates the properdin system]
Echinacea aktiviert das Properdinsystem
Med Monatsschr 1976 Jan;30(1):32-3 (Published in German)

Coeugniet EG Elek E
Immunomodulation with Viscum album and Echinacea purpurea extracts.
Onkologie 1987 Jun;10(3 Suppl):27-33

Heinzer F Chavanne M Meusy JP Maitre HP Giger E Baumann TW
[The classification of therapeutically used species of the genus Echinacea]
Pharm Acta Helv 1988;63(4-5):132-6 (Published in German)

Tragni E Galli CL Tubaro A Del Negro P Della Loggia R
Anti-inflammatory activity of Echinacea angustifolia fractions separated on the basis of molecular weight.
Pharmacol Res Commun 1988 Dec;20 Suppl 5:87-90

Bauer R Foster S
Analysis of alkamides and caffeic acid derivatives from Echinacea simulata and E. paradoxa roots.
Planta Med 1991 Oct;57(5):447-9

Schulthess BH Giger E Baumann TW
Echinacea: anatomy, phytochemical pattern, and germination of the achene.
Planta Med 1991 Aug;57(4):384-8

Wacker A Hilbig W
[Virus-inhibition by Echinacea purpurea (author's transl)]
Planta Med 1978 Feb;33(1):89-102 (Published in German)

Verelis C Becker H
[N-Alkanes of Echinacea angustifolia (author's transl)]
Planta Med 1977 May;31(3):288-9 (Published in German)

Samochowiec E Urbanska L Manka W Stolarska E
[Evaluation of the effect of Calendula officinalis and Echinacea angustifolia extracts of Trichomonas vaginalis in vitro]
Wiad Parazytol 1979;25(1):77-81 (Published in Polish)

ELDERBERRY - Sambucus canadensis, S. spp.

Bibliography

Ellingwood; pg. 451
Grieve; pp. 265-276
Holmes; pp. 172-175
Hutchens; pp. 114-117
King's; pg. 706
Kloss; pp.212-213
N. Am. Plants; pp. 121-125
Potters; pg. 106
Santillo; pp. 113-115

Citations from the Medline database

Sata T Roth J Zuber C Stamm B Heitz PU
Expression of alpha 2,6-linked sialic acid residues in neoplastic but not in normal human colonic mucosa. A lectin-gold cytochemical study with Sambucus nigra and Maackia amurensis lectins.
Am J Pathol 1991 Dec;139(6):1435-48

Shibuya N Goldstein IJ Broekaert WF Nsimba-Lubaki M Peeters B Peumans WJ
The Elderberry (Sambucus nigra L.) bark lectin recognizes the Neu5Ac(alpha 2-6)Gal/GalNAc sequence.
J Biol Chem 1987 Feb 5;262(4):1596-601

Jensen SR Nielsen BJ
Cyanogenic glucosides in Sambucus nigra L.
Acta Chem Scand 1973;27(7):2661-2

Harada H Kondo M Yanagisawa M Sunada S
Mucin-specific bark lectin from Elderberry Sambucus sieboldiana and its applications to the affinity chromatography of mucin.
Anal Biochem 1990 Sep;189(2):262-6

Kolodynska M Pasieczna W
[The determination of rutin and quercetin in selected galenic preparations of Sambucus nigra flowers]
Ann Univ Mariae Curie Sklodowska [Med] 1967;22:127-30

Kolodynska M Praczko J
[A quantitative estimation of valeric acid and tannins in some galenic preparations of the bark of Sambucus nigra]
Ann Univ Mariae Curie Sklodowska [Med] 1966;21:207-11

Kaku H Peumans WJ Goldstein IJ
Isolation and characterization of a second lectin (SNA-II) present in Elderberry (Sambucus nigra L.) bark.
Arch Biochem Biophys 1990 Mar;277(2):255-62

Shibuya N Goldstein IJ Broekaert WF Nsimba-Lubaki M Peeters B Peumans WJ
Fractionation of sialylated oligosaccharides, glycopeptides, and glycoproteins on immobilized Elderberry (Sambucus nigra L.) bark lectin.
Arch Biochem Biophys 1987 Apr;254(1):1-8

Tunmann P Grimm HJ
[A hydroxysteroid ketone in the radix of Sambucus ebulus L]
Arch Pharm (Weinheim) 1974 Dec;307(12):966-9

Mach L Scherf W Ammann M Poetsch J Bertsch W Marz L Glossl J
Purification and partial characterization of a novel lectin fromelder (Sambucus nigra L.) fruit.
Biochem J 1991 Sep 15;278 (Pt 3):667-71

Broekaert WF Nsimba-Lubaki M Peeters B Peumans WJ
A lectin from elder (Sambucus nigra L.) bark.
Biochem J 1984 Jul 1;221(1):163-9

Devine PL Harada H
Reactivity of mucin-specific lectin from Sambucus sieboldiana with simple sugars, normal mucins and tumor-associated mucins. Comparison with other lectins.
Biol Chem Hoppe Seyler 1991 Oct;372(10):935-42

Iatskovskii AN Lutsik AD
[A method of selective histochemical analysis of sialoglycoproteins using lectins from elder (Sambucus nigra L.)]
Biull Eksp Biol Med 1991 Jan;111(1):71-4

Lalaurie M Berlan J Janicot M
[Sambucus ebulus L. lectin: detection of H character of newborn red cells]
C R Soc Seances Soc Biol Fil 1981;175(4):490-5 (Published in French)

Altosaar I Bohm BA Taylor IE
Isolation and properties of a ferredoxin from leaves of Sambucus racemosa L.
Can J Biochem 1977 Feb;55(2):159-64

Peumans WJ Kellens JT Allen AK Van Damme EJ
Isolation and characterization of a seed lectin from Elderberry (Sambucus nigra L.) and its relationship to the bark lectins.
Carbohydr Res 1991 Jun 25;213:7-17

Scawen MD Ramshaw JA Brown RH Boulter D
The amino-acid sequence of plastocyanin from Sambucus nigra L. (Elder).
Eur J Biochem 1974 May 2;44(1):299-303

Mumcuoglu M Manor D Slavin S
Enrichment for GM-CFU from human bone marrow using Sambucus nigra agglutinin: potential application to bone marrow transplantation.
Exp Hematol 1986 Nov;14(10):946-50

Paulo E
Effect of phytohaemagglutinin (PHA) from the back of Sambucus nigra on embryonic and foetal development in mice.
Folia Biol (Krakow) 1976;24(2):213-22

Shibuya N Tazaki K Song ZW Tarr GE Goldstein IJ Peumans WJ
A comparative study of bark lectins from three Elderberry (Sambucus) species.
J Biochem (Tokyo) 1989 Dec;106(6):1098-103

FENNEL—Foeniculum vulgare

Bibliography

Grieve; pp. 293-297
Holmes; pp. 301-302
Hutchens; pg. 246
King's; pg. 625
Kloss; pp. 125-126
Porcher; pg. 46
Potters; pg. 114
Santillo; pp. 118-119

Citations from the Medline database

Croteau R Felton M Ronald RC
Biosynthesis of monoterpenes: preliminary characterization of i-endo- fenchol synthetase from Fennel (Foeniculum vulgare) and evidence that no free intermediate is involved in the cyclization of geranyl pyrophosphate to the rearranged product.
Arch Biochem Biophys 1980 Apr 1;200(2):534-46

Croteau R Felton M Ronald RC
Biosynthesis of monoterpenes: conversion of the acyclic precursors geranyl pyrophosphate and neryl pyrophosphate to the rearranged monoterpenes fenchol and fenchone by a soluble enzyme preparation from Fennel (Foeniculum vulgare).
Arch Biochem Biophys 1980 Apr 1;200(2):524-33

Croteau R Miyazaki JH Wheeler CJ
Monoterpene biosynthesis: mechanistic evaluation of the geranyl pyrophosphate:(-)-endo-fenchol cyclase from Fennel (Foeniculum vulgare).
Arch Biochem Biophys 1989 Mar;269(2):507-16

Annusuya S Vanithakumari G Megala N Devi K Malini T Elango V
Effect of Foeniculum vulgare seed extracts on cervix & vagina of ovariectomised rats.
Indian J Med Res 1988 Apr;87:364-7

Malini T Vanithakumari G Megala N Anusya S Devi K Elango V
Effect of Foeniculum vulgare Mill. seed extract on the genital organs of male and female rats.
Indian J Physiol Pharmacol 1985 Jan-Mar;29(1):21-6

Shah AH Qureshi S Ageel AM
Toxicity studies in mice of ethanol extracts of Foeniculum vulgare fruit and Ruta chalepensis aerial parts.
J Ethnopharmacol 1991 Sep;34(2-3):167-72

Abdul-Ghani AS Amin R
The vascular action of aqueous extracts of Foeniculum vulgare leaves.
J Ethnopharmacol 1988 Dec;24(2-3):213-8

Betts TJ
Anethole and fenchone in the developing fruits of Foeniculum vulgare Mill.
J Pharm Pharmacol 1968 Jun;20(6):469-72

Abdallah N El-Gengaihi S Sedrak E
The effect of fertilizer treatments on yield of seed and volatile oil of Fennel (Foeniculum vulgare Mill.).
Pharmazie 1978 Sep;33(9):607-8

El-Gengaihi S Abdallah N
The effect of date of sowing and plant spacing on yield of seed and volatile oil of Fennel (Foeniculum vulgare Mill.).
Pharmazie 1978 Sep;33(9):605-6

Trenkle K
[Recent studies on Fennel (Foeniculum vulgare M.) 2. The volatile oil of the fruit, herbs and roots of fruit-bearing plants]
Pharmazie 1972 May;27(5):319-24 (Published in German)

Beitz H Pank F
[Residues of herbicides in medicinal and spice plants. Residues of methylparathion in Fennel (Foeniculum vulgare Mill.) and in Peppermint (Mentha piperita L.)]
Pharmazie 1972 Aug;27(8):532-4 (Published in German)

Trenkle K
[Contents of Fennel root (Foeniculum vulgare Mill.)]
Pharmazie 1969 Dec 12;24(12):782 (Published in German)

Trenkle K
[Recent studies in Foeniculum vulgare. Organic acids, especially phenyl carbonic acids]
Planta Med 1971 Dec;20(4):289-301 (Published in German)

Karlsen J Svendsen AB Chingova B Zolotovitch G
Studies on the fruits of Foeniculum species and their essential oil.
Planta Med 1969 Aug;17(3):281-93

Toth L
[Studies on the essential oil from Foeniculum vulgare. I. Composition of fruit-and root oil]
Planta Med 1967 May;15(2):157-72 (Published in German)

Toth L
[Studies on the etheric oil of Foeniculum vulgare. II. Changes of different Fennel oils beforeand after harvest]
Planta Med 1967 Nov;15(4):371-89 (Published in German)

Sharma AK Sharma KD
Effects of fungal metabolites on the germination of sweet Fennel (Foeniculum vulgare Mill.) seeds.
Toxicol Lett 1983 Jun;17(1-2):81-4

Chakurski I Matev M Koichev A Angelova I Stefanov G
[Treatment of chronic colitis with an herbal combination of Taraxacum officinale, Hipericum perforatum, Melissa officinaliss, Calendula officinalis and Foeniculum vulgare]
Vutr Boles 1981;20(6):51-4 (Published in Bulgarian)

Kunzemann J Herrmann K
[Isolation and identification of flavon(ol)-O-glycosides in caraway (Carum carvi L.), Fennel (Foeniculum vulgare Mill.), anise(Pimpinella anisum L.), and coriander (Coriandrum sativum L.), and of flavon-C-glycosides in anise. I. Phenolics of spices (author's transl)]
Z Lebensm Unters Forsch 1977 Jul 29;164(3):194-200 (Published in German)

GARLIC—Allium sativum

Bibliography

Duke; pg. 411
Grieve; pg. 342
Heinerman; pg. 244
Holmes; pg. 375
PDR-HM; pg. 626
Potters; pg. 124
Santillo; pg. 122

Citations from the Medline database

Mahady GB, et al.
Garlic and Helicobacter pylori.
Am J Gastroenterol. 2000 Jan;95(1):309

Miron T, et al.
The mode of action of allicin: its ready permeability through phospholipid membranes may contribute to its biological activity.
Biochim Biophys Acta. 2000 Jan 15;1463(1):20-30.

Wang HX, et al.
Natural products with hypoglycemic, hypotensive, hypocholesterolemic, antiatherosclerotic and antithrombotic activities.
Life Sci. 1999;65(25):2663-77.
Department of Microbiology, China Agricultural University, Beijing.
This article reviews compounds of botanical origin which are capable of lowering plasma levels of glucose and cholesterol and blood pressure, as well as compounds inhibiting atherosclerosis and thrombosis. Hypoglycemic natural products comprise flavonoids, xanthones, triterpenoids, alkaloids, glycosides, alkyldisulfides, aminobutyric acid derivatives, guanidine, polysaccharides and peptides. Hypotensive compounds include flavonoids, diterpenes, alkaloids, glycosides, polysaccharides and proteins. Among natural products with hypocholesterolemic activity are beta-carotene, lycopene, cycloartenol, beta-sitosterol, sitostanol, saponin, soybean protein, indoles, dietary fiber, propionate, mevinolin (beta-hydroxy-beta-methylglutaryl coenzyme A reductase inhibitor) and polysaccharides. Heparins, flavonoids, tocotrienols, beta-hydroxy-beta-methylglutaryl coenzyme A reductase inhibitors (statins), Garlic compounds and fungal proteases exert antithrombotic action. Statins and Garlic compounds also possess antiatherosclerotic activity.

Ankri S, et al.
Antimicrobial properties of allicin from Garlic.
Microbes Infect. 1999 Feb;1(2):125-129.

Irion CW.
Growing alliums and brassicas in selenium-enriched soils increases their anticarcinogenic potentials.
Med Hypotheses. 1999 Sep;53(3):232-5.

Klein JO.
Management of acute otitis media in an era of increasing antibiotic resistance.
Int J Pediatr Otorhinolaryngol. 1999 Oct 5;49 Suppl 1:S15-7.
Development of resistance to available antimicrobial agents has been identified in every decade since the introduction of the sulfonamides in the 1930s. Current concerns for management of acute otitis media (AOM) are multi-drug resistant Streptococcus pneumoniae and beta-lactamase producing Haemophilus influenzae and Moraxella catarrhalis. In the USA, amoxicillin remains the drug for choice for AOM. Increasing the current dose to 80 mg/kg/day in two doses provides increased concentrations of drug in serum and middle ear fluid and captures additional resistant strains of S. pneumoniae. For children who fail initial therapy with amoxicillin an expert panel convened by the Centers for Disease Control and Prevention suggested amoxicillin-clavulanate, cefuroxime axetil or intramuscular ceftriaxone. To protect the therapeutic advantage of antimicrobial agents used for AOM, it is important to promote judicious use of antimicrobial agents and avoid uses if it is likely that viral infections are the likely cause of the disease, to implement programs for parent education and to increase the accuracy of diagnosis of AOM. Conjugate polysaccharide pneumococcal vaccines are currently in clinical trial; early results indicate protective levels of antibody can be achieved with a three dosage schedule beginning at 2 months of age. Finally, alternative medicine remedies may be of value for some infectious diseases including AOM; Garlic extract is bactericidal for the major bacterial pathogens of AOM but is heat- and acid-labile and loose activity when cooked or taken by mouth.

Jiang C, et al.
Selenium-induced inhibition of angiogenesis in mammary cancer at chemopreventive levels of intake.
Mol Carcinog. 1999 Dec;26(4):213-25.

Drouin E.
Helicobacter pylori: novel therapies.
Can J Gastroenterol. 1999 Sep;13(7):581-3.

Denisov LN, et al.
[Garlic effectiveness in rheumatoid arthritis].
Ter Arkh. 1999;71(8):55-8. Russian.

Salman H, et al.
Effect of a Garlic derivative (alliin) on peripheral blood cell immune responses.
Int J Immunopharmacol. 1999 Sep;21(9):589-97.

Gao CM, et al.
Protective effect of allium vegetables against both esophageal and stomach cancer: a simultaneous case-referent study of a high-epidemic area in Jiangsu Province, China.
Jpn J Cancer Res. 1999 Jun;90(6):614-21.

Koscielny J, et al.
The antiatherosclerotic effect of Allium sativum.
Atherosclerosis. 1999 May;144(1):237-49.

Ali M, et al.
Effect of raw versus boiled aqueous extract of Garlic and onion on platelet aggregation.
Prostaglandins Leukot Essent Fatty Acids. 1999 Jan;60(1):43-7.

Chung JG.
Effects of Garlic components diallyl sulfide and diallyl disulfide on arylamine N-acetyltransferase activity in human bladder tumor cells.
Drug Chem Toxicol. 1999 May;22(2):343-58.

Siegers CP, et al.
The effects of Garlic preparations against human tumor cell proliferation.
Phytomedicine. 1999 Mar;6(1):7-11.
The growth of the human lymphatic leukemia cell line CCRF CEM was significantly inhibited in a dose-dependent manner by both Garlic powder and Garlic extract at concentrations as low as 30 micrograms/ml. However, no potentiation of this effect occurred upon mixing of the two preparations. Our results suggest that the antiproliferative effects of Garlic may be due to breakdown products of alliin, such as allicin or polysulfides, rather than alliin itself, since the addition of an alliinase system (Garlic powder) to an alliin enriched preparation without alliinase (Garlic extract) potentiated the effects observed with the two preparations alone.

MANY, MANY MORE RESEARCH PAPERS ON Garlic ARE AVAILABLE ON MEDLINE

GRAVEL ROOT—Eupatorium purpureum

Bibliography

Christopher; pp. 338, 485
Culpeper; pg. 207
Grieve; pg. 374
Holmes; pg. 307
Millspaugh; pg. 305
Potters; pg. 133
Santillo; pg. 128

Citations from the Medline database

Habtemariam S.
Cistifolin, an integrin-dependent cell adhesion blocker from the anti-rheumatic herbal drug, Gravel Root (rhizome of Eupatorium purpureum).
Planta Med. 1998 Dec;64(8):683-5.
During routine screening of medicinal plants for small molecular weight inhibitors of cell adhesion, the crude ethanolic extract of the anti-rheumatic herbal drug Gravel Root (rhizome of Eupatorium purpureum), was identified as a potent inhibitor of some beta 1 and beta 2 integrin-mediated cell adhesions.

Wagner H, et al.
[Immunostimulating action of polysaccharides (heteroglycans) from higher plants].
Arzneimittelforschung. 1985;35(7):1069-75. German.

Kupchan SM, et al.
Tumor inhibitors. 33. Cytotoxic flavones from eupatorium species.
Tetrahedron. 1969 Apr;25(8):1603-15.

HAWTHORN—Crataegus spp.

Bibliography

Culpeper; pg. 127
Duke; pp. 118, 246, 254
Grieve; pg. 385
Heinerman; pg. 271
Holmes; pg. 276
PDR-HM; pg. 779
Potters; pg. 138
Santillo; pg. 129

Citations from the Medline database

Tauchert M, et al.
[High-dose Crataegus extract WS 1442 in the treatment of NYHA stage II heart failure].
Herz. 1999 Oct;24(6):465-74; discussion 475. German.

Muller A, et al.
Crataegus extract blocks potassium currents in guinea pig ventricular cardiac myocytes.
Planta Med. 1999 May;65(4):335-9.

Gildor A.
Crataegus oxyacantha and heart failure.
Circulation. 1998 Nov 10;98(19):2098.

Popping S, et al.
Effect of a Hawthorn extract on contraction and energy turnover of isolated rat cardiomyocytes.
Arzneimittelforschung. 1995 Nov;45(11):1157-61
Within a range of 30-180 microg/ml, the Hawthorn extract exhibited a positive inotropic effect on the contraction amplitude accompanied by a moderate increase of energy turnover both for mechanical and ionic processes. In comparison with other positive inotropic interventions, such as application of the beta-adrenergic agonist isoprenaline, or of the cardiac glycoside ouabain (g-strophantin), or elevation of the extracellular $Ca++$-concentration, the effects of the Hawthorn extract were significantly more economical with respect to the energetics of the myocytes. Furthermore the extract prolonged the apparent refractory period in the presence and the absence of isoprenaline, which be indicative for an antiarrhythmic potential.

Schussler M, et al.
Myocardial effects of flavonoids from Crataegus species.
Arzneimittelforschung. 1995 Aug;45(8):842-5.

Chiu KW, et al.
Observations on blood pressure responses to injections of medicinal plant extracts in rats.
Am J Chin Med. 1995;23(1):91-9.

Blesken R
[Crataegus in cardiology] Crataegus in der Kardiologie.
Fortschr Med (1992 May 30) 110(15):290-2
The fact that the effectiveness of numerous phyto-preparations, so-called, has been demonstrated to the satisfaction of traditional medicine has led to increasing interest in phytotherapy. This also applies to Crataegus (whitethorn), the effects of which have been demonstrated in numerous pharmacological studies. These effects, produced mainly by the flavonoids, indicate a simultaneous cardiotropic and vasodilatory action, as confirmed clinically in controlled double-blind studies. This means that Crataegus can be employed for cardiological indications for which digitalis is not (yet) indicated.

Ciplea AG Richter KD
The protective effect of Allium sativum and crataegus on isoprenaline-induced tissue necroses in rats.
Arzneimittelforschung (1988 Nov) 38(11):1583-92
Possible protective effects of Allium sativum and Crataegus—alone and in combination--on isoprenaline (isoproterenol)-induced heart, liver and pancreas damage were studied using rats as test animals.
Pretreatment with Allium sativum alone, or in combination with Crataegus, resulted in protective effects on isoprenaline-induced damage of heart, liver, and pancreas. These effects proved to be dose-dependent. The following parameters were used to evaluate the protective effect: Clinical signs, qualitative histological and histoenzymatical findings, as well as quantitative microphotometric determination of enzymatic activities of succinate dehydrogenase, NADH-NBT reductase, acid phosphatase and glucose-6-phosphate dehydrogenase in cardiac, hepatic and pancreatic tissues. The underlying mechanisms are discussed. The results suggest that Allium sativum, resp. Allium sativum plus Crataegus exert a pronounced protective effect.

Vanhaelen M Vanhaelen-Fastre R
TLC-densitometric determination of 2,3-cis-procyanidin monomer and oligomers from Hawthorn (Crataegus spp.).
J Pharm Biomed Anal (1989) 7(12):1871-5

Glatzel H.
[Effect of bitters on cardiac output, heart rate and blood pressure].
Planta Med. 1968 Feb;16(1):82-94.

HOPS—Humulus lupulus

Bibliography

Christopher; pp. 435-437
Culpeper
Duke; pg. 298
Ellingwood; pg. 124
Heinerman; pp. 275-277
Holmes; pp. 558-560
Potters; pg. 145
Santillo; pp. 130-131

Citations from the Medline database

Hansel R Wohlfart R Coper H
[Sedative-hypnotic compounds in the exhalation of Hops, II]
Z Naturforsch [C] (1980 Nov-Dec) 35(11-12):1096-7

Wohlfart R Hansel R Schmidt H
[The sedative-hypnotic action of Hops. 4. Pharmacology of the hop substance 2-methyl-3-buten-2-ol]
Planta Med (1983 Jun) 48(2):120-3

Hansel R Wagener HH
[Attempts to identify sedative-hypnotic active substances in Hops]
Arzneimittelforschung (1967 Jan) 17(1):79-81

Schmidt HE
[Investigations on the therapy of virus infected hop (Humulus lupulus L.) by heat treatment of cuttings and shoot tips (author's transl)]
Zentralbl Bakteriol Parasitenkd Infektionskr Hyg (1974) 129(3-4):259-70

Caujolle F Pham-Huu-Chanh Duch-Kan P Bravo-Diaz L
[Spasmolytic action of hop (Humulus lupulus, Cannabinacees)]
Agressologie (1969 Sep-Oct) 10(5):405-10

Bravo L Cabo J Fraile A Jimenez J Villar A
[Pharmacodynamic study of the lupulus' (Humulus lupulus L.) tranquilizing action]
Boll Chim Farm (1974 May) 113(5):310-5

HOREHOUND—Marrubium vulgare

Bibliography

Christopher; pp. 379-382
Grieve; pp. 415-417
Holmes; pp. 240-242
Hutchens; pp. 154-156, 199
King's; pg. 1240
Potters; pp. 146-147
Tierra; pg. 380

Citations from the Medline database

Bird GW Wingham J
More Tn-specific lectins from seeds of the genus Labiatae: Hyptis sp.Chan, Salvia lyrata and Marrubium velutinum.
Clin Lab Haematol (1982) 4(4):403-4

Bird GW Wingham J
Anti-Tn from Marrubium candidissimum.
Rev Fr Transfus Immunohematol (1981 Jun) 24(3):347-8

Cahen R
[Pharmacologic spectrum of Marrubium vulgare L]
C R Soc Seances Soc Biol Fil (1970) 164(7):1467-72

Bartarelli M
[Marrubium vulgare and its pharmaceutical uses. I.]
Boll Chim Farm (1966 Nov) 105(11):787-98

HORSETAIL—Equisetum arvense

Bibliography

Culpeper; pg. 136
Duke; pp. 118, 246, 254
Grieve; pg. 385
Heinerman; pp. 80, 107, 342
Holmes; pg. 642
PDR-HM; pg. 830
Potters; pg. 138
Santillo; pg. 133

Citations from the Medline database

Graefe EU, et al.
Urinary metabolites of flavonoids and hydroxycinnamic acids in humans after application of a crude extract from Equisetum arvense.
Phytomedicine. 1999 Oct;6(4):239-46.
Flavonoids and hydroxycinnamic acids are polyphenolic compounds present in our daily diet in form of tea and vegetables as well as in herbal remedies used in phytomedicine. A wide range of in-vitro activities, in particular their antioxidant properties, have been studied intensively. However, in-vivo-data on absorption, bioavailability and metabolism after oral intake are scarce and contradictory. In order to examine the metabolism and renal excretion of these compounds a standardized extract from Horsetail (Equisetum arvense) was administered to 11 volunteers following a flavonoid-free diet for 8 d. 24 h urine samples were collected and analyzed by HPLC-DAD. The putative quercetin metabolites, 3,4-dihydroxyphenylacetic acid or 3,4-dihydroxytoluene could not be detected in urine in any sample. The endogenous amount of homovanillic acid, generally regarded as one of the main quercetin metabolites, was 4 +/- 1 mg/d and did not increase significantly. However, hippuric acid, the glycine conjugate of benzoic acid, increased twofold after drug intake. Thus, the degradation to benzoic acid derivatives rather than phenylacetic acid derivatives seems to be a predominant route of metabolism. The results of this pilot study give rise to additional, substantial pharmacokinetic investigations in humans.

Nitta A Yoshida S Tagaeto T
A comparative study of crude drugs in Southeast Asia. X. Crude drugs derived from Equisetum species.
Chem Pharm Bull (Tokyo) 1977 May;25(5):1135-9

Franck Bakke IL Kringstad R Nordal A
Water-soluble acids from Equisetum arvense L.
Acta Pharm Suec 1978;15(2):141-7

Piekos R Paslawska S Grinczelis W
Studies on the optimum conditions of extraction of silicon species from plants with water. III. On the stability of silicon species in extracts from Equisetum arvense herb.
Planta Med 1976 Jun;29(4):351-6

Kaufman PB LaCroix JD Dayanandan P Allard LF Rosen JJ Bigelow WC
Silicification of developing internodes in the perennial scouring rush (Equisetum hyemale var. affine).
Dev Biol 1973 Mar;31(1):124-35

JEWELWEED—Impatiens capensis

Bibliography

Duke; pp. 262-263, 358-359
Grieve; pp. 449-450
Heinerman; pp. 290-291
Peterson; pp. 120, 154-155
Porcher; pg. 139
Potters; pp. 159-160
Tierra; pp. 214, 232

Citations from the Medline database

Long D, Ballentine NH, Marks JG Jr.
Treatment of poison ivy/oak allergic contact dermatitis with an extract of Jewelweed.
Am J Contact Dermat. 1997 Sep;8(3):150-3.

Tailor RH, Acland DP, Attenborough S, Cammue BP, Evans IJ, Osborn RW, Ray JA, Rees SB, Broekaert WF.
A novel family of small cysteine-rich antimicrobial peptides from seed of Impatiens balsamina is derived from a single precursor protein.
J Biol Chem. 1997 Sep 26;272(39):24480-7.

Ishiguro K, Ohira Y, Oku H.
Antipruritic dinaphthofuran-7,12-dione derivatives from the pericarp of Impatiens balsamina.
J Nat Prod. 1998 Sep;61(9):1126-9.

Oku H, Ishiguro K.
Screening method for PAF antagonist substances: on the phenolic compounds from Impatients balsamina L.
Phytother Res. 1999 Sep;13(6):521-5.

Oku H, Ishiguro K.
Antipruritic and antidermatitic effect of extract and compounds of Impatiens balsamina L. in atopic dermatitis model NC mice.
Phytother Res. 2001 Sep;15(6):506-10.

Lobstein A, Brenne X, Feist E, Metz N, Weniger B, Anton R.
Quantitative determination of naphthoquinones of Impatiens species.
Phytochem Anal. 2001 May-Jun;12(3):202-5.

Mitchell-Olds T, et al.
Statistical genetics of an annual plant, Impatiens capensis. II. Natural selection.
Genetics. 1990 Feb;124(2):416-21.

Donohue K, et al.
Evidence of adaptive divergence in plasticity: density- and site-dependent selection on shade-avoidance responses in Impatiens capensis.
Evolution Int J Org Evolution. 2000 Dec;54(6):1956-68.

Mitchell-Olds T, et al.
Statistical genetics of an annual plant, Impatiens capensis. I. Genetic basis of quantitative variation.
Genetics. 1990 Feb;124(2):407-15.

JUNIPER BERRIES—Juniperis communis

Bibliography

Culpeper; pg. 141
Duke; pp. 43, 451
Grieve; pg. 452
Heinerman; pp. 80, 107, 342
Holmes; pg. 351
PDR-HM; pg. 918
Potters; pg. 160
Santillo; pg. 135

Citations from the Medline database

Gardner DR, et al.
Abortifacient effects of lodgepole pine (Pinus contorta) and common juniper (Juniperus communis) on cattle.
Vet Hum Toxicol. 1998 Oct;40(5):260-3.

Jones SM, et al.
Dietary juniper berry oil minimizes hepatic reperfusion injury in the rat.
Hepatology. 1998 Oct;28(4):1042-50.

Nelson RR.
In-vitro activities of five plant essential oils against methicillin-resistant Staphylococcus aureus and vancomycin-resistant Enterococcus faecium.
J Antimicrob Chemother. 1997 Aug;40(2):305-6.

Schilcher H.
[Juniper berry oil in diseases of the efferent urinary tract]?
Med Monatsschr Pharm. 1995 Jul;18(7):198-9.

Takacsova M, et al.
Study of the antioxidative effects of Thyme, Sage, juniper and oregano.
Nahrung. 1995;39(3):241-3.

Sanchez de Medina F, et al.
Hypoglycemic activity of juniper "berries."
Planta Med. 1994 Jun;60(3):197-200.
This work studies the hypoglycemic activity of a decoction from juniper "berries" (Juniperus communis) both in normoglycemic and in streptozotocin-diabetic animals. Juniper decoction decreases glycemic levels in normoglycemic rats at a dose of 250 mg/kg. This effect can be achieved through: a) an increase of peripheral glucose consumption; b) a potentiation of glucose-induced insulin secretion. The administration of the decoction (125 mg total "berries"/kg) to streptozotocin-diabetic rats for 24 days results in a significant reduction both in blood glucose levels and in the mortality index, as well as the prevention of the loss of body weight. This effect seems to be mediated by the peripheral action of juniper.

Agrawal OP Bharadwaj S Mathur R
Antifertility effects of fruits of Juniperus communis.
Planta Med 1980;Suppl:98-101

Lamer-Zarawska E
Biflavonoids in Juniperus L. sp (Cupressaceae).
Pol J Pharmacol Pharm 1975 Jan-Feb;27(1):81-7

LEMON BALM—Melissa officinalis

Bibliography

Culpeper; pg. 21
Duke; pp. 211, 387
Grieve; pg. 76
Holmes; pg. 530
PDR-HM; pg. 967
Potters; pg. 22
Santillo; pg. 139

Citations from the Medline database

Koytchev R, et al.
Balm mint extract (Lo-701) for topical treatment of recurring herpes labialis.
Phytomedicine. 1999 Oct;6(4):225-30.

Hohmann J, et al.
Protective effects of the aerial parts of Salvia officinalis, Melissa Officinalis and Lavandula angustifolia and their constituents against enzyme-dependent and enzyme-independent lipid peroxidation.
Planta Med. 1999 Aug;65(6):576-8.
The antioxidant effects of aqueous methanolic extracts from three medicinal Lamiaceae species were investigated in enzyme-dependent and enzyme-independent lipid peroxidation systems. All these extracts caused a considerable concentration-dependent inhibition of lipid peroxidation. Phenolic components present in the plant extracts were evaluated for antioxidant activity and were found effective in both tests. Their concentrations in each extract were determined by TLC-densitometry

Perry EK, et al.
Medicinal plants and Alzheimer's disease: Integrating ethnobotanical and contemporary scientific evidence.
J Altern Complement Med. 1998 Winter;4(4):419-28.

Yamasaki K, et al.
Anti-HIV-1 activity of herbs in Labiatae.
Biol Pharm Bull. 1998 Aug;21(8):829-33.
The anti-HIV-1 activity of aromatic herbs in Labiatae was evaluated in vitro. Forty five extract from among 51 samples obtained from 46 herb species showed significant inhibitory effects against HIV-1 induced cytopathogenicity in MT-4 cells. In particular, the aqueous extracts of Melissa officinalis, a family of Mentha x piperita "grapefruit mint," Mentha x piperita var. crispa, Ocimum basilicum cv "cinnamon," Perilla frutescens var. crispa f. viridis, Prunella vulgaris subsp. asiatica and Satureja montana showed potent anti-HIV-1 activity (with an ED of 16 microg/ml). The active components in the extract samples were found to be water-soluble polar substances, not nonpolar compounds such as essential oils. In addition, these aqueous extracts inhibited giant cell formation in co-culture of Molt-4 cells with and without HIV-1 infection and showed inhibitory activity against HIV-1 reverse transcriptase.

Larrondo JV, et al.
Antimicrobial activity of essences from labiates.
Microbios. 1995;82(332):171-2.
Bacteria, filamentous fungi and yeasts were subjected to the action of Lavandula officinalis, Melissa officinalis and Rosmarinus officinalis essences in a steam phase, using a microatmospheric technique. Due to the methodology employed, L. officinalis essence was more active in filamentous fungi than the other essential oils studied. All three essences possessed a similar degree of activity against the micro-organisms tested, though a relatively higher activity was seen in the case of M. officinalis.

Dimitrova Z, et al.
Antiherpes effect of Melissa officinalis L. extracts.
Acta Microbiol Bulg. 1993;29:65-72.

Auf'mkolk M, et al.
Extracts and auto-oxidized constituents of certain plants inhibit the receptor-binding and the biological activity of Graves' immunoglobulins.
Endocrinology. 1985 May;116(5):1687-93.

Chlabicz J Galasinski W
The components of Melissa officinalis L. that influence protein biosynthesis in-vitro.
J Pharm Pharmacol 1986 Nov;38(11):791-4

Mulkens A Kapetanidis I
[Flavonoids of the leaves of Melissa officinalis L. (Lamiaceae)]
Pharm Acta Helv 1987;62(1):19-22

Chakurski I Matev M Koichev A Angelova I Stefanov G
[Treatment of chronic colitis with an herbal combination of Taraxacum officinale, Hipericum perforatum, Melissa officinaliss, Calendula officinalis and Foeniculum vulgare]
Vutr Boles 1981;20(6):51-4
Twenty four patients with chronic non-specific colitis were treated with a herb combination. As a result from the treatment, the spontaneous and palpable pains along the large intestine disappeared in 95.83 per cent of the patients by the 15th day of their admission to the clinic. Defecation became daily in the patients with obstipation syndrome, but a combination of Rhamus frangula, Citrus aurantium, C. carvi was added to the herb combination already indicated. Defecation was normalized in patients with diarrhea syndrome. The pathological admixtures in feces disappeared.

Chlabicz J Rozanski A Galasinski W
Studies on substances of plant origin with anticipated cyto- and oncostatic activity. Part 1: The influence of water extracts from Melissa officinalis on the protein biosynthesis in vitro.
Pharmazie 1984 Nov;39(11):770

Morelli I
[Constituents and uses of Melissa officinalis]
Boll Chim Farm 1977 Jun;116(6):334-40

Herrmann EC Jr Kucera LS
Antiviral substances in plants of the mint family (labiatae). II. Nontannin polyphenol of Melissa officinalis.
Proc Soc Exp Biol Med 1967 Mar;124(3):869-74

LOBELIA—L. inflata, L. spp.

Bibliography

Christopher; Chpt. 10, pp. 393-405, 452
Ellingwood; pg. 235
Heinerman; pp. 313-314
Holmes; pp. 505-507
King's; pg. 1199
Peterson; pp. 207-208
Porcher; pp. 401-403
Potters: pg. 175
Santillo; pp. 141-142

Citations from the Medline database

Dwoskin LP, et al.
A novel mechanism of action and potential use for lobeline as a treatment for psychostimulant abuse.
Biochem Pharmacol. 2002 Jan 15;63(2):89-98.

Teng L, et al.
Lobeline displaces [3H]dihydrotetrabenazine binding and releases [3H]dopamine from rat striatal synaptic vesicles: comparison with d-amphetamine.
J Neurochem. 1998 Jul;71(1):258-65.

Subarnas A, et al.
Pharmacological properties of beta-amyrin palmitate, a novel centrally acting compound, isolated from Lobelia inflata leaves.
J Pharm Pharmacol. 1993 Jun;45(6):545-50.

Subarnas A, et al.
An antidepressant principle of Lobelia inflata L. (Campanulaceae).
J Pharm Sci. 1992 Jul;81(7):620-1.

Sopranzi N De Feo G Mazzanti G Braghiroli L
[The biological and electrophysiological parameters in the rat chronically treated with Lobelia inflata L.]
Clin Ter (1991 May 31) 137(4):265-8

Karawya MS Abdel-Wahab SM Zaki AY
Colorimetric method for the estimation of alkaloids in Lobelia and its pharmaceutical preparations.
J Assoc Off Anal Chem (1971 Nov) 54(6):1423-5

Melendez EN Carreras L Gijon JR
New alkaloid from Lobelia portoricensis Urban.
J Pharm Sci (1967 Dec) 56(12):1677-80

Desjobert A
[Volumetric determination of total alkaloids in Lobelia inflata in non-aqueous media]
Ann Pharm Fr (1968 May) 26(5):367-75

Hlavackova Z
[Variability of some characteristics in Lobelia inflata L]
Cesk Farm (1972 Sep) 21(7):319-24

Simon IS
[Obtaining lobeline from Lobelia cultivated in the USSR]
Farm Zh (1965) 20(2):66-9

O'Donovan DG Long DJ Forde E Geary P
The biosynthesis of Lobelia alkaloids. Part III. Intermediates in the biosynthesis of lobeline; biosynthesis of 8, 10-diethyl-lobelidione.
J Chem Soc [Perkin 1] (1975) (5):415-9

Weinges K Bahr W Ebert W Kloss P
[Norlobelanidine, the main alkaloid from Lobelia polyphylla Hook and Arn]
Justus Liebigs Ann Chem (1972 Feb) 756:177-80

Tschesche R Kloden D Fehlhaber HW
[On the alkaloids of Lobelia syphilitica L. II. Syphilobin A and syphilobin F]
Tetrahedron (1964 Dec) 20(12):2885-93

MARSHMALLOW—Althea officinalis

Bibliography

Christopher; pp. 354-365
Duke; pp. 84, 96, 147, 165, 396, 406
Ellingwood; pg. 431
Grieve; pp. 507-509
Heinerman; pp. 326-327
Holmes; pp. 464-466
King's; pg. 157
Potters; pp. 185-186

Santillo; pp. 144-145
Shook; pp. 119-124

Citations from the Medline database

Wang DF Shang JY Yu QH
[Analgesic and anti-inflammatory effects of the flower of Althaea rosea (L.) Cav.]
Chung Kuo Chung Yao Tsa Chih (1989 Jan) 14(1):46-8, 64

Kantee H
[Althaea, ipecac, senega and Thyme as cough medicines]
Sairaanhoitaja (1973 Mar 26) 49(5):32

Guarnieri A Chiarini A Burnelli S Amorosa M
[Mucilage of Althaea officinalis]
Farmaco [Prat] (1974 Feb) 29(2):83-91

Khaut Gla Kulachek GV
[Determination of polysaccharides in the dry mucilage of Althaea]
Farmatsiia (1971) 20(3):27-30

MULLEIN—Verbascum thapsus

Bibliography

Christopher; pp. 344-351, 485
Culpeper; pg. 174
Duke; pp. 180, 306
Grieve; pg. 562
Holmes; pg. 470
PDR-HM; pg. 1210
Potters; pg. 196
Santillo; pg. 149

Citations from the Medline database

Galasinski W, et al.
The substances of plant origin that inhibit protein biosynthesis.
Acta Pol Pharm. 1996 Sep-Oct;53(5):311-8.

Klimek B.
6'-O-apiosyl-verbascoside in the flowers of Mullein (Verbascum species).
Acta Pol Pharm. 1996 Mar-Apr;53(2):137-40.

Warashina T, et al.
Phenylethanoid and lignan glycosides from Verbascum thapsus.
Phytochemistry. 1992 Mar;31(3):961-5.

Zgorniak-Nowosielska I, et al.
Antiviral activity of Flos verbasci infusion against influenza and Herpes simplex viruses.
Arch Immunol Ther Exp (Warsz). 1991;39(1-2):103-8.
The lyophilized infusion from flowers of Verbascum thapsiforme Schrad. (FVI) showed antiviral activity in in vitro studies against Fowl plague virus, several influenza A strains, influenza B strain as well as Herpes simplex virus. Influenza

viruses titer decreased by 1-3 log units, while of H. simplex virus by 2.3 log. FVI has shown virucidal activity on H. simplex virus at 300 micrograms/ml, but did not inactivate influenza viruses. Phytochemical investigations of FVI have shown the presence of flavonoids, iridoids, phenolic acids, saponins, amino acids and free sugars.

Slagowska A, et al.
Inhibition of herpes simplex virus replication by Flos verbasci infusion.
Pol J Pharmacol Pharm. 1987 Jan-Feb;39(1):55-61.
The preliminary phytochemical investigations have revealed the presence of flavonoids, iridoids, phenolic acids, saponins, amino acids, free sugars, and mucilages in the lyophilized infusion obtained from flowers of Verbascum thapsiforme Schrad. (FVI). Antiviral activity of the FVI on Herpes simplex type 1 virus (HSV-1) was studied in vitro by the yield reduction test. Decrease in the virus titer amounted to about 2.5 log at the non-toxic concentrations of FVI. The inhibitory effect of FVI on HSV studied by plaque reduction test in Vero cells showed that 50% inhibition of virus plaques occurred at 190 micrograms/ml. The virucidal effect of FVI on HSV was also shown.

NETTLES—Urtica dioica

Bibliography

Christopher; pg. 335
Duke; pp. 40, 53-59, 225, 263, 371
Ellingwood; pg. 446
Grieve; pp. 574-582
King's; pg. 2032
Millspaugh; pp. 611-614
Peterson; pp. 239-240
Porcher; pp. 268-273
Potters; pg. 200
Santillo; pp. 151-152
Tierra; pp. 332-334

Citations from the Medline database

Czarnetzki BM Thiele T Rosenbach T
Immunoreactive leukotrienes in nettle plants (Urtica urens).
Int Arch Allergy Appl Immunol (1990) 91(1):43-6

Beintema JJ Peumans WJ
The primary structure of stinging nettle (Urtica dioica) agglutinin. A two-domain member of the hevein family.
FEBS Lett (1992 Mar 9) 299(2):131-4

Oliver F Amon EU Breathnach A Francis DM Sarathchandra P Black AK Greaves MW
Contact urticaria due to the common stinging nettle (Urtica dioica)--histological, ultrastructural and pharmacological studies.
Clin Exp Dermatol (1991 Jan) 16(1):1-7

Le Moal MA Truffa-Bachi P
Urtica dioica agglutinin, a new mitogen for murine T lymphocytes: unaltered interleukin-1 production but late interleukin 2-mediated proliferation.
Cell Immunol (1988 Aug) 115(1):24-35

Mittman P
Randomized, double-blind study of freeze-dried Urtica dioica in the treatment of allergic rhinitis.
Planta Med (1990 Feb) 56(1):44-7

Wagner H Willer F Kreher B
[Biologically active compounds from the aqueous extract of Urtica   dioica]
Planta Med (1989 Oct) 55(5):452-4

Shibuya N Goldstein IJ Shafer JA Peumans WJ Broekaert WF
Carbohydrate binding properties of the stinging nettle (Urtica dioica) rhizome lectin.
Arch Biochem Biophys (1986 Aug 15) 249(1):215-24

Bousquet J Hewitt B Guerin B Dhivert H Michel FB
Allergy in the Mediterranean area. II: Cross-allergenicity among Urticaceae pollens (Parietaria and Urtica).
Clin Allergy (1986 Jan) 16(1):57-64

Maitai CK Talalaj S Njoroge D Wamugunda R
Effect of extract of hairs from the herb Urtica massaica, on smooth muscle.
Toxicon (1980) 18(2):225-9

Piekos R Paslawska S
Studies on the optimum conditions of extraction of silicon species from plants with water. V. Urtica dioica.
Planta Med (1976 Dec) 30(4):331-6

Barsom S Bettermann AA
[Prostatic adenoma. The conservative therapy with urtica extract]
ZFA (Stuttgart) (1979 Nov 30) 55(33):1947-50

Vialli DM Barbetta F Zanotti L Mihalyi K
[Extensibility of enterochromaffine cell system concept to plants. I.Histochemical knowledge of the stings of the nettle (Urtica dioica L.)]
Acta Histochem (1973) 45(2):270-82

Barlow RB Dixon RO
Choline acetyltransferase in the nettle Urtica dioica L.
Biochem J (1973 Jan) 132(1):15-8

Oregon Grape ROOT—Mahonia aquifolia (Berberis aquifolium)

Bibliography

Christopher; pp. 80-82
Duke; pg. 376
Ellingwood; pg. 107
Grieve; pg. 369
Holmes; pp. 697-698
King's; pg. 1439
Kloss; pg. 198
Potters; pg. 193
Santillo; pp. 153-154

Citations from the Medline database

Upadhyay L, Mehrotra A, Srivastava AK, Rai NP, Tripathi K.
An experimental study of some indigenous drugs with special reference to hydraulic permeability.
Indian J Exp Biol. 2001 Dec;39(12):1308-10.

Kim SH, Lee SJ, Lee JH, Sun WS, Kim JH.
Antimicrobial activity of 9-O-acyl- and 9-O-alkylberberrubine derivatives.
Planta Med. 2002 Mar;68(3):277-81.

Yesilada E, Kupeli E.
Berberis crataegina DC. root exhibits potent anti-inflammatory, analgesic and febrifuge effects in mice and rats.
J Ethnopharmacol. 2002 Feb;79(2):237-48.

Soffar SA, Metwali DM, Abdel-Aziz SS, el-Wakil HS, Saad GA.
Evaluation of the effect of a plant alkaloid (berberine derived from Berberis aristata) on Trichomonas vaginalis in vitro.
J Egypt Soc Parasitol. 2001 Dec;31(3):893-904 + 1p plate.

Singh B, Srivastava JS, Khosa RL, Singh UP.
Individual and combined effects of berberine and santonin on spore germination of some fungi.
Folia Microbiol (Praha). 2001;46(2):137-42.

Janbaz KH, Gilani AH.
Studies on preventive and curative effects of berberine on chemical-induced hepatotoxicity in rodents.
Fitoterapia. 2000 Feb;71(1):25-33.

Stermitz FR, Beeson TD, Mueller PJ, Hsiang J, Lewis K.
Staphylococcus aureus MDR efflux pump inhibitors from a Berberis and a Mahonia (sensu strictu) species.
Biochem Syst Ecol. 2001 Aug;29(8):793-798.

Anis KV, Rajeshkumar NV, Kuttan R.
Inhibition of chemical carcinogenesis by berberine in rats and mice.
J Pharm Pharmacol. 2001 May;53(5):763-8.

Ivanovska N, Philipov S, Hristova M.
Influence of berberine on T-cell mediated immunity.
Immunopharmacol Immunotoxicol. 1999 Nov;21(4):771-86.

Fukuda K, Hibiya Y, Mutoh M, Koshiji M, Akao S, Fujiwara H.
Inhibition of activator protein 1 activity by berberine in human hepatoma cells.
Planta Med. 1999 May;65(4):381-3.

Sohni YR, Bhatt RM.
Activity of a crude extract formulation in experimental hepatic amoebiasis and in immunomodulation studies.
J Ethnopharmacol. 1996 Nov;54(2-3):119-24.

Ivanovska N, Philipov S.
Study on the anti-inflammatory action of Berberis vulgaris root extract, alkaloid fractions and pure alkaloids.
Int J Immunopharmacol. 1996 Oct;18(10):553-61.

Khan I, Qayum A, Qureshi Z.
Study of the hypotensive action of berbamine, an alkaloid isolated from berberis lycium.
Life Sci. 1969 Sep 1;8(17):993-1001.

PASSION FLOWER—Passiflora incarnata

Bibliography

Duke; pp. 296, 353-354, 388
Grieve; pg. 618
Heinerman; pp. 366-367
Holmes; pp. 839-841
Hutchens; pp. 240-241, 250, 267
Peterson; pg. 27
Potters; pp. 209-210
Santillo; pp. 155-156
Tierra; pp. 117, 355

Citations from the Medline database

Nicolls JM Birner J Forsell P
Passicol, an antibacterial and antifungal agent produced by Passiflora plant species: qualitative and quantitative range of activity.
Antimicrob Agents Chemother 1973 Jan;3(1):110-7

Birner J Nicolls JM
Passicol, an antibacterial and antifungal agent produced by Passiflora plant species: preparation and physicochemical characteristics.
Antimicrob Agents Chemother 1973 Jan;3(1):105-9

Bennati E Fedeli E
[Gas chromatography of fluid extract of Passiflora incarnata]
Boll Chim Farm 1968 Nov;107(11):716-20 (Published in Italian)

Aoyagi N Kimura R Murata T
Studies on passiflora incarnata dry extract. I. Isolation of maltol and pharmacological action of maltol and ethyl maltol.
Chem Pharm Bull (Tokyo) 1974 May;22(5):1008-13

Sopranzi N De Feo G Mazzanti G Tolu L
[Biological and electroencephalographic parameters in rats in relation to Passiflora incarnata L.]
Clin Ter 1990 Mar 15;132(5):329-33 (Published in Italian)

Perry NB Albertson GD Blunt JW Cole AL Munro MH Walker JR
4-Hydroxy-2-cyclopentenone: an anti-Pseudomonas and cytotoxic component from Passiflora tetrandra.
Planta Med 1991 Apr;57(2):129-31

Oga S de Freitas PC Gomes da Silva AC Hanada S
Pharmacological trials of crude extract of Passiflora alata.
Planta Med 1984 Aug;50(4):303-6

Speroni E Minghetti A
Neuropharmacological activity of extracts from Passiflora incarnata.
Planta Med 1988 Dec;54(6):488-91

Lutomski J Malek B
[Pharmacological investigations on raw materials of the genus passiflora. 4. The comparsion of contents of alkaloids in some harman raw materials (author's transl)]
Planta Med 1975 Jun;27(4):381-6 (Published in German)

Lutomski J Malek B
[Pharmacochemical investigations on raw materials genus passiflora. 3. Phytochemical investigations on raw materials of passiflora edulis forma flavicarpa (author's transl)]
Planta Med 1975 May;27(3):222-5 (Published in German)

Lutomski J Malek B Rybacka L
Pharmacochemical investigations of the raw materials from passiflora genus. 2. The pharmacochemical estimation of juices from the fruits of Passiflora edulis and Passiflora edulis forma flavicarpa.
Planta Med 1975 Mar;27(2):112-21

Lutomski J Malek B Stachowiak Z
[Pharmacochemical investigation of the raw materials from passiflora genus. 1. New method of chromatographic separation and fluorometric- planimetric determination of alkaloids and flavonoids in harman raw materials
Planta Med 1974 Dec;26(4):311-7 (Published in German)

Poethke W Schwarz C Gerlach H
[Components of Passiflora bryonioides. 2. Flavone derivatives]
Planta Med 1970 Nov;19(2):177-88 (Published in German)

Poethke W Schwarz C Gerlach H
[Contents of Passiflora bryonioides. 1. Alkaloids]
Planta Med 1970 Aug;18(4):303-14 (Published in German)

Glotzbach B Rimpler H
[Flavenoids from Passiflora incarnata L., Passiflora quandrangularis L. and Passiflora pulchella H. B. V. A chromatographic study]
Planta Med 1968 Feb;16(1):1-7 (Published in German)

PEPPERMINT—Mentha piperita

Bibliography

Christopher; pp. 238, 241, 429
Culpeper; pg. 166
Heinerman; pp. 331-333
Holmes; pg. 155
Kloss; pg. 165
PDR-HM; pg. 971
Potters; pg. 213
Santillo; pg. 158

Citations from the Medline database

Atta AH, et al.
Anti-nociceptive and anti-inflammatory effects of some Jordanian medicinal plant extracts.
J Ethnopharmacol. 1998 Mar;60(2):117-24.
The anti-nociceptive effect of ethanolic extract of 11 traditionally used Jordanian plants was studied by using the acetic acid-induced writhing and hot-plate test in mice. The anti-inflammatory effect of these plants was determined by xylene-induced ear oedema in mice and cotton pellet granuloma test in rats. Mentha piperita, Cinnamomum zeylanicum, Apium graveolens, Eucalyptus camaldulentis, and Ruta graveolens possess an anti-nociceptive effect against both acetic acid-induced writhing and hot plate-induced thermal stimulation. M. piperita, Jasminum officinale, Commiphora molmol, and Beta vulgaris possess an anti-inflammatory effect against acute (xylene-induced ear oedema) and chronic (cotton-pellet granuloma) inflammation. The anti-nociceptive and anti-inflammatory effects were dose dependent. These data affirm the traditional use of some of these plants for painful and inflammatory conditions.

Tassou CC, et al.
Effects of essential oil from mint (Mentha piperita) on Salmonella enteritidis and Listeria monocytogenes in model food systems at 4 degrees and 10 degrees C.
J Appl Bacteriol. 1995 Jun;78(6):593-600.

Rai MK Upadhyay S
Laboratory evaluation of essential oil of Mentha piperita Linn. against Trichophyton mentagrophytes.
Hindustan Antibiot Bull 1988 Aug-Nov;30(3-4):82-4

Sarbhoy AK, et al.
Efficacy of some essential oils and their constituents on few ubiquitous molds.
Zentralbl Bakteriol [Naturwiss]. 1978;133(7-8):723-5.

Six essential oils of Mentha arvensis, Mentha piperita, Anethum sowa, Cymbopogon winterianus, Nardostachys jatamansi, and Commiphora mukul were selected and tested for their efficacy against Aspergillus flavus, A. fumigatus, A. sulphureus, Mucor fragilis, and Rhizopus stolonifer. These oils were fungistatic or fungicidal to one or the other molds, depending upon the concentrations.

Beitz H Pank F
[Residues of herbicides in medicinal and spice plants. Residues of methylparathion in Fennel (Foeniculum vulgare Mill.) and in Peppermint (Mentha piperita L.)]
Pharmazie 1972 Aug;27(8):532-4

Herrmann EC Jr Kucera LS
Antiviral substances in plants of the mint family (labiatae). 3. Peppermint (Mentha piperita) and other mint plants.
Proc Soc Exp Biol Med 1967 Mar;124(3):874-8

Gella EV Makarova GV Borisiuk IuG
[Flavonoids of Mentha piperita]
Farm Zh 1967;22(4):80-5

Ruminska A Nieweglowska A
[Effect of shading on morphological features, yield and volatile oil content and reducing sugars of the Peppermint plant (Mentha piperita L.)]
Acta Pol Pharm 1965;22(4):373-9

PLANTAIN—Plantago spp.

Bibliography

Christopher; pp. 57-61
Grieve; pp. 640-644
Heinerman; pp. 373-375
Holmes; pg. 619
Millspaugh; pg. 419
PDR-HM; pg. 1050
Potters; pg. 218
Santillo; pg. 160

Citations from the Medline database

Wegener T, et al.
[Plantain (Plantago lanceolata L.): anti-inflammatory action in upper respiratory tract infections].
Wien Med Wochenschr. 1999;149(8-10):211-6.
Plantain (Plantago lanceolata L.) is used for the therapy of infections of the upper respiratory airways. While only few clinical data are available, results of experimental research confirm e.g. antiinflammatory, spasmolytic and immunostimulatory actions. A positive benefit-risk-ratio allows the recommendation of Plantain in moderate chronic irritative cough, also especially for children.

Fernandez-Banares F, et al.
Randomized clinical trial of Plantago ovata seeds (dietary fiber) as compared with mesalamine in maintaining remission in ulcerative colitis. Spanish Group for the Study of Crohn's Disease and Ulcerative Colitis (GETECCU).
Am J Gastroenterol. 1999 Feb;94(2):427-33.
OBJECTIVE: Butyrate enemas may be effective in the treatment of active distal ulcerative colitis. Because colonic fermentation of Plantago ovata seeds (dietary fiber) yields butyrate, the aim of this study was to assess the efficacy and safety of Plantago ovata seeds as compared with mesalamine in maintaining remission in ulcerative colitis. A significant increase in fecal butyrate levels (p = 0.018) was observed after Plantago ovata seed administration. CONCLUSIONS: Plantago ovata seeds (dietary fiber) might be as effective as mesalamine to maintain remission in ulcerative colitis.

Ringbom T, et al.
Ursolic acid from Plantago major, a selective inhibitor of cyclooxygenase-2 catalyzed prostaglandin biosynthesis.
J Nat Prod. 1998 Oct;61(10):1212-5.

Rodriguez-Moran M, et al.
Lipid- and glucose-lowering efficacy of Plantago Psyllium in type II diabetes.
J Diabetes Complications. 1998 Sep-Oct;12(5):273-8.
The beneficial effect of dietary fiber in the management of type II diabetes is still controversial and has not been totally demonstrated. Our results show that 5 g t.i.d. of Psyllium is useful, as an adjunct to dietary therapy, in patients with type II diabetes, to reduce plasma lipid and glucose levels, resolving the compliance conflict associated with the ingest of a great amount of fiber in customary diet.

Bol'shakova IV, et al.
[Antioxidant properties of plant extracts].
Biofizika. 1998 Mar-Apr;43(2):186-8.

Murai M, et al.
Phenylethanoids in the herb of Plantago lanceolata and inhibitory effect on arachidonic acid-induced mouse ear edema.
Planta Med. 1995 Oct;61(5):479-80.

Ponce-Macotela M, et al.
[In vitro effect against Giardia of 14 plant extracts].
Rev Invest Clin. 1994 Sep-Oct;46(5):343-7.

Nikulin AA, et al.
[A comparative pharmacological evaluation of sea buckthorn, rose and Plantain oils in experimental eye burns].
Eksp Klin Farmakol. 1992 Jul-Aug;55(4):64-6.

Lithander A.
Intracellular fluid of waybread (Plantago major) as a prophylactic for mammary cancer in mice.
Tumour Biol. 1992;13(3):138-41.
The investigations were performed on female mice of the strain C3H Strong. Only the breeders were used in the experiments. A number of mice were given intracellular fluid of way-bread in subcutaneous injections. The controls received no treatment. The age at which mammary cancer appeared was noted and also how often the tumors occurred. The frequency of tumor formation was 93.3% in the controls and 18.2% in the treated mice. The difference is significant.

Hriscu A, et al.
[A pharmacodynamic investigation of the effect of polyholozidic substances extracted from Plantago sp. on the digestive tract].
Rev Med Chir Soc Med Nat Iasi. 1990 Jan-Mar;94(1):165-70.
From the leaves and seeds of some Plantago species (Plantago major, media, lanceolata) the polyholozidic fraction was separated. A statistically significant gastroprotective action was found both in the case of the polyholozide obtained from seeds and leaves in two experimental models. At higher doses a laxative action was also obtained.

Karpilovskaia ED, et al.
[Inhibiting effect of the polyphenolic complex from Plantago major (plantastine) on the carcinogenic effect of endogenously synthesized nitrosodimethylamine].
Farmakol Toksikol. 1989 Jul-Aug;52(4):64-7.
Amidopyrine administered in combination with sodium nitrite in the long-term experiment produces the toxic damage of the liver and tumors in rats in connection with endogenic synthesis of carcinogenic nitrosodimethylamine. The inclusion into the animal diet of the polyphenolic complex from Plantago major--plantastine as an inhibitor of the carcinogen synthesis reduced the toxic damage of the liver that was indicated by normalization of biochemical parameters and also decreased the tumor yield from 87.5% to 33.3%. The data obtained may be the basis for the combined use of plantastine with nitrosated drugs that would contribute to carcinogenesis prevention.

Matev M, et al.
[Clinical trial of a Plantago major preparation in the treatment of chronic bronchitis].
Vutr Boles. 1982;21(2):133-7.
Plantago major, according to literature data, has expectorant, antiphlogistic, pain-relieving effect. The experimental studies confirmed a spastic effect upon the smooth musculature of bronchi as well. Twenty five patients with chronic bronchitis were examined, with or without spastic character, with light and moderately severe deviations in ventilation indices. The treatment period was 25-30 days. A rapid effect on subjective complaints and objective findings was obtained in 80 per cent. Some indices of external respiration were favourably affected. The preparation is with a good tolerance, with no toxic effect on gastrointestinal tract, liver, kidneys, hemopoiesis.

Shipochliev T.
[Uterotonic action of extracts from a group of medicinal plants].
Vet Med Nauki. 1981;18(4):94-8.
Water extracts (infusions) from a group of medicinal plants were studied in terms of their activity enhancing the uterine tonus in a series of experiments with a preparation of an isolated rabbit and guinea pig uterine horn. In a final extract concentration of 1 to 2 mg crude drug per 1 cm3 the plants ranked in the following descending order with regard to their tonus-raising effect on the uterus: camomile (Matricaria chamomilla L.), potmarigold Calendula (Calendula officinalis L.) cockscomb (Celosia cristata L.), Plantain (Plantago lanceolata L. et Plantago major L.), symphytum (Symphytum officinale L.), shepherdspurse (Capsella bursa pastoris L.), St.-John's wort (Hypericum perforatum L.).

Shipochliev T, et al.
[Anti-inflammatory action of a group of plant extracts].
Vet Med Nauki. 1981;18(6):87-94.
Use was made of Wistar albino rats in which an inflammation was induced via the simultaneous injection of caraginan and prostaglandin E1 in order to evaluate the antiinflammatory activity of 6 freeze dried plant extracts. It was found that with such model of inflammation the inflammatory effect of caraginan was strongly enhanced, which was accompanied by the rapid and prolific white blood cell extravasates. The freeze-dried extracts of St. John's-wort (Hypericum perforatum L.), potmarigold Calendula (Calendula officinalis L.), camomile (Matricaria chamomilla L.) and Plantain (Plantago lanceolata L. et Pl. major L.) were found to suppress both the inflammatory effect and the leukocyte infiltration.

Duckett S.
Plantain leaf for poison ivy.
N Engl J Med. 1980 Sep 4;303(10):583.

Grigorescu E, et al.
[Phytochemical and microbiological control of some plant species used in folk medicine. II. Plantago lanceolata L., Plantago media L., Plantago major L].
Rev Med Chir Soc Med Nat Iasi. 1973 Oct-Dec;77(4):835-41.

Maksiutina NP.
[Polyphenol compounds of Plantago major L. leaves].
Farm Zh. 1972 Jan-Feb;27(1):59-63.

PLEURISY ROOT—Asclepias tuberosa

Bibliography

Ellingwood; pg. 250
Grieve; pp. 64, 647
Holmes; pp. 238-240
King's; pg. 984
Kloss; pp. 168-169
Millspaugh; pp. 538-543
Porcher; pp. 485-488
Potters; pg. 219
Santillo; pp. 161-162
Tierra; pg. 161

Citations from the Medline database

Kelley BD Appelt GD Appelt JM
Pharmacological aspects of selected herbs employed in hispanic folk medicine in the San Luis Valley of Colorado, USA: II. Asclepias asperula (inmortal) and Achillea lanulosa (plumajillo).
J Ethnopharmacol (1988 Jan) 22(1):1-9

 Pagani F
[Phyto-constituents of Asclepias tuberosa L. (Asclepiadaceae)]
Boll Chim Farm (1975 Aug) 114(8):450-6

Petricic J
[On the cardenolides of roots of Asclepias tuberosa L.]
Arch Pharm Ber Dtsch Pharm Ges (1966 Dec) 299(12):1007-11

POKE—Phytolacca americana

Bibliography

Christopher; pp. 65-70
Grieve; pg. 648
Holmes; pg. 730
Kloss; pg. 169
PDR-HM; pg. 1030
Potters; pg. 220
Santillo; pg. 162

Citations from the Medline database

Rajamohan F, et al.
Pokeweed antiviral protein isoforms PAP-I, PAP-II, and PAP-III depurinate RNA of human immunodeficiency virus (HIV)-1.
Biochem Biophys Res Commun. 1999 Jul 5;260(2):453-8.
Pokeweed antiviral protein (PAP) is a naturally occurring broad-spectrum antiviral agent with potent anti-human immunodeficiency virus (HIV)-1 activity by an as yet undeciphered molecular mechanism. Our study prompts the hypothesis that the potent antiviral activity of PAP may in part be due to its unique ability to extensively depurinate viral RNA, including HIV-1 RNA.

Wang P, et al.
Pokeweed antiviral protein cleaves double-stranded supercoiled DNA using the same active site required to depurinate rRNA.
Nucleic Acids Res. 1999 Apr 15;27(8):1900-5.

Wang P, et al.
Reduced toxicity and broad spectrum resistance to viral and fungal infection in transgenic plants expressing Pokeweed antiviral protein II.
Plant Mol Biol. 1998 Dec;38(6):957-64.

Yamaguchi K, et al.
The amino acid sequence of mitogenic lectin-B from the roots of Pokeweed (Phytolacca americana).
Biosci Biotechnol Biochem. 1997 Apr;61(4):690-8.

Zhao Y, et al.
[Effects of processing on toxicity and pharmacological action of Phytolacca americana L].
Chung Kuo Chung Yao Tsa Chih. 1991 Aug;16(8):467-9, 511.
The experimental results have shown that the toxicity of variously processed Phytolacca americana is lower than that of the original rude drug, i.e. the local irritability tends to decrease by 16.7-83.3%; LD50 to elevate by 1.66-10.47 times; expectoration to increase by 1.10-1.57 times; but diuresis mostly to decrease by 16.0-45.0%. This reveals that the main object of processing Phytolacca americana is to lower toxicity, increase expectoration and relieve diuresis to reduce fluid retention.

Kung SS, et al.
The complete amino acid sequence of antiviral protein from the seeds of Pokeweed (Phytolacca americana).
Agric Biol Chem. 1990 Dec;54(12):3301-18.

Ready MP, et al.
Extracellular localization of Pokeweed antiviral protein.
Proc Natl Acad Sci U S A. 1986 Jul;83(14):5053-6.
Pokeweed antiviral protein is an enzyme of Mr 29,000 known to inactivate a wide variety of eukaryotic ribosomes. We have used electron microscopy to show that the antibody specific for the protein is bound within the cell wall matrix of leaf mesophyll cells from Phytolacca americana. Any penetration or breakage of the cell wall and membrane could allow the enzyme to enter the cytoplasm, where it is likely to inhibit protein synthesis in the damaged cell. We speculate that Pokeweed antiviral protein is a defensive agent whose principal function is probably antiviral.

Hostettmann K.
On the use of plants and plant-derived compounds for the control of schistosomiasis.
Naturwissenschaften. 1984 May;71(5):247-51.

Ekiert H, et al.
[Cultivation and preliminary phytochemical analysis of Phytolacca sp].
Acta Pol Pharm. 1984;41(5):581-3.

Irvin JD, et al.
Purification and properties of a second antiviral protein from Phytolacca americana which inactivates eukaryotic ribosomes.
Arch Biochem Biophys. 1980 Apr 1;200(2):418-25.

Sayed MD.
Traditional medicine in health care.
J Ethnopharmacol. 1980 Mar;2(1):19-22.

Funayama S, et al.
Hypotensive principles of Phytolacca roots.
J Nat Prod. 1979 Nov-Dec;42(6):672-4.

Tomlinson JA, et al.
The inhibition of infection by cucumber mosaic virus and influenza virus by extracts from Phytolacca americana.
J Gen Virol. 1974 Feb;22(2):225-32.

RED CLOVER—Trifolium pratense

Bibliography

Christopher; pp. 61-65
Grieve; pp. 207-208
Heinerman; pp. 390-393
Hutchens; pp. 233-235
Kloss; pp. 172-173
Potters; pg. 233
Santillo; pp. 166-167

Citations from the Medline database

Oleszek W, Stochmal A.
Triterpene saponins and flavonoids in the seeds of Trifolium species.
Phytochemistry. 2002 Sep;61(2):165.

Howes J, Waring M, Huang L, Howes LG.
Long-term pharmacokinetics of an extract of isoflavones from Red Clover (Trifolium pratense).
J Altern Complement Med. 2002 Apr;8(2):135-42.

Moyad MA.
Complementary/alternative therapies for reducing hot flashes in prostate cancer patients: reevaluating the existing indirect data from studies of breast cancer and postmenopausal women.
Urology. 2002 Apr;59(4 Suppl 1):20-33. Review.

Risbridger GP, Wang H, Frydenberg M, Husband A.
The in vivo effect of Red Clover diet on ventral prostate growth in adult male mice.
Reprod Fertil Dev. 2001;13(4):325-9.

Husband AJ.
Phytoestrogens and menopause. Published evidence supports a role for phytoestrogens in menopause.
BMJ. 2002 Jan 5;324(7328):52.

Burdette JE, Liu J, Lantvit D, Lim E, Booth N, Bhat KP, Hedayat S, Van Breemen RB, Constantinou AI, Pezzuto JM, Farnsworth NR, Bolton JL.
Trifolium pratense (Red Clover) exhibits estrogenic effects in vivo in ovariectomized Sprague-Dawley rats.
J Nutr. 2002 Jan;132(1):27-30

Robb-Nicholson C.
By the way, Doctor. I've seen advertisements for Red Clover as a treatment for menopausal symptoms. Is it an effective alternative to hormone replacement therapy (HRT)?
Harv Womens Health Watch. 2001 Dec;9(5):7. Review.

Widyarini S, Spinks N, Husband AJ, Reeve VE.
Isoflavonoid compounds from Red Clover (Trifolium pratense) protect from inflammation and immune suppression induced by UV radiation.
Photochem Photobiol. 2001 Sep;74(3):465-70.

Liu J, Burdette JE, Xu H, Gu C, van Breemen RB, Bhat KP, Booth N, Constantinou AI, Pezzuto JM, Fong HH, Farnsworth NR, Bolton JL.
Evaluation of estrogenic activity of plant extracts for the potential treatment of menopausal symptoms.
J Agric Food Chem. 2001 May;49(5):2472-9.

Mueller RL, Scheidt S.
History of drugs for thrombotic disease. Discovery, development, and directions for the future.
Circulation. 1994 Jan;89(1):432-49.

Cassady JM, Zennie TM, Chae YH, Ferin MA, Portuondo NE, Baird WM.
Use of a mammalian cell culture benzo(a)pyrene metabolism assay for the detection of potential anticarcinogens from natural products: inhibition of metabolism by biochanin A, an isoflavone from Trifolium pratense L.
Cancer Res. 1988 Nov 15;48(22):6257-61.

RED RASPBERRY —Rubus spp.

Bibliography

Christopher; pp. 156-165
Duke; pp. 326-333, 361-366
Ellingwood; pg. 345
King's; pg. 1682
Potters; pg. 35, 232
Santillo; pp. 165-166
Shook; pp. 104-110
Tierra; pp. 263, 332-334

Citations from the Medline database

Zhu Z Zhang H Yuan M
[Pharmacological study of Rubus parvifolius L.]
Chung Kuo Chung Yao Tsa Chih (1990 Jul) 15(7):427-9, 447

Chou WH Oinaka T Kanamaru F Mizutani K Chen FH Tanaka O
Diterpene glycosides from leaves of Chinese Rubus chingii and fruits of R. suavissimus, and identification of the source plant of the Chinese folk medicine "fu-pen-zi."
Chem Pharm Bull (Tokyo) (1987 Jul) 35(7):3021-4

Zhu MS
[The analysis of styptic medicinal herbs Hong Mian Teng (Rubus rufo-lanatus) by mass spectrometry, (I) Yao Hsueh Hsueh Pao (1981 Jun) 16(6):471-3

Alonso R Cadavid I Calleja JM
A preliminary study of hypoglycemic activity of Rubus fruticosus.
Planta Med (1980) Suppl:102-6

Kallio H Linko RR Pyysalo T Puntari I
Identification of keto acids in arctic bramble, Rubus arcticus L. as methyl esters of their 2,4-dinitrophenylhydrazones.
Anal Biochem (1978 Oct 1) 90(1):359-64

Anderson AC Abdelghani AA Hughes J Mason JW
Accumulation of MSMA in the fruit of the blackberry (Rubus sp.).
J Environ Sci Health [B] (1980) 15(3):247-58

Pyysalo T Honkanen E
The influence of heat on the aroma of cloudberries (rubus Chamaemorus l.).
Z Lebensm Unters Forsch (1977) 163(1):25-30

Pyysalo T
Identification of volatile compounds in hybrids between raspberry (Rubus idaeus, L.) and arctic bramble (Rubus arciticus, L.).
Z Lebensm Unters Forsch (1976 Nov 24) 162(3):263-72

SAGE—Salvia officinalis

Bibliography

Christopher; pp. 256-259
Culpeper; pg. 228
Duke; pp. 40, 79, 116
Grieve; pg. 700
Heinerman; pp. 410-416
Holmes; pg. 773
Kloss; pg. 178
PDR-HM; pg. 1113
Potters; pg. 240
Santillo; pg. 171

Citations from the Medline database

Hohmann J, et al.
Protective effects of the aerial parts of Salvia officinalis, Melissa Officinalis and Lavandula angustifolia and their constituents against enzyme-dependent and enzyme-independent lipid peroxidation.
Planta Med. 1999 Aug;65(6):576-8.
The antioxidant effects of aqueous methanolic extracts from three medicinal Lamiaceae species were investigated in enzyme-dependent and enzyme-independent lipid peroxidation systems. All these extracts caused a considerable concentration-dependent inhibition of lipid peroxidation. Phenolic components present in the plant extracts were evaluated for antioxidant activity and were found effective in both tests. Their concentrations in each extract were determined by TLC-densitometry.

Perry EK, et al.
Medicinal plants and Alzheimer's disease: from ethnobotany to phytotherapy.
J Pharm Pharmacol. 1999 May;51(5):527-34.
Old European reference books, such as those on medicinal herbs, document a variety of other plants such as Salvia officinalis (Sage) and Melissa officinalis (balm) with memory-improving properties, and cholinergic activities have recently been identified in extracts of these plants. This article considers not only the value of an integrative traditional and modern scientific approach to developing new treatments for dementia, but also in the understanding of disease mechanisms. Long before the current biologically-based hypothesis of cholinergic derangement in Alzheimer's disease emerged, plants now known to contain cholinergic antagonists were recorded for their amnesia- and dementia-inducing properties.

Wang M, et al.
Antioxidative phenolic glycosides from Sage (Salvia officinalis).
J Nat Prod. 1999 Mar;62(3):454-6.

Then M, et al.
[Plant anatomical and phytochemical evaluation of Salvia species].
Acta Pharm Hung. 1998 May;68(3):163-74.

De Leo V, et al.
[Treatment of neurovegetative menopausal symptoms with a phytotherapeutic agent].
Minerva Ginecol. 1998 May;50(5):207-11.
In this study, the efficacy has been tested of a plant product based on extracts of the leaves of Salvia officinalis (Sage) and Medicago sativa (alfalfa) in the treatment of hot flushes in 30 menopausal women with these symptoms. RESULTS: Hot flushes and night sweating completely disappeared in 20 women: four women showed good improvement and the other six showed a reduction in symptoms

Bol'shakova IV, et al.
[Antioxidant properties of plant extracts].
Biofizika. 1998 Mar-Apr;43(2):186-8.

Daniela T.
[Salvia officinalis l. I. Botanic characteristics, composition, use and cultivation].
Cesk Farm. 1993 Jun;42(3):111-6.
The drug contains mainly ethereal oil (1-2%), diterpenes, triterpenes and tannin. The pharmacopoeial criterion of quality is the content of essential oil, which is produced in an increased amount in the plant in warm summer months. Herba salviae and the extracts prepared from it are used as an antiseptic agent, an antiphlogistic agent, in the inflammations of the oral cavity and gingivitis and also as a stomachic and an antihydrotic agent. Its utilization in cosmetics and food industry is also of importance.

Schwarz K, et al.
Antioxidative constituents of Rosmarinus officinalis and Salvia officinalis. II. Isolation of carnosic acid and formation of other phenolic diterpenes.
Z Lebensm Unters Forsch. 1992 Aug;195(2):99-103.

Osawa K, et al.
The inhibitory effect of plant extracts on the collagenolytic activity and cytotoxicity of human gingival fibroblasts by Porphyromonas gingivalis crude enzyme.
Bull Tokyo Dent Coll. 1991 Feb;32(1):1-7.
The present study examined the inhibitory effects of natural plant extracts against the collagenolytic activity of Porphyromonas gingivalis. The enzyme was isolated from a culture supernatant of P. gingivalis 381. The aqueous and 50% ethanolic extracts of Ginkgo biloba, Mosla chinensis, Salvia officinalis, Cinnamomum cassia, and a catechin extract of Camellia sinensis exhibited strong inhibitory effects on collagenolytic activity. The activities of these plant extracts were higher than that of tetracycline-HCl.

Todorov S, et al.
Experimental pharmacological study of three species from genus Salvia.
Acta Physiol Pharmacol Bulg. 1984;10(2):13-20
Future studies of substances isolated from Salvia officinalis and Salvia triloba are promising with a view to their spasmolytic and hypotensive actions.

Tucakov J, et al.
[Comparative pharmacognostic studies on Sage officinalis (Salvia officinalis L.) of Pastrovici].
Glas Srp Akad Nauka [Med]. 1977;(27):47-60.

Murko D, et al.
[Tannins of Salvia officinalis and their changes during storage].
Planta Med. 1974 May;25(3):295-300.

ST. JOHN'S WORT—Hypericum perforatum

Bibliography

Culpeper; pg. 139
Duke; pp. 157, 213, 265-268, 354
Grieve; pg. 707
Heinerman; pg. 421
Holmes; pg. 565
Kloss; pg. 188
Millspaugh; pg. 114
PDR-HM; pg. 905
Potters; pg. 220
Santillo; pg. 162

Citations from the Medline database

Ernst E.
Herbal medications for common ailments in the elderly.
Drugs Aging. 1999 Dec;15(6):423-8.

Tripathi YB, et al.
Role of alcoholic extract of shoot of Hypericum perforatum Linn on lipid peroxidation and various species of free radicals in rats.
Indian J Exp Biol. 1999 Jun;37(6):567-71.
The alcoholic extract of the shoot of H. perforatum shows strong antioxidant property. It possesses the iron chelation property with more affinity to the ferrous form. It has scavenging property for both superoxide and for hydroxyl radicals but the response is more towards the superoxide radicals. Thus in addition to the anti-depressant property it has strong antioxidant property also.

Grube B, et al.
St. John's Wort extract: efficacy for menopausal symptoms of psychological origin.
Adv Ther. 1999 Jul-Aug;16(4):177-86.
Herbal remedies such as St. John's Wort preparations can be used successfully to relieve the psychological and vegetative symptoms of menopause. Substantial improvement in psychological and psychosomatic symptoms was observed. Climacteric complaints diminished or disappeared completely in the majority of women (76.4% by patient evaluation and 79.2% by physician evaluation). Of note, sexual well-being also improved after treatment with St. John's Wort extract.

Philipp M, et al.
Hypericum extract versus imipramine or placebo in patients with moderate depression: randomised multicentre study of treatment for eight weeks.
BMJ. 1999 Dec 11;319(7224):1534-8.
OBJECTIVES: To assess the efficacy and safety of hypericum extract (STEI 300, Steiner Arzneimittel, Berlin) compared with imipramine and placebo in patients in primary care with a current episode of moderate depression. CONCLUSIONS: At an average dose of 350 mg three times daily hypericum extract was more effective than placebo and at least as effective as 100 mg imipramine daily in the treatment of moderate depression. Treatment with hypericum extract is safe and improves quality of life.

Firenzuoli F, et al.
Safety of Hypericum perforatum.
J Altern Complement Med. 1999 Oct;5(5):397-8.

Rezvani AH, et al.
Attenuation of alcohol intake by extract of Hypericum perforatum (St. John's Wort) in two different strains of alcohol-preferring rats.
Alcohol Alcohol. 1999 Sep-Oct;34(5):699-705.
Depression and alcoholism have some neurochemical similarities, such as low brain serotonin activities. Thus, we hypothesized that SJW extract, which contains 0.22% hypericin and 4.05% hyperforin, also may be effective in suppressing alcohol intake. To test this hypothesis, the effects of SJW extract on voluntary alcohol intake were studied in two different genetic animal models of human alcoholism. The oral administration of SJW extract significantly (P < 0.0001) reduced alcohol intake in both FH and HAD rats. In a third study, FH rats did not develop tolerance to the suppressant effects of SJW on alcohol intake and preference following oral administration of (400 mg/kg) of the extract for 15 consecutive days. These promising findings suggest that SJW extract should be evaluated clinically as a potential therapeutic agent in the treatment of alcoholism.

Kim HL, et al.
St. John's Wort for depression: a meta-analysis of well-defined clinical trials.
J Nerv Ment Dis. 1999 Sep;187(9):532-8.
Studies concluding that St. John's Wort (Hypericum perforatum) is an effective antidepressant can be challenged due to questionable methodology. We attempt to correct this by a meta-analysis utilizing only well-defined clinical trials. The meta-analysis also showed that there was a higher dropout rate in the TCA group and that the TCAs were nearly twice as likely to cause side effects, including those more severe than hypericum. Hypericum perforatum was more effective than placebo and similar in effectiveness to low-dose TCAs in the short-term treatment of mild to moderately severe depression.

Yesilada E, et al.
Screening of Turkish anti-ulcerogenic folk remedies for anti-Helicobacter pylori activity.
J Ethnopharmacol. 1999 Sep;66(3):289-93.

Schempp CM, et al.
Hypericin levels in human serum and interstitial skin blister fluid after oral single-dose and steady-state administration of Hypericum perforatum extract (St. John's Wort).
Skin Pharmacol Appl Skin Physiol. 1999 Sep-Oct;12(5):299-304.

Wheatley D.
Hypericum in seasonal affective disorder (SAD).
Curr Med Res Opin. 1999;15(1):33-7.
Volunteers from the membership of the SAD Association took part in a postal survey, before and after eight weeks' treatment with Hypericum (Kira), using an 11-item rating scale. On the results of this survey, Hypericum would appear to be an effective treatment for SAD.

Bernd A, et al.
Phototoxic effects of Hypericum extract in cultures of human keratinocytes compared with those of psoralen.
Photochem Photobiol. 1999 Feb;69(2):218-21.

Schellenberg R, et al.
Pharmacodynamic effects of two different hypericum extracts in healthy volunteers measured by quantitative EEG.
Pharmacopsychiatry. 1998 Jun;31 Suppl 1:44-53.
These experimental findings suggest that hypericum extracts with a high hyperforin content have a shielding effect on the central nervous system.

Mueller BM.
Effects of hypericum extract HYP 811 in patients with psychovegetative disorders.
Adv Ther. 1998 Jul-Aug;15(4):255-60.
By study end, 83.1% of patients had experienced a reduction in symptom severity, and the frequency of symptoms had improved by an average of 37.3%. After 3 weeks of treatment, the dosage could be reduced to one capsule per day in 35.8% of patients.

Bol'shakova IV, et al.
[Antioxidant properties of plant extracts].
Biofizika. 1998 Mar-Apr;43(2):186-8.

Czekalla J, et al.
The effect of hypericum extract on cardiac conduction as seen in the electrocardiogram compared to that of imipramine.
Pharmacopsychiatry. 1997 Sep;30 Suppl 2:86-8.
Our results indicate that for the treatment of patients with a pre-existing conductive dysfunction or elderly patients, high-dose hypericum extract is safer with regard to cardiac function than tricyclic antidepressants.

Taylor RS, et al.
Antiviral activities of Nepalese medicinal plants.
J Ethnopharmacol. 1996 Jul 5;52(3):157-63.
In a screening of plants used traditionally in Nepal to treat diseases that could be caused by viruses, methanol extracts from 21 species were assayed for activity against three mammalian viruses: herpes simplex virus, Sindbis virus and poliovirus. Assays were performed in UV-A or visible light, as well as dark. Individual species of Hypericum, Lygodium, and Maesa exhibited impressive antiviral activities, although their selective effects on the three viruses suggested that the antiviral ingredients were different in each extract. In addition, many of the other extracts showed partial inactivation of one or more test viruses.

Krylov AA, et al.
[The use of an infusion of St.-John's-wort in the combined treatment of alcoholics with peptic ulcer and chronic gastritis].
Lik Sprava. 1993 Feb-Mar;(2-3):146-8.

Smyshliaeva AV, et al.
[The modification of a radiation lesion in animals with an aqueous extract of Hypericum perforatum L. 1].
Biol Nauki. 1992;(4):7-9.

Melzer R, et al.
Vasoactive properties of procyanidins from Hypericum perforatum L. in isolated porcine coronary arteries.
Arzneimittelforschung. 1991 May;41(5):481-3.

Meruelo D, et al.
Therapeutic agents with dramatic antiretroviral activity and little toxicity at effective doses: aromatic polycyclic diones hypericin and pseudohypericin.
Proc Natl Acad Sci U S A. 1988 Jul;85(14):5230-4.
Two aromatic polycyclic diones hypericin and pseudohypericin have potent antiretroviral activity; these substances occur in plants of the Hypericum family. Both compounds are highly effective in preventing viral-induced manifestations that follow infections with a variety of retroviruses in vivo and in vitro. Hypericin and pseudohypericin have low in vitro cytotoxic activity at concentrations sufficient to produce dramatic antiviral effects in murine tissue culture model systems that use radiation leukemia and Friend viruses. Administration of these compounds to mice at the low doses sufficient to prevent retroviral-induced disease appears devoid of undesirable side effects. This lack of toxicity at therapeutic doses extends to humans, as these compounds have been tested in patients as antidepressants with apparent salutary effects. Our observations to date suggest that pseudohypericin and hypericin could become therapeutic tools against retroviral-induced diseases such as acquired immunodeficiency syndrome (AIDS).

Shipochliev T.
[Uterotonic action of extracts from a group of medicinal plants].
Vet Med Nauki. 1981;18(4):94-8.

Shipochliev T, et al.
[Anti-inflammatory action of a group of plant extracts].
Vet Med Nauki. 1981;18(6):87-94.

Matei I, et al.
[Value of Hypericum perforatum oil in dermatological preparations. I].
Rev Med Chir Soc Med Nat Iasi. 1977 Jan-Mar;81(1):73-4.

Derbentseva NA, et al.
[Action of tannins from Hypericum perforatum L. on the influenza virus].
Mikrobiol Zh. 1972;34(6):768-72.

Gurevich AI, et al.
[Antibiotic hyperforin from Hypericum perforatum L].
Antibiotiki. 1971 Jun;16(6):510-3.

Aizenman BIu.
[Antibiotic preparations from Hypericum perforatum L].
Mikrobiol Zh. 1969 Mar-Apr;31(2):128-33.

Chaplinskaia MG, et al.
[Study of the photodynamic action of Hypericum in its external use].
Farm Zh. 1965;20(2):47-53.

SASSAFRAS—S. officinale

Bibliography

Christopher; pp. 86-91
Grieve; pg. 715
Heinerman; pg. 424
Holmes; pg. 356
PDR-HM; pg. 1123
Potters; pg. 244

Santillo; pg. 173
Shook; pp. 269-272

Citations from the Medline database

Klepser TB, et al.
Unsafe and potentially safe herbal therapies.
Am J Health Syst Pharm. 1999 Jan 15;56(2):125-38;

Carlson M, et al.
Liquid chromatographic determination of safrole in Sassafras-derived herbal products.
J AOAC Int. 1997 Sep-Oct;80(5):1023-8.

Farag SE, et al.
Degradation of the natural mutagenic compound safrole in spices by cooking and irradiation.
Nahrung. 1997 Dec;41(6):359-61
Safrole was determined using gas-liquid chromatography in some common spices as star anise, cumin, black pepper and ginger. Safrole concentration in these spices was 9,325, 3,432, 955 and 500 mg.kg-1, respectively. Black pepper was chosen to use in the following experiments. Finally, these results proved that the mutagenicity of some spices due to presence of safrole can be destructed during drying of the washed seeds or during cooking either with or without any additional treatment as irradiation.

Haines JD Jr.
Ipecac, Indian turnip, and Sassafras: a sampling of American Indian medicine.
J Okla State Med Assoc. 1996 Sep;89(9):326-7.

Kamdem DP, et al.
Chemical composition of essential oil from the root bark of Sassafras albidum.
Planta Med. 1995 Dec;61(6):574-5.

Haines JD Jr.
Sassafras tea and diaphoresis.
Postgrad Med. 1991 Sep 15;90(4):75-6.

Kapadia GJ, et al.
Carcinogenicity of some folk medicinal herbs in rats.
J Natl Cancer Inst. 1978 Mar;60(3):683-6.

Segelman AB, et al.
Sassafras and herb tea. Potential health hazards.
JAMA. 1976 Aug 2;236(5):477.

Hoke M, et al.
[A new study on Sassafras root].
Arch Pharm (Weinheim). 1972 Jan;305(1):33-9.

THYME—Thymus vulgaris

Bibliography

Christopher; pp. 250-256
Culpeper; pg. 139
Duke; pp. 85, 204, 408

Grieve; pp. 808-813
Heinerman; pp. 445-449
Holmes; pg. 219
King; pg. 1939
Kloss; pg. 191
PDR-HM; pg. 1184
Potters; pg. 220
Santillo; pg. 183

Citations from the Medline database

Youdim KA, et al.
Dietary supplementation of Thyme (Thymus vulgaris L.) essential oil during the lifetime of the rat: its effects on the antioxidant status in liver, kidney and heart tissues.
Mech Ageing Dev. 1999 Sep 8;109(3):163-75.
This study aimed not only to identify age-related changes in certain antioxidant systems, but to assess whether dietary supplementation of Thyme oil could address the unfavourable antioxidant-pro-oxidant balance that occurs with age. A general feature of these various antioxidant parameters measured was that their activities remained higher in rats whose diets were supplemented with Thyme oil, suggesting that they retained a more favourable antioxidant capacity during their life span.

Meister A, et al.
Antispasmodic activity of Thymus vulgaris extract on the isolated guinea-pig trachea: discrimination between drug and ethanol effects.
Planta Med. 1999 Aug;65(6):512-6.

Marino M, et al.
Antimicrobial activity of the essential oils of Thymus vulgaris L. measured using a bioimpedometric method.
J Food Prot. 1999 Sep;62(9):1017-23.
The essential oils obtained from Thymus vulgaris L. harvested at four ontogenetic stages were evaluated for their biological activity and chemical composition. The Thyme essential oils were tested for their inhibitory effects against nine strains of gram-negative bacteria and six strains of gram-positive bacteria. All the Thyme essential oils examined had a significant bacteriostatic activity against the microorganisms tested. This activity was more marked against the gram-positive bacteria. The oil from Thyme in full flower was the most effective at stopping the growth of the microbial species examined. The oils tested were also shown to have good antibacterial activity by direct contact, which appeared to be more marked against the gram-negative bacteria. Only a few of the species were capable of recovering at least 50% of their metabolic function after contact with the inhibitor, while most of the strains were shown to have been inactivated almost completely. Escherichia coli O157:H7 was the most sensitive species, given that after contact with even the lowest concentration of oil cells could not be recovered.

Lall N, et al.
In vitro inhibition of drug-resistant and drug-sensitive strains of Mycobacterium tuberculosis by ethnobotanically selected South African plants.
J Ethnopharmacol. 1999 Sep;66(3):347-54.
Acetone as well as water extracts of Cryptocarya latifolia, Euclea natalensis, Helichrysum melanacme, Nidorella anomala and Thymus vulgaris inhibited the growth of M. tuberculosis.

Manou I, et al.
Evaluation of the preservative properties of Thymus vulgaris essential oil in topically applied formulations under a challenge test.
J Appl Microbiol. 1998 Mar;84(3):368-76.
The preservative properties of Thyme essential oil (3%) with a known composition were evaluated in two types of final formulations, suitable for use as pharmaceutical or cosmetic vehicles, by means of a standard challenge test proposed by the latest European Pharmacopoeia. The required preservation efficacy criteria were satisfied against the bacterial strains, against the yeast in one of the formulations, but not against the mould strain involved in this study.

Agnihotri S, et al.
A novel approach to study antibacterial properties of volatile components of selected Indian medicinal herbs.
Indian J Exp Biol. 1996 Jul;34(7):712-5.
Of the four herbs selected (Eugenia caryophyllus, Thymus vulgaris, Cinnamonum zeylanium, Cuminum cyminum), volatile components of Thymus vulgaris were most effective againsts all the seven test organisms.

Panizzi L, et al.
Composition and antimicrobial properties of essential oils of four Mediterranean Lamiaceae.
J Ethnopharmacol. 1993 Aug;39(3):167-70.
Essential oils from Satureja montana L., Rosmarinus officinalis L., Thymus vulgaris L., and Calamintha nepeta (L.) Savi, were chemically analysed and their antimicrobial and fungicide activities evaluated on the basis of their minimum inhibitory concentration (MIC) and minimum bactericidal concentration (MBC). All four oils have a biotoxic effect, the most active being those from Calamintha and Thymus.

Van Den Broucke CO, et al.
Spasmolytic activity of the flavonoids from Thymus vulgaris.
Pharm Weekbl Sci. 1983 Feb 25;5(1):9-14.

VITEX—Vitex agnus-castus

Bibliography

Duke; pp. 41, 91, 324, 327, 364
Grieve; pg. 188
Holmes; pg. 597
PDR-HM; pg. 1222

Citations from the World Wide Web

Summary of Scientific Studies
PMS- 1542 women, 90% had improvement or complete relief of symptoms, 2% side effects,some improvement of symptoms in an average of 25 days
Abnormal menstrual cycles-186 women, 140 had normalization of their cycles Infertility- 45 women, 7 were pregnant after 3 months of treatment
Hyperprolactinemia- Prolactin release significantly reduced in a study of 52 women
Poor lactation- Most women in one controlled study effectively increased milk production with Vitex
http://www.herbcraft.com/Vitex.html#Summary

Menopause - Alternative Medicine - 09/06/99
Why take these risks if there's a more natural way to go through this
URL: http://altmedicine.about.com/library/weekly/aa090699.htm

Chaste (Vitex agnus-castus) - Herbs for Health - 05/08/98
A historical herb great for treating womens complaints , from your About.com Guide
URL: http://herbsforhealth.about.com/library/weekly/aa050898.htm

Herbs for Fertility, Pregnancy and Child Birth - Herbs for Health Net Links
Your resource for herbs for prenancy, fertility, and childbearing, from your About.com Guide.
URL: http://herbsforhealth.about.com/msubpreg.htm

WILD CHERRY—Prunus serotina

Bibliography

Christopher; pp. 383-387
Eclectic Manual, No. 6, Fyfe; pg. 115
Grieve; pg. 191
Heinerman; pg. 470
Holmes; pg. 509
King; pg. 1583
PDR-HM; pg. 1069
Potters; pg. 281
Santillo; pg. 190

Citations from the Medline database

Haupt H.
[Toxic and less toxic plants. 39. Prunus padus, Prunus serotina].
Kinderkrankenschwester. 1998 Nov;17(11):504-5.

Turner NJ, et al.
Contemporary use of bark for medicine by two Salishan native elders of southeast Vancouver Island, Canada.
J Ethnopharmacol. 1990 Apr;29(1):59-72.

Wills RB, et al.
Nutrient composition of stone fruit (Prunus spp.) cultivars: apricot, cherry, nectarine, peach and plum.
J Sci Food Agric. 1983 Dec;34(12):1383-9.

Buchalter L.
Identification of monomeric and polymeric 5,7,3'4'-tetrahydroxyflavan-3,4-diol from tannin extract of Wild Cherry bark USP, Prunus serotina Erhart, family Rosaceae.
J Pharm Sci. 1969 Oct;58(10):1272-3.

WILLOW—Salix alba, Salix spp.

Bibliography

Culpeper; pg. 271
Duke; pp. 197, 231, 245, 454
Eclectic Manual, No. 6, Fyfe; pg. 127
Grieve; pg. 847
Heinerman; pp. 473-474
Holmes; pg. 659
Kloss; pg. 231
Millspaugh; pg. 645
PDR-HM; pg. 1111
Potters; pg. 283
Santillo; pg. 189

Citations from the Medline database

Rohnert U, et al.
Superoxide-dependent and -independent nitrite formation from hydroxylamine: inhibition by plant extracts.
Z Naturforsch [C]. 1998 Mar-Apr;53(3-4):241-9.

Hedner T, et al.
The early clinical history of salicylates in rheumatology and pain.
Clin Rheumatol. 1998;17(1):17-25.
The first clinical reports on the treatment of fever and pain with salicylate-containing natural Willow bark remedies were made by the English clergyman Edward Stone in 1763. The pharmacologically active principles were isolated from natural sources by Italian, German and French scientists between 1826 and 1829. Salicylic acid was first synthesised by the German Gerland in 1852 and a year later the Frenchman Gerhardt synthesised acetylsalicylic acid. The first reports on the clinical use of salicylic acid in rheumatic disorders were made independently by the two German physicians Stricher and Reiss in 1876. Acetylsalicylic acid was rediscovered by Hoffmann in 1897 and by the turn of the century it had gained worldwide recognition in the treatment of pain and rheumatological disorders. Reports on adverse events relating to gastrointestinal intolerance and bleeding appeared early, but were largely neglected until the 1950s. Today, salicylates are still widely used as analgesic, antipyretic and anti-inflammatory drugs. New indications, such as thrombosis prophylaxis, have emerged during the last decades, and yet others are being explored.

Vainio H, et al.
Aspirin for the second hundred years: new uses for an old drug.
Pharmacol Toxicol. 1997 Oct;81(4):151-2.

Aronson SM.
The miraculous Willow tree.
R I Med. 1994 Jun;77(6):159-61.

Mueller RL, et al.
History of drugs for thrombotic disease. Discovery, development, and directions for the future.
Circulation. 1994 Jan;89(1):432-49.

Decker JL.
From the Willow bark to cytotoxics: the management of rheumatoid arthritis.
Med Times. 1977 Nov;105(11):28-34.

Thieme H.
[On the tannin content of Willow cortex].
Pharmazie. 1968 Apr;23(4):212.

Logan A.
Around the Willow tree.
N S Med Bull. 1966 Aug;45(8):207-8.

YARROW—Achillea millefolium

Bibliography

Christopher; pp. 234-239
Ellingwood; pg. 355
Heinerman; pp. 480-482
Holmes; pp. 748-751
Potters; pg. 290

Santillo; pp. 195-196
Tierra; pg. 161

Citations from the Medline database

Verzar-Petri G Cuong BN
On the quantitative determination of chamazulene and prochamazulenes in essential oils and crude drugs from Yarrow (Achillea sp.--Compositae). II.: A new colorimetric method of high sensitivity for determination of chamazulene in the essential oils.
Acta Pharm Hung 1977 May;47(3):134-41

Lamaison JL Carnat AP
[Study of azulen in 3 subspecies of Achillea millefolium L.]Recherche d'azulene chez les trois sous-especes d'Achillea millefolium L.
Ann Pharm Fr 1988;46(2):139-43 (Published in French)

Ibragimov DI Kazanskaia GB
[Antimicrobial action of cranberry bush, common Yarrow and Achillea biebersteinii]
Antibiotiki 1981 Feb;26(2):108-9

Rucker G Manns D Breuer J
[Peroxides as plant constituents. 8. Guaianolide-peroxides from Yarrow,Achillea millefolium L., a soluble component causing Yarrow dermatitis]
Arch Pharm (Weinheim) 1991 Dec;324(12):979-81

Kraus L Perenyi F
[Determination of azulene in the oil of milfoil (Achillea millefolium) by thin-layer chromatography]
Cesk Farm 1965 Oct;14(8):423-4 (Published in Czech)

Bohlmann F Zdero C
[Polyacetylene compounds, 215. New components from Achillea species]
Chem Ber 1973;106(4):1328-36 (Published in German)

He SQ
[Treatment of acute tonsillitis with total organic acid capsules of Achillea]
Chung Yao Tung Pao 1987 May;12(5):55-6 (Published in Chinese)

Barel S Segal R Yashphe J
The antimicrobial activity of the essential oil from Achillea fragrantissima.
J Ethnopharmacol 1991 May-Jun;33(1-2):187-91

Kelley BD Appelt GD Appelt JM
Pharmacological aspects of selected herbs employed in hispanic folk medicine in the San Luis Valley of Colorado, USA: II. Asclepias asperula (inmortal) and Achillea lanulosa (plumajillo).
J Ethnopharmacol 1988 Jan;22(1):1-9

Chandler RF Hooper SN Hooper DL Jamieson WD Flinn CG Safe LM
Herbal remedies of the Maritime Indians: sterols and triterpenes of Achillea millefolium L. (Yarrow).
J Pharm Sci 1982 Jun;71(6):690-3

Falk AJ Smolenski SJ Bauer L Bell CL
Isolation and identification of three new flavones from Achillea millefolium L.
J Pharm Sci 1975 Nov;64(11):1838-42

Goldberg AS Mueller EC Eigen E Desalva SJ
Isolation of the anti-inflammatory principles from Achillea millefolium (Compositae).
J Pharm Sci 1969 Aug;58(8):938-41

Bejnarowicz EA Smolenski SJ
Gas chromatographic analysis of the essential oil from Achillea millefolium L.
J Pharm Sci 1968 Dec;57(12):2160-1

Falk AJ Bauer L Bell CL Smolenski SJ
The constituents of the essential oil from Achillea millefolium L.
Lloydia 1974 Dec;37(4):598-602

De Pasquale R Ragusa S Iauk L Barbera R Galati EM
Effect of cadmium on germination, growth and active principle contents of Achillea millefolium L.
Pharmacol Res Commun 1988 Dec;20 Suppl 5:145-9

Haggag MY Shalaby AS Verzar-Petri G
Thin layer and gas-chromatographic studies on the essential oil from Achillea millefolium.
Planta Med 1975 Jun;27(4):361-6

Oswiecimska M
[Correlation between number of chromosomes and prochamazulene in Easteuropean Achillea (author's transl]
Planta Med 1974 Jun;25(4):389-395 (Published in German)

Plchova S Spurna V Karpfel Z
Intra- and interspecific differentiation within the Achillea genus.
Planta Med 1970 Oct;19(1):75-82

Kozlowski J Lutomski J
[On the content of etheric oils, azulene and bitter principle in selected clones of Achillea millefolium L. s.l]
Planta Med 1969 Aug;17(3):226-9 (Published in German)

Oswiecimska M
[Achillea collina Becker--a proazulene containing taxon from Achillea Millefolium L.S.I.]
Planta Med 1968 May;16(2):201-7 (Published in German)

YELLOW DOCK—Rumex crispus

Bibliography

Christopher; pp. 102-107
Culpeper; pg. 90
Duke; pg. 444
Grieve; pg. 259
Heinerman; pg. 482
Holmes; pg. 682
King's; pg. 1683
Millspaugh; pg. 574
PDR-HM; pg. 1106
Potters; pg. 291
Santillo; pg. 196

Citations from the Medline database

Reig R, et al.
Fatal poisoning by Rumex crispus (curled dock): pathological findings and application of scanning electron microscopy. Vet Hum Toxicol. 1990 Oct;32(5):468-70.

Citations from the World Wide Web

Hepatics- HealthWorld Online
Abstract: Hepatics. David L. Hoffman, M.N.I.M.H.. Hepatics are herbal remedies which in a wide range of ways aid the work of the liver. They tone, strengthen and in some cases increase the flow of bile. In a broad holistic approach to health they are of great importance.
http://www.healthy.net/hwlibrarybooks/hoffman/actions/hepatic.htm

HerbalGram - Number 35 - 1995 - HealthWorld Online
Abstract: The Journal of the American Botanical Council and the Herb Research Foundation Number 35 - Fall, 1995 Seventy-Five Pervent of Rural Mississippi Residents Report Use of Plant Remedies. by Barbara
http://www.healthy.net/hwlibraryjournals/herbalgram/herbalgram35/features/plantremedies.htm

Skin Enhancement -- Nutritional Programs - HealthWorld Online
Abstract: Skin Enhancement. Color. Organ. Element. Increased Water Needs. Decreased Water Needs. SKIN-SUPPORTING NUTRIENTS. Elson M. Haas, M.D.. Diet and Supplements. Common Skin Conditions. Herbs. Skin Enhancement Program.
http://www.healthy.net/hwlibrarybooks/haas/perform/skinenha.htm

Detoxification Programs: General Detoxification & Cleansing - HealthWorld Online
Abstract: General Detoxification and Cleansing. OUR GENERAL DETOXIFICATION SYSTEMS. SIGNS AND SYMPTOMS OF TOXICITY. PROBLEMS RELATED TO CONGESTION / STAGNATION / TOXICITY. Other Programs by Elson M. Haas, M.D.. Elson M. Haas, M.D.. Who Is Best Suited for Detoxification?. What Is Detoxification?.
http://www.healthy.net/hwlibrarybooks/haas/detox/general.htm

Herbal Phytotherapy and the Elderly- HealthWorld Online
Abstract: Herbal Phytotherapy and the Elderly. Prevention and Treatments of Disease. David L. Hoffman, M.N.I.M.H.. The Biology of Aging. Psychology of Aging
http://www.healthy.net/hwlibrarybooks/hoffman/elders/elders.htm

APPENDIX C

Abrasions 107, 116, 197, 274
Abscess Root 70
Abscesses 103, 151, 206, 212, 218, 230, 257
Acerola 183
Achillea millefolium 295
Acidosis 173, 305
Acne 103, 112, 140, 211, 229, 230, 257, 277, 302
Activated Charcoal 281, 294
Agar 76, 306
Agrimony 73, 74, 80, 87, 263
AIDS 65, 112, 200, 306, 338, 363, 424
Ajuga reptans 105
Alcohol Withdrawal 178, 273
Alder 70
Alfalfa 66, 83, 84, 212, 257, 263, 269
Algae 83, 307
Allergies 156, 196, 218
Allium sativum 164
Aloe 45, 76, 87, 107, 121, 133, 274
Alopecia 93, 307
Althea officinalis 207
Alum Root 73, 80, 85, 103, 104, 187, 224, 225, 299
Alzheimer's 140, 224, 269
Amenorrhea 98, 144, 183, 196, 263, 285, 308
American Wormseed 68
Anemia 140, 224, 302, 308
Anethum graveolens 142
Angelica 67, 69, 73, 74, 76, 78, 80, 82, 83, 98, 99, 113, 126, 179, 229, 263
Angostura 74

Anise 69, 70, 72, 73, 79, 145, 162, 277
Anxiety 126, 178, 200, 234, 273, 311
Apple 67, 72
Apricot
  kernels 68
  seeds 87
Arctium lappa 109
Arnica 70, 272
Arrhythmia 173, 290, 312
Arteriosclerosis 121, 166, 173, 312
Arthritis 67, 98, 112, 121, 132, 166, 170, 173, 196, 205, 211, 224, 251, 252, 293, 298, 312
Asclepius tuberosa 245
Asthma 98, 121, 132, 183, 202, 205, 218, 224, 248, 257, 281, 289, 312
Astragalus 274
Athlete's Foot 151

Bad Breath 144, 269
Balmony 70, 229
Balm of Gilead 70
Balsam of Peru 71
Barberry 66, 67, 69, 71, 72, 73, 74, 75, 80, 86, 166, 179, 205, 227, 228, 230, 243, 298, 302, 303
Basil 73, 144
Bayberry 66, 69, 73, 78, 80, 82, 93, 103, 258, 263, 264, 302, 303
Bedwetting 137, 187, 196, 273, 298, 314
Beet Greens 229
Beets 75
Bell's Palsy 274

Benzoin 53, 54, 55, 73, 79, 84, 87, 157
Berberis aquifolium 227
BET 274
Betula alba, Betula spp. 90
Bilberry 70, 196
Birch Bark 71, 77, **90–94**, 137, 374
Bistort 69, 71, 80, 85
Bites 116, 150, 192, 243
  insect 55, 116, 192
Bitter Orange 70
Bitter Root 68, 80
Bittersweet 69
Black Cohosh 66, 68, 70, 72, 75, 77, 78, 80, 82, 83, 86, 93, **95–99**, 103, 121, 150, 162, 179, 183, 196, 212, 234, 239, 260, 285, 298, 376
Black Currants 81
Black Haw 70, 72, 78, 82, 86, 99
Black Pepper 82, 84, 277
Black Walnut 66, 68, 69, 71, 73, 77, 81, 83, 87, 93, **100–104**, 112, 166, 167, 183, 196, 253, 293, 377
Blackberry 68, 71, 73, 77, 80, 81, 85, 86, 259, 260, 262, 264, 277, 298, 299
Blackberry Root 80, 85, 262, 277, 298, 299
Bladder
  infection 93, 196
  irritability 178
Bladderwrack 66, 67, 71
Bleeding 85, 116, 121, 187, 225, 243, 263, 264, 293, 299, 315
  blood in urine 187
  excessive 263
  heavy 225, 298
  internal 225, 293
  nosebleed 104, 225, 299
Blepharitis 162, 315
Blessed Thistle 66, 74, 76, 78, 79, 80, 87, 162, 179, 212, 285
Bloating 126, 229
Blood Alkalizer 257
Blood Cleanser 257
Blood Poisoning 151
Blood Pressure 99, 140, 173, 200, 224, 234, 269, 298
Blood Purifier 74, 129, 132, 140, 147, 277
Blood Root 69, 80, 98

Blood Thinner 257
Blood Toxicity 252
Bloodroot 257
Blue Cohosh 72, 77, 78, 82, 83, 98, 144, 263, 285, 298
Blue Flag 66, 68, 75, 80, 151, 181, 253, 258
Blue Vervain 76
Boils 57, 93, 103, 112, 133, 140, 151, 212, 218, 234, 257, 277, 303
Boneset 72, 75, 76, 79, 82, 126, 151, 157, 169, 170, 177, 196, 205, 238, 248, 298
Borage 69, 70, 84, 200, 273
Bramble Root 252
Broken Bones 107, 132, 133
Bronchial Spasms 98
Bronchitis 79, 98, 126, 132, 144, 179, 183, 205, 211, 218, 238, 248, 269, 281, 289, 302, 316
Bruises 107, 133, 157, 218, 234, 273, 274
  internal 107
Buchu 71, 73, 76, 77, 81, 86, 137
Buckbean 68
Buckthorn 68, 81, 86
Bugle 55, 67, 70, 71, 72, 73, 74, 76, 80, 87, 98, **105–108**, 116, 121, 132, 133, 179, 183, 187, 200, 230, 243, 244, 249, 273, 274, 293, 298, 299, 302, 303, 377
Bugleweed 73, 75, 82, 85, 107, 200
Burdock 66, 68, 69, 72, 76, 77, 86, 93, 99, **109–113**, 129, 132, 140, 151, 170, 212, 224, 229, 234, 244, 252, 257, 258, 277, 285, 302, 303, 378
Burns 107, 113, 116, 133, 167, 183, 197, 218, 225, 264, 274, 299
Bursitis 187, 224, 316
Butcher's Broom 72, 77, 81, 112, 157, 218, 253
Butternut 68

Cajuput 68, 71
Calcium Deficiency 133
Calcium Deposits 187
Calculi 277

Calendula 44, 54, 55, 67, 70, 72, 73, 76, 87, 93, 107, 112, 113, **114–117**, 129, 133, 151, 157, 179, 187, 192, 197, 206, 211, 212, 218, 224, 230, 243, 244, 253, 257, 274, 277, 298, 299, 303, 379, 380, 387, 390, 394, 404, 414

Calendula officinalis 114

Camphor 71, 84

Cancer 151, 257, 258
 skin 93

Candida 104, 375, 389

Candidiasis 281, 317, 367

Canker Sores 93, 243, 263, 269, 281, 293

Capsicum 44, 55, 66, 68, 69, 70, 72, 73, 80, 82, 84, 99, **118–122**, 126, 133, 157, 162, 166, 173, 178, 205, 206, 212, 218, 224, 225, 234, 239, 257, 263, 265, 269, 281, 290, 298, 299, 381, 382

Capsicum frutescens, C. annum 118

Caraway 67, 145, 238

Cardamon 82

Carline Thistle 86

Carob 72

Carrot 40, 68, 80, 144

Cascara 66, 72, 80, 81, 86, 218, 228, 229, 243, 257

Cassia Oil 83

Catnip 67, 70, 72, 76, 79, 82, 98, 112, **123–126**, 137, 144, 145, 162, 183, 200, 212, 219, 229, 238, 239, 263, 298, 383

Cat's Claw 166, 170

Celery 77, 82, 86, 144, 224, 298

Celery Seed 77, 144, 224, 298

Chamomile 67, 70, 72, 74, 76, 78, 82, 86, 99, 126, 179, 212, 219, 225, 239, 257, 298

Chaparral 28, 66, 68, 69, 70, 71, 72, 73, 77, 78, 81, 83, 93, 112, 151, 249, 257

Chickweed 52, 66, 70, 76, 77, 84, 87, 129, 157, 218, 253, 258, 269, 299, 303

Chicory 72, 77

Chilblains 157

Chills 238

Cholesterol 166, 243, 320

Chorea 98

Cimicifuga racemosa 95

Cinnamon 70, 73, 83, 104, 269, 275, 277

Cirrhosis 253, 320

Clary Sage 72

Cleavers 66, 72, 77, 80, 86, 93, 112, **127–129**, 137, 140, 157, 170, 187, 225, 226, 229, 244, 253, 257, 263, 277, 298, 302, 303, 383

Clove Oil 167, 218, 239

Cloves 67, 68, 69, 70, 73, 82, 264

Coffee 82

Cold Extremities 121

Colds 126, 129, 151, 154, 156, 166, 183, 196, 238, 248, 281, 289, 298
 head cold 129

Colic 126, 144, 162, 183, 238, 245, 321

Colitis 133, 212, 238, 321, 413

Colloidal Silver 69, 151, 230

Colon
 ballooned 103
 relaxed 103

Coltsfoot 69, 72, 76, 79, 98

Comfrey 28, 40, 44, 45, 49, 52, 54, 55, 66, 67, 69, 70, 71, 73, 76, 79, 83, 86, 87, 93, 98, 103, 105, 107, 108, 112, 113, 116, 117, 129, **130–134**, 140, 151, 157, 167, 170, 182, 183, 184, 187, 192, 196, 197, 200, 205, 211, 212, 218, 223, 225, 229, 230, 234, 238, 239, 243, 244, 248, 249, 253, 257, 263, 264, 269, 273, 274, 277, 281, 289, 290, 298, 299, 302, 303, 383, 384

Composition Powder 261, 263, 264

Condurango 71

Congestive Heart Failure 173

Conjunctivitis 103, 162, 212, 218, 281, 322

Constipation 74, 103, 140, 156, 212, 218, 229, 243, 252, 302, 322

Convulsions 205, 234

CoQ10 173

Coriander 69, 73, 145, 162, 281

Cornsilk 70, 76, 77, 81, 93, 112, 129, 133, **135–137**, 140, 150, 170, 178, 187, 196, 212, 225, 243, 263, 274, 293, 298, 384

Cotton Root 83

Cough 98, 107, 133, 144, 166, 183, 196, 205, 212, 218, 234, 257, 281, 290, 323
 persistent 290

Crabs 281

Cradle Cap 257

Crampbark 72, 73, 82, 98, 179, 285

Cramps 72, 98, 116, 162, 205, 206, 239, 263, 277, 281

Cranberry 84, 93, 137, 196
Cranesbill 69, 73, 80, 85, 86, 225, 263, 299
Crataegus spp. 172
Cubebs 69
Culver's Root 66, 68, 71, 75
Cumin 79, 277
Cuts 71, 234, 243, 274
CVA 121, 365
Cystitis 137, 187, 196, 324
Cysts 140

Damiana 77, 86
Dandelion 42, 66, 68, 72, 74, 75, 77, 79, 80, 81, 86, 93, 99, 112, 121, 129, 133, 137, **138–141,** 162, 166, 170, 173, 183, 187, 196, 211, 212, 224, 225, 226, 229, 243, 253, 263, 269, 274, 277, 293, 298, 302, 385, 387
Delirium Tremens 121, 178
Dementia 269, 325
Deodorant 281, 325
Depression 121, 200, 273, 274, 422
Dermatitis 112, 192, 230, 244, 326
Devil's Claw 66, 77, 81, 82, 298
Diabetes 112, 140, 196, 212, 243, 263, 326, 413
Diaper Rash 133, 192
Diarrhea 93, 103, 107, 126, 133, 212, 218, 224, 243, 247, 248, 263, 290, 293, 298, 326
Digestive Inflammation 116
Dill 44, 67, 69, 73, 126, **142–145,** 162, 163, 196, 387
Discoloration 157
Diverticulitis 238, 327
Dizziness 238, 327
Dong Quai 78, 83, 86, 99, 170, 200, 225, 257, 274, 277, 285
Dropsy 110, 112, 140, 173, 187, 224, 327
Dulse 68, 269
Dysentery 133, 212, 248, 277, 293, 328
Dysmenorrhea 98, 162, 239, 263, 277, 328
Dyspepsia 67, 145, 328

E. Coli 281
Ear Infection 218
Earache 116, 179, 218
Echinacea 66, 67, 69, 71, 81, 83, 84, 112, 126, **146–152,** 157, 167, 183, 196, 218, 248, 249, 253, 269, 273, 281, 298, 302, 388, 389, 390
Echinacea angustifolia 146
Eczema 93, 103, 112, 116, 129, 133, 140, 192, 197, 212, 224, 229, 244, 253, 257, 277, 302
Edema 112, 129, 137, 140, 170, 187, 328
Elder 66
  bark 71
  berries 72, 81, 155, 252
  flowers 44, 67, 69, 70, 76, 79, 82, 84, 93, 99, 112, 151, 155, 200, 211, 234, 238, 248, 298
Elderberry **153–158,** 390, 391, 392
Elecampane 66, 68, 69, 72, 73, 77, 79, 82, 86, 87, 183, 212
Emphysema 133, 157, 166, 183, 205, 218, 248, 269, 302, 329
Endometriosis 170, 329
Enuresis 137, 187, 196, 273, 330
Ephedra 76, 79, 82, 196, 218, 269, 330
Equisetum arvense 185
Erysipelas 206, 331
Eucalyptus 71, 281, 411
Eupatorium purpureum 169
Evening Primrose Oil 166, 274, 285
Excessive Sweating 269
Eye
  disorders 103
  eyewash 264, 332
  inflammation 290
  irritation 218
  sore 126, 212
Eyebright 69, 73, 86, 202, 218, 264, 281, 290

False Unicorn 77, 78, 80, 82, 83, 86, 99, 285

Fatigue 239
Fatty Tumors 253
Fennel 44, 67, 69, 70, 72, 73, 75, 77, 79, 80, 82, 126, 142, 144, 145, **159–163,** 166, 167, 183, 208, 212, 238, 239, 263, 392, 393, 394, 412
Fenugreek 70, 76, 79, 86, 87, 145, 162, 166, 196, 212
Fever 77, 81, 84, 112, 116, 126, 129, 151, 157, 167, 170, 196, 200, 205, 224, 238, 248, 269, 277, 281, 293, 298, 332
Feverfew 200, 239, 281
Fibroid Growths 112
Figs 69, 72
Flatulence 145, 162, 166, 196, 229, 238, 333
Flax Seed 67, 69, 72, 76, 112, 113, 132, 166, 173, 178, 187, 196, 243, 285
Flu 126, 151, 156, 166, 183, 196, 238, 248, 281, 289, 298
Foeniculum vulgare 159
Food Poisoning 205, 281
Foot Odor 293
Fo-ti 86
Fresh Wounds 107, 187
Fringe Tree Bark 229
Fungal Conditions 116
   infections 167, 281

Galium aparine 127
Gall Bladder 133, 141, 229, 302, 303
   stones 140
Gangrene 151
Garlic 51, 66, 68, 69, 70, 71, 72, 76, 77, 79, 81, 82, 83, 86, 87, 103, 104, 113, 121, 151, **164–167,** 173, 183, 197, 212, 229, 230, 234, 238, 243, 244, 249, 269, 281, 293, 307, 394, 395, 396
Gas 73, 126, 145, 162, 196, 229, 238, 410, 431
Gelatin 132
Gentian 68, 69, 70, 74, 75, 78, 80, 83, 87, 179, 253
Ginger 67, 69, 70, 73, 76, 82, 84, 119, 121, 126, 133, 151, 166, 167, 183, 187, 196, 200, 212, 224, 225, 238, 239, 249, 263, 264, 269, 277, 290, 293, 303

Gingivitis 293, 334
Ginkgo 99, 121, 140, 173, 224, 234, 238, 257, 269, 420
Ginseng 42, 66, 82, 85, 86, 269, 274, 302
Glandular Swelling 253
Goiter 253, 335
Gold Thread 74
Goldenseal 42, 66, 69, 70, 71, 75, 78, 85, 86, 87, 140, 166, 187, 196, 228, 230, 243, 289, 302
Gotu Kola 66, 84, 140, 173, 234, 238, 274, 293
Gout 93, 112, 162, 170, 212, 224, 298, 335
Gravel Root 43, 73, 77, 81, 82, 93, 112, 133, 137, **169–170,** 187, 196, 212, 238, 243, 253, 273, 274, 277, 293, 396
Grave's Disease 200
Graying 269
Green Tea 269
Guarana 82
Gum Disease 269
Gymnema 212, 263

Hair Loss 225, 269, 299
Halitosis 239, 336
Hangover 293
Hawthorn 44, 72, 73, 75, 77, 82, 85, 107, 121, **172–174,** 183, 187, 200, 205, 224, 234, 290, 293, 397, 398
Hay Fever 156, 196, 218, 224
Headache 98, 126, 205, 234, 239, 247, 269, 293, 336
Heart
   disease 121
   palpitations 173, 183, 290
   poor circulation 238
   protection 293
   tonic 173
Heart Attack 121
Heartburn 239, 337
Heartsease 66, 69, 70, 77, 79
Hemlock Spruce 67, 264
Hemorrhage 107, 116, 121, 133, 218, 225, 298, 299, 337

Hemorrhoids 103, 116, 192, 218, 243, 263, 264, 298, 299, 302, 303, 337
Hepatitis 80, 140, 183, 337
Herpes 121, 151, 229, 230, 239, 273, 338, 406, 407
Hiccough 234
Hiccups 239
High Blood Pressure 99, 140, 200, 224, 234, 269, 298
HIV 92, 93, 112, 151, 200, 274, 338, 403, 416
Hives 112, 192, 224, 338
Hoarseness 162
Hollyhock 76, 87
  flowers 76
Honey 69, 87, 103, 104
Hops 67, 68, 69, 70, 74, 75, 80, 82, 86, 98, 99, 126, 147, 158, 173, **175–179**, 200, 212, 218, 234, 296, 398
Horehound 68, 72, 73, 74, 76, 79, **180–184**, 211, 224, 226, 234, 248, 257, 290, 399
Horsenettle 67
Horseradish 69, 70, 71, 75, 76, 77, 79, 82, 303
Horsetail 68, 73, 77, 78, 80, 81, 83, 85, 86, 87, 93, 107, 132, 137, **185–188**, 196, 225, 244, 253, 263, 269, 273, 299, 302, 399, 400
Hot Flashes 99
Houndstongue 192
Humulus lupulus 175
Hydrangea 43, 68, 77, 81, 93, 137, 140, 170, 187, 212, 277
Hyperactivity 200, 234
Hypericum perforatum 271
Hyperthyroidism 200, 339
Hyssop 66, 68, 69, 70, 72, 75, 76, 79, 80, 81, 82, 103, 125, 126, 183, 274, 281

Impatiens capensis 189
Indigestion 126, 140, 162, 166, 179, 183, 200, 243, 263, 290
  nervous 290
Infection 151, 167

Infertility 285, 427
Inflammation 70, 133, 151, 179, 230
Insomnia 126, 145, 173, 179, 200, 218, 234, 341
Intestinal Griping 162
Ipecac 78, 425
Irish Moss 67, 68, 69, 70, 76, 83, 86, 87, 187
Irregular Heartbeat 205
Irritable Bowel 133, 166, 212, 243
Itching 239, 269, 303
Ivy Berries 71

Jaundice 140, 179, 183, 205, 229, 298, 302, 342
Jewelweed 44, 55, 113, 129, **189–193**, 206, 223, 224, 225, 230, 241, 400
Joe Pye Weed 79
Joint
  pain 293
  problems 196
Juglans nigra 100
Juniper Berries 44, 67, 69, 70, 71, 73, 77, 81, 82, 83, 101, 116, 137, 140, 151, 170, **194–197**, 200, 212, 230, 243, 244, 263, 293, 298, 401
Juniperis communis 194

Kava 67, 72, 77, 82, 86, 200, 234, 281
Kelp 66, 76, 77, 83
Kidney
  infections 293
  inflamed 112, 133
  stones 93, 112, 137, 140, 170, 212, 225
Kidney / Bladder
  inflammation 129, 243
  troubles 170
Kola Nut 82
Kudzu 178, 273
  root 178

Labor Pains 99, 263
Lactation 145, 162, 212
Lady's Mantle 70, 73, 80, 170, 243, 253
Lady's Slipper 82, 189
Laryngitis 107, 121, 162, 212, 239, 269, 281, 342
Lavender 54, 55, 70, 125, 197
Lavender Essential Oil 197
Lemon Balm 43, 47, 70, 72, 76, 82, 84, 93, 98, 103, 104, 112, 121, 126, 151, 178, 183, 192, 196, **198–201,** 205, 218, 219, 229, 230, 234, 238, 239, 243, 248, 263, 269, 273, 274, 277, 281, 289, 290, 293, 298, 402
Lemons 84
  juice 129
  peel 73
Lesions 112
Leukorrhea 104, 196, 197, 229, 244, 263, 302
Lice 167, 281
Licorice 66, 68, 70, 72, 76, 79, 84, 151, 163, 182, 184, 187, 200, 205, 211, 212, 218, 224, 225, 230, 243, 269, 274, 277, 285, 293
Life Root 196
Limes 84
Linden 72, 140, 173, 200, 298
Liver
  congestion 166, 253, 302
  difficulties 183
  problems 179, 229, 243
Liverwort 80, 344
Lobelia 43, 57, 67, 69, 70, 72, 78, 79, 81, 82, 86, 98, 112, 113, 118, 121, 126, 132, 133, 151, 166, 169, 179, 183, 196, **202–206,** 211, 212, 218, 224, 234, 248, 249, 257, 274, 281, 289, 290, 298, 303, 404, 405
Lobelia inflata 202
Lock Jaw 205
Lovage 73, 229
Lung Congestion 121
Lungwort 69, 73, 76, 79, 80, 86, 87, 214
Lymphatic Congestion 57, 112, 151, 253, 302
Lymphatics 64, 81, 218

Magnesium 173, 297
Mahonia aquifolia 227
Male Fern 68
Mandrake 66, 82, 222
Marrubium vulgare 180
Marshmallow 66, 69, 70, 72, 76, 77, 81, 83, 87, 93, 107, 112, 126, 129, 133, 166, 169, 174, 182, 183, 196, 200, **207–213,** 218, 225, 229, 239, 243, 248, 257, 263, 277, 281, 285, 290, 299, 302, 405
Mastitis 151, 212, 253, 345
Meadowsweet 67, 68, 73, 77, 112, 126, 205, 226, 249
Measles 116, 298, 345
Melancholy 200
Melissa officinalis 198
Melon Seeds 68
Menopause
  discomfort 99, 285
  issues 257
Menorrhagia 225, 263, 298, 346
Menstruation
  cramps 239, 263, 285
  difficulty 126
  heavy 107, 121, 187
  pain 170, 274
Mentha piperita 236
Mescal 78
Migraine 200, 239, 281, 346
Milk Thistle 44, 69, 80, 229, 243, 253
Miscarriage 263
Mistletoe 72, 78, 82
Morning Sickness 126, 239, 263
Motherwort 72, 75, 76, 78, 81, 82, 85, 86, 183, 212
Mouth Ulcers 243, 263, 269, 281, 293
Mugwort 70, 72, 74, 76, 78, 87, 347
Mulberry Bark 68
Mullein 57, 67, 69, 70, 71, 72, 73, 76, 77, 79, 80, 81, 83, 86, 87, 107, 112, 113, 116, 121, 126, 132, 144, 151, 157, 179, 183, 205, 206, 211, 212, **214–219,** 224, 238, 239, 249, 253, 257, 258, 274, 289, 290, 302, 303, 406

Muscle
  pain 121, 162, 239, 273, 293
  spasms 205, 206, 281
  tension 234
Mustard Seeds 84
Myrrh 53, 54, 69, 70, 71, 73, 78, 79, 82, 87, 116, 117, 121, 151, 218, 263, 264, 269, 274

Nausea 70, 239, 263, 269, 349
Nepeta cataria 123
Nephritis 196, 349
Nerve deficiency 285
Nervous Distress 218
Nervous Exhaustion 269
Nervousness 126
Nettle Rash 192, 225
Nettles 66, 70, 71, 79, 80, 83, 84, 85, 93, 99, 112, 121, 137, 191, 211, 212, **220–226**, 234, 241, 257, 298, 299, 407
Neuralgia 99, 179, 212, 234, 293, 349
Neuropathy 274, 350
Nicotine Withdrawal 218
Night Sweats 225, 269
Nightmares 281
Nursing 285
Nutmeg 73, 86

Oat Bran 166
Oat Grass 86
Oats 72, 82, 86
Obstructions 140
Old Sores 133, 151, 187, 244, 281
Olive Leaf 71, 73, 93, 121, 196, 200, 212
Olive Oil 51, 52, 72, 121, 192, 211
Onion 82, 165
Oranges 84
Oregano 73, 224

Oregon Grape 54, 66, 69, 71, 72, 74, 75, 80, 81, 85, 86, 87, 93, 103, 104, 112, 113, 116, 117, 121, 129, 133, 137, 140, 151, 179, 183, 187, 192, 197, 205, 206, 211, 212, 224, **227–230**, 248, 253, 257, 258, 277, 281, 298, 299, 302, 408
Osteoporosis 133, 187, 225, 351
Ox-eye Daisy 70, 72

Papaya 162, 239
Parasites 93, 103, 166, 167, 183, 196, 197
Parkinson's 234, 274, 353, 385
Parsley 67, 77, 79, 81, 85, 86, 93, 137, 144, 167, 187, 196, 208, 269
Parturient 263, 353
Passiflora incarnata 231
Passion Flower 67, 72, 76, 82, 86, 112, 121, 126, 140, 145, 173, 179, 200, 205, 218, 224, **231–235**, 273, 274, 277, 281, 290, 410
Pau D'Arco 77, 83, 93, 104, 112, 151, 167, 192, 229, 244, 263, 281, 293
Paw Paw 83
Peach 68, 70, 74, 76, 81, 82
Pennyroyal 70, 72, 73, 76, 78, 82, 124, 126, 183
Peppermint 43, 47, 55, 57, 67, 70, 72, 73, 76, 79, 82, 84, 99, 103, 113, 119, 126, 129, 140, 145, 156, 162, 166, 179, 183, 184, 196, 205, 206, 229, 234, **236–239**, 243, 263, 269, 290, 302, 393, 411, 412
Periwinkle 73
Pertussis 133, 354
Peruvian Bark 234
Phytolacca americana 250
Piles 264, 355
Pipsissewa 66, 74, 77, 86
Plantago lanceolata 240
Plantain 44, 52, 55, 66, 71, 74, 77, 85, 87, 98, 103, 113, 116, 126, 129, 133, 150, 157, 170, 192, 206, 218, 223, 225, 230, 238, 239, **240–244**, 263, 264, 269, 273, 274, 277, 293, 298, 303, 412, 413, 414
Pleurisy 121, 157, 205, 246, 249, 356
Pleurisy Root 69, 70, 71, 72, 76, 77, 79, 82, 86, 157, 183, **245–249**, 415

PMS 99, 170, 257, 284, 285, 427
Pneumonia 212, 356
Podophyllum 75, 78, 80, 86
Poison Ivy 44, 55, 113, 129, 192, 206, 241, 242, 277
Poke 43, 66, 67, 78, 80, 81, **250–253**, 257, 277, 302, 415
Poor Appetite 145
Poppy 179, 212
Post-partum Pain & Depression 274
Pregnancy 263, 427
Prickly Ash 66, 71, 72, 74, 78, 82, 84, 99, 234, 263, 298
Prickly Pear 84, 112
Prostate
  enlargement 225
  issues 170
  problems 187, 257
Prostatitis 137, 293, 357
Prunes 72
Prunus serotina 287
Pruritis 269, 303, 357, 358
Psoriasis 93, 103, 112, 116, 129, 133, 140, 192, 197, 212, 224, 229, 244, 253, 257, 277, 302, 358
Psyllium 72, 76, 140, 212, 218, 241, 244, 413
Pulsatilla 67, 72
Pumpkin 166
  seed 68, 93, 103
Purslane 84
Pygeum 170, 293

Quaker Button 86
Queen of the Meadow 78

Raisins 69, 72
Rashes 55, 112, 113, 129, 206, 218, 244

Red Beet 302
Red Clover 66, 67, 70, 72, 77, 82, 83, 99, 112, 129, 132, 140, 151, 252, **254–258**, 277, 285, 298, 303, 417, 418
Red Poppy 67
Red Raspberry 66, 67, 70, 72, 74, 79, 80, 82, 83, 87, 99, 170, 212, **259–265**, 274, 298, 418
Red Raspberry Leaf 99, 212
Red Root 72, 80
Respiratory
  infection 249
  inflammation 107
  problems 112, 166
Restless Leg 179, 274
Restlessness 234
Rheumatic Pains 93, 234
Rheumatism 96, 111, 113, 121, 157, 179, 224, 249, 252, 277, 298, 360
Rhubarb 66, 72, 74, 82, 86, 103, 212, 303
Ringworm 104, 167, 192, 360
Rock Rose 258
Rose Hips 72, 83, 183
Rosemary 32, 53, 69, 71, 72, 73, 74, 77, 82, 84, 87, 223, 225, 269
Rubus idaeus 259
Rue 68, 72, 73, 74, 78, 82, 83, 84
Rumex crispus 300

S. uplandicum 130
Safflower 69, 72, 76, 78, 302
Sage 43, 53, 68, 69, 70, 71, 72, 73, 74, 86, 93, 99, 103, 104, 112, 121, 151, 157, 162, 170, 179, 183, 200, 212, 218, 223, 224, 225, 229, 234, 243, 264, **266–270**, 277, 281, 284, 290, 293, 298, 299, 402, 419, 420, 421
St. John's Wort 66, 73, 74, 77, 82, 87, 107, 116, 151, 157, 160, 167, 183, 200, 215, 218, 234, 244, **271–274**, 285, 293, 303, 421, 422
Salivation
  dry mouth 121
  excessive 269
Salix alba 291
Salvia officinalis 266

Sambucus canadensis   153
Sandalwood   74
Sarsaparilla   66, 68, 69, 76, 81, 86, 269
Sassafras   28, 66, 67, 70, 73, 76, 77, 79, 82, 113, 129, 192, 226, 248, 252, 253, **275–277**, 424, 425
Sassafras officinale   275
Savory   145
Saw Palmetto   68, 71, 77, 82, 86, 137, 170, 187, 225, 257, 293
Scalds   113, 116, 133, 167, 197, 225, 274
Scalp Problems   269
Sciatica   113, 234, 362
Scrofulas Swelling   258
Scullcap   67, 68, 72, 82, 99, 179, 200, 205, 224, 234, 239
Seizure   205, 234, 363
Self Heal   70, 72, 74, 80, 87
Senna   81
Sheep Sorrel   68, 257
Shepherd's Purse   74, 77, 79, 80, 82
Shingles   103, 112, 121, 200, 229, 230, 277, 363
Shortness of Breath   183
Siberian Ginseng   82, 274, 302
Sinus Congestion   218, 239, 269
Sinus Lavage   116
Sinusitis   157, 363
Skin
   blemishes   157
   diseases   116, 140, 151, 206, 212, 253
   disorders   253, 303
   eruptions   116, 129, 140, 277, 298, 302
   infections   281
   ulcers   57, 277
Skunk Cabbage   67, 72
Slippery Elm   67, 76, 83, 87, 103, 107, 133, 156, 212, 218, 224, 252, 263, 264, 281, 293, 298, 302
Slow Healing Wounds   107, 212
Smartweed   71, 74
Smoking Cessation   205, 274
Solomon's Seal   67, 70, 74, 192
Sore Nipples   212, 299
Sore Throat   103, 104, 107, 121, 151, 157, 174, 183, 212, 239, 264, 269, 281
Sores   93, 107, 133, 151, 187, 218, 230, 243, 263, 269, 281, 293

Sorrel   68, 69, 70, 77, 81, 82, 84, 257
Sour milk   157
Southernwood   71, 73, 234
Spasms   98, 205, 206, 232, 234
Spastic Colon   281
Spearmint   70, 72, 73, 76, 82
Spinal Injury   274
Spirulina   83
Splinters   174
Sprains   133, 157
Spring Tonic   157
Squaw Vine   66, 74, 77, 78, 83, 86, 151, 285
STD's   113
Stillingia   66, 78, 257
Stings   55, 116, 192, 243
   bee   116
Stomach Cramps   126
Stomachache   183
Stoneroot   74, 77, 86
Stone Root   81
Stones   93, 112, 137, 140, 170, 187, 212, 225, 229, 277
Stress   83, 178, 234
Stroke   121, 365
Sty   281, 365
Suma   82, 269, 274
Sumac Berries   84, 252
Sunburn   116, 274
Supporations   179
Sweet Basil   70
Sweet Cicely   73
Sweet Flag   73, 183, 212
Sweet Marjoram   67
Swelling   57, 129, 140, 258
Swollen Breasts   253
Swollen Glands   113, 126, 218, 274
Symphytum officinale   130
Syphilis   113, 366
Systemic Skin Issues   229

Tachycardia   234, 366

Tansy   68, 72, 78, 82, 83
Taraxacum officinale   138
Tea Tree Oil   83, 104, 151, 167, 197, 281
Teething   205
Tendonitis   187, 367
Thrush   263, 367
Thyme   68, 69, 71, 72, 76, 79, 82, 83, 84, 103, 104, 129, 132, 137, 144, 151, 166, 212, 218, 230, 234, 257, 263, 269, **278–282**, 285, 289, 290, 293, 402, 406, 425, 426
Thymus vulgaris   278
Tinea   151, 192, 368
Tinnitus   99, 368
Tobacco   67, 71, 202
Tonsillitis   103, 121, 293, 368
Toothache   126, 167, 179, 205, 218, 239, 244
Tormentil   80, 81, 85
Tormentil Root   80
Trauma   187
Trifolium pratense   254
Trillium   66, 71, 74, 78, 85, 86, 263
True Unicorn   86
Tuberculosis   24, 151, 249, 281, 290, 368
Tumors   77, 112, 157, 167, 206, 218, 253, 258, 269, 303
Turkey Rhubarb   68, 81
Turmeric   187, 224, 234, 293, 298
Turpentine   68, 71

Urinary Tract Infection   137, 212, 263
Urticaria   192, 225, 369
Urtica dioica   220
Uterine Tonic   170, 243
Uva Ursi   70, 74, 77, 80, 81, 86, 93, 137, 150, 170, 196, 212, 293

Vaccination Reaction   151
Vaginal Discharge   116, 197
Vaginitis   212, 302, 369
Valerian   67, 72, 82, 86, 126, 137, 176, 179, 234
Vanilla   73, 86
Varicose Veins   116, 244
Varicosity   107
Verbascum thapsus   214
Vertigo   173, 238, 370
Vervain   67, 72, 74, 75, 76, 79
Vinegar & Honey   69
Violet   258
Viral infections   200
Virginia Snake Root   67, 72, 82
Vitex   44, 83, 98, 99, 126, 162, 170, 196, 225, 239, 257, 269, 274, 277, **283–286**, 427
Vitex agnus-castus   283

Ulcerations   116, 290
Ulcers   93, 107, 112, 116, 121, 151, 166, 179, 187, 230, 244, 257, 263, 269, 277, 281, 293, 303
   indolent   93, 112, 151
   purulent   257
Una de Gato   151, 229
Urethritis   187, 369
Uric Acid Excess   137
Urinary Issues
   deficiency   274
   discharges   298
   retention   293
   scalding urine   112

Warts   93, 103, 167, 192
Wash Wounds   116
Water Retention   140, 170
Watercress   83
Watermelon   72, 77
Weak Digestion   229
Weaning   269
White Birch   68, 90
White Oak   70, 71, 74, 77, 80, 85, 93, 103, 116, 264
White Pond Lily   67, 71, 77

White Poplar 67
White Willow 67, 71, 76, 77, 79, 291, 294
Whooping Cough 205, 212, 218, 257
Wild Carrot 40, 68, 144
Wild Cherry 44, 69, 74, 79, 82, 86, 87, 98, 132, 133, 144, 166, 183, 196, 205, 212, 218, 248, 269, 281, **287–290**, 302, 428
Wild Lettuce 67
Wild Yam 67, 69, 70, 72, 75, 76, 78, 80, 85, 99, 113, 211, 212, 230, 234, 263, 298
Willow 43, 71, 76, 77, 79, 93, 99, 113, 121, 187, 196, **291–294**, 428, 429
Wintergreen 68, 69, 70, 71, 73, 91, 121, 162, 226, 293
Witch Hazel 70, 74, 80, 82, 85
Wood Betony 66, 67, 72, 73, 80, 82, 83, 86, 212, 239, 269
Wood Sage 68, 71
Wood Sorrel 69
Woodruff 77
Wormwood 68, 70, 71, 73, 74, 75, 80, 82, 87, 93, 103, 157
Wounds 87, 107, 116, 121, 179, 183, 187, 197, 212, 218, 225, 230, 243, 264, 269, 299

Yarrow 44, 66, 69, 74, 76, 79, 80, 82, 85, 87, 98, 103, 104, 113, 121, 126, 137, 156, 170, 179, 187, 192, 218, 224, 225, 243, 248, 264, 269, **295–299**, 429, 430
Yeast Infection 104, 151, 167, 229
Yellow Dock 44, 66, 68, 74, 75, 80, 81, 83, 103, 112, 113, 140, 151, 170, 212, 224, 229, 253, 257, 277, **300–303**, 431
Yellow Parilla 257
Yellow Root 74, 75, 86, 228, 230
Yerba Santa 69, 79, 82, 257
Yohimbe 86
Yucca Root 68

Zea mays 135
Zedoary 73
Zinc 151

NOTES

*"What remains now,
but that you labor to glorify God
each in your own places,
and do good to yourselves first
by increasing your Knowledge,
and to your Neighbors afterwards
by helping their Infirmities.*

*Many such as you,
I hope this Nation is worthy of,
and to such as you
shall I remain a Friend for life,
ready always to help
as my own poor power allows."*

– Nicholas Culpeper, 1652